PSYCHOLOGICAL DNA

LOS ANGELES

Ambassador hotel

A COLD CASE ANALYSIS OF WHO KILLED ROBERT F. KENNEDY

JOHN C. BRADY, II, PHD, D. CRIM.

PSYCHOLOGICAL DNA: A COLD CASE ANALYSIS OF WHO KILLED ROBERT F. KENNEDY
COPYRIGHT © 2023/2024 DR. JOHN C. BRADY, II

Published by:
Trine Day LLC
PO Box 577
Walterville, OR 97489
1-800-556-2012
www.TrineDay.com
TrineDay@icloud.com

Library of Congress Control Number: 2024938417

Brady, John C., II.
—1st ed.
p. cm.

Epub (ISBN-13) 978-1-63424-488-6
Trade Paperback (ISBN-13) 978-1-63424-487-9
1. Kennedy, Robert F., (1925-1968) Assassination. 2. Sirhan, Sirhan Bishara, (1944-). 3. Diamond, Bernard L (1912-). 4. Forensic Psychiatry. 5. Expertises Californie Jurisprudence. 6. Assassination Investigation History 20th century. I. Brady, Jiohn C. II. Title

FIRST EDITION
10 9 8 7 6 5 4 3 2 1

Printed in the USA
Distribution to the Trade by:
Independent Publishers Group (IPG)
814 North Franklin Street
Chicago, Illinois 60610
312.337.0747
www.ipgbook.com

Publisher's Foreword

"Have you news of my boy Jack?"
Not this tide.
"When d'you think that he'll come back?"
Not with this wind blowing, and this tide.

"Has any one else had word of him?"
Not this tide.
For what is sunk will hardly swim,
Not with this wind blowing, and this tide.

              –"My Boy Jack, " Rudyard Kipling (1916)

If any question why we died,
Tell them, because our fathers lied.
      – "Epitaphs of the War," Rudyard Kipling (1918)

And even in our sleep,
pain which cannot forget
falls drop by drop upon the heart,
until in our own despair,
against our will,
comes wisdom through the awful grace of God.

           – Aeschylus

What does it take for us to understand our fate? When do we know? Will we ever learn?

I was 18 in June of 1968 – a heady year. The Vietnam "police action" was over the top: almost 300,000 kids drafted, over half-million US troops in country, 16,899 US deaths – the bloodiest year of *that* war.

It was bloody at home too. Dr. Martin Luther King, Jr., was murdered in Memphis, Tennessee in April. There were riots. Then Robert Francis Kennedy was gunned down after a stirring political victory – leaving hopeful aspirations devastated and in disarray.

It *was* a wild political year. President Johnson had announced he wasn't going to run for re-election the end of March, two weeks after RFK joined the fray – the race was on. I was too young to vote but stayed abreast of the news. Oregon held it's primary on May 28, just a week before the California primary. Eugene McCarthy won Oregon. Bobby was second, and the chatter was that if he won California, RFK had a path to his party's nomination, pitting him against Richard Nixon.

Well, we all know what happened. *The Smithsonian Magazine* declared 1968: THE YEAR THAT SHATTERED AMERICA.

Dr. John C. Brady II has written and TrineDay is honored to publish his comprehensive analysis into the wilderness of mirrors surrounding Sirhan Bishara Sirhan, the accused and convicted assassin of RFK: *Psychological DNA: A Cold Case Analysis of Who Killed Robert F. Kennedy.*

Dr. Brady's book is the first to truly explore, edify and elucidate the fractured mental state and psychology of Sirhan. Dr. Brady is a California licensed forensic psychologist and a Doctor of Criminology, and as a young graduate student became involved in the state's attempt to understand this seemingly mild but tortured soul.

With the advancement of psychological testing and knowledge, plus his background and access to the many tests given to Sirhan, Dr. Brady has produced an amazing detailed volume that speaks to what happened, not only on that troubling day, but also examines and forensically explains the motivations of other sensational murderers.

Dr Brady delves into the question of "Manchurian Candidates" and probes the possibilities and history of personality disorders. Was Sirhan a manufactured killer? Was he used? Maybe ... there is much in his psychological make-up that could lead one to make that conclusion, but then there is much more to the story.

Psychological DNA: A Cold Case Analysis of Who Killed Robert F. Kennedy brings a trained eye to a fateful moment of our history.

> *And I to my pledged word am true,*
> *I shall not fail that rendezvous.*
> – Alan Seeger (1917)

Onward to the Utmost of Futures,
Peace,
Kris Millegan
Publisher
TrineDay
5/4/24

DEDICATION

Naturally, each subject I approach to write about is done from a different perspective making each one special in its own way. *Psychological DNA: A Cold Case Analysis of Who Killed Robert F. Kennedy* stands out from the others because of the research necessary to complete the book – extending back five decades – required a concerted time commitment not to mention the time necessary to write the first drafts. Of course, during those blocks of time I was alone separated from my family – not physically, but mentally – who often asked, "Is the Kennedy book almost finished?" My standard answer, "It's almost there." Because of my family's selflessness I did finish the book, and for that "release time," I am grateful.

Acknowledgements

First, I must acknowledge Dr. Bernard L. Diamond, my major professor at UC Berkeley's School of Criminology, who introduced me to Sirhan Bishara Sirhan (Sirhan) when I was a graduate student and he was the lead psychiatrist in Sirhan's murder trial. He also provided ample support to my continued interest in examining why some individuals choose homicide as a solution to resolve their unconscious conflicts. Marly Cornell, my first editor and cheerleader, steered me in the right direction during the two years it took to produce an initial draft stating, "It's ready, now find a publisher and get it out there." William M. Law – wrote the Foreword – passed on new information concerning the Sirhan case based on his thirty years of careful research. For his contribution, I'm thankful. And last, to Kris Millegan – who wrote the generous Publisher's Foreword – and provided support and encouragement for this project kindly stamping the TrineDay mark on *Psych DNA*.

CONTENTS

FOREWORD

by Willim Matson Law

Iwas honored when TrineDay LLC publisher, Kris Millegan, kindly asked me if I could write an in-depth foreword to Dr. John Brady's new release *Psychological DNA: A Cold Case Analysis of Who Killed Robert F. Kennedy* (*PsychDNA*) on the fifty-sixth anniversary of Robert Kennedy's assassination June 5, 2024. I agreed, taking this challenge seriously because I have extensively researched this case for more than thirty years and I am always hungry to learn more about Robert Kennedy's assassination, especially from a new criminological perspective written by the author who was there at the beginning.

My interest in the Kennedy assassinations-both President Kennedy (JFK) and Robert F. Kennedy (RFK) culminated in the publishing my first book *In the Eye of History: Disclosure in the JFK Assassination Medical Evidence* in 2004 that concerned the autopsy of JFK and had led me into some strange territory to say the least. Reading Dr. Brady's new release, *Psych DNA*, also opened up some additional territory for me – this time from a psychological-criminal perspective.

In the Eye of History had taken me six years to research and write. I was working full-time and my wife and I were raising three small children, so I had to do research and write when I had the time. I was told by a fellow researcher of the Robert Kennedy case, "You're gonna fall in love with Bobby," but what my friend may not have known was that I already had.

In review, Robert Kennedy was killed by assassin's bullets in the pantry of the Ambassador Hotel in Los Angeles, California. I remember the news of Kennedy's killing, watching the funeral train as it carried the senator's body to Washington. I remember the men and women and children who stood at the side of the tracks on either side as the train passed by. I remember some people holding signs that read "Goodbye Bobby," "We love you Bobby" and "So long Bobby" with their hands over their hearts in silent respect.

Mostly I remember the sadness. I couldn't really grasp at the age of 10 what it meant, but I knew it was something terrible. As I write these lines in my 66th year and 57 years after the event, I can explain the sadness. I'm not sure I can really do justice to the explanation of the loss or how the assassination has affected the country from then until now, but I know we lost not only a man on that dirty pantry floor, but we also lost hope for a better world. Robert Kennedy's death has led us into the world we live in today.

When noted film director Mark Sobel and I decided to join together and interview the witnesses to Kennedy's assassination who were still alive, we began with Larry Teeter, Sirhan's attorney. When I contacted Teeter somewhere around 2005, he said yes to our request once he understood the idea was to film him as he was trying to get a new trial for Sirhan Sirhan. Somewhere along the way we hoped that there would be a meeting with Sirhan in his jail cell, one that could be filmed for a documentary and have an experience that I could write about.

Two months before I was to leave for California to start filming, I received information that Larry Teeter had died. I made some calls and found that was indeed the case. Teeter had died. I had talked to Teeter some months before and Larry had said nothing to me as far as concerning the fact that he was ill. All I could figure is that his illness had progressed quickly, and he had passed soon after the diagnosis. However, it happened or when, with Teeter gone, Mark and I had no direction to go in. It was Mark Sobel who came up with the idea to follow me while I tried to find witnesses to Robert Kennedy's murder and interview them. I said yes because I would have a record of practically everything we did that could then prompt my memory for a proposed book. And I liked the idea of being the subject of a film that fellow historians could look at long after I had stepped off into the great beyond. Politicians, writers, and film-makers think about their legacy a lot and I'm no different.

Robert Francis Kennedy's role as President Kennedy's protector, keeper of the secrets, his time as Attorney General, and later as a US Senator is well known. The legacy of what could have been, what RFK could have become, that part of Kennedy's legacy belongs to the mists of time. The legacy of RFK, unlike his brother John F. Kennedy, has dimmed as the decades have passed. Ask a millennial or a Gen Z'er today who JFK and RFK were. I've asked a lot of people over 40 and have gotten blank stares and perhaps a comment like, "I've heard of them, but I don't really know." I understand the loss of that unfulfilled opportunity for all Americans in the world of the 1960s and the generations who have come after them.

For those of us from that time what we now hold are the memories we have of a man who at least some of us felt could change the world for the better. For those of us still on this ever-turning planet in the three and a half decades I've been researching and writing about the Kennedy brothers, I've become more than a little aware of what our country lost by their assassinations, even more by Bobby's loss than John's. Why? Because I've come to believe that through his grief over his brother's death, Robert Kennedy became empathetic (something he was not before the tragedy of November 22, 1963) towards the pain of the poor, the downtrodden, and those who often experience the weight of a life changing event.

In 1963 on November 20th, Robert Kennedy celebrated his 38th birthday. A friend observed that he was in a dark mood, his mind already turning to the difficult task of getting his brother reelected in the coming year. Two days later Bobby Kennedy was having lunch at Hickory Hill, his home in Virginia, when a call came from FBI Director J. Edgar Hoover. "I have news for you," Hoover said, his voice devoid of emotion, "The president's been shot." Kennedy's body contorted with grief. A few minutes later he mumbled to aide Ed Guthman, "There's so much bitterness. I thought they'd get one of us. I thought it would be me." After Bobby had gone to meet Air Force One and Jackie Kennedy and the casket containing his brother's remains, the next night in the White House his friend Ted Spaulding said, "I was with Bobby, and I talked with him a while.

Then it came time to go to bed and I closed the door. I walked outside and I heard him sobbing and he was saying, "Why, why God, why?'" His friend John Seigenthaler said, "It was a physical blow to him, the loss of his brother. An emotional blow, intellectual blow, but it took a toll on him. He was physically in pain." Another man who knew RFK intimately, John Morgenthau, believed Bobby was haunted by doubt for the rest of his life. "Was there something I could have done to prevent it? Was there something I did to encourage it? Was I to blame?"

In researching and writing about the mystery of the Kennedys' deaths, I've had glimpses of truth I wish I'd had never known. I've become more affected over the years by the loss of Bobby Kennedy than I have by John. Perhaps because I was older when Bobby Kennedy was murdered. All I know is when I look at John Kennedy's picture or film of him, I look at his image with a clinical eye. When I look at pictures or film of Bobby, I can never see his image without my heart hurting. Robert Kennedy knew the risk he was taking when he decided to run for the presidency. I think he was afraid and yet fought the fear ... and ran anyway.

Robert Blair Kaiser was the first writer to delve into the case of Sirhan Sirhan. Kaiser explained in the reissue of his book *RFK Must Die*, first published in 1970, "I woke up that June morning, turned on NBC's *Today Show*, and learned that yet another Kennedy had been gunned down and in Los Angeles. My friends at *Time*'s sister publication, *Life*, called me into the story and soon I was way into it, with far deeper access than anyone could have dreamed of, right up close and personal with the assassin himself and those who were probing him: Police, prosecutors, defense attorneys, psychiatrists, and psychologists, reporters. I had wangled my way inside the assassin's defense team. I did so out of curiosity, mainly, and out of a suspicion that the public would learn something less than the whole truth if it had to rely on either the assassin's unchallenged version or even the story told by the police and the prosecutors."

Kaiser goes on to write, "I became a participant observer in the attorneys' own private working sessions; I conferred closely with the psychologists, and psychiatrists in the case and served as a kind of bridge between the assassin's doctors and his lawyers. I had access to police and FBI files, which would remain out of public view for the next 22 years, and, most important of all, I was able to visit Sirhan in his cell two or three times a week until he left Los Angeles for San Quentin, condemned to die."

I first read *RFK Must Die*, I believe, around 1986. I found Kaiser's journey down the rabbit hole of RFK's assassination fascinating, especially his one-on-one conversations with the alleged assassin Sirhan Bishara Sirhan.

The first time the defense psychiatrist Dr. Bernard Diamond had hypnotized Sirhan Sirhan in his cell, Sirhan was told to concentrate on a quarter that Dr. Diamond held in his hand; Sirhan went under almost immediately. That doesn't usually happen with the subject unless the subject has been put under hypnosis before. Robert Blair Kaiser in *RFK Must Die* writes, "On Saturday January 11th I visited the cell for the third time and while the jailhouse radio blared in the background, I watched Diamond put Sirhan into a trance almost immediately. Then to check the authenticity of the hypnotic state, Diamond pulled a safety pin from his jacket, sterilized it with an alcohol-soaked pad he had brought along for the purpose and stuck the pin through the skin on the top of Sirhan's left hand. He told Sirhan he would feel no pain." Apparently, he did not. After asking Sirhan some questions while in the trance state, Diamond brought him out and when Sirhan woke up he was astounded to see the safety pin stuck in his hand.

"'Jesus Christ!" he cried. "What's that?" "Sirhan was upset by the trickle of blood that flowed when he jiggled the pin, and he ran excitedly over to the bars to show the guard what Diamond had done to him." During a tape-recorded hypnosis session held on February 28th, 1969 Diamond suggested that when Sirhan was awakened from hypnosis that he climb the bars of his cell like a monkey. Kaiser continues, "Diamond brought Sirhan out of his trance, who then started climbing on the bars of his cell."

"He was up there," he explained to Diamond, "for exercise."

Diamond replayed the tape and let Sirhan hear how he'd been programmed and said, "It wasn't your idea at all Sirhan, you were just following suggestions."

Sirhan responded, "Oh it frightens me doc. It's very scary."

"It's very real," Diamond said. "It's not fake and it's not a trick."

"But goddammit Sir, killing people is different than climbing up bars," said Sirhan.

"There's this difference Sirhan," Diamond said, "I couldn't force you to do something you were opposed to, but if you wanted to do it, you could if under hypnosis."

* * *

I remember a story told to me by Laurie Dusek, Sirhan's co-counsel who told me, "I went to the prison where Sirhan was being held, I had been there a few times before with Dr. Daniel Brown, but this was the first time I had gone to the prison by myself. I was in the jail cell with Sirhan asking him questions, when all of a sudden, he … Sirhan got up from the table and went into what I call "range mode." He acted as if he were pulling a pistol from his waistband, pointing it and firing it."

Alarm bells went off in my head, listening to this story. I find it not credible that Laurie Dusek, who is a small quiet person, finds herself alone for the first time with Sirhan and that Sirhan suddenly is triggered by a question and goes into range mode, like what Kaiser and Diamond experienced with Sirhan while under Diamond's hypnotic state back in 1968. When Sirhan received the death penalty, he was transported to San Quentin's death row, where he was tested by Dr. Simson-Kallas, chief of the psychological assessment team made available to death penality inmates. He found almost zero confirming evidence of Sirhan's previously diagnosed paranoid schizophrenia. This finding was consistent with the diagnostic opinion provided by the prison's chief psychiatrist. After spending 20 to 30 hours with Sirhan, Dr. Simson-Kallas concluded there was nothing psychiatrically wrong with him although he was highly hypnotizable, and importantly he did not present with any schizophrenic-related symptoms. It looked like original team of defense-prosecution doctors including Dr. Diamond may have been wrong – labeling their errant opinions Dr. Simson-Kallas said, "This is the psychiatric blunder of the century."

Dr. Simson-Kallas further speculated Sirhan could have been a "Manchurian candidate" who had somehow been programmed to serve as a "distractor" that night in RFK's assassination. In a clip from the documentary film *The Real Manchurian Candidate*, Dr. Simson-Kallas stated, "My own hypothesis is that there had to be other people involved. Someone had to set him up. He would be the ideal person for the purpose because he could be exploited with the background of Jews, Arabs – intense conflict. He is the ideal person because he's a follower essentially."

The late Dr. Daniel P. Brown, who has written four textbooks on hypnosis, and had spent more than a hundred and fifty hours with Sirhan over a three year period, concluded that Sirhan had indeed been under hypnotic influence or in a trance state when he shot at RFK. He used the standard tests to access hypnnotizability that Diamond had used in 1968 and, unlike Dr. Brown, Dr. Diamond found that Sirhan was diagnosed with schizophrenia and used diminished capacity as his defense. Dr. Brown did a double-blind test in which he sent Sirhan's standardized test results given by two psychologists used by Dr. Diamond to a colleague without telling him whose tests they were, and that in the colleagues' opinion Sirhan was not schizophrenic. There was nothing wrong with Sirhan's brain.

To complete this foreword to *Psych DNA*, I interviewed Dr. John C. Brady, criminologist, forensic psychologist, and author of this book. During the Sirhan murder trial he was a doctoral graduate student and studied under the guidance of Dr. Diamond while at Berkeley. At the time, Dr. Diamond was the Dean of the School of Criminology at Berkeley and served as Dr. Brady's academic advisor and major professor. As a graduate student he was involved in the Sirhan case from the beginning, working with and under Dr. Diamond for five years.

Based on this essential background history, Dr. Brady was made aware of Dr. Diamond's innermost thoughts on the Sirhan case during the confusing, 1969 trial. As Sirhan's trial proceeded, the defense brought in six psychologists and Dr. Diamond, as a defense psychiatrist, and four review psychologists; ten doctors in all who rendered their individual psychiatric opinions. The persistent question: "What was wrong with Sirhan?" As to the diagnosis of paranoid schizophrenia, collectively they were leaning in that direction, but there remained some controversy as to Sirhan's secondary condition, his dissociative state.

On this diagnostic point, Dr. Diamond and currently Dr. Brady believed that Sirhan was in a disassociated state at the time he shot at Robert Kennedy, and in the process Sirhan became a kind of Dr. Jeykll-Mr. Hyde having two different and distinct personalities. The cause of this splitting seemed to derive from the profound and recurring trauma Sirhan had experienced as a child in Palestine. For his own professional reasons, Diamond did not want to present what amounted to a diagnosis of multiple personality disorder, MPD, to the jury because as a defense concept in a murder case the diagnosis generated both professional and public controversy. Later this was established in the famous but highly disputed Sybil MPD case (allegedly involving a woman possessed with sixteen personalities). Although not in a homicide case, the Sybil saga was supported by the financially-motivated Dr. Cornelia Wilbur, a New York psychiatrist, who above all "wanted to be famous."[1]

Later the Sybil case turned out to be proven a fraud orchestrated just to make money on book sales and promotion of a successful TV mini-series. There was additional controversy in the Sirhan case because there was no real hard evidence, or diagnostic support, that Sirhan suffered from any form of schizophrenia. Nevertheless, his doctors moved forward believing that schizophrenia was a convenient and acceptable diagnosis clinically available at the time, but grossly overused to label Sirhan even though it didn't quite match his symptoms.

After graduation from Berkeley, Dr. Brady went on to become a forensic psychologist as well as a criminologist called on to diagnose many murder defendants' mental states similar to Sirhan. After reading *Psych DNA*, it is clear that the author has been able to provide valuable new insights into Sirhan's mental status compared with other analyses put forth during the past fifty-five years. Indeed, as Dr. Brady pointed out to me, that there has not been a single book written unmasking the specific criminal drivers that explain Sirhan's homicidal behavior.

Dr. Brady also pointed out that interestingly enough, at one point Sirhan, saw RFK as a savior of down-trodden people, and his hero – "He looked like a saint to me." Later this initial affection took a dark turn and Sirhan began to hate RFK who he deemed as a traitor to the Palestinian people (Sirhan's people). This split in his consciousness formed the foundation of Sirhan's split personality. In Dr. Brady's opinion, in effect, Sirhan had unconsciously cleaved his personality into two separate Sirhans. Sirhan's core personality number one, was the good, law-abiding, conforming identity, and personality number two, his alter, was the angry young man who could be sullen, impolite, loud, and ultimately violent. Dr. Brady mentioned that, "In the end,

---

1   "Real'Sybil'AdmitsMultiplePersonalitiesWereFake"https://www.npr.org/2011/10/20/141514464/
real-sybil-admits-multiple-personalities-were-fake

this multiple personality viewpoint is supported by my retrospective study of Sirhan's multi-dimensional sides that he, Sirhan, was experiencing some type of disassociated condition leading to the establishment of the two Sirhans. In addition to the split personality, I also identified four different criminological conditions that factored into Sirhan's homicidal behavior. "

Casting light into the Sirhan case, I recall the story of John Shear, which I found in an obscure interview. It seems that Shear hired Sirhan as a hot walker at Santa Anita racetrack the summer of 1968.

Quoting Shear:

"There was this young man comes round about and he says, 'I'm looking for work. Do you need anybody?' 'So, I looked at him. He was a guy not much taller than me. I said, 'The only job we have is as a hot walker.' A hot walker is a man, a person that walks the horses after they're exercised, then washed off and then walk them around the ring until they're calmed down and cooled out. And I said, 'Well that's the only job I have.' And it 'paid $200 a month.' And I said, 'If you're interested, I need a hot walker.'" He said, "I'll take it."

"We called him Saul. Very quiet and he was like subservient in a way. Not only would he walk the horses, but he'd clean all our racing tack. He'd sweep out our little office. He'd sweep the shed room. He'd do all this work for nothing because he liked to work.

"When we were in the tack room one day, a friend of mine and I, we were sitting in the office there and he was reading the *Los Angeles Times*. And the first page, I think it was, he shouted out, 'Hey, Bobby Kennedy is arming Israel,' or something like that. And as he said that Sirhan went into a rage. He raged and he shouted, and he screamed. How wicked a man Kennedy is: 'The man should be dead. He's killing my people,' because he (Sirhan) is Palestinian. I looked at my friend and I looked over at, we looked over with our mouths wide open because he'd been, he went from a mouse to a lion in a matter of seconds. And finally, I said, 'Calm down.' 'What do you know about politics?'

"Sirhan reacted. He rattled off every senator and congressman in the United States and what state they were from. He knew everything about politics. So eventually he calmed down and we calmed down. We were over at Hollywood Park. I saw him up the steps with these people and I asked my wife, I saw Saul at the racetrack dressed up. He had money and he doesn't seem to be working yet. He's got a couple of hoodlums with him. I can't remember who they were. I've seen these people before. I think they had been thrown out off the track once.

"The day Kennedy was shot, I was working at the racetrack and they flashed a picture on the TV. 'Do you know this man?' My wife saw it and she knew who it was. She called Hollywood Park and she said, 'I'd like to talk to my husband. It's very important.'

"So, they got me to the phone, and she said, 'Guess what? Bobby Kennedy's just been shot and guess who shot him? Saul. Saul, you have to tell somebody.' So, I put the phone down in a hurry. I ran down to the security office, and I told the man inside, 'I know who shot Kennedy!' I told them who he was, and I told him 'he worked for me.'"

If John Shear's story is true, that could be a revealing clue that Dr. Brady's diagnostic opinion is correct in his analysis that there were two, distinctly separate Sirhans – one good, one bad. Then again, there is the part in Shear's story of seeing "Saul" (Sirhan) with a couple of hoodlums who were dressed up and had money. That could point in the direction of others besides Sirhan being involved in RFK's murder.

Although *Psych DNA*, as carefully researched, and then written by Dr. Brady, he does not directly delve into the question of any conspiracy angles in RFK's death; the book is, in Dr. Brady's words, "My book deals with the previously untapped psychological-criminological aspects of Sirhan's deeply troubled personality, especially the hidden, unconscious facets of his personality probably still unavailable to him in a conscious state of awareness. I deal with the result of my research findings that when Sirhan's assassinated Senator Kennedy he was in an altered state of awareness and what factors contributed to that troubling dissociative state. To substantiate this opinion, I used Sirhan's in-depth autobiographical data and three, well-documented tests to verify the presence of Sirhan's split personality type. The results of Sirhan's results on these specific tests confirms the existence of a dissociative profile similar to what Drs. Diamond and Brown found. These different scales were based on Sirhan's extensive autobiographical information, which chronicled his multiple, and severe trauma issues that I attribute his personality fragmentation to."

Yes, Sirhan could be identified as an assassin with a dissociated personality disorder, or a multiple personality, and yet Dr. Brady remains open to the possibility that Sirhan was not alone in assassinating RFK.

Dr. Brady continues, "If you can, look at it this way: there's another Sirhan, a very different one, his personality number two filled with rage and hatred momentarily aimed at his target, Kennedy, who he felt had betrayed him by supporting Israel's side in the never ending war against the Palestinian people. It's pretty much the same as it is today (2024) in the war against Hamas. And there certainly could be another side to this. Whether or not there was a second gunman involved in the assassination, or if there was in fact a conspiracy plot I don't doubt if any of that could be representative. However, I'm not a ballistics expert presenting physical evidence at trial. I'm a forensic psychologist presenting a criminological picture of Sirhan. And I don't doubt that maybe, for instance, that Thane Cesar, a kind of suspicious security guard in close contact with Kennedy when he was fatally wounded, might have taken a shot at Kennedy, but that's the 'sexy tabloid stuff,' but it's not what my information, my analysis has concluded." Is Dr. Brady's assessment of Sirhan's two personalities, correct?

Of course, Dr. Brady, then a graduate student, was in the unique position of being informed by Dr. Diamond's lectures and he had a continuing relationship with him during and after Sirhan's confusing 1969 trial. It appears from my research into this case that Dr. Brady is the first criminologist-psychologist to have truly analyzed all of Sirhan's prior psychological tests and used new ones to confirm his professional opinions. It looks to me as if he has done the psychological work that should have been done five decades ago. In this regard, Dr. Brady also told me: "In my view, if these results had been presented to the jury at trial a different outcome may have resulted – a conviction of second-degree murder not necessitating the death penalty sentence." Finally, has the good doctor given us the final clue as to what really happened in one of the most puzzling assassination mysteries of the 1960s? Read *Psychological DNA; A Cold Case of Who Killed Robert F. Kennedy*, and judge for yourself.

INTRODUCTION

In my long career as a forensic psychologist, I have often been called upon to do psychological postmortems and provide written reports on sometimes aging, cold cases to help determine whether a particular suspect or perpetrator fits a certain psychological profile (i.e., a rapist or murderer), or to find out a perpetrator's intent and motive for engaging in a specific crime or series of crimes. *Psychological DNA: A Cold Case Analysis of Who Killed Robert F. Kennedy (Psych DNA)* offers a deeper understanding of the psychodynamics of Robert F. Kennedy's convicted assassin, Sirhan Bishara Sirhan.

Like all Americans in the summer of 1968, I was upset by the news of the assassination of Robert F. Kennedy (RFK), a former US Attorney General and current New York Senator running for President of the United States. In the Ambassador Hotel in Los Angeles in the early hours of June 5, 1968, Senator Kennedy, who had just won the California Democratic Party primary, finished delivering his victory speech to hundreds of loyal supporters. From all eyewitness accounts, it appeared that a lone gunman caught up with Senator Kennedy in a crowded pantry area of the hotel and emptied an eight-shot revolver almost point blank at him. The world saw heart-wrenching photos of the mortally wounded Kennedy lying on the floor.

Troubling historical events associated with the assassination of Senator Kennedy were that his brother, John Fitzgerald Kennedy (JFK), the thirty-fifth President of the United States, had been assassinated a mere five years before; the war in Vietnam was raging; and the death of Martin Luther King Jr., who was assassinated only two months before RFK, on April 4, 1968, was followed by race riots. The killing of Senator Kennedy left an indelible stain on the American experience.

My personal interest and professional insight into Sirhan's criminal case began during his 1969 trial in Los Angeles. I was a doctoral student at that time in the School of Criminology at the University of California, Berkeley, and Sirhan's lead defense psychiatrist, Dr. Bernard L. Diamond, was my major professor and academic advisor.

During graduate seminars, Dr. Diamond often presented nonconfidential information on the Sirhan case to his graduate students. During lengthy discussions with Professor Diamond, I became aware of many psychological details of the case; much of the same information on which he relied in the preparation and subsequent expert testimony in the case.

"Diminished capacity" was the unique criminal defense Dr. Diamond more or less pioneered in California several years before. His primary rationale for using this unique California defense was to save Sirhan from the death sentence – an effort to help defense attorneys convince the trial jury that the defendants diminished mental state prevented him from "knowingly" committing the crime, and was thus not guilty of first-degree murder, but second-degree murder, which carried a life sentence rather than death in San Quentin's ominous gas chamber.

However, Sirhan was convicted of murder in April 1969 and sentenced to death, though his conviction was commuted to life in prison in 1972. More than a half-century after Sirhan's confusing murder trial, I focused on the salient psychological aspects of the Sirhan case, specifically, his multilayered personality dynamics, by using psychological DNA. In doing so, I arrived at a different psychological portrayal of Sirhan than the previous doctors and investigators who took up the challenge to figure out why Sirhan assassinated RFK.

I share this perspective in detail, reconstructing a comprehensive, new mental picture of the man who gunned down Robert Kennedy in cold blood in a crowded hotel pantry, where the killer's chance of escape was almost zero.

Maybe escape was never part of the plan. Sirhan claimed from the start, and still claims, more than a half-century later, to have no memory of planning the crime, or of having a loaded gun in his possession. In addition, he has no recollection of the murder scene itself, even though he was physically caught with the literal smoking gun until it was wrestled out of his hand after he fired all eight shots.

I have tracked Sirhan's meandering journey over the years as he was shuffled through the California Department of Corrections and Rehabilitation and moved from one correctional institution to another.

The psychological DNA process relies on the verification of explanatory, psychological, and criminological factors located somewhere perhaps far back in a criminal's distant past, most probably during childhood, which explain the radical switch from a law-abiding lifestyle to a deviant one. That somewhere on every criminal's road is an identifiable turning point is well understood by criminologists.

Sirhan, always fighting an uphill battle, was also being tried in the court of public opinion. Celebrity crime writer Truman Capote (*In Cold Blood*) chimed in on the case, speculating on *The Tonight Show* that Sirhan had accomplices, and that he was somehow hypnotized and then brainwashed to kill Senator Kennedy as part of a wider plot to assassinate US political leaders.

Even Dr. Diamond, as lead psychiatrist for the defense, in a statement perhaps gone too far, characterized his own analysis of Sirhan's case, saying, "I agree that this is an absurd and preposterous story, unlikely and incredible. I doubt that Sirhan himself agrees with me as to how everything happened."

Almost lost in the courtroom drama sparked by these true-crime figures was the fact that RFK's accused killer's life was at stake. Sirhan's life became obscured, lost in the confusing testimony presented by the dueling, ego-driven psychiatric experts. Day after day these "well-intentioned" doctors hired by the defense paraded conflicting theories on Sirhan's mental state in front of a progressively bewildered jury. By the end of the stressful four-month trial, they had heard nonstop psychobabble, and their frustration showed.

Sirhan's uneven case percolated in my thoughts for many years, and important aspects just didn't seem to make cohesive, psychological or criminological sense to me. So in revisiting this case that still has so many unanswered questions, I wanted to seek out and provide helpful psychological answers to what seemed an enigma.

My psychological search slowly evolved into what I describe as a type of "criminal-psychosocial autopsy," labeled psychological DNA – a methodology not specifically available when Sirhan was tried for first-degree murder. My research into Sirhan's psychodynamics turned up many new domains of psychological evidence that informed my opinions about *Who is Sirhan? And why did he murder the man he once so admired?*

If the new information provided in this book had been exposed to Sirhan's jury, I believe that it could have made a substantial difference in their guilty verdict and the imposition of the death penalty.

"I killed Robert F. Kennedy willfully, premeditatedly, with twenty years of malice aforethought, that is why," answered Sirhan Bishara Sirhan to the trial judge Herbert Walker's question: "Now, when we come to accepting a plea, you have to give me a reason!"

So, begins the twisted, psychological saga of why Sirhan Bishara Sirhan assassinated RFK.

To the judge's question: "What do you want to do about the penalty?," Sirhan responded flippantly, "I will ask to be executed, Sir!"

I wanted to know, *What distorted psychological reasoning led Sirhan to make these and other equally outrageous statements during the trial?*

The elevated emotions swirling around Sirhan's high-profile assassination trial were fueled by a media that demanded nothing less than a swift – fair or not fair – trial, a conviction, and imposition of the death sentence for the young Arab man who inexplicably continued to deny recall of any of the factual circumstances of the shooting.

A missing key element in the comprehensive assessment of Sirhan's case is derived from the results of extensive, psychological testing administered by the two defense-hired psychologists, who (in my view) missed diagnosing Sirhan's most important psychological conditions. Oddly enough, the primary diagnostic opinions affecting Sirhan's mental state did not came from the two original psychologists, but from seven "blind diagnostic" review doctors. One of these review doctors, Dr. Georgene Seward, stated: "I proceeded as if I were dealing with the patient in a hospital on whom I was asked to make a blind diagnosis. That means I examined each of the tests by each of the examiners, and I compared them. I noted the differences and the similarities that were shown." The diagnostic impressions of Sirhan at the time of the trial were sufficiently flawed because they were partially based on the incomplete and confusing psychological testing results provided by the defense psychologists and the "second opinion" review doctors.

In retrospect, this created a significant diagnostic dilemma that was especially the case when I reexamined the scattered results on Sirhan's Thematic Apperception Test (TAT), a well-researched personality scale. The results from this specific test, when accurately presented and scored, could have provided enhanced insight into Sirhan's troubled personality structure.

In addition to the faulty testing issues, more strategic legal troubles arose during Sirhan's trial. For example, over Sirhan's noisy courtroom outbursts and protests, the trial judge allowed the prosecution to present some limited, but devastating, evidence against Sirhan, based on his own damaging words written in his diary (the controversial "RFK Must Die" document). Then inexplicably, the defense made the unwise decision to introduce into evidence even more disturbing statements from Sirhan's diary, further enraging him. This single, disputable decision by the defense team to open up Sirhan's innumerable incriminating diary entries to the jurors may have unduly influenced their decision to impose a death sentence.

This major defense blunder made by Sirhan's combined legal and psychiatric team appeared to sink any meaningful chances for Sirhan to receive a fair trial.

Why would the defense doctor-lawyer team deliver up their client on a silver platter to the prosecution, ultimately pushing Sirhan toward an awaiting executioner in charge of San Quentin's ominous gas chamber?

Somehow the defense team, using convoluted logic, had convinced themselves that by exposing Sirhan's "crazy-sounding" incriminating verbal statements, combined with written statements taken from his diary, this damaging information would in some way lend support for Sirhan's psychiatric, "diminished capacity" defense. They couldn't have been more wrong.

My research into Sirhan's complex criminological-psychological mental status culminated in my developing five criminal-psychologically explanatory categories missed by all the experts. Absent the detailed exploration into these unique, explanatory conditions, no possible path can explain why Sirhan committed a single, homicidal act that changed the fabric of twentieth century American political history.

These five conditions, when combined, provide a very different picture of the criminal mind of this assassin. The corroboration of these newly constructed criminal and mental destabilizers are supported by the results of my current research.

When I began to research the literature about the RFK assassination, I found a glaring absence of books by professionally trained criminologists, forensic psychologists, or psychiatrists familiar with the "right fit" methodology to best integrate the facts of Sirhan's case.

My goal after all these years is to share the new criminological and psychological facts and findings I concluded from my research compiled in *Psych DNA*. I can now offer an evidence-based interpretation of the original psychological testing results, having reevaluated these assessment conclusions and the psychiatric diagnoses, using current psychological systems and contemporary psychiatric classifications not available in 1969. Similar to Dr. Seward's viewpoint, my second-opinion ("cold case") psychological picture of Sirhan may be understood as a unique contribution to reconstructing Sirhan's complex psychodynamics, and better answer the more than fifty-year-old question: Why did he kill Senator Kennedy?

CHAPTER 1

SETTING THE STAGE IN RETROSPECT

The period in January of 1969, when Sirhan's trial began in a Los Angeles Superior Courtroom, was a significant time for me because, as Dr. Diamond's graduate student when he was selected as Sirhan's lead psychiatrist, I had special access to some psychological information, including Sirhan's mixed psychiatric diagnoses, which was unavailable at the time to the press or the general public.

Additionally, during Senator Kennedy's California campaign for the Democratic Party nomination, I had volunteered to work a Kennedy for President table, set up on Bancroft Avenue not far from the University of California's Law School, taking donations and distributing fliers and other pamphlets in support of Kennedy's California campaign. This had been an exciting time for all of us "true believers" that Robert Kennedy could make a difference if he became President of the US.

When I thought back to those hectic academic days, I recall how much I learned about the Sirhan case during Dr. Diamond's many informative seminars delving into his particular analysis of Sirhan's mental status, placing particular emphasis on Sirhan's psychological confusion before and at the time of the murder. This was especially true during Dr. Diamond's informative lectures when he laid out the legal precedent cases leading to the criminal defense of diminished capacity that he helped introduce into law via a California Supreme Court decision.

Still, the abundance of physical evidence and eyewitness accounts of what transpired in a tiny pantry in the Ambassador Hotel where Senator Kennedy was shot seemed overwhelmingly destined to lead to a guilty verdict. Reflecting back on this notorious case in US political history, and on the nature of those valued lectures delivered by Dr. Diamond, I wondered whether I could supplement the copious opinions on the case done during the past fifty-five years and bring a fresh psychological interpretation of what I learned about Sirhan's complicated mental health status while studying under the direction of Dr. Diamond and in combination with my own long career experiences as a California-based forensic psychologist.

Many of the important psychodiagnostic decisions made by the defense team's medical experts were based on troubling and incomplete psychological testing data, skewed testing results, and various reports that were submitted specifically by two psychologists: Drs. Martin Schorr and Roderick Richardson. During cross examination by Assistant District Attorney David Fitts, Dr. Diamond pointed out the significance of these incomplete testing results: "Dr. Schorr and Dr. Richardson presented their psychological findings in great detail, and I insisted that I wished to have the raw data that is Sirhan's actual responses to these tests rather than Dr. Schorr's conclusions. I had some problems in my mind accepting their conclusions."[1] I concur with Dr. Diamond's reservations.

The death of Senator Kennedy represented the end to his idealistic dream for America's new direction of peaceful coexistence in the 1960s-torn society. The year 1968 was the beginning of a fifty-five-year nightmare (and counting) for Sirhan Sirhan, a then-twenty-four-year-old Palestinian and wannabe jockey, who was misdiagnosed and portrayed by the media as "a fanatic Arab terrorist, paranoid crazy loser, and crazed-psychopathic killer."

Although more than five decades have passed since Sirhan was convicted of killing Senator Kennedy and sent to San Quentin's death row, the fresh psychological analysis of Sirhan's representative mental state adds important, new psychological concepts negatively affecting him at the time he shot Senator Kennedy. Many of Sirhan's actual psychological, mental conditions eluded the efforts of the "best and brightest" psychiatric team of that time and could not be professionally addressed during what I consider Sirhan's 1969 "show trial."

To sort out this cold case, I used updated psychiatric and criminal classifications based on newly constructed psychological tests, and contemporary research methods (particularly the psychological DNA methodology), and completed a revised psychological profile of Sirhan's personality dynamics that embraced a complete review of all the doctors' diagnoses. The revised testing results helped form a different picture of the man who in the end was not proven "crazy" at all. The retrospective analysis and reinterpretation of Sirhan's assessment results convinced me that Sirhan's original paranoid schizophrenic diagnosis was errant and way off the mark.

The discovery of erroneous diagnoses were news to me and not where I planned to go when I originally outlined my concept for the direction

---

1   *Trial*, Vol 25, March 27, 1969.

of this book. Perhaps the jury's verdict in Sirhan's trial might have turned out quite differently if my newly uncovered psychological conditions, or at least some of them, had found their way into the defense arguments in support of Sirhan's very disturbed personality – a volatile, antisocial personality operating below his own personal level of awareness – when he killed Senator Kennedy. The reformulated psychological conditions explained here, not entered as mitigating, psychiatric evidence at trial, might have constituted grounds for judicial appeal motions if made by the defense team.

The extensive use of Sirhan's court testimony and the testimony of many additional witnesses cited throughout this book represent my effort to recapture many counterproductive courtroom moments that sealed Sirhan's fate. The defenses' unforced strategic and legal-psychiatric mistakes only compounded as the trial moved forward, serving to further confuse the skeptical jury who seemed perplexed by the divergent and what seemed at times an unstopped stream of "psychobabble" delivered by the psychiatric defense team.

A notable factor affecting the outcome of Sirhan's trial is the turbulent time in American history during which Sirhan was tried and convicted of first-degree murder. The entire country appeared to be on edge, and a noticeable undercurrent of a societal prejudice worked against the obviously foreign immigrant defendant. Worsening the situation were the innumerable race riots. The Watts riots of 1965, for instance, that raged through the mostly Black neighborhoods in South-Central Los Angeles, resulted in almost fifty deaths and thousands injured. Racially charged riots spread rapidly across the nation, igniting prejudice against African-Americans and other minority groups in proportions not experienced since the end of the Civil War, a hundred years before. Like most of us living through those turbulent times, Sirhan was of course well aware of the impact of these riots and the rapidly building racism fostering hopelessness in millions of disenfranchised people of color – because he was one of them!

During the Sirhan trial, racial discrimination could not be factored out. This potentially damaging issue may have negatively affected the jurors, or at least reinforced the presence of inherent juror bias by the twelve ordinary citizens who would determine Sirhan's fate. As the trial proceeded, the rising tide of racial bias began to wash over it.

At the beginning of the trial, the possibility of potential juror bias was palpable, and it became a real concern raised by attorney Abdeen Jabara, Sirhan's designated Arab representative. To offset or minimize the presence of prejudicial bias, Jabara proposed a number of questions that defense attorneys, Grant Cooper and Emile Zola Berman, might pose to the potential members of the jury pool during the *voir dire* (preliminary exam of a juror or a witness) process.

In response to his request, Jabara stated, "Cooper and Berman laughed when I gave them these questions and paid no attention to them at all. In selecting the jury, Cooper restricted his questioning on racism to the simple leading question: 'The fact that this man is a Palestinian won't affect your consideration of this case, will it?'"

"Parsons [Russell Parsons, also a defense attorney] didn't do much better.... What followed after the selection of the jury was the opening of the case by the prosecution and weeks of tedious reconstructing of the shooting of Kennedy...."[2]

Jabara stated that from the outset of the trial, it was apparent that: "... Their main responsibility was to avoid the theoretical possibility of his judicial execution: as they had to strive officiously to keep him alive."[3]

Jabara maintained an inside track, assessing the jury's mindset as he sat next to Sirhan at critical times during the trial. He said of the jury: "A number of jurors were totally confused by the psychiatric testimony. After the trial, juror Benjamin Glick told Martin Kasindorf of *Newsweek* magazine that "not even the experts could get together among themselves."

Another juror, Albert Frederico, stated emphatically, "All those psychiatrists! They really had us stirred up. It was confusing. It stunk!"[4]

As the trial progressed, Jabara strongly believed that the defense team disagreed on the best strategy to use to present evidence consistent with the diminished capacity defense as a novel psychiatric plea, and why it failed: "Everyone had an opinion as to why the defense had failed. Cooper saw it as a backlash of the jurors against the violence in the United States."

Robert Blair Kaiser, a journalist and appointed defense investigator who was commissioned to write a book on the case, thought political considerations in the trial had mitigated "the only real defense Sirhan ever had."[5]

Sirhan was portrayed by members in the news media as a politically motivated assassin, a "sleeper terrorist," vindictive, and maybe the first Arab terrorist to strike the US homeland. In a rush to judgment, news

---

2   Jansen, G. (1970). *Why Robert Kennedy Was Killed: The Story of Two Victims*. The Third Press, Joseph Okpaku Publishing Company, Inc., New York.
3   Ibid.
4   Ibid.
5   Ibid.

media outlets falsely claimed that Sirhan was supported in his desire to kill Senator Kennedy by the fledgling Palestine Liberation Organization (PLO) founded only a few years prior to the assassination. The PLO goal was to eliminate Zionists, who they believed illegally occupied large swaths of former Palestinian territories, and retaliate against those who supported the State of Israel.

Though Sirhan had a firm pro-Palestinian view, there is no evidence that Sirhan was ever a member of the radical PLO or any other subversive organizations. Responding to the allegation, Sirhan told defense investigator Robert Kaiser quite a different story: that his hope for the future was always connected to the United States where there were better opportunities and he was not in any way tethered to violent, Arab terrorist groups: "I don't identify with the Arabs politically or any other way except for the fact that their blood flows through my veins.... Their religion? I'm a Christian. Their language, I don't speak very well. Hell, I'm an American."[6]

In spite of his strong denial of an Arab political connection, or affiliations and not forming allegiances with subversive groups, Sirhan was deeply affected by the Palestinian defeat in the Six-Day War between Israel and a coalition of Arab states only a year before the assassination.,

The feeling across the nation was that nothing less than swift, retributive justice, and the imposition of capital punishment would be acceptable for this foreigner who murdered an American political icon. And that's exactly how it turned out for the twenty-four-year-old, diminutive would-be jockey and transplant from war-torn Jordan.

Similar to the assassination of JFK five years earlier, Sirhan's murder trial attracted considerable international attention as well. But unlike the fate of the killer in that case, Lee Harvey Oswald, himself murdered, the fact remains: the Sirhan case, shaped by a drawn-out criminal trial, provided an enduring record, yielding considerable new psychological information that, for some reason, has not previously been addressed by forensic psychologists familiar with the case.

From the outset, my intention was specifically focused on the most-salient psychological information that would provide renewed insight into Sirhan and why he assassinated RFK.

Dr. Diamond connected the "diminished capacity" defense to Sirhan's tangled mental state wherein he could be guilty of the lesser murder charge of second-degree, thereby negating the death penalty. Back then,

---

6   Kaiser, R.B. (1970). "R.F.K. Must Die!": A History of the Robert Kennedy Assassination and Its *Aftermath.* E.P. Dutton, New York.

most of us nodded affirmatively that, on some level, we intellectually grasped Dr. Diamond's nuanced meaning concerning the lessening of criminal responsibility dependent on the nature and severity of the defendant's mental symptoms. Assuredly Dr. Diamond hoped the jury would likewise understand this defense was formulated as part philosophic, part legal, and part psychiatric. His initial optimism was dashed by the jury's seemingly confused reaction of what diminished capacity was really all about and, even more essential, how its application might lessen Sirhan's responsibility for killing a national hero.

The jury took four days to render a guilty verdict for first-degree murder, and five additional guilty verdicts for criminal assault with the intent to commit murder, condemning Sirhan to death in San Quentin's feared gas chamber – clearly not the optimistic outcome the "high-powered" defense doctors, especially Dr. Diamond, envisioned.

Over time, as I looked deeper into Sirhan's personality dynamics, examining his strange collection of psychiatric symptoms, I wondered if he was experiencing a different, previously undiagnosed psychiatric condition, or several undiagnosed conditions. This prompted additional areas of concern:

Who really is Sirhan Bishara Sirhan?

Was he actually mentally ill at the time of the murder?

And why did he desire to kill Senator Kennedy in the first place and then could not remember the actual killing scene?

In my retrospective view, the collective efforts of the psychologists and psychiatrists at the time only further clouded the already murky psychodynamics of this murder case. Many of the basic, psychological, and the criminological drivers (in particular) contributed to this case remaining an unsolved, psychological cold-case mystery.

Naturally, Dr. Diamond lent his considerable psychiatric weight as the lead psychiatrist heading the well-advertised defense team was labeled "a dream team." He gladly welcomed the opportunity to work for Sirhan's defense team pro bono, but his efforts were not enough to reach the hoped-for second-degree murder verdict.

CHAPTER 2

SIRHAN'S MOTIVE – PURELY POLITICAL?

Almost anyone who has followed this case has been informed that Sirhan Bishara Sirhan was the alleged single shooter in the killing of Senator Kennedy, yet theories persist that he was not the only person involved. The relevant information sources included here and used throughout this psychological reappraisal of the Sirhan case, particularly his mental state, were carefully selected as factually confirmed with actual timelines, specific dates, key players, court testimony, and actual locations.

Sirhan's case continued to command my professional attention and concerted criminological interest over the years. I took this opportunity to probe into Sirhan's psychiatric background, guided by a psychological lens for considering a complete reconstructing of previous, unconsidered forensic facts that were likely unavailable to other writers.

Immediately evident to anyone examining the facts of the Sirhan case is the inordinate amount of investigative time spent tying Sirhan's "hatred of Jews and the Israeli State" to his motivational reasoning for the murder of Senator Kennedy. Allegedly, Sirhan's motivation to kill Senator Kennedy was based on the statement Kennedy made to a Jewish gathering in Beverly Hills during a campaign speech, saying that he supported sending at least fifty US bombers to Israel to be used to attack the Palestinian people (Sirhan's people).

During his sessions with Dr. Diamond, Sirhan seemed to acknowledge his guilt in the assassination (quoted by Dr. Diamond): "Because Sirhan was quite prepared to admit to me or anybody who would ask him that he killed Senator Kennedy, that he hated Senator Kennedy, and he had done this to prevent Senator Kennedy from getting elected to the presidency and sending fifty bombers to Israel."[1]

Later when questioned by Robert Kaiser about why Sirhan wrote "RFK Must Die" many times throughout the diary, Sirhan gave confusing and off-putting answers.

"After that, I forgot it all.... The idea of killing Kennedy never crossed my mind, Sir. I just wanted, Sir, to stop him from sending planes to Isra-

---
1   Kaiser. (1970).

el." This approximates the statement he openly provided to Dr. Diamond, referencing the often-promoted, "jet bomber theory" of the crime motivation that has been almost universally accepted, especially among Sirhan's legal team and the psychologists and psychiatrists who assessed his mental state.

Explanations for why Sirhan continuously admitted to shooting Senator Kennedy, and why he said a number of times that he could not remember committing the homicidal act, seemed incongruous at best, and did not reconcile with eyewitness accounts of the shooting. Apparently, Sirhan was told by so many people and so many times, including his defense team, the police, investigators, and others, that he was guilty of killing RFK, he automatically internalized this inculpatory evidence and said, "Yes, I am the one who killed Senator Kennedy," but guess what?, "I can't recall it, or doing it!"

In reviewing Sirhan's extensive trial record, it became apparent that his professional defense team clearly downplayed or outright rejected any competing notions or theories examining his antisocial traits that might explain why he committed the crime or what his true mental state was. From the start, they chose not to explore alternative motivational patterns that may have influenced Sirhan's homicidal drive. This is significant in that he had no history of committing assaultive crimes and was characterized by many people who knew him as somewhat "passive and nonconfrontational by nature."

Peculiarly, during long periods in the trial, Sirhan seemed to sleepwalk through the tedious legal proceedings, appearing sometimes dazed, out of sorts, and at times, "kind of out of this world." Other times, suffused with rage and anger, he momentarily erupted, became agitated, rebellious, confused, somewhat uncontrolled, and seemingly perplexed by the complex legal wrangling: "I don't know. I don't understand all this legality … Sirhan said. "I still maintain my original point. I plead guilty to murder and asked to be executed; that's it!"

During the past forty-plus years, I have been called upon to analyze and diagnose similar, select murder cases by the Santa Clara County Superior Court in San Jose, California, to ascertain a credible psychological theory for why a crime was committed, and why the perpetrator did it. I have been baffled at how many of the criminal defendants I assessed, tested, and diagnosed had vague or no conscious comprehension of why they took the life of another human being – a Rubik's Cube of my business!

Generally, in those cases, the more apparent or surface reasons were usually linked to the most common criminal motivational patterning: jealousy, money, rage, revenge, and sex. These reasons provided by defendants proved to be more conveniently descriptive than psychologically explanatory to me. I pondered whether the Sirhan case might fall into the conveniently descriptive category.

During my career, I have found that a criminal's covert motivation pattern to kill often remains buried somewhere deep in their unconscious mind. During the 1968-1969 academic year, when I was first introduced to the Sirhan case, I was still learning the theories (of why people kill and how they came to form criminal intent) and searching for homicidal motivational patterns. Over time, Dr. Diamond delved into more aspects of the criminal mind in cases similar to Sirhan's. From his standpoint, the common denominator connecting his choice of cases seemed to be centered on one aspect or another of the bad actor's mental state when the crime was committed. The primary analysis of the Sirhan case was quite naturally centered on issues related to his demonstrable mental state at the time he murdered Robert Kennedy.

Appropriately, Dr. Diamond drew from his vast experience as a military psychiatrist, diagnosing and rendering professional opinions concerning sanity issues, especially as a US Army psychiatrist serving in World War II. The issues raised by Dr. Diamond in his seminars were the same complex mental issues I struggled with later as a forensic psychologist. Though the issues facing forensic psychologists do not change, new methodologies used to answer the key question do change, i.e., Was Sirhan sane or insane at the time he shot Robert F. Kennedy?

Sometimes when approaching a new case, the reason/motive for the criminal behavior is self-evident and quite easy for professionals to agree on, thereby making an informed opinion. Consider one Silicon Valley case I was asked to diagnose by a defense attorney, which involved a female defendant accused of first-degree murder.

For twenty years, she had remained a devoted wife who raised two teenagers and saw herself as a supportive wife and mother. Suddenly she found out that her husband had taken a mistress and squandered their life savings in Las Vegas. She decided to eliminate the philanderer, cash in the two-million-dollar life insurance funds, and simply start her life over again. The motive for her crime seemed fairly easy to grasp.

The unmasking of this woman's killer motive for why she did it doesn't really meet the stress test to trigger our imaginative, psychological investigative skills necessary to locate her underlying dangerous behavior. This simple example, demonstrating where this homicidal motive originated and was harbored by this woman, is certainly *not* what we find when analyzing the complexities of the true motive underlying Sirhan's case.

A TRAGIC YEAR IN HISTORY

In their book, *Crimes of the Century*, authors Gilbert Geis and Leigh Beinen pose an essential question: "What is it that catapults a crime – or, at times, an event that allegedly is criminal – into a realm where it remains deeply embedded into our collective imagination many decades later?"[2]

By any historical viewpoint, 1968 was a year marked by tragedy and political upheaval directly impacting the American mindset. The mood of the nation, especially its youth, during that critical year was negatively impacted by the violence continuing to rage in Vietnam as the body count approximated fifty thousand dead US soldiers returned to our shores in body bags.

Accompanying the turmoil in South East Asia, the civil rights movement began to gather momentum with demands for change – that America strive to become a more racially balanced and equal society after a century of racism and color discrimination. Espousing high ideas to achieve equality for all African-Americans, a charismatic Southern Baptist preacher, Dr. Martin Luther King Jr., began his quest, presenting a number of speeches culminating in his now famous "I Have a Dream" speech delivered on the steps of Washington's Lincoln Memorial on August 28, 1963, in front of 250,000 devoted civil rights supporters. Bob Dylan's lyrics in his song, "The Times They Are a-Changing," in 1964, served notice that the changes were likely not for the better in the short run.

As 1968 progressed, changes advocated by Dr. King, using peaceful, nonviolent protests combined with the nationwide demonstrations to pull out of the Vietnam conflict, and the immediate changes prophesied by Dylan portended a rising dark cloud marked by domestic violence, widespread street riots, and social turmoil with little blue sky in sight!

Americans could see this dark cloud manifesting in a number of political assassinations characterized by a malaise and disbelief, leading to the questions, "Can this really be happening to our country? And what can stop it from tearing our nation apart?"

The 1960's assassination case that has fostered the most controversy and generated the most conspiracy theories over time is the tragic assas-

---

2   Geis, G. and L. B. Bienen. (1998). *Crimes of the century.* Northeastern University Press, Boston.

sination of President John Fitzgerald Kennedy (JFK), on November 22, 1963, as he waved to his supporters who lined the streets in Dealey Plaza in Dallas, Texas, on a sunny afternoon. In the past six decades, more books have been written about President Kennedy's killing than almost any noteworthy assassination save the crucifixion of Jesus Christ.

Two years after President Kennedy's assassination, Malcolm X, an African-American Muslim leader; and like Dr. King a civil rights activist, was assassinated on February 21, 1965, representing the loss of another American hero to many African-Americans and civil rights advocates. X's transformation from a local street hustler to a figure of national prominence, spreading the word of Islam as a prophet of hope to millions of African-Americans, was a dramatic rise.

As Malcolm X prepared to deliver a speech to 400 attendees of the Organization of Afro-American Unity at Manhattan's Audubon Ballroom, he was shot multiple times by three gunmen. He died at the scene. His wife and four children in the crowd witnessed the murder. An autopsy established that at least twenty-one bullets entered his body.

The three gunmen were arrested and subsequently convicted of murder and sentenced to life in prison. However, this did not end the probing into who really killed Malcolm X? And why? Initially it was believed, contrary to police evidence, that the Nation of Islam was the culprit, then an alleged connection to local drug dealers was proffered. A number of additional conspiracy theories emerged shortly after his death, this time pointing the finger at three more of the usual suspects – the CIA, the police (NYPD), and the FBI.

CHAPTER 3

BACKGROUND OF THE CASE

RFK MUST DIE

Though the case against Sirhan Sirhan is rife with controversy and loaded with enduring conspiracy theories, the circumstantial facts surrounding the case as we know them are these: At approximately 12:15 a.m., after consuming "four or five" strong Tom Collins drinks, Sirhan ended up in the LA Ambassador Hotel pantry just as Senator Kennedy passed through. Suddenly Sirhan wielded a snub-nosed, Iver Johnson .22 caliber hand gun, from his waistband, and unloaded eight shots in the direction of Senator Kennedy. Less than twenty-four hours later, Kennedy was pronounced dead.

According to the LA County Coroner, Dr. Thomas Noguchi, who later became a controversial figure in the case, three of these bullets ripped into Senator Kennedy, and the remaining shots wounded another five people: a United Auto Worker executive and Kennedy supporter, Paul Schrade; an American Broadcasting Company (ABC) newsperson, William Weisel; seventeen-year-old Irwin Stroll; nineteen-year-old Ira Goldstein; and Mrs. Elizabeth Evans. Because this tragedy was covered by multiple local, state, and national media services, headline reports immediately flew around the globe that Bobby Kennedy, the much-beloved democratic candidate for the 1968 presidential nomination was shot after finishing an uplifting victory speech to well-wishers, ardent supporters and hangers on, having just won the California Democratic primary.

Several people who witnessed the shooting screamed, "No, please God, not another Dallas!"

Senator Kennedy, only forty-two years old and well on his way to winning the approaching Democratic nomination for president scheduled for Chicago in August, was immediately taken by ambulance to Central Receiving Hospital, a close by but limited trauma center located on West 6th Street. The other gunshot victims were also rushed there to treat what initially appeared to be lesser, gunshot-inflicted, non-life-threatening injuries.

Because of the obvious head wounds seen by the medical triage team, Kennedy was then rushed to Good Samaritan Hospital, a larger full-scale trauma facility, only three blocks away. Dr. Henry Cuneo, a surgeon, was dispatched to Good Samaritan to take charge of Senator Kennedy's trauma treatment and immediately instructed the hospital staff to place the senator on an ice bed to avoid a spike in temperature.

At first, some positive indication that his medical condition was improving led the doctors to think they might be able to stabilize him. Kennedy was moved to the ninth floor of Good Samaritan Hospital where Dr. Cuneo, assisted by Dr. Maxwell Andler and Dr. Nat Reid, made an incision in the back of the senator's head and carefully removed a large blood clot, bone shards, and several metal pieces (presumably bullet fragments). The doctors were not able to remove all the small metal shards lodged in the brain, yet there was still hope. The initial optimism was short-lived as the senator's vital signs quickly worsened, and he was barely clinging on to life. At 1:27 a.m. on June 6, his pulse, breathing, and cardiac function failed, and all lifesaving measures were stopped. Tragically, at 1:44 a.m., Senator Kennedy was pronounced dead.

At 2:00 a.m. Senator's Kennedy's press secretary, Frank Mankiewicz, provided the final update to the gathered press that aired it live, saying simply, "Robert Francis Kennedy died at 1:44 a.m. today, June 6, 1968."

Two Parallel Killers: Richard Speck and Sirhan Sirhan

My initial interest in the psychology of murder cases like Sirhan's was ignited by the brutal murder of eight student nurses in Chicago two years before Sirhan's case. Richard Franklin Speck, a mentally challenged drifter with a violent history was charged in 1966 with first-degree murder for the mass homicides of the nurses. Individually they were killed in their supposedly safe student nurses' dormitory.

Clearly, in addition to his violent potential, Speck, like Sirhan, had a variety of serious mental issues. Also similar to Sirhan, the Chicago media called for an immediate trial and would not accept anything less that capital punishment for the gangly, pockmarked defendant who they labeled, "Born to Raise Hell" from the tattoo prominently inked on his left forearm.

Less than a month after the Born to Raise Hell case made nationwide headlines, the public's conscience was again shocked. In Austin, Texas, Charles Whitman stood at the top of a clock tower overlooking the University of Texas's usually tranquil campus and killed thirteen people. Later in 1966, a disgruntled high-school senior executed four women and a child in a beauty salon in Mesa, Arizona. In both the Austin and Mesa cases, the victims were selected randomly with no relationship between the killer and victims, and no apparent motive.

To some degree, Speck's mass murder changed the American understanding of violent crime remembering, quite naturally, that this was a pre-Ted Bundy serial killing rampage, accounting for at least twenty-eight female murders across the country between 1974 and 1978. It was never made exactly clear why, on July 13, 1966, Speck chose to victimize eight student nurses which made the crime seem like a purely random event rather than a rationally planned attack. However, Ted Bundy was selective in his choice of victims, only choosing a similar type of young women with long, brown hair.

In many ways, these tragedies helped to change society's comprehension of violent crimes: *If it can happen there, then maybe it's possible here too?*

Richard Speck was confined in the Cook County Jail, where he was extensively interviewed by Dr. Martin Ziporyn, an experienced psychiatrist assigned by the county to the jail facility, and the psychiatrist who knew the most about Speck's brain dysfunction, low IQ, and multiple psychiatric disorders.

Dr. Ziporyn concluded that Speck was suffering from an organic brain syndrome due to his chronic ingestion of alcohol and other toxic agents he used. Added to the brain syndrome, Dr. Ziporyn stated that Speck's cerebral damage was worsened, based on his history of repeated head trauma.

Unexpectedly during Speck's trial, little attention was devoted to diagnosing his obviously disturbed mental state when he murdered the student nurses. His defense attorney did not even call Dr. Ziporyn as a professional witness, thus losing the opportunity to present the mitigating psychiatric factors that negatively affected Speck during the commission of the murders. The trial judge even disallowed mitigating psychiatric testimony from Dr. Ziporyn.

Sirhan, on the other hand, found himself in the opposite situation, because he was deluged with almost daily mental probing from a steady stream of prosecution and defense doctors, none who seemed to agree on an accepted diagnosis. For Sirhan, additional doctors didn't insure a better result.

Richard Speck, the rejected drifter with a compromised IQ, a host of psychiatric problems, and possible organic brain damage, who sexually assaulted then killed eight defenseless student nurses, was (like Sirhan) twenty-four years old at the time of the murders. The legal process in which their respective criminal cases were adjudicated paralleled each other, and their respective outcomes, capital punishment, were the same. Strong societal forces pushing for eye-for-an-eye retaliation in both head-line-grabbing murder cases were simply too powerful to allow Richard Speck, a mass killer of innocent young women; or Sirhan Bishara Sirhan, the man who killed RFK, to marshal the ability to present credible and convincing psychiatric defenses to save their lives.

Sirhan's team of defense doctors failed to locate and delve into the mainsprings of Sirhan's criminal motivation, and far too much court testimony that was confusing, difficult to understand and, at times, contradictory, stretched the jury's sense of incredulity to the breaking point. When all the testimony was presented during Sirhan's four-month trial, the jury, in a collective act of frustration, apparently threw up their hands and declared, "Guilty as charged, send him to the gas chamber; and now can we please go home?"

Like millions of other Americans, I had a simple question regarding the Speck case: How could Richard Speck, a lone criminal, control, bind, and then rape several victims and then systematically murder a total of eight women in one night?

As Speck began his assault, a ninth student nurse managed to hide under a bed and remain quiet as Speck methodically murdered her classmates one by one. As the State's principal witness, this survivor could identify Speck at his 1969 trial from the distinctive tattoo on his left forearm, "Born to Raise Hell!"

Unfortunately, we will never know why Speck engaged in his homicidal acts, which made the crime seem like a purely random event rather than a rationally planned attack. Similar to Sirhan' s psychodynamics, Speck claimed he had no recollection of the events leading up to or committing the eight grisly murders. When interviewed, he said, "I can't remember anything that happened that night. I musta blacked out!"

Was this memory deficit claim, also made by Sirhan, a conscious ploy to avoid responsibility for their heinous crimes?

Similar to the Speck case, Sirhan was spared the death penalty (in Illinois it was carried out using the electric chair) this time by a US Supreme Court decision ruling in June 1971 that the death penalty was unconstitutional. Speck was resentenced to Statesville Correctional Center in Joliet, Illinois, for fifty to one hundred years for each murder.

In both the Sirhan and Speck cases, psychiatric testimony was not exactly aimed to better explain the perpetrators' actions at the time of their offenses. Interestingly, before the trial, the issue of Speck's sanity and general mental capacity was addressed when the trial court made its own motion to have Speck examined by an appointed panel of six experts, including specialists in the field of neurology and psychiatry. They all testified, expressing their opinions that defendant Speck was able to understand the nature of charges against him and that he was able to cooperate with counsel in the preparation of his criminal defense.

On appeal, the convicted Speck claimed that the testimony by the State's experts during cross-examination provided sufficient grounds to challenge his mental competency to stand trial in the first place. His appeal based on mental incompetency was rejected by the Supreme Court of Illinois in a decision issued on November 22, 1968.

The rejection of Speck's insanity defense was challenged by Dr. Ziporyn, who had extensively interviewed Speck in jail. Dr. Ziporyn concluded that Speck suffered from chronic brain damage caused by a long history of drug and alcohol abuse and repeated head traumas, extending back to when he was fifteen years old, and he was not responsible for his longstanding violent inclination, including the murderous actions on the day of the mass killings.

Speck's direct damage to his brain caused by the chronic ingestion of drugs, multiple head traumas, and chronic alcohol ingestion, according to Dr. Ziporyn, may have negatively impacted his remote memory, thus affecting his moral compass and judgment at the time of the murders.

Glancing back, Sirhan's sophisticated team of psychologists and one designated psychiatrist, ostensibly hired to help him with his defense, seemed to fall short in their charge. For instance, results of two of the tests given to Sirhan to assess possible organic brain damage were never given much focus, nor adequately explained to the jury. Were their results even considered by Sirhan's defense attorneys?

Such potentially vital omissions make one wonder how many more omissions and unintentional oversights were made in the presentation of Sirhan's important testing results? Perhaps like the Speck case, where Dr. Ziporyn, who knew the most about Speck's mental status and possible organic brain damage, was blocked from presenting important court testimony that might have proved invaluable to the defense. This key witness who could have helped explain Speck's clear antisocial personality and turn to mass murder.

Because of these and additional unanswered questions in the Speck case, Dr. Ziporyn contends that Speck's confinement to a mental facility and not a death sentence could yield the real reason or reasons why he took the lives of eight young women.[1]

Although the circumstances and the nature of the wanton mass murder committed by Speck differ from Sirhan's assassination of RFK, perhaps the real reasons both engaged in their crimes were not the apparent ones popularized and repeated ad nauseam by dueling doctors and spread widely by an eager press that demanded answers. The drumbeat by the press and the public may have, in the end, choked off viable exploration into reasonable alternative psychological avenues to help explain why Speck and Sirhan did what they did. A simple rush to judgment seemed to follow: that Speck killed predicated on his unstable, criminal background; and that Sirhan, an ardent supporter of the Palestinian plight, acted because Senator Kennedy supported military aid for Israel.

The theories to account for Sirhan's and Speck's behavior advanced at the time of their respective trials may have been descriptive enough of these two criminal actors' psychiatric histories, but doggedly clinging to these theories alone may have disallowed further exploration into more explanatory criminological-psychological streams of thought, providing alternative trails of criminal causation.

During one of his first graduate seminars at Berkeley, Dr. Diamond, in another of his penetrating lectures, delved into how a person's psychological state goes to the core of their capacity to form criminal intent, an essential element to be held legally responsible for committing a crime. In Sirhan's case, Dr. Diamond strongly believed that the issue of criminal intent and responsibility for his actions, resulting in RFK's death, should have figured prominently in the defense strategy. But it did not.

A basic understanding of Sirhan's criminal intent appeared to be the key to best analyzing the case. How fortunate for myself and my graduate colleagues to be right in front of the doctor who played such a decisive role in determination of Sirhan's ultimate fate. During lectures and face-to-face conferences throughout Sirhan's trial and after his conviction, Dr. Diamond conveyed as much psychological information as he could concerning the construction and foundation of a psychological portrait of the man who shot RFK.

Based on Dr. Diamond's pivotal role as a representative of Sirhan's defense team, and because the trial was held in Los Angeles County Superior

---

1   Altman, K. and M. Ziporyn. (1967). *Born to Raise Hell: The Untold Story of Richard Speck.* New York,: Grove Press, Inc.

Court, he had to shuttle between the Berkeley campus and LA. Though Dr. Diamond's court testimony became a part of the public record, his theories, insightful ideas, and conceptualization of Sirhan's case remained private and stayed confidential.

During these seminars, Dr. Diamond was able to sketch out relevant psychological constructs that, in a general way, were also applicable to what was taking place in the LA courtroom. Obviously, as a graduate student, my role as an observer was to absorb as much information as I could, and then at some point draw my own academic conclusions based on what I learned from Dr. Diamond's analysis, following the twisting psychological contours of the case. At a later point, I was able to proffer questions to him to help clarify many of the complex and challenging legal-psychological issues facing the struggling defense team during the duration of the trial, which was in session from January 7, to April 14, 1969.

During the trial testimony, Dr. Diamond laid out his well-conceived vision of Sirhan's psychiatric defense to the jury. The prosecution presented their psychological evidence using the State's hired doctors, including psychiatrists and psychologists who individually or collectively mostly disagreed with Dr. Diamond's professional opinions. That is how issues are sorted out in a courtroom when there is a constant battle of experts. Quite naturally, several doctors hired by the prosecution's team took exception to Dr. Diamond's psychiatric testimony, taking an adversarial position to refute his analysis and conclusions as presented, a tactic that was baked into their job description.

As Dr. Diamond's core lectures continued, he presented additional material, exploring the mental concept of *mens rea* (the guilty mind), referring to the essential mental element of a person's volitional intent or knowledge that one's action or lack of action would result in a crime. Mens rea is the established legal doctrine of whether a criminal defendant is capable of possessing and maintaining the required mental elements necessary to commit a crime.

The doctrine of mens rea is combined with *actus rea* (the guilty act) or one's conduct of engaging in a prohibited act, a crime, and is required to constitute a criminal act. Mens rea, as interpreted under The California Penal Code, must be established for those crimes that require specific intent such as homicide as listed in Code Section 187. Both of these essential mental concepts (criminal intent and mens rea) played essential roles and impacted the Sirhan case as to his mental state when he killed RFK.

CHAPTER 4

THE DIMINISHED CAPACITY DEFENSE

HOW DOES IT WORK?

The unique criminal defense presented at the trial by Sirhan's defense attorneys was legally known in California as diminished capacity or diminished responsibility. Dr. Diamond's decades of work in psychiatry and the law had led to the adoption of this truly unique defense finding its way into California law when it was passed by the California legislature. A complete description of this defense was explained to his students by Dr. Diamond prior to his explaining the concept to Sirhan's jury.

If the diminished capacity defense could be introduced as a legal doctrine, Sirhan could be tried for second-degree murder, or even voluntary manslaughter, not first-degree murder. Dr. Diamond realized this was somewhat of a long shot, but worth it if it could save Sirhan from the gas chamber. To present a convincing case for diminished capacity to the jury, the defense team needed to get all the doctors thinking on the same page – not easy in that each witness testimony did not seem to support the essential elements of the diminished capacity doctrine.

Back at Berkeley, Dr. Diamond lectured us at length, unraveling the psycho-legal foundation of the diminished capacity enigma to make complex psycho-legal concepts easier to grasp. He told us that diminished capacity required redefining some basic historical, philosophical, and psycho-legal premises that needed modification and updating.

He explained that the doctrine of diminished capacity reshaped the historical definition of culpability and responsibility for committing a criminal act. For example, he described how, for too many years, a strict legal dichotomy dictated that criminals were viewed as either "completely responsible for their actions or at the opposite end, not at all responsible." He said the not guilty by reason of insanity concept (the so-called NGRI defense) "leaves a lot of marginal behaviors in the middle."

That led to the notion that a person's responsibility for a particular behavior or action could be assessed incrementally on a flexible scale, or continuum (from totally responsible to not responsible) – and modifying the idea that psychosis means "not responsible," and nonpsychotic behavior means responsible. Behavioral responsibility, at least in California, would no longer be seen as a polar concept.

This is not an easy process to explain, but if Dr. Diamond, the intellectual force behind California's diminished capacity defense, failed to explain it to me and my graduate colleagues, then how could a jury of twelve laypersons sort through the nuances of this complicated and somewhat philosophical/legal defense? We tried and finally got it, but for the Sirhan jury, comprehension of this defense was met with mixed results and some vacuous stares.

Dr. Diamond was careful to point out that such a new defense as diminished capacity was not adopted into California law overnight. He hammered home how arduous it was to adopt a precedent of legal court decisions that added to or amended old legal defenses. He told us that setting the legal precedent for diminished capacity as a defense in California began with a series of criminal cases leading to the Wells-Gorshen Rule of Doctrine, which he also helped establish.

At the time that Dr. Diamond testified in the *People versus Wells* appeal case, the settled law regarding insanity trials in California constituted a two-part trial system for defendants who pled the NGRI defense. The first trial, he explained, "was the guilt phase to determine whether the defendant had committed the crime for which he was charged. During this phase in the trial, no psychiatric testimony is presented by the defense attorneys; however, if the defendant is found guilty, then this triggers the second phase, the insanity phase." This phase takes up the issue of what constitutes legal insanity.

Dr. Diamond brought to the jury's attention precedent cases related to the historical development of diminished capacity in California. During one three-hour presentation, he attempted to establish that the admissibility of psychiatric information in California trials could diminish or reduce, not eliminate, a defendant's responsibility for committing murder, although not abdicate *all* responsibility.

During intensive interviewing and hypnosis sessions with Sirhan, Dr. Diamond somewhat unrealistically anticipated garnering all the relevant information concerning Sirhan's specific account of the assassination scene. But the many answers he pursued remained tightly locked up, maybe forever, in Sirhan's unconscious mind, increasing a sense of frustration in the doctor and in the defendant.

Key Diminished Capacity Cases

According to Dr. Diamond, six chief cases formed the core of the defense of diminished capacity, and are presented here in chronological order.

The Controversial M'Naghten Case, 1843: Knowing Right From Wrong

The M'Naghten case established the rule of insanity in a criminal court. The case involved Daniel M'Naghten, who attempted to kill England's prime minister but accidentally shot the leader's secretary. At the time, M'Naghten appeared to be suffering from what now could be labeled paranoid ideations and delusions of persecution. He firmly believed that the prime minister and the entire government was out to get him for unknown reasons.

This test or legal insanity rule found its way into American law in 1851, after Daniel M'Naghten's acquittal in England for murder on the grounds of insanity. The test likely reached its high point when accepted by the US federal court system, which was followed by a majority of state jurisdictions.

M'Naghten was not held responsible for the murder because he was deemed to be insane at the time he shot the secretary. This ruling angered the English public, leading to a generally acceptable definition of what constituted insanity and how it could be used to exculpate a defendant, relieving them of personal responsibility for their actions. The societal outrage caused Queen Victoria to prompt the English House of Lords to define insanity, answering the question: Did the defendant know what he was doing, and if so, that it was wrong?

The essential findings of the House of Lords noted how the new M'Naghten Rule could define insanity. Three key elements of this ruling survive:

1) Determination whether the defendant knows the crime they committed was wrong.

2) The initial presumption that a sane defendant is responsible for his criminal acts.

3) At the time of the crime, the defendant must have been suffering from a disease of the mind.

The M'Naghten Rule presumed that every man was sane; and to put forth a defense of legal insanity, the new criteria must be met. To establish a defense on the grounds of insanity, it must be clearly proven that, at the time of committing the act, the accused person was laboring under such a defect of reason, from disease of the mind, and did not know the nature and quality of their act; or if he knew it, he did not know what he was doing was wrong. Further, a defendant who labors under partial delusions only, and is not in other respects insane, must be considered in the same situation as to responsibility as if the facts with respect to which the delusions exists were real. M'Naghten became the accepted English standard for criminal responsibility.

The court's acceptance of the M'Naghten Rule assumes an "all or nothing mental responsibility polarity," that Dr. Diamond soundly rejected, yet a person can be mentally ill under M'Naghten and still legally know right from wrong.

Innumerable criticisms of the M'Naghten Rule arose over the years. One specific criticism pointed out by Dr. Diamond was that it did not allow complete and adequate psychiatric testimony at trial; also the Rule was formulated as a legal term, not a psychiatric one.

The Wells Case:
Capital Punishment While in Prison?

The 1949 California Supreme Court decision in the *People versus Wells* altered the way psychological testimony could be used at trial in a non-NGRI case, and went far beyond the M'Naghten rules. Dr. Diamond was convinced that the Wells decision could have an impact on Sirhan's case if the jury could wade through a hard-to-grasp, abstract mixture of legalese and psychiatric reasoning. The Wells decision, according to Dr. Diamond, would remove the absurd restrictions on psychiatric testimony to a very few mental conditions that met the archaic 1843 M'Naghten definition of insanity that amounted to a "right versus wrong" test.

Prior to the M'Naghten test, no clear method or set of psychological standards existed to determine insanity in a court of law. Only a few capital cases approximated the legal concept of diminished capacity in California, thus it did not begin with Wells. Dr. Diamond noted "the first case," which involved a "quarrel between two homosexual men. One struck the other, who fell and hit his head on a fireplace hearth, fractured his skull, and died."

A psychoanalyst, Dr. Meyer Zeligs, testified at the murder trial about what is now called the "diminished capacity defense." He carefully detailed the psychodynamics that led to the quarrel and the death. "The verdict was manslaughter," Dr. Diamond asserted, "which is all that one hopes for in such a diminished capacity defense."[1]

Wesley Robert Wells was a forty-six-year-old Black man with an extensive history of violence and subsequent incarceration, starting as a teenager when he was committed to the California Youth Authority, then later to the Adult Authority. His criminal rap sheet was filled with charges for receiving stolen property, and additional more-aggressive crimes.

As a state prisoner at California's Folsom Prison, Wells was involved in an altercation with other inmates resulting in the death of one man. Wells was singled out as being responsible for this killing, quickly convicted of manslaughter, and sentenced to ten additional years in prison. He was granted parole in 1941 but, within a few weeks, he was arrested again for grand theft auto.

When confined in various prisons, he was continuously involved in acting-out offenses that resulted in ten to fifteen disciplinary hearings per year, leading to multiple stints in solitary confinement. In 1944 he injured another inmate in a stabbing incident, assaulted a prison doctor, and committed violence against a prison guard. A year later, he assaulted several prison guards with a metal rod he'd removed from his bed. After three months in solitary in 1947, he showed visible signs of stress, manifesting as irritability and tenseness, and he became obsessed over why his prison term remained on an indeterminate status as opposed to a "fixed" term.

Wells heard a rumor via the grapevine that a letter was sent from the District Attorney's Office to the Adult Authority, advising them not to fix his sentence, so that he would be technically eligible for capital punishment if he should ever commit another assault. And such a letter actually was sent to the Adult Authority. Because of Wells' odd stressful behaviors and tendency to act out, he was evaluated by the prison doctor and a consulting psychiatrist, who found him to be in an emotionally dysfunctional state of tension.

At that point, the doctors recommended that Wells be sedated and removed from solitary and put back in the general prison population. Both treatment plans were ignored. Sufficient evidence was found that the prison guards taunted Wells by flashing bright lights in his eyes as he slept, resulting in his angry outbursts, screaming at them to stop. Wells felt that the California Adult Authority, the district attorney, the warden, and the guards were all against him.

1   Diamond, B.L. (1978). "Psychoanalysis in the Courtroom." Dialogue. J. San Francisco Psychoanalytic Society, Spring: 2–15. *In Quen*, J.M. (1994). The psychiatrist in the courtroom. (Ed.) The Analytic Press. Hillsdale, NJ, and London.

Two days after his most-recent outburst, at another disciplinary hearing held in the warden's office, Wells lost control again, displaying anger and hostility. He became hysterical to such an elevated degree that the warden expelled him from his office. On his way out, as the guards attempted to quiet him down in a narrow hallway, a struggle began, and Wells threw a cuspidor at one guard, causing an injury. Wells was subsequently indicted for malicious assault and moved to trial.

During the trial, his defense team desired to introduce medical and psychiatric testimony verifying that he was experiencing a high state of tension, and that he was overly sensitized to react with fear and suspiciousness to situations around him when feeling threatened. However, all professional psychiatric defense testimony, including Dr. Diamond's, was excluded by the trial judge, leading to Wells being convicted and sentenced to death.

"On appeal, the California Supreme Court rules that Dr. Diamond's testimony should have been admitted during the guilt phase of the bifurcated trial."

Further, the Court stated, "While the insanity of the defendant is not an issue under the general plea, yet this does not preclude evidence tending to establish his mental condition...."[2]

Dr. Diamond had occasion to visit Wells in prison. "I was impressed by Wells' great strength – both physical and mental. Though he had little formal education, his IQ was over 120. He showed remarkable shifts in identity. One moment he was angry, belligerent and threatening, an almost animal-like person; confused, acting on impulse, and having utter disregard for consequences.... At another time, he appeared to be a sincere, friendly, and wholly rational person...."

Dr. Diamond described Wells as able to intelligently discuss the racial discrimination in the prison system, saying, "Wells is an excellent reminder of the close similarities between the traumata of military life and prison confinement ... and Wells's symptoms were strikingly similar to those of soldiers whose evil, aggressive identity may be a last stand against total psychotic disintegration."[3]

When Dr. Diamond served as a medical officer during WWII, he dealt with troubled combat soldiers, which no doubt sensitized his diagnostic lens on Wells's profound stress-related symptoms, and considered some type of a stress disorder that fell short of psychosis. However, at the time Dr.

---

2   Ibid.
3   Ibid.

Diamond interviewed and diagnosed Wells, the concept of post-traumatic stress disorder (PTSD), was not yet an established psychiatric diagnosis.

The importance of the Wells decision, particularly in relation to insanity, in Dr. Diamond's view, centered on three essential elements. First, this decision did not change the existing rules relating to legal insanity as a defense. Second, the psychiatric issues in the Wells case did not involve lack of capacity for malice aforethought, but rather that Wells did not have malice aforethought because of his nervous tension and fears; and that the medical testimony concerning the tension and fears was relevant to the determination of this. Thirdly, regardless of the statutory restrictions that exist as to the admissibility of testimony concerning insanity, medical, psychiatric, and other evidence pertinent to the existence of premeditation, deliberation, intent, and malice aforethought must be admitted and can be considered by the jury in determining the question of guilt.

"Thus in California, psychiatrists who were formerly excluded from testifying in the main portion of the trial (being able to testify after a verdict of guilt was reached) can now bring evidence to bear on these basic elements of guilt itself … the issue must be whether this individual, under the special circumstances of the crime, in his particular frame of mind, did or did not have the necessary design or intent, that is, malice."

The Wells case represented a breakthrough decision, because it allowed the admissibility of critical psychological testimony where the issue of insanity was not an issue before the court, regardless of what insanity rules were applied. Instead, direct psychiatric testimony was allowed concerning the key concept in "diminished capacity, malice aforethought." Specifically, the Wells case centered on the presentation of psychological evidence concerning malice aforethought, even though an insanity defense was not introduced.

As Dr. Diamond said, "The decision has already produced a radical improvement in the use of psychiatric testimony and, although the direct effect of this decision applies only in California, it is reasonable to suppose that similar decisions may be won in other jurisdictions as well."

Dr. Diamond added, "The door was opened by the Wells case to the possibility of using psychoanalytic and psychodynamic testimony to comment on these mental states, which relate to the criminal act itself. Such an abnormal mental state may be far short of insanity and quite different from the delusions, hallucinations, and other conventional symptoms of insanity."

Dr. Diamond continued, "Now, the testimony for the defense is for the purpose of negating or canceling out the mental states specified by the definition of the crime, permitting conviction only for a lesser offense. The effect is to eliminate what has always been the worst feature of the legal concept of responsibility: its dichotomous, all-or-none quality ... there can be degrees of responsibility, varying all the way from first-degree murder punishable by death to misdemeanor manslaughter, which may mean only a brief stay in jail or even probation."

The Wells case made psychiatric testimony more readily available to California courts, facilitating a jury's better comprehension that the strict insanity defense may be an all-or-nothing proposition. But by using Wells, gradations of gray mental areas vis-à-vis criminal responsibility exist. The Wells case is especially unique because, at the time he was charged, Wells was a prisoner in San Quentin, existing under the prevailing, sordid conditions that included racism, random corporeal punishment meted out by guards, arbitrary suspensions of even minimal privileges, long stretches in solitary confinement for almost no apparent reason, as well as the creation of an atmosphere of constant fear that "you might be next in line for brutal treatment." Apparently, the prison guards were on their own to mete out punishments for the slightest infractions of an unwritten but pervasive "prison conduct code."

The decision in the Wells case ushered in the use of mitigating psychiatric testimony in all murder cases in California where the issue of the mental capacity of the defendant regarding their premeditation, deliberation, malice, or intent are called into question. Dr. Diamond felt that the "the tragic case of Wesley Robert Wells" represented the most enlightened and most comprehensive of the various opinions on these matters.

THE GORSHEN CASE:
WHEN WORDS CAN KILL

Prior to the Sirhan case, Dr. Diamond applied explanatory reasoning related to the production of trance states in the several select cases he was charged to analyze for defense purposes in key trials decisions.

In these cases, Dr. Diamond served in an advisory capacity as a psychiatric consultant to the defense teams, and in some cases as a direct expert witness. It is well-established that, for an individual with dissociative personality, a "fracture" takes place, yielding certain altered dissociative states, and is not a volitional on-demand process. As Dr. Diamond stated,

"It's not like turning on and off a switch." On some psychological level, patients experiencing various dissociative reactions begin to realize that this process is a last resort as a pathway to escape from a set of adverse circumstances that continue to recur no matter what they do.

The facts of the Nicholas Gorshen case: Mr. Gorshen after consuming a pint of gin was reprimanded for his inappropriate and drunken behavior by his boss, longshoreman foreman, Joseph "Red" O'Leary. The two men began arguing, and then O'Leary carried the argument a step further, hitting Gorshen and knocking him down, then kicking him as he laid on the ground. Gorshen collected himself, leaving the work site only to return with a gun and kill O'Leary in cold blood on the spot.

This homicidal scene happened in the presence of two uniformed police officers who failed to notice that Gorshen had a gun. Though this seemed to be an open-and-shut case for the prosecution on a first-degree murder charge, Dr. Diamond argued that (psychologically) Gorshen had acted somewhat "like an irrational robot" when he gunned down O'Leary. He also argued persuasively that, at the time of the crime, Gorshen did not possess the requisite mental state required for malice aforethought and mental deliberation, as necessitated under the criminal laws of the State of California as a foundation for a first-degree murder charge.

Dr. Diamond noticed this same irrational robotic tendency in Sirhan's dissociated behavior when under hypnosis accompanied by the prosecution's psychiatrist, Dr. Seymour Pollack. He asked Sirhan the simple task to write a few sentences on a piece of paper. Dr. Diamond described this experience to defense attorney, Mr. Berman: "So I asked him, 'Write your name.' ... So he proceeded to write his name at the top of the page here, 'Sirhan B. Sirhan,' and then started to write it again, 'Sirhan B. Sirhan,' ... Sirhan had now sort of flipped automatically into a hypnotic trance. He continued to write his name, 'Sirhan B. Sirhan, Sirhan B. Sirhan,' and this sort of astonished me. He wrote like a robot writes, in a stiff mechanical way, his eyes fixed on the paper, and writing mechanically...."[4]

Dr. Diamond testified concerning Gorshen's multiple trancelike episodes regarding the killing as a psychological defense mechanism. Surprisingly, the trial judge agreed with Dr. Diamond: "Up to the time Dr. Diamond testified ... there was no explanation of why this crime was committed. [Diamond] is the first person that has any explanation. Whether it's correct or not I don't know."[5]

4   Trial Vol 24, 649, March 24, 1969.

5   Bromberg, W. (1992). "Diminished Capacity as an Alternative to McNaghten in California Law." *Bull Am Acad Psychiatry Law*, Vol 29, No.2, 1992.

During his court testimony, Dr. Diamond emphasized that Gorshen was protecting himself from further perceived mental deterioration and had to kill O'Leary, who had traumatized him with sexual innuendos concerning his masculinity. Dr. Diamond had "discovered [similar to Sirhan] that Gorshen was prone to dissociated, or trance states in which he experienced himself as the sexual plaything of the devil. Gorshen feared that if these states became known, his transportation to that evil world would become permanent."

"Only through killing [O'Leary]," Diamond said, "could he [Gorshen] retain his sanity and avoid eternal incarceration in the hell of his trance states."[6]

Dr. Diamond asserted, "The Gorshen case involved a homicide committed by a middle-aged man who was undergoing a sexual decline and who was also subject to very strange hallucinatory episodes, visions in which he was being put to the test by various demonological half-animal, half human creatures. There was a rich variety of bizarre material – of distortions of body image and sexual peculiarities in the visions, which lasted only moments."[7]

Dr. Diamond added: "The defendant suffers from chronic paranoid schizophrenia.... For twenty years the defendant had trances during which he heard voices and experienced visions ... devils in disguise committing abnormal sexual acts, sometimes on the defendant."[8] According to Dr. Diamond, Gorshen acted like an automaton during the shooting, absent the mental state required for malice aforethought and deliberation.

The California Supreme Court allowed the testimony of psychiatric experts, establishing what became known in California as the Wells-Gorshen Doctrine of Diminished Capacity. Dr. Diamond had established the value of expert testimony in determination of all aspects of a criminal case especially, once again, breaking with the traditional and archaic M'Naghten rules.

THE MELKONIAN CASE:
INFIDELITY CAN BE DEADLY

D r. Diamond, testifying in the 1953 Melkonian case, presented a summary of the facts in Melkonian's troubled life. He emphasized that this murder case presented a perfect opportunity to apply the Wells decision. Lewon Melkonian, a Russian-Armenian, in a fit of anger and mental

6   Quen, J.M. (1994). (Ed.) *The psychiatrist in the courtroom*. Hillsdale, NJ and London: The analytic press. xxxiv-xxxv.
7   Diamond. (1978). 16.
8   Bromberg. 180.

confusion, killed his wife and the man he believed was her lover. After the double murder, many witnesses came forward with information to help establish Melkonian's criminal intent and premeditation.

Melkonian testified in his trial, openly admitting that he committed the murders. Naturally, this revelation did not facilitate his defense. In fact, his defense was largely based on expert psychiatric testimony, arguing that, because of Melkonian's poor mental state, he did not manifest capacity to premeditate or malice aforethought – both components necessary to be convicted of first-degree murder.

In the absence of these two factors, he could only be convicted of manslaughter. At first, the prosecution strongly objected to the introduction of any psychiatric testimony. According to Dr. Diamond, the prosecution did not anticipate a psychiatric defense as viable. The prosecuting attorney admitted that he had not heard of a previous attempt to use psychiatric evidence to negate the concept of malice aforethought, however the prosecution did not call a medical-psychiatric witness to challenge the defense's theory. Melkonian was not examined by a State-appointed psychiatrist.

Aside from admitting to the crimes, Melkonian presented as a sympathetic figure, seemingly sincere, though emotionally labile. The defense counsel cited the Wells decision as the reason for the psychiatric testimony and, subsequent to considerable back and forth, argued that the trial judge allowed Dr. Diamond to testify over many objections from the prosecution.

Dr. Diamond was able to shape his psychiatric findings and present these to the jury, although the prosecuting attorney challenged Dr. Diamond's appearance as an expert witness rendering an opinion that the prosecution believed was basically a "legal" view. Dr. Diamond was interrogated, forcing him to define and provide the exact legal definitions of insanity, malice aforethought, and the penal code definition of homicide. The prosecuting attorney argued that the concept of malice had never been raised in a California case.

Dr. Diamond provided a detailed history of the defendant, including being born in Russia, as a child losing both parents, forced to live in a harsh orphanage until age twenty when he was conscripted into the Russian Army during WWII, then captured by the Germans and spending almost a year in a prison camp until he escaped in 1944.

At that time he fell in love and married, and he and his wife were both committed to a concentration camp where he experienced the horrors of Nazi brutality. In 1945 the concentration camp was liberated, and he and his wife were taken to a displaced persons (DP) camp, where their three children were born. In 1949, with the help of a refugee organization, the Melkonian family was relocated to Fresno, California, among a growing number of Russian-Armenian residents. Unfortunately, during the voyage to America, Melkonian discovered that his wife had entertained a strange man in their stateroom. Later, while living in Fresno, he felt that an Armenian male friend was becoming far too friendly with his wife.

Dr. Diamond's impression of his story of possible infidelity was based in actual facts leading to Melkonian's paranoid ideation concerning his wife who he considered to be serially unfaithful. He became depressed and suspicious of not just his wife, but that certain people wanted to harm him.

In 1952 he moved the family to San Francisco to escape from his wife's temptations. They moved in with an old friend, Usunian and his wife. For Melkonian, this was a seemingly happy moment. He said he was so close to Usunian that he described him as his "blood brother."

However, almost immediately he developed the same paranoid impression he had in Fresno: he suspected that his blood brother had a more-than-casual physical interest in his wife. He now thought that his wife and Usunian were plotting to kill him. For his own safety, he purchased a gun. On Sunday morning, January 23, 1953, Melkonian left his house to attend church services, but unexpectedly returned a few minutes later only to discover Usunian and his wife in each other's arms.

He said that, upon seeing this scene, his blood began to boil, and he feared for his life as Usunian attempted to choke him. Melkonian retrieved his gun from the kitchen, shot both of them, then shot himself in the neck. The neck wound was superficial. He bandaged it himself as police arrived, and he admitted what he had done.

Dr. Diamond's opinion was that Melkonian had a brief psychotic break – an acute confused, paranoid psychosis and, "I had no hesitation telling the jury that the killings were the result of his abnormal mental state and that there had been no conscious voluntary, deliberative action. I also testified that the purchase of the gun and the threat he had made were of similar origin, bringing the results of mental disease rather than volition."

When the verdict was recorded, the jury came in with a conviction of manslaughter and not first-degree murder. A motion of insanity was never offered. Why not?

Dr. Diamond explained: "The defense counsel and I agreed that it would be very difficult to fit him into the rigid California rule of right and wrong." Application of the Wells decision enabled Dr. Diamond to move forward the defense of diminished capacity by obviating the strict

M'Naghten rule as to who is insane and who is not. The next grizzly case of Ronald Dennis Wolff, who murdered his mother in cold blood, reinforced the diminished capacity defense.

THE WOLFF CASE:
THE AXE HANDLE MURDER

The Ronald Dennis Wolff case in Southern California was the first diminished capacity defense involving a minor. Wolff was a fifteen-year-old, previously diagnosed with schizophrenia, who smashed his mother with an axe handle, then strangled her as he chased her throughout their house. Wolff's apparent motive was to eliminate his intrusive mother so he could entertain a series of girls, take nude photographs of them, then sexually assault and rape them. There was no question that he planned the murder in advance, taking an axe handle from the garage and placing it under his mattress until the propitious moment arrived. That moment arrived during the morning of May 15, 1961, in their house.

The stated facts of the case as Wolff reported them: On Sunday night, May 14, 1961, he retrieved the axe handle he had hidden from his bedroom and proceeded to the dining room, where his mother was sitting quietly, and he raised the weapon in a threatening manner.

As she turned around, she asked him, "What is that?"

Wolff said nothing, returned to his bedroom, again hid the axe handle, and went to sleep.

The next day, as usual, he ate the breakfast his mother prepared for him; then as she stood facing the sink, washing dishes, she turned her head and Wolff struck her several times on the back of the head. Wolff said he wanted to knock her unconscious, then kill her. He hit her again as she screamed, and he believed he hit her twice more. To stop the screaming, he put his hand over her mouth and began choking her as she tried to move across the kitchen to the stove area.

He said, "I know I shouldn't be doing this," as he laid down next to her on the floor. Suddenly she got up and ran to the dining room where Wolff caught her, and they struggled. He began to choke her as she lay dying. He stated that, at that point, he said to her, "God loves you, He loves me, you love me; Dad, I love you!"

At about 9:20 a.m. on May 15, 1961, Wolff went to the Glendale Police Department, stating that he had something to report, "I just killed my mother with an axe handle!"

The police went to his house where they found his mother deceased on the floor as Wolff described. She was covered with blood, and it was obvious that she had been severely beaten. Her hair was matted with large a large amount of drying blood. The blood-soaked axe handle was still on the kitchen floor where he left it. The autopsy report stipulated that the death was caused by asphyxiation resulting from strangulation, and the case was filed as a murder.

Wolff admitted hitting his mother approximately six times with the axe handle until he was sure she was dead. Later he told police that he "didn't get along with her!"

He told investigating officers that he killed his mother so he could bring seven girls to the house and have sex with them. He made a list of these girls, none of whom knew him. He said that he also thought about knocking his aunt unconscious, because she had a car that he could use to pick up the girls on the street. He mentioned that he had never had a real date with a girl.

Wolff was examined by four independent psychiatrists, and all four agreed that he fell somewhere along the schizophrenic spectrum of mental illness. Dr. J. M. Nielsen testified about Wolff's complete disassociation between his intellectual and emotional grounding with a clear intellect and without any emotional attachment to the terrible thing he had done. He believed that Wolff knew what he was doing, because he examined his mother to see whether she was dead; and when she was not, he finished her.

Dr. Daryl D. Smith, a court-ordered psychiatrist, conducted a California Penal Code section 1027 assessment to determine if Wolff was insane at the time of the crime. His impression was that the defendant was legally insane at the time of the murder, and he was not able to appreciate the nature and consequences of his act. A third expert, Dr. George Maculans, a staff psychiatrist for the California Youth Authority also confirmed that, in his opinion, Wolff was schizophrenic because he was unable to judge the quality and nature of his actions and could not distinguish between right and wrong – the M'Naghten standard.

The fourth psychiatrist, Dr. Blake Skrdla, under a similar court appointment by the superior court, examined Wolff in October 1961, concluding that Wolff was suffering from chronic undifferentiated schizophrenia, disallowing his ability to appreciate the quality and nature of his act. Dr. Skrdla added to his testimony however, that the defendant probably did know the difference between right and wrong at the time of the crime.

In his opinion, after the commission of the murder, Wolff realized it was wrong, and that is why he contacted the police. In Wolff's defense, each doctor testified that he was schizophrenic, although Dr. Nielsen also testified that Wolff's schizophrenia was episodic and, between episodes, he could be considered legally sane. However, as noted here, some variegation existed in the testimony of witnesses.

Again, after turning himself in to police, Wolff made a number of statements to the effect that he did "know right from wrong." For example, when questioned on the issue, Wolff told police that he knew it was wrong, "but I wasn't thinking of it. I was aware of it." Wolff was convicted in a jury trial of first-degree murder because all the elements to substantiate the crime seemed to be there – planning and malice aforethought.

An appeal to the California Supreme Court was made and, in a review of the Wolff matter, the court ruled: "There is no question that the defendant had the intent to kill; but … the true test must include consideration of the somewhat limited extent to which this defendant could maturely and meaningfully reflect upon the gravity of his contemplated act.… He knew the difference between right and wrong; he knew the intended act was wrong, and nevertheless carried it out. But the extent of his understanding, reflection upon it and its consequences, with realization of the enormity of the evil, appears to have been materially … vague and detached."[9]

The court's decision reduced Wolff's conviction from first-degree murder to second-degree murder, and this led to a redefining the concept of premeditation, and firmly broadened the defense of diminished capacity by allowing expert testimony to challenge the fundamental concept of what really constitutes premeditation. The court's decision in Wolff could now challenge the concept of malice aforethought.

Presumably Dr. Diamond's work on diminished capacity could lead to exploration into additional aspects of a crime, such as motivational issues and additional avenues leading away from the binary, forced-choice stricture of the M'Naghten test to a reformed diminished capacity defense strategy.

THE FRED KIPP BASSETT CASE: "MY PARENTS HAD TO GO!"

The 1964 decision in the Wolff case was followed by the California Supreme Court decision in People versus Bassett, decided on August 8,

9   Klaber, W. and P. Melanson. (1997). *Shadow Play: The Murder of Robert F. Kennedy, The Trial of Sirhan Sirhan, And the Failure of American Justice.* St. Martin's Press, New York, 196.

1968, a few months before the official opening of Sirhan's trial on January 7, 1969. The facts in the case revealed the mentally addled eighteen-year-old, Fred Bassett, who ritualistically murdered his parents, then tried to stage the crimes as a murder-suicide killing.

Bassett was charged with two counts of murder and pleaded not guilty, and not guilty by reason of insanity to both charges. The trial jury returned verdicts of first-degree murder on both counts and fixed the death penalty. In California, the appeal of every capital punishment sentence is automatic.

This calculated parricide case is reminiscent of the Menendez brothers who, twenty years later, murdered their unsuspecting parents. The high-profile Menendez case was unique because it happened in upscale Beverly Hills, California, where multiple murders "just don't happen here!"

The Menendez murders were also special because of social status, Hollywood fame, societal power, capitalism, and unimagined, in-your-face affluence. Because their parents were almost physically unidentifiable due to the fifteen blasts from two 12-gauge-shotguns the brothers fired, reloaded, and then fired again, the police thought initially that the killings might be a "mob hit."

The Menendezs' unrestrained violence against their parents was more of an execution slaughter than another multiple killing. Their first four-and-a-half-month trial in 1993 was televised nationwide, exposing the public to the brothers' wild allegations of mental and sexual abuse paraded daily on the new Court-TV channel. The two combined juries, one for each brother, came back hung. The prosecution planned a retrial, the 1995 retrial yielded a different result: both bothers were convicted of first-degree murder and sentenced to life without the possibility of parole.

The sordid details in the Menendez case would be hard to top, but as the details of the Bassett parricide case emerged, they came gruesomely close. After the murders, Fred Bassett was quoted as telling a chilling tale to a psychiatric technician that, "he enjoyed doing it; that they deserved to die because all crumbs deserve to die; and that they drank a lot, and argued a lot, and were cold towards him ... that killing them was one of the most glorious or heightened or wonderful experiences of his life." Then he added, "He had been planning to kill his parents since he was about eight years old."[10]

These were shocking statements from a seemingly remorseless defendant who was facing the death penalty. Based on his history of multiple

---

10   California Supreme Court, People V. Bassett, 69 Cal. 2nd 122, August 8, 1968.

childhood psychological conditions, Bassett was diagnosed as a paranoid schizophrenic and (similar to Sirhan's misdiagnosis), he was assessed by numerous professionals (twelve in his case) during various phases of his trial on the issue of his mental status at the time of the murders.

During his childhood, Bassett was enveloped progressively into a deep paranoid delusional system where he saw his enemies everywhere, and this included his parents. This case introduced the defense doctrine of diminished capacity that Dr. Diamond worked on for years to reinterpret the meaning of criminal responsibility. Unfortunately, the California Supreme Court stated, "To an accusation charging a defendant with the crime of murder [California Penal Code 187, Murder], there is yet no statutory plea of 'not guilty of first degree murder by reason of diminished mental capacity.'"

Apparent in this case, the use of diminished capacity could serve as a psychiatric mitigator, lessening the first-degree murder charge to second-degree murder to spare Bassett's life. Dr. Daryl D. Smith, a court-appointed psychiatrist, was one of the professionals tasked with the responsibility to evaluate Bassett to determine whether he had the capacity to form criminal malice aforethought and form intent to kill his parents.

During Dr. Smith's assessment about a month after the killings, he concluded that Bassett had been mentally ill for many years. "As evidence of this, he explained that hallucinations and delusions, such as the defendant exhibited, only arise in an illness out of earlier maladaptation." He termed this as Bassett's "fluctuating reality contact," and connected it to his early life trauma. He concluded that Bassett, based on the extent and duration of his mental illness, did not have the capacity to give careful thought to and weigh the consideration for and against killing his parents, or to maturely and meaningfully deliberate and reflect upon the gravity of his contemplated act.[11]

Dr. Nicholas M. Langer, a psychiatrist who conducted a number of interviews with Bassett, presented another diagnostic picture of the defendant that cast light on what seems to be a missed opportunity to present an alternative diagnosis. From reading the detailed account of Dr. Langer's findings, Bassett perhaps had an undiagnosed second personality or even additional alter personality structures differing from his host or foundation personality that dominated him from time to time. In this sense, Bassett looked psychologically a lot like Sirhan from the dissociated, diagnostic perspective.

11   Ibid.

Over time, Bassett told Dr. Langer that he could identify and name at least four more of these differing voices, or possibly multiple personalities (MPD) or alters. A week before the shootings, he had been listening to music in the record library at school, when the voice of "Christopher Chamberlain" told Bassett to write out the plan [to kill his parents] ... "Christopher Chamberlain wouldn't let me sleep." Bassett gave his alters different names. Two alters were friendly; and two were unfriendly, one of which was Christopher Chamberlain, who began telling Bassett to kill his parents. It is conceivable that this was the intrusive, evil alter encouraging him to kill his parents as his host, the un-dissociated self, was pressed into committing the acts of violence, just as he stated, "It was Christopher Chamberlain who told me!"

Dr. Langer analogized Bassett's mental state at the time of the crimes to a person placed in a hypnotic trance who "neither really knows what he is doing, let alone why he is doing it. One is an outside command, the other one is a command coming from within, but he has no power resist it...."

Dr. Langer concluded, like Dr. Smith, that Bassett did not, at the time of the double murder, manifest the necessary mental capacity to give careful thought to and weigh the consideration for and against killing his parents, to form an intention to kill unlawfully, or to meaningfully and maturely deliberate and premeditate and reflect upon the gravity of his contemplated act and to harbor malice aforethought.[12]

Another psychiatrist, Dr. Joseph Krofcheck, engaged by the defense to examine Bassett two months after the murders, concurred with the other two defense doctors that he believed Bassett "was suffering from paranoid schizophrenia. Such a person ... becomes so concerned with this own inner feelings and thoughts, he gives less credence to the reality of the ... actions of people and objects...."

The prosecution presented three witnesses in rebuttal to the defenses' experts: George Y. Abe, Edwin E. McNeil, and Marcus Crahan. Dr. Crahan was court-ordered to interview Bassett after Bassett's attorney entered an NGRI plea. In opposition to defense witnesses, when asked for his professional opinion, Dr. Crahan stated that Bassett had the mental capacity to deliberate, premeditate, and harbor malice aforethought.

As Dr. Abe was the psychiatric director at Norwalk State Hospital, he was well acquainted with various types of psychiatric patients, including convicted felons and defendants in similar legal situations to Sirhan's. Dr.

---

12   Ibid.

Abe did not actually interview Bassett, but rendered the same opinion as Dr. Crahan that the defendant could actually deliberate, premeditate, and had the ability to harbor malice aforethought. Dr. McNeil concurred with both opinions, so now the California Supreme Court had to present its legal ruling on the case.

"Under our established rules and from an appraisal of the entire record in this case, we find no substantial evidence to support the verdicts of murder in the first degree. The evidence does support, however, a conviction of murder in the second degree, and it is our duty to modify the judgment accordingly. The judgment is modified by reducing the degree of the crimes to murder in the second degree and, as so modified, is affirmed...."[13]

The ruling in Bassett, contingent on the diminished capacity defense, helped his legal team save his life.

Now we turn to Sirhan's psychological profile connecting the results of his psychological testing to his diagnoses as measured by the experts at the time.

---

13   Ibid.

CHAPTER 5

SIRHAN'S PSYCHOLOGICAL PROFILE: EXPERT PERSPECTIVES

Rich literature exists about Sirhan Sirhan, consisting of thousands of pages of interviews with him, videos, documentaries, and hundreds of sworn court testimonies from too many witnesses to begin to list here. The integrated areas of criminology, psychology and psychiatry have not remained static fields of professional inquiry over the past half-century. The evolution of these fields since the murder of RFK has led to the creation of multiple new psychiatric diagnostic categories that capture and reclassify various contemporary symptoms and focus on new explanatory reasons why good people sometimes turn to "the dark side" and engage in criminal behaviors.

Similarly, the world of psychological assessment has seen the development of many new psychodiagnostic instruments. I was able to use several current tests to retrospectively assess Sirhan's "disorders" and form a clearer picture of Sirhan's diagnostic profile. The professional opinions, and impressions of Sirhan's mental state expressed throughout this book derive from the author's clinical experience and on the prospective assessment results obtained and presented here. This same "blind analysis" was used by several review doctors to validate Sirhan's test results.

* * *

While confined in jail after his arrest, Sirhan was assessed by two expert psychologists hired by the defense team, Drs. Schorr and Richardson, who employed a standard psychological testing protocol that likely included these tests in an assessment battery: the Rorschach Test, often referred to as the inkblot test, because the test is comprised of ten abstract ink blot cards presented on a hard card stock; the Thematic Apperception Test (TAT), a projective test used to analyze a patients psychological responses to a series of a maximum of thirty-one photos presented on 9x11-inch cardboard stock, depicting various provocative scenes, some happy and some not so much; the Bender Visual Motor Gestalt test (BVMGT) to check for gross signs of neurological dysfunction; and the Minnesota Multiphasic Personality Inventory (MMPI), a standard personality test comprised at the time (1960s) of 504 true-false questions; and the Wechsler Adult Intelligence Scale (WAIS), a standard intelligence test commonly used in most comprehensive psychological assessments. The results of these tests helped form the basis of the psychologists' later psychiatric diagnoses of Sirhan.

A substantial sample of the Rorschach results were preserved, thanks to the efforts of defense investigator Robert Kaiser, in his comprehensive 634-page book on the RFK assassination and the Sirhan trial, first published in 1970. However, when I reexamined these testing results, even Kaiser's comprehensive reportage falls somewhat short. For example, the recorded MMPI results are merely fragmentary, thus not open to a detailed, analytical reinterpretation.

Equally important, no reliable or complete record exists of Sirhan's results on the TAT – no exact responses or how they were scored. I tried to remedy this important deficit regarding the TAT results by reconstructing Sirhan's TAT testing responses based on the doctors' descriptive and anecdotal testimony as presented during the trial and from additional sources. The complete scoring protocol of Sirhan's Rorschach is presented with a simplified, self-scoring system (see Appendix).

The Hooper Visual Organization Test (HVOT), and the Menninger Diagnostic System (MDS) were both presented to Sirhan by Dr. Richardson, but few scorable results were reported. By reexamining Dr. Richardson's descriptions of these tests' results, I was able to piece together, then retro-score these results as well so that the results of these two tests, plus the TAT results, can now be examined.

Most likely due to the complex testing protocols used by Dr. Richardson, the results of these two assessment tools were inadvertently minimized and somehow obscured during his testimony, and they stayed buried until their recent discovery deep in the trial transcript.

From the outset of Sirhan's trial, the insanity issue was the core psychological concept framing the defense attorneys' strategy to save Sirhan from San Quentin's gas chamber. In the pursuit of this goal, the defense team was faced with two principal challenges.

First, the prosecution team handpicked Dr. Seymour Pollack to head the psychiatric team. Like defense expert, Dr. Diamond, Dr. Pollack was also a well-respected forensic psychiatrist practicing in the Los Angeles area. Second, the defense had to deal directly with Sirhan's strong protestations that he was not suffering from a mental defect or some form of diagnosable legal insanity.

The basis of Sirhan's entire defense rested on the complicated psycho-legal doctrine (diminished capacity or diminished responsibility) that had been introduced into California law through the tireless efforts of Dr. Diamond. Yet as Dr. Diamond mentioned, Sirhan admitted to anyone who would listen that he killed Kennedy, adding, "I killed Robert Kennedy with twenty years of malice aforethought!"

The origin of this and many other odd statements about harboring malice aforethought and criminal intent at the time of the crime remains unknown. There has been no confirmation that Sirhan understood this complex psychiatric-legal doctrine of "diminished capacity," or the specific definition of "malice aforethought." But we do know that, during the course of his investigation and continuing into the trial phase, Sirhan uttered additional and equally bizarre declarations portending his guilt.

During innumerable interviews with attorneys and doctors, Sirhan appeared momentarily dazed and confused, giving conflicting information particularly about the salient events proceeding and during the assassination. For instance, during his initial session with lead defense attorney Grant Cooper, responding to the query, "I am interested in when you first decided you were going to kill Kennedy, because it is written down in books and everything, and they [the prosecution] have it, so you tell me...."

Sirhan responded, "I honestly did not decide to do it, Sir ... objectively, I had no awareness of what I was doing that night."

Cooper followed up, asking, "Who do you think killed him?"

Sirhan answered, "Obviously, I must have – but I have no exact – no objective [memory] of what I was doing."

The Defense Team's Investigators Left a Lot to Be Desired

In addition to Robert Kaiser, who was given the rights to write a book about Sirhan's trial, the defense team hired two more investigators: Ronald Allen and Michael McCowan who had formed a private investigation firm. McCowan was a former Marine with a ten-year history with the LAPD. Three years before the Sirhan trial, he had been forced to retire from the department after his arrest and conviction for theft and mail fraud, stemming from a "diamond ring caper," wherein he stole several valuable diamond rings allegedly from two different women he was having affairs with – they were beyond upset, and he was arrested. In addition, he was involved in a land swindling scandal. During the defense of his criminal case, McCowan had retained Russell Parsons.

McCowan was actually on parole when Parsons then selected him as a chief investigator for the defense. Regarding the Sirhan case, McCowan told Parsons that, "You need help. I'm here to help, and I'll drop everything I'm doing."

McCowan had also presumably agreed to serve as an inside informant to the LAPD as a kind of double agent while working on the Sirhan case. But in the end, McCowan's licensed private eye affiliation ended due to the tumult and bad press from working on the Sirhan team, which included multiple death threats.

Grant Cooper, though a highly respected trial lawyer and former president of the LA Bar Association, was facing his own legal issues and reputation smear based on his representation of a defendant in a fraudulent Beverly Hills-based gambling scam involving several LA high rollers with mob connections. Prior to entering private practice, Cooper was a distinguished member of the LA District Attorney's Office with a proven track record. Cooper was definitely a member in good standing in *Who's Who in the Legal Profession*.

Cooper had to know that McCowan was serving a court-ordered probation when he took him on as an investigator (or he should have known). In my view, the hire of McCowan reflected another in a series of defense missteps prior to and during Sirhan's trial.

Robert Kaiser wasn't a professional criminal investigator or a private eye. He was a well-traveled, savvy, and seasoned investigative reporter and a contributor to *Time* magazine. This LA-based journalist performed a remarkable task with regard to the Sirhan trial – he left a preserved, detailed record of almost all aspects of "everything Sirhan Sirhan." In fact, the only (nonclinical) active, day-to-day record of Sirhan's psychological assessment and test results were documented by Kaiser.

Though Kaiser reproduced limited sections of Sirhan's total assessment records conducted by the psychologists, he provided ample data to reanalyze Sirhan's testing results some fifty years later. But for this historic psychological information, and Kaiser's description of Sirhan's testing, and reproducing some of the testing protocols, we would have no testing record to draw upon, review, or reassess Sirhan's test results for inclusion in this book. Absent this critical information, my reanalysis, or any analysis by another forensic psychologist, of Sirhan's testing results would not have been possible.

More than an observer, Kaiser became an active participant during the trial proceedings, who did not hide his intent to write a tell-all book about the Sirhan trial. Kaiser also had a monetary interest in working the Sirhan case. Nor was he alone in his desire to write a book covering the trial. McCowan was also intent on doing a book.

The money Kaiser sought wasn't entirely for himself; he wanted most of the future book royalties to help defray the legal fees necessary to provide an adequate defense for Sirhan. In return for his work, he wanted the exclusive rights to write a book about the case. As an appointed investigator on the case, Kaiser had unlimited access to Sirhan, so why not choose him to chronicle the case and later publish a book?

Prior to the trial, defense attorney Parsons wanted to get the investigation moving; and to do that, he said, "We need money!"

Kaiser wanted Parsons to draw up an exclusive contract for him to do the proposed book focusing on all aspects of the Sirhan case. Kaiser drafted a contract and showed it to Parsons and Cooper. Cooper said he did not want to be compensated for his work on the case, but Kaiser insisted he take at least a share.

However, the Sirhan family had their own plan, because McCowan promised the Sirhan's $100,000 on his proposed book deal. Kaiser was upset to think the family could even dream of profiting from Robert Kennedy's death, and McCowan's deal was quashed.

During what turned out to be a showdown meeting attended by Sirhan's older brother, Adel, along with Parsons and McCowan at Parsons' legal offices, Adel made an interesting proposal to Kaiser: "Why can't you take one-third, and let us split fifty-fifty with the attorneys?"

Kaiser pondered a moment then agreed; and Parsons and McCowan took the contract to show Sirhan for his review and approval. He signed it without reservations, saying that any percentage of monies from Kaiser's book was fine with him because he wanted the attorneys to get paid to save him from the gas chamber. He added another odd comment, "If I go to the gas chamber, I'll take the whole fuckin' world with me!"

Shortly after Kaiser finalized his book deal in mid-April 1969, he wrote to J. Edgar Hoover, the director of the Federal Bureau of Investigation, to request additional information concerning the Senator Kennedy assassination. He hoped he could tap into any new information produced by the FBI's ongoing, parallel investigation into the RFK assassination.

Kaiser clearly referenced that he was writing a book on the case, but needed additional investigative information that the FBI had obtained.

Kaiser wrote, "In order to write the best possible book, however, I feel I should get other points of view. I would like the FBI to consider helping me with information and some evaluation. I'd like to know how the FBI went into action, who got the word first, where you were when the news came, what orders you gave, who carried them out, and how. It is part of the story which I imagine the FBI would not want me to overlook ... I became an investigator for the defense. In that role, it became necessary for me to engage in long interviews with Sirhan, to work in close cooperation with the psychologists and psychiatrists in the case and, of course, with the lawyers ... I was happy to help them in that because at the same time I was helping myself gather material for my book."[1]

Apparently, Hoover and the FBI were not in a particularly sharing mood. Whatever information Kaiser wished to gather from the FBI's investigative efforts into RFK's assassination would not be forthcoming, as affirmed in J. Edgar Hoover's terse response dated ten days later: "Your letter of April 19, 1969, has been received, and I appreciate the interest which prompted you to write. In reference to your inquiry, the files of the FBI are confidential pursuant to regulations of the Department of Justice, and it will not be possible to furnish the information regarding Sirhan Bishara Sirhan you desire. Sincerely yours, J. Edgar Hoover."[2]

Without Kaiser's book deal, it would have been an insurmountable task for any psychologist to reaccess even small amounts of data from the psychologists' testing sessions with Sirhan, what conclusions they reached, how they arrived at their psychiatric diagnoses and, most essential, how the assessment results supported those conclusions. We can thank Kaiser for memorializing records that would have otherwise been permanently lost to later psychologists like myself who searched for answers to still unsettled questions about Sirhan's mental state when he killed Robert Kennedy – and how the experienced defense team simply "lost track" of their central defense strategy: diminished capacity.

A Look into Sirhan's Psychological Testing

Since Sirhan was exposed to a number of psychological tests given by the two principal psychologists, who presented uneven results that did very little to clarify all aspects of his personality, the question I posed concerning the extensive psychological testing was: What new information can we gain from a reassessment of Sirhan's original psychological testing results?

---

1 Robert Blair Kaiser letter to J. Edgar Hoover, FBI director, April 19, 1969.
2 J. Edgar Hoover, FBI director, letter to Robert Blair Kaiser, April 29, 1969.

To understand the significance of the psychological tests given to Sirhan in his jail cell when he was still a defendant, I wanted to (where appropriate) simplify, condense, and make comprehensible the oftentimes confusing psychological jargon used to explain psychological testing results as expressed in the writings and testimony of the doctors.

Though Kaiser did a good job preserving most of these materials available for a later interpretation, many of the tests and assessment results that he described in a general way needed considerably more detail, specificity, and accuracy to be best understood. For example, the description of results from certain psychological tests are presented by Kaiser as generalities not tied directly to specific test responses or to assessment criteria. This is especially the case with regard to the TAT, where Kaiser recorded general statements concerning Sirhan's responses to one or more TAT images.

The identification of specific TAT cards is necessary to determine Sirhan's accurate responses to the individual cards he was presented. As one example, Kaiser generally reported that, "In another [TAT card], Sirhan saw someone standing under a street light. ..." This card was identified as TAT image number twenty, and the content was described by the test's author as "a dimly illuminated figure of a man (or woman) in the dead of night, leaning against a lamppost."[3]

Many additional references to TAT cards failed to identify which card Sirhan is responding to, or what his responses were. Using the Kaiser information, I have clarified what TAT card was being discussed, as well as Sirhan's responses.

THE AMAZING DR. MARTIN SCHORR FALLS OFF A CLIFF

The following is a reporting of the testing results either directly given to Sirhan by defense psychologists, or results that were reviewed by other doctors. I started with the psychological testing results based on Dr. Martin Schorr's assessment of Sirhan.

The defense's selection of expert witnesses failed to be in concert with the principal defense strategy put forward in the concept of diminished capacity by Dr. Diamond. Specifically, a "well-respected" although somewhat odd-mannered, clinical psychologist, Dr. Martin Schorr, from San Diego, had positive letters of recommendation from several San Diego judges, two of which said Dr. Schorr was able to comport himself with ease in a courtroom.

---

3   Kaiser. (1970). 441.

Apparently, Dr. Schorr had helped screen inmates for San Diego County. He was advertised as the doctor who could titrate complex psychological issues into comprehensible facts easy for the jury to get. He had some limited staff privileges at several psychiatric hospitals and clinics in Southern California and belonged to several professional organizations: the Rorschach exchange, the Society of Projective Techniques, and the Transactional Analysis Association. On paper, he looked great! Reality was something else again.

When defense attorney Parsons first contacted him, Dr. Schorr more or less pleaded with Parsons to bring him into the case, after all his credentials spoke volumes. At the outset, Parsons was reluctant: "I'm not sure I want Schorr in this case … he's too goddamn eager."

From his initial contacts, defense investigator Michael McCowan showed an open dislike for Dr. Schorr, questioning, "Why he was selected in the first place?"

McCowan was everything Dr. Schorr was not: a former Marine and ex-cop, and he had worked for the LAPD for ten years prior to finishing law school. He exuded a "tough guy" macho image, whereas Dr. Schorr seemed more like a "marshmallow" kind of guy. Sirhan's first reaction to Dr. Schorr also ran from cold to freezing.

During a preliminary meeting between Schorr and Parsons, Parsons was heard saying, perhaps in jest, "I don't know who is crazier, you or Sirhan?"

Dr. Schorr took no offense at the not-so-subtle comment.

Dr. Schorr's expert fees became an issue; he would not consult on the case pro bono, as Parsons suggested. During a personal conversation, Parsons reiterated to Dr. Schorr that he was fortunate to be in this case because the publicity alone was probably worth $100,000. Parsons quipped, "We could get 50,000 psychologists for free. In fact, they'd pay us!"

But Schorr wasn't convinced, responding something to the effect that when he is "on the stand, it'll look more professional." Dr. Schorr said he'd invoice Parsons's office for his time; but for now he'll put it on the cuff.

After Schorr's performance "on the stand," as he put it, I found no record that Dr. Schorr was paid even a dime; and the publicity value of his appearance quickly plummeted. Displaying a variety of odd personal, psychological, and medical symptoms himself, Dr. Schorr did not present a strong physical presence in the courtroom. For instance, he suffered from an acute anxiety reaction, acrophobia, and wore poorly fitted contact lenses that caused him to crane his neck around, like a long-necked bird, into a contorted position when making direct eye contact with anyone, especially the jurors.

He presented himself at court with a variety of props like a stage entertainer might use. Hoping to dazzle the jury, he put up a number of confusing graphs and equally baffling charts supposedly representing some aspect of Sirhan's various mental conditions. He came equipped with a handy silver telescopic pointer to march through his endless points to the jury; but even with his magic pointer, he struck the image of a one-man band obviously playing to an audience of one – himself!

A witness's overall physical appearance and size, gestures, movements, attire, ability to hold eye contact, and general continence and demeanor are often referred to as "expressive cues." Jurors as well as judges and attorneys pay close attention to these sometimes subtle factors that are often equally important to what a witness actually has to say when providing testimony.

Dr. Schorr had lots to say and was not afraid to talk. His circuitous testimony was characterized as wordy, windy, and pedantic, often leaving jurors scratching their heads, seeking relief from endless lectures. As his testimony continued, it was obvious that he didn't score many points with the jury. His deficits in physical appearance were just the tip of a perilous iceberg he later slammed into headlong, which negated whatever importance the jury may have given to his testimony concerning Sirhan's mental state.

Pretrial preparation is an absolute key. In Dr. Schorr's situation, this step was obviously not taken. Once a key witness's credibility is discredited (as Dr. Schorr's was), the defense's job is to rehabilitate the injured party if possible. Experience has repeated shown me that this is why witness pretrial preparation is profoundly important to making the best possible case to a jury – to set up possible antagonistic scenarios and hypotheticals to test the potential witness and, where possible, insulate them from falling into preset traps set by the opposition. The process can counteract or mitigate the anticipated hostile cross-examination tactics that at times can become argumentative, facilitating the witness' ability to not have holes punched in their testimony. This is especially important to avoid a witness impeachment, for instance, by being caught in a distortion of the facts; identification of a witness caught in a lie usually represents a fatal wound where the bleeding simply cannot be stopped.

In some cases when testifying as an expert witness, the amount of time I spent in trial preparation with representing attorneys often took more time than my actual court testimony. Whether testifying for the defense, the prosecution, or in a civil matter, I was always sensitized to listen to the representing attorneys' pretrial recalcitrant attacks on my potential testimony that could undermine or jeopardize the impact of my testimony. I was always careful to listen to their suggestions and pay close attention to how my real-time testimony might be received in court.

Probably the most cardinal sin that can sink a witness's testimony faster than anything is a certain sense of arrogance, as if: "Don't you realize that I know it all? Why bother me with these trivial questions?" And Dr. Schorr checked all the boxes on what not to do as an expert witness providing trial testimony. In the end, because of his poor performance, he embarrassed himself and the well-intentioned defense attorneys who unfortunately hired him.

In Dr. Schorr's case, he just could not help himself; not listening to his attorney handlers was only the beginning. He unwittingly set up his own fatal trap, and the prosecution did its job, following through, and sprang it, which led to his demise as a credible witness, helping to materially sink the defense case, contributing to an almost total collapse of Sirhan's defense, which had drastically departed further from the diminished capacity defense as the trial progressed.

For Dr. Schorr, the real fireworks began when one of the prosecutors, John Howard, during cross-examination led him down a road of no return. During Dr. Schorr's windy cross-examination, he presented a meandering discussion of the psychological tests given to Sirhan. His complete test results, diagnosis, and professional opinions were integrated into his lengthy psychological report, as directed by the defense, and marked and submitted as a defense exhibit for the court record. Just when prosecutor Howard's cross examination could have moved on to other issues, Dr. Schorr insisted that it was important if not essential for him to read his entire psychological report in open court, particularly for the edification of the jury.

Perhaps sensing that two paragraphs from page 3, which had already been bracketed, were the parts Dr. Schorr was most eager to read aloud, Howard handed the report to Dr. Schorr and asked him to read that section in his December 18 report.

Dr. Schorr began to read, "By killing Kennedy, Sirhan kills his father, takes his father's place as heir to his mother. The process of acting out this problem can only be achieved in a psychotic, insane state of mind. Essentially the more he railed and stormed, the more he withdrew into her protection. He hated his father and feared him. He would never consciously entertain the idea of doing away with him, but somewhere along the line, the protecting mother fails her son. The mother finally lets down the son. She whom he loved never kept her pledge, and now his pain has to be repaid with pain. Since the unconscious always demands maximum penalties, the pain has to be death. Sirhan's prime problem becomes a conflict between instinctual demand for his father's death and the realization through his conscience that killing the father is not socially acceptable. The only real solution is to look for a compromise. He does. He finds the symbolic replica of his father in the form of Kennedy, kills him and also removes the relationship that stands between him and his most possession, his mother's love."[4]

As soon as Dr. Schorr finished reading the passage from his report, Howard queried, "Who wrote that?"

"I did," Dr. Schorr replied.

Howard answered with a dubious, "UH HUH," [author's capitals] convinced that these were not Dr. Schorr's original words as written in his report.

His intuition was correct.

The characterization of Sirhan's projected Oedipal aggression against his father and love for his mother was immediately reported by the hungry press who couldn't wait to print Dr. Schorr's mother-father-son Greek tragedy analysis.[5]

Newspapers carrying this kind of TV soap opera coverage quickly sold out, and the evening TV news played and replayed the recounting of Sirhan's Oedipal complex. The public's thirst for this racy trial update wasn't quenched. More was to come, quite possibly tied to Dr. Schorr's own ethical issues. These were raised when the trial resumed on March 18 when the real bombshell struck its target.

A fact checker from the *New York Times* discovered that Dr. Schorr had not credited, or had outright plagiarized, a considerable part of his psychological report on Sirhan, which he put on public display, from a crime textbook written by Dr. James A. Brussel, titled *Casebook of a Crime Psychiatrist*. Dr. Brussel was a well-known, East Coast-based forensic psychiatrist, probably best known to Dr. Schorr from his work on the Albert DeSalvo case, the 1967 Boston Strangler trial.

---

4   Klaber and Melanson. (1997). 200.
5   Dr. Schorr had hoped to write a book on his forensic experiences, *Murder Is a Family Affair*, with a main thesis that men kill in order to symbolically get even with their cold, hostile, rejecting mothers. Being humiliated as a plagiarist in front of the Sirhan jury apparently did not figure into his proposed book pitch.

The *New York Times* printed Dr. Schorr's words right next to the unquoted passages from Dr. Brussel's book – they were identical. Brussel's publisher jumped into the plagiarism fray, claiming it was intent on suing Schorr for copyright infringement; but Dr. Brussel took a rather humorous, high-road position, stating that he was flattered that his words were lifted without credit and made their way into Sirhan's famous criminal trial.

For the prosecution in Sirhan's case, the trap was unfolding and, before Dr. Schorr could shrug his shoulders and say, "I didn't do it!," John Howard made an additional direct request: "Your Honor, here we have a book, *Casebook of a Crime Psychiatrist* by James A. Brussel, MD, and may it be marked as People's next order 101."

The similarities of descriptions in Dr. Brussel's book to those appearing in Dr. Schorr's psychological report were striking if not word-for-word identical. Howard made his point when Dr. Schorr took the stand, "At the time you prepared your report, were you aware of a book called *Casebook of a Crime Psychiatrist* by James A. Brussel?"

Dr. Schorr clipped back, "Oh yes, I read it."

Howard pressed the issue: "Doctor, you copied right out of the book, didn't you?"

Dr. Schorr's convoluted answer proved the case: "I took materials from the book that applied to the paranoid mechanism, and I redesigned it to fit with what I had already said."

Dr. Schorr was drowning hopelessly, going down for the third time, and beyond rescue. Lead defense attorney, Grant Cooper, later said, "At that point, I could have crawled under a table!"

Given the negative, undisputable facts of the moment, Dr. Schorr ignominiously fell on his sword, and reluctantly confessed, using ambiguous language in order to save face. But it was too little, and far too late. He said weakly that Dr. Brussel had used precise psychological language that more or less captured his own perspective on Sirhan's mental state.

With Dr. Schorr still on the stand, Howard twisted the sword in a little deeper, having Dr. Schorr read additional sections of his report and then read corresponding sections from Dr. Brussel's book.

Howard had a beaten-down Dr. Schorr, reading verbatim parts of Brussel's case, "The Christmas Eve Killer" and "The Mad Bomber," each virtual matches to what Dr. Schorr wrote in his report. Dr. Schorr was finally forced to admit to the jury that he had borrowed or misappropriated Dr. Brussel's words without attribution to the real author.

Howard twisted the sword deeper: "Doctor, by the time you graduated from college, did you know how to put quotation marks around or use footnotes to indicate that you had taken from another source?"

Dr. Schorr gave another oblique response that made little sense, "I wanted to make a statement that one would not disbelieve!"

In the end, almost everything he said was disbelieved due to his plagiarism from Dr. Brussel's clinical cases.

At that point, as Dr. Schorr was quickly excused from the witness stand and, as subsequently described by a *Newsday* reporter, "Dr. Martin M. Schorr had the sick look of a man who has just taken a hard right to the belly yesterday when he stepped off the elevator on the first floor of the Hall of Justice at exactly 12:07 P.M. He was just getting used to contact lenses, and he had to tilt his head backward to focus correctly before starting walking. A mob of interviewers tried to hold him back. But he kept shaking his head and broke into an awkward trot toward the street door. His petite, gray-haired wife, Dolores, put her arm around his waist and squeezed. He sagged for a moment and then squeezed back ... they left the building without looking back."[6]

One fact became clear to Parsons, the jury, and the press: Dr. Schorr definitely didn't have the right stuff, thereby discrediting the balance of his psychological report.

In spite of this humiliating impeachment backdrop, his testing profile of Sirhan was fairly accurate. Prior to Dr. Schorr's self-immolation, he had administered five individual psychological tests to Sirhan: the BVMGT, the TAT, MMPI, WAIS, and the Rorschach. When these assessment tools are presented in a nonthreatening atmosphere, they can help establish rapport with the defendant and glean considerable additional information concerning the person, reaching far beyond cold clinical facts.

I have incorporated these same tests with hundreds of criminal defendants for more than four decades as a forensic psychologist. The TAT especially presents an open-ended opportunity to explore a person's responses in depth, particularly helping test takers better understand themselves and even stimulate personal development. The TAT administration provides multiple moments when the psychologist can unobtrusively probe in a passive manner without threatening the client. Sirhan's being born in the Middle East and having different cultural values, one can imagine his reaction when confronted with a request to submit to a battery of strange-appearing psychological tests. Whether Dr. Schorr used

---

6   Bob Greene, *Newsday*, March 19, 1969.

the TAT in this manner as a self-enhancement, door-opening technique is not known.

Dr. Schorr's first attempt to establish rapport with Sirhan during the initial session was not met with great expectations perhaps because Sirhan (like Parsons and McCowan) seemed to be upset with him. Almost immediately the following day, Sirhan summoned Parsons and made an incredible statement: "I want to plead guilty, and I don't want a trial. I don't want the doctors trying to prove I'm insane!"

All of Dr. Schorr's assessment sessions with Sirhan were conducted on the thirteenth floor of the Hall of Justice where the County jail was located. Schorr had alluded to the fact that his five psychological tests were all recognized projective techniques, forming what he claimed was a kind of representative mental picture of Sirhan, capable of deeply penetrating "the mask of sanity or conformity or getting down to the root feeling and attitudes of the true personality."

The reason these projective tests have prevailed for so many decades is that the process remains a completely projective, or a stimulus-driven technique, urging the patient to unfold sometimes hard to reach material unavailable using other methods. There is a low probability for the subject to tell the examiner what they "wanted" to hear, no right or wrong answers. The answers give the examiner the best possible insight into that person's unconscious depths. It wasn't the Rorschach that yielded specious results; it was Dr. Schorr's deceptive testimony that mostly negated the good work he did using the Rorschach and the other psychological tests.

Dr. Schorr was not quite accurate when he claimed that all these psychological tests in their format were projective in methodologies; in fact, only the TAT and Rorschach are clearly identified by psychologists as distinctively projective tests where clients are encouraged to immerse themselves in a series of abstract photo representations (TAT) or ambiguous inkblots (Rorschach).

The BVMGT is not commonly classified as a projective test using the meaning described here, however interpretative hypotheses concerning possible clinical psychiatric diagnoses can be extrapolated from an analysis of a client's projective responses to this test.

The WAIS is a standard, comprehensive measure of intelligence in eleven specific areas related to an individual's intelligence quotient (IQ). These eleven areas are divided into two sets of subscales comprising a verbal IQ (six areas) and a performance IQ (five areas). The summation of these two scales yields a full-scale IQ score. At times, WAIS results have been used to generate psychological hypotheses regarding personality dysfunction.

I was instructed on how to administer and score the WAIS in graduate school, about the same time the Sirhan trial was in progress. Generally accepted by my professors was that the WAIS was to be used specifically as a measurement of a client's global intellectual functioning, and only secondarily to gather any diagnostic information leading to psychiatric theories.

Dr. Schorr assessed Sirhan using the WAIS version available at that time, reporting that his verbal IQ was fixed at 109, and his performance IQ was fixed at only 82. Schorr attributed this large IQ differential between verbal and performance scores to either some form of brain damage or a psychotic process.

Two years before the assassination, Sirhan was thrown from a horse at Corona where he worked as a horse groomer and want-to-be jockey. He suffered a marginal head injury, received medical attention, and was awarded $1,705 by the State of California as compensation. A review of Sirhan's medical records verify that his head injury was superficial and not serious, but he sustained more-serious injuries to both eyes. Sirhan seemed depressed over the fact that the injury to his eyes might end his quest to be a jockey.

To rule out the presence of an organic brain syndrome, Parsons ordered that Sirhan be given an electroencephalogram (EEG), administered in his jail cell.

Oddly, prior to the administration of the EEG, Sirhan asked defense investigator, Michael McCowan, if he should prepare for the upcoming test by banging his head against the cell's bars, perhaps just to make sure the EEG findings would confirm he had some form of active brain damage.

McCowan dissuaded Sirhan's plan, saying, "No, it's not a good idea. You either got it, or you don't, period."

The judge approved the EEG procedure, and Dr. Edward Davis appeared at Sirhan's cell along with his EEG machine and his technician, Ms. Helga Kaye, who both explained the EEG technology to him. Dr. Davis, a well-respected Beverly Hills neurologist, conducted the test using a portable brain-wave machine. The results, taken over a one-hour period, proved negative for brain trauma.

On the night of the assassination, Sirhan said he had consumed approximately four strong drinks while attending one of the concurrent political events that night at the Ambassador Hotel, which he inadvertently happened upon: a political celebration for Max Rafferty in the Ambassador's Venetian Room, and not Robert Kennedy's party. Sirhan said that he paid for and drank four Tom Collins while at the Rafferty party. As a nondrinker, this was way out of character for Sirhan. In any case, he downed the gin-based beverages one after another, as he said, "They were like lemonade!"

If Sirhan's story is representative of what he actually did, then he consumed the alcoholic drinks before finding his way to the Embassy Ballroom where Robert Kennedy was to deliver a victory speech to his supporters, having just won the California Democratic primary. Was Sirhan using the drinks to fortify his nerve, knowing that he was now one step closer to fulfillment of his plan to kill Senator Kennedy in cold blood?

Dr. Davis had Sirhan consume the same approximate amount of alcohol that he consumed at the Ambassador Hotel's Venetian bar. After Sirhan consumed the alcohol from a paper cup within eight minutes, Dr. Davis reassessed him for more than one hour and reached the same conclusion as in the sober test: no noticeable signs of EEG irregularities, and thus no verification of brain damage.

Though Sirhan had steadfastly desired to have a positive EEG finding that he had incurred some form of brain damage as a result of the Corona accident, unfortunately (also for Cooper) the EEG results did not confirm any abnormal brain waves.

Sirhan, though not a good student, had apparently cultivated an enhanced appetite for reading. His verbal acumen, comprising his vocabulary depth and word fluency, is later discussed when the Rorschach is taken up. All the verbatim responses to the Rorschach given to Sirhan by Dr. Schorr, and later by Dr. Richardson, are from Kaiser's reporting. This also applies to Sirhan's responses on the MMPI and the TAT.

Dr. Schorr's description of Sirhan's Rorschach responses could at best be characterized as confusing, and at worst it descended into a strange word salad, mixing arcane Rorschach percentages with meaningless statistics, only further confusing the jury. His covert language describing Sirhan's Rorschach responses seemed more appropriate for a sophisticated graduate school seminar, not for LA jurors.

If Dr. Schorr became confused by the inquiries from the defense attorney who hired him, then the prosecution would have a clear opening to discredit his testimony. At that point in the testimony, Dr. Schorr referenced his many visual aids – graphs and charts, trying to illustrate his case using his handy pocket telescopic pointer.

An example of Dr. Schorr's uneven testimony referring to Sirhan's test scores: "But this is most significant ... here we have 41 percent – and the total here should always be under ten; less than ten. It's forty-one. So taking the upper limit of the norm, ten, forty-one is four times excessively wrong."

Listening to this word salad, Berman simply shook his head and asked, "Four times what?"

Indignantly, Dr. Schorr bristled, "Wrong ... four times excessively abnormal. This is what I tried to say earlier; there are no right or wrong things; there are no good or bad. This is bad in terms of the norm, but it is not bad in and of itself; it depends on what kind of value you place on this kind of personality profile. I haven't even given it a name yet!"

Even with his magic pointer, it is doubtful at the end of this meandering statement whether he still had an audience, especially the puzzled jury holding back their snickers.

Dr. Schorr told the jury that the psychological tests revealed a man basically trapped in "a rigid, persistent, persuasive system of false beliefs with a personality structure that was in high degree of fragmentation."

Ultimately disappointing to the defense's position, Dr. Schorr, still under questioning by Berman, acknowledged that Sirhan was able to "maturely and meaningfully reflect upon the gravity of his crime!"

That was not a positive sign for the defense side. Given the entire defense position, constructed around the premise of diminished capacity, Sirhan could not have demonstrated malice aforethought; and the negation or limiting of criminal intent was just the opposite of what Dr. Schorr was testifying to.

This was one of many strategic breaks from the original plan to convince the jury that Sirhan was guilty of a lesser crime, e.g., second-degree murder or voluntary manslaughter, neither meeting California Penal Code criteria for a death sentence. The defense's attempt to overwhelm or saturate the jury with psychological expertise using various witnesses, including Dr. Schorr, simply didn't work.

Even the results of Dr. Schorr's psychological testing of Sirhan were controversial. On November 26, 1968, Dr. Schorr administered the ten ink blot cards comprising the Rorschach Test to Sirhan in his jail cell. During his testimony, he described Sirhan's responses and reactions to the cards. He copied the ten miniature ink blots and Sirhan's Individual Record Blank, the revised edition, and proudly presented these handouts to the jury for their careful inspection.

Dr. Schorr made it very clear that the Rorschach Test was his "psychological Bible," used to interpret Sirhan's personality structure. The jury closely examined the Rorschach cards, then began to take copious notes as they rotated and turned the cards from side to side and upside-down in an unserious manner.

Dr. Schorr painstakingly explained to the jury that he believed the test revealed the inner or hidden facets in Sirhan's subterranean personality structure – who he really was. As the jury continued to turn and rotate the miniature ink blots, Dr. Schorr flashed colored slides visually depicting what they were seeing on paper. He provided a confusing "expert" narrative to ostensibly clarify what the jury was completely missing. His description drifted into an arcane, technical introspective of what Sirhan saw on each ink blot. This only added to their bewilderment as they squirmed in the jury box, shaking their heads as if wondering, *What in the world is this supposed doctor talking about? We just don't get it.*

At the bottom of the Individual Record Blank, Dr. Schorr had typed in his diagnostic impression of Sirhan: "Percentages all point to a paranoid state of psychosis and the trend is toward further deterioration. Concept of NGRI [not guilty by reason of insanity] could be considered as percepts conceivably reach beyond M'Naghten."

His even more confusing testimony did not help clarify his points. The jurors' reaction seemed confused and, at the same time, they wanted to know just exactly what this Rorschach proved anyhow.

The *coups de grace* to his challenged testimony came when Dr. Schorr went over select Rorschach responses apparently made by Sirhan during the assessment. Dr. Schorr, who audio taped all his jail sessions with Sirhan, including the administration of the Rorschach test, was pressed by prosecutor Fitts as to one of Sirhan's responses to card IV, which Dr. Schorr said was a Frankenstein monster. But there was no record of this response. Apparently Schorr either lost or destroyed the recording that could corroborate the Frankenstein monster image.

Launching into an attack on Dr. Schorr's professional credibility, Fitts said, "Maybe Dr. Schorr's got a good memory. There are no notes whatsoever to indicate that Sirhan said 'Frankenstein monster.' What are we getting here? ... I say it's deplorable."[7]

Although the major damage to the defense had already been inflicted, Dr. Schorr was still sitting nervously on the stand, being questioned on redirect examination by defense attorney Emile Zola Berman. Berman did

---

7   Kaiser. (1970). 481.

not care to pursue the fine points of Dr. Schorr's damaging testimony, his professional integrity, or the disappearing records, but instead knew the best thing he could do was to get Schorr off the stand quickly, and tell him to get lost!

The prosecuting attorney summed up Dr. Schorr's performance as centered on "entertainment, and this is not appropriate in a capital case. So far as I'm concerned, Dr. Schorr is consigned to oblivion."[8]

Sadly, the concept of diminished capacity was continually clouded with the testimony of additional doctors who just couldn't stay on the same page, perhaps confusing the jury with complicated terminology hard even for some professionals to grasp.

DR. RODERICK RICHARDSON TAKES THE STAND

Dr. Schorr's ignominious testimony didn't make it any easier for Dr. Roderick Richardson, who was called to testify as the next defense expert. Quite naturally his testimony would be highly scrutinized especially by the prosecution attorneys.

Sirhan had been questioned, verbally probed, challenged, tested and analyzed, and reanalyzed by a steady stream of what he contended were "a bunch of plotting Jewish shrinks!" But Sirhan took an immediate liking to Dr. Richardson, a tall, athletic figure, who had a winning demeanor, nonabrasive personality, and pleasing manner. As his sessions with Sirhan progressed, the trust factor increased.

Dr. Richardson's most persuasive diagnostic information about Sirhan was garnered from the psychological tests he used to gather psychological information and hopefully restore the credibility of Sirhan's mental defense of diminished capacity. After Richardson finished testing Sirhan, he was asked to write a report to be presented to lead defense attorney Grant Cooper. At that point, Dr. Richardson turned the questioning around and posed a more-or-less loaded question to Mr. Berman: "Would it be permissible to read the report first and then to handle the tests one by one?"

With Dr. Schorr's plagiarism debacle still fresh in Mr. Berman's mind (certainly still in the jurors' minds), and knowing that the credibility of psychologists' testimony had taken a severe hit, Berman was understandably nervous.

Dr. Richardson asked again: "Would it be permissible to read the report?"

Mr. Berman: "AND IT WAS MADE BY YOU?" [author's capitals]

---

8   Ibid.

Dr. Richardson: "Yes, it was."

Mr. Berman presses the point: "It is your work product?"

Dr. Richardson: [emphatic] "Yes!"[9]

• • •

Dr. Richardson was initially consulted in order to verify psychiatric diagnoses, using empirical methods that could be reverified by other psychologists. Forensic psychologists know that raw testing data obtained by one doctor can be reinterpreted by a second or third psychologist. On the other hand, the information drawn by the psychiatric community more or less rests on the opinions and conclusions put forth by an individual psychiatrist, sometimes with greatly divergent outcomes.

Berman continued his examination of Dr. Richardson, inquiring about the specifics of Sirhan's assessment. He said, "Tell us what tests you performed; the circumstances under which they were performed; and the results that you came to in each specific test."

Dr. Richardson responded, "All right. I tested Mr. Sirhan in his cell at the Hall of Justice, I think on the 13th floor, I think on July 20, 1968. I spent three hours with him, the hours from 11:00 until 2:00 that day. Subsequent to that, the tests that I administered were selective-subtests from the Wechsler Adult Intelligence Scale; the Rorschach; the TAT; the Hooper Visualization Test; and the Bender Visual-Motor Gestalt Test."[10]

Dr. Richardson's testimony came off almost seamlessly, save one possible professional misstep. He omitted a discussion or analysis of two additional psychological assessment tools he used to evaluate Sirhan. Richardson actually presented Sirhan with six individual psychological tests: the Rorschach, TAT, WAIS, BVMGT, HVOT, and the MDS and the MMPI, just as Dr. Schorr did. Dr. Richardson had actually administered the first Rorschach several months before Dr. Schorr did.

To establish rapport, he tried to cultivate a positive assessment milieu with Sirhan by beginning the assessment session with the Rorschach, because it was nonstructured and fairly nondemanding of the test taker. Dr. Richardson, like Dr. Schorr, placed a lot of emphasis on how the Rorschach could be used to analyze a client's personality as he said, "A good Rorschach can give a psychologist perhaps a deeper insight into the patient than any other of the series of perhaps thirty to forty tests currently at his disposal. In a Rorschach, the subject is merely supposed to say what he 'sees' in the ink blots."[11]

---

9   *People vs. Sirhan Bishara Sirhan*, Certified trial transcript. Vol 22: 6330–6336. March 17–19 , 1969.

10   Ibid.

11   Kaiser. (1970). 179.

Unlike Dr. Schorr's Rorschach results, where only his "Individual Record Blank-Revised" and "Tabulation and Scoring Sheet" were preserved, Dr. Richardson's Rorschach results provided a detailed description of each of Sirhan's responses to the ten Rorschach cards.

This important data, concerning Sirhan's responses to what he saw in each ink blot, was recorded by Dr. Richardson, and the scoring was preserved by Kaiser.

Equally important to this analysis, Sirhan's Rorschach responses are also compared with a cross-cultural sample of Middle Eastern clients. Dr. Meloy's more recent comparison and reanalysis of the original Rorschach data conducted by Dr. Richardson provide new insights and valuable information to help clarify the complex mosaic of Sirhan's personality.

Dr. Richardson was concerned that Sirhan might be reluctant to respond to the second Rorschach presentation coming months later. But as Richardson began the presentation of the ten Rorschach cards to Sirhan, his multiple and varied responses to each of the ten cards were anything but disappointing. Dr. Richardson stated, "I was afraid to get into the most important case in my life and find my patient telling me they [Rorschach cards] just looked like a lot of ink blots to him. Instead, he came through with a torrent of response."[12]

In keeping with Rorschach guidelines, when Sirhan was finished giving his first impressions – content data – to the cards, Dr. Richardson represented them a second time, probing for more specific information and to clarify any ambiguous meaning or content of Sirhan's initial responses. This phase of the Rorschach administration is presented on the scoring sheet to the right of Sirhan's original responses. The scoring sheet displayed two distinct columns; one for Sirhan's verbatim or direct responses, and one for the examiner's secondary inquiry.

When asked about the two-phase administration of the Rorschach, Dr. Richardson explained, "That means that when the Rorschach was administered [to Sirhan], it was divided into two parts. In the administration proper, it's where you go through and ask an individual what he sees.... Then you go back to the second phase ... called 'inquiry' and then ask in more detail, trying to get a patient to say what it [a card image] is about, the blot that helped him get his ideas. That is where you determine where he sees it, what quality there is in the blot that brings the idea to mind, that kind of thing."[13]

---

12   Ibid.
13   Trial Vol 22: 6203–6502, March 17–19, 1969.

Dr. Richardson's complete Rorschach examination of Sirhan was re-analyzed using the most widely accepted Rorschach scoring system employed by forensic psychologists: the Exner system.[14] An updated scoring of Dr. Richardson's Rorschach record of Sirhan's performance was professionally reanalyzed in 1992 by Dr. Reid Meloy, a San Diego-based forensic psychologist and researcher. His detailed reassessment of Sirhan's Rorschach responses is referenced here and compared with Dr. Richardson's.[15] Dr. Meloy used this same system to reanalyze Sirhan's Rorschach responses as Dr. Richardson's.[16] The present analysis represents a hybrid of Exner's general Rorschach interpretation and the specific analysis of Sirhan's response results made by Dr. Meloy.

Ample information from Dr. Richardson's administration of Sirhan's Rorschach results includes a complete test record to facilitate this reanalysis. Using the updated Exner scoring system, my goal was to determine if this reassessment of Sirhan's Rorschach can help us uncover those hidden aspects of Sirhan's personality and help create a better understanding of who he is and, most importantly, his criminal proclivities – what motivated him to shoot Robert Kennedy. To accomplish this task, Sirhan's Rorschach responses have been reassessed and grouped into clinical areas to better understand how he saw and interpreted his negative psychological world in 1968.

Perhaps Dr. Schorr was correct at least once during his circuitous testimony, when he claimed the Rorschach represents a kind of mental X-ray, enabling psychologists to peer deeply into unknown regions of a client's personality to uncover "the mask of sanity or insanity."

---

14   Exner, J. (1978). *The Rorschach: A Comprehensive System*. NY: John Wiley & Sons, NY; Exner, J. (2003). *Basic Foundations and Principles of Interpretation: The Rorschach: A Comprehensive System*. 4th Ed. John Wiley & Sons, Hoboken, NJ.
15   Meloy, J.R. (1992). "Revisiting the Rorschach of Sirhan Sirhan." *Journal of Personality Assessment*, 58 (3), 548–570.
16   Ibid.

CHAPTER 6

THE RORSCHACH RESULTS

THE RORSCHACH – NOT JUST TEN INKBLOTS!

The Rorschach test is actually an interpretive technique used to access the unconscious areas of a person's psyche. When mental expansiveness is encouraged, the Rorschach "trip" can prove insightful and rewarding for the client as well as the psychologist. The optimal use of the Rorschach can provide an exciting journey into mental spaces for the client and the psychologist, allowing both to learn unanticipated information that may have been pushed deep into areas of the client's mind and remained otherwise unavailable.

Dr. Hermann Rorschach's seminal work, *Psychodiagnostics: A Diagnostic Test Based on Perception*, first published as a research article in September 1921, laid the foundation for one of the most unique psychological tests ever developed. His complete Rorschach results were later published in book form in 1942.[1] Because of its time-tested validity as a diagnostic tool, the Rorschach test has become the "go-to" evaluative measure for psychologists around the world. This was particularly true during the late 1960s when Sirhan was assessed.

According to J. E. Exner in his book, *The Rorschach: A Comprehensive System* (2003), "The greatest utility of the Rorschach is when an understanding of a person, as an individual, becomes important for the purpose of selecting treatment strategies or targets, or when that sort of information is important to other decisions concerning the individual."[2]

Obviously, in addition to the Rorschach test, many contemporary psychological tests are used by forensic psychologists to facilitate the unfolding of valuable clinical information about a client; but the Rorschach remains in the clinicians' armamentarium to access the less obvious aspects of a client's personality.

---

1   Rorschach, H. (1942). *Psychodiagnostics: A Diagnostic Test Based on Perception*. Verlag Hans Huber, Berne, Switzerland.

2   J.E. Exner (2003). *The Rorschach: A Comprehensive System*. 4th ed. John Wiley & Sons, Inc., Hoboken, NJ.

Dr. Rorschach's original work stems from his tireless inkblot experimentation during the 1920s in Switzerland. He studied medicine at Nerenburg, Zurich, Berne, and Berlin, finishing his medical education in 1910, the same year he married. He accepted a position in a private hospital in Moscow, returning to Switzerland a year later. At that time, during the pilot phase, Dr. Rorschach developed up to one hundred sample inkblots later pared down to the ten in current use.[3]

He explained, "Every figure in the series has to fulfill certain special requirements as these general ones, and each, as well as any whole series, must be thoroughly tried out before it can be used as apparatus for the test.... From the method of preparation it will be apparent that the figures will be symmetrical, with very little difference between the two halves."

With regard to the administration of the test, he provides this guidance: "The subject is given one plate after the other and asked, What might this be? He holds the plate in his hand and may turn it about as much as he likes. The subject is free to hold the plate near his eyes or far away as he chooses; however it should not be viewed from a distance."[4]

Dr. Rorschach said, "An attempt is made to get at least one answer to every plate, though suggestion in any form is, of course, avoided. Answers are taken down as long as they are produced by the subject. It has proven unwise to set a fixed time for exposure of each Rorschach card. All coercion should be avoided as much as possible."

During the development of the test, Dr. Rorschach noted that his findings were only preliminary as he had more work to do for final development. Unfortunately, on April 1, 1922, at the age of thirty-seven he died of acute peritonitis. After his death, the ten original Rorschach plates were published by the Swiss company, Verlag Hans Huber. I continue to use these Rorschach cards in my practice with defendants like Sirhan.

THE RORSCHACH 1.0

The Rorschach, a valuable diagnostic tool used by psychologists worldwide to assess personality variables, is of special importance in the Sirhan case because his Rorschach results were used by the defense team doctors to help diagnose him.

"Essentially, this broad-reaching test is composed of a stimulus that allows the examiner's traits and styles to be expressed. When interpreting the data, the examiner cannot focus solely on one small aspect of the ex-

---

3   Rorschach. (1942).
4   Ibid. 15, 16.

aminee or one small coded variable; each aspect can be understood only in context of the examinee's other features...."[5]

Hopefully this information can help demystify certain obscure aspects of the Rorschach to add clarity and promote a better understanding of Sirhan's Rorschach responses. Also presented here is an abbreviated scoring of Sirhan's Rorschach results as administered by Dr. Richardson.

When viewing Sirhan's specific Rorschach results in the right-hand column (the inquiry section) a variety and sometimes a combination of letters and symbols (+ and –) contribute to the overall scoring pattern. The specific areas described here are only some of the coding categories used, for instance, by Drs. Schorr and Richardson, to help develop their diagnostic impression of Sirhan's mental state when they tested him, and retrospectively his mental state at the time of the assassination. Drs. Schorr and Richardson rendered their final diagnostic decisions based on several psychological tests, but their professional opinions, derived in large measure from the Rorschach, relied on seven coding variables. 1. Location and Developmental Quality; 2. Determinants; 3. Form Quality; 4. Contents; 5. Popular Responses; 6 and 7, Organizational Activity (Z score), and Special Scores. For my own analysis, I focused on Sirhan's specific content coding (This denotes the test taker's choice of responses based on a class of objects chosen).

SIRHAN'S RORSCHACH RESULTS

The essential four clinical areas as suggested by Exner in the Rorschach investigation phase include:

1. predatory inclination, which examines such areas as psychopathic behavior, prior offenses, signs of impulse control dysfunction, and emotional tone (fluctuations in affect – highs to lows or manic episodes;

2. deception;

3. depression; and

4. anxiety level.

Each of these areas is evaluated against Rorschach content responses (what images he actually sees on the ten cards). The process is similar to retrospectively using new information to piece together the elements of a cold case criminal file. Using a forensic DNA case analysis, my goal

5   Rose, T., N. Kaser-Boyd, and M. Maloney. (2001). *Essentials of Rorschach Assessment*. John Wiley & Sons, New York, 37.

was to reevaluate the mountain of psychological evidence, using updated psychological assessment techniques like Dr. Exner's. I went through this data to see if the original team of doctors during the trial missed something, or if my fresh analysis might tell a different story about Sirhan's criminal pathology. Because the Rorschach seemed to be the centerpiece of Sirhan's previous psychological assessment, that's where I began. Using four select areas, this analysis was blended into Dr. Meloy's more specific analysis of Sirhan's Rorschach responses.

SIRHAN'S RORSCHACH CODING

The basis for many of the new clinical opinions I include here were formed by a clarification of Sirhan's psychological tests and rescoring and interpreting his original tests. This information, so essential to making Sirhan's psychiatric diagnoses, has not been explored or categorized in any comprehensive way by other professionals.

A glaring gap by prior experts, including Dr. Diamond, was that they relied on contradictory psychological testing results. I was able to supplement this informational gap by focusing attention on specific firsthand testimony from those select doctors who analyzed and tested Sirhan. Much of the psychological testimony presented here is derived from the actual trial transcript and parts not previously accessed by investigators.

The goal of the psychological testing in Sirhan's murder case was to augment the professional diagnoses rendered by defense psychiatrist, Dr. Bernard Diamond, and prosecution psychiatrist, Dr. Seymour Pollack. Neither were trained in the use of psychometric assessments, therefore they had to rely on input from psychologists trained in psychological assessment, and that meant they had to rely on the expertise of Drs. Schorr and Richardson, each of whom presented Sirhan with several key assessment instruments. Though some aspects of the psychological testing yielded hazy results that were confusing to the jury, nevertheless the testing results are some of the more intriguing factors in Sirhan's case. The Rorschach test is the first test explained here.

The general theory underlying the Rorschach test and the Thematic Apperception Test (TAT), as projective assessment tools, is their unique capacity to present a kind of three-dimensional personality X-ray of a person's inner mental structure. With so many unanswered psychological questions in Sirhan's case, the psychologist team hoped the testing would help clarify Sirhan's underlying psychodiagnostic picture; sometimes it did and sometimes it didn't. However, based on my review, the results from the Rorschach test proved to be a valuable psychometric asset in helping to diagnose Sirhan's psychiatric condition(s).

As discussed in some detail previously, Dr. Richardson presented his summary of Sirhan's Rorschach results during his court testimony when examined by defense attorney Berman on March 18, 1969, noting,

> Indications from the psychological tests are that Mr. Sirhan is of bright-normal to superior intellectual endowment. At the present time, however, his ability to think abstractly, to concentrate adequately, and thought process is shown to have significant reduction in efficiency. Psychological testing is indicative at this time of very severe emotional and mental disturbance ... so that his best and most adequate level of functioning is not stable or reliable, but subject to episodes of acute and rapid deterioration. At such times, his behavior and thinking become psychotic and are characterized by paranoid, projective distortion of the characteristics and motives of others, loss of judgment, loss of discrimination, loss of control over impulses, particularly hostile, aggressive impulses.[6]

A complete, annotated record of Sirhan's Rorschach Coding (real-time scoring), showing his complete Rorschach protocol card by card, is included in the Appendix.

To confirm the validity of his Rorschach results, Dr. Richardson also had two additional psychologists in the LA area review his work: Dr. Steven Howard and Dr. William Crain. In order to get a representative second opinion and a fresh diagnostic view on the Rorschach results from Sirhan first analyzed by Drs. Schorr and Richardson, the defense team also requested that the raw testing data be given to two additional psychologists unfamiliar with the case for a "blind diagnostic analysis." Because the defense team did not elect to plead Sirhan under the California not guilty by reason of insanity rules, the two psychologists, Drs. Georgene Seward and George DeVos, were asked to only review the psychological testing results.

As a matter of court procedure, the expert doing a "blind diagnostic assessment" doesn't know the diagnostic opinions of the original doctors. When Dr. Georgene Seward took the witness stand, she was questioned by lead attorney, Grant Cooper, about the report she wrote for the defense team. When he asked her how she made her evaluation of the raw data, she confirmed, "I proceeded as if I were dealing with the patient in a hospital on whom I was asked to make a blind diagnosis. That means I ex-

---

6 Trial Vol 22: 6203–6502, March 17–18, 1969.

amined each of the tests by each of the examiners, and I compared them. I noted the differences and the similarities that were shown."[7]

The review doctors knew the testing protocol they were double-checking was Sirhan's, therefore their principal focus was predicated on confirmation or disconfirmation of Dr. Richardson's and Dr. Schorr's primary psychiatric diagnosis of paranoid schizophrenia.

After Dr. Richardson presented his psychological conclusions, Berman delved into the critical area, asking, "I want to ask your opinion as a doctor in psychology, could any such person as you have described have the mental capacity to maturely and meaningfully deliberate and reflect upon the gravity of his contemplated act, that is of a murder on June 5, 1968; and by murder you may assume the unlawful killing of any human being with malice aforethought?"

Dr. Richardson replied, "As I understand those terms, my answer would be that he is not able to maturely and meaningfully premeditate." This was a definite plus for the defense team.

Berman continued the inquiry, "In your opinion, Doctor, could any such individual, particularly Sirhan, as described by you, have the mental capacity and ability to comprehend his duty to govern his actions in accord with the duty imposed by law, and thus have the mental capacity to act with malice aforethought?"

Dr. Richardson answered, "My general feeling is that, for at least a year or two, Mr. Sirhan couldn't be characterized as capable of maturely premeditating or comprehending his duty as most of us would understand it."[8]

After questioning Dr. Richardson concerning his diagnosis of Sirhan, Berman commented that "there is no denying that the first thing that would pop to mind is a paranoid personality – to a psychologist. Since we know that assassins far back in US history are people who tend to be paranoid, and this is what we read in our textbooks, and so the assumption is paranoid ... the most probable diagnosis is paranoid."

SIRHAN'S FOUR RORSCHACH CLINICAL AREAS REVISITED

1. PREDATORY INCLINATION:
AGGRESSIVENESS

One major psychological factor associated with predatory behavior is victim stalking. My research confirmed that Sirhan stalked Sena-

---

7   Trial Vol 25: 7726 March 26–28, 1969.
8   Trial Vol 25: 6438 March 26-28, 1969.

81

tor Kennedy on at least four occasions, the last being the night of June 4, 1968. As Kaiser stated, "It was becoming clearer to me that Sirhan stalked Kennedy and that he wasn't necessarily alone."

Previously, on May 20, 1968, Sirhan was seen in the company of a woman at Robbie's Restaurant in the City of Pomona where Senator Kennedy was to dine and give a short speech. Four days later on May 24, Sirhan attended a Kennedy political event held at the LA Sports Arena where at least two witnesses placed him; and on Monday June 2, he was driven to the Ambassador Hotel where he claimed he "wanted to see a friend who worked in the hotel kitchen."[9]

During a personal interview twenty-five years later, investigative reporter Dan Moldea confronted Sirhan, "Did you know anyone who worked at the Ambassador Hotel back then?"

Sirhan answered, "I never knew anyone who worked at that hotel. I had never been to the Ambassador before. I had heard about the Coconut Grove, but I had never been there."[10]

When questioned about those dates, Sirhan gave various conflicting accounts to investigators of where he was and why he went to these different locations. Defense investigator, Michael McCowan, speculated that on June 3, 1968, Sirhan drove from LA to San Diego to attend what was to be still another Kennedy rally where he was scheduled to address a crowd at the El Cortez Hotel. Senator Kennedy, exhausted from being on the long campaign trail, canceled his appearance at the last minute. McCowan based his suspicion of the trip on the extra 350 miles he noted on Sirhan's car odometer, about or a little more than a round trip to San Diego.

Predatory inclination can also be evidenced by the aggressor's own words. This is particularly relevant in Sirhan's case because in his diary he wrote, "My determination to eliminate RFK is becoming more of an obsession."[11] According to Dr. Meloy, Sirhan's Rorschach responses were marked by grandiosity, malevolence, and high aggression; and the object of this aggression was RFK. Dr. Meloy also characterized Sirhan's Rorschach content analysis as suggestive of predatory violence, although Sirhan did not reflect psychopathic signs. Sirhan's stalking and rehearsal of his future violent event is consistent with predation.

Sirhan's Rorschach content analysis also portends an aggressive motif when he projects into one of his responses: "a rocket, guns, mortars and

---

9   Kaiser. (1970). 534.
10   Moldea, D. E. (2018) *The Killing of Robert F. Kennedy: An Investigation of Motive, Means, and Opportunity*. Moldea.com, 4th Ed.
11   Meloy. (1992).

very dark, and serpents look ready to strike." His responses keep flowing when he notes: "This is madness, anger – the teeth are showing."

Are Sirhan's violent Rorschach images a reflection of what he's already done (killed Senator Kennedy?). Or are these fact-based images emanating from his own troubled earlier life ("a rocket, guns and mortars") that he witnessed on a daily basis when growing up in war-torn Jordan?

2. <u>DECEPTIVENESS/DEFENSIVENESS</u>

Ironically, deceptiveness is a special psychological defense mechanism, yet not easily identified. Here defensiveness is defined as guarding or shielding ourselves from real or perceived verbal attacks. Defending oneself is usually quite natural because we need to protect or insulate from the negative consequences of what we perceive as a personal threat. The ego is the real part of the personality that we carefully seek to protect, and all information that contradicts our perception of ego has to be neutralized or be completely eliminated.

Sirhan's defensiveness is important to analyze when we consider how many defensive responses he made on the Rorschach test. His total defensive responses were rated by Meloy using the Rorschach Defense Scale scoring system.

Sirhan's scores using the Rorschach Defense Scale suggest a defensive framework constructed around a neurotic system marked by personal isolation, devaluation, denial, and projection. For example, Sirhan's isolation fits with his loner, self-identification patterning and a near-psychotic massive denial score. His results also suggest personal devaluation that involves his attempt to neutralize attempts to fracture his fragile ego. Again, on Rorschach card X (number 10), Sirhan develops a projection tied to an overly suspicious or paranoid theme: "It's a cacophony of colors. A hodgepodge. All those legs, this here [probably pointing] looks like some kind of a rat (brown area). No, not a rat – it flies – a bat.... Everybody wants to catch on to you – with those legs! The minute you're within reach you're in their clutches."

The Rorschach Defense Scale also does not support a clinical diagnosis of a psychosis, such as schizophrenia. Rather, a diagnosis of borderline personality disorder (BPD) might better characterize Sirhan's personality, including overcompensation and his sense of omnipotence.

The high rating on defensiveness here is indicative of how Sirhan desperately tries to defend his ego from real or fantasized outside attacks. Additionally, this connects to his paranoid thought process, projection, and the rejection of those who may hurt him before they reject him. But how does this pattern of rejecting others before they reject him fit into the assassination scheme? Was Sirhan's violent act his way of fulfilling an ultimate plan to reject RFK?

Sirhan's deceptiveness was addressed by Dr. Diamond who tied this concept to his having lied during his testimony. During a sharp exchange with prosecutor David Fitts, Dr. Diamond dodged questions about Sirhan's truthfulness when he testified, denying being at the shooting range earlier on the day of the assassination. Upon being questioned about this distortion or defensiveness, Dr. Diamond admitted that Sirhan had at times lied on the witness stand when he denied prosecution witnesses' testimony that he practiced rapid-firing at the San Gabriel Range on June 4, 1968, the day of the assassination.

Dr. Diamond stated that Sirhan lied because he feared that the truth of what he had done might reveal "the degree and depth of his true mental illness." Above all, Sirhan did not want to acknowledge the seriousness of his perceived psychiatric illness. He was willing to admit that he killed RFK, but he did not want his own disturbed mental state to figure into the crime. Although Sirhan was willing to accept a plea of guilty to first-degree murder, he remained indifferent so long as "the shrinks didn't think I was crazy!"

Sirhan was defensive but, in his poorly constructed self-diagnosis, he wasn't insane. For Sirhan, insanity meant weakness, and he wanted to convey the image of power, self-mastery, and personal control. Dr. Diamond stated, "He tells lies when it comes to revealing anything that shows an indicator of mental illness; anything which shows that he is crazy, then he conceals and denies this and all things that are related to this."[12]

3. DEPRESSION

Sirhan's depression was deeply rooted into his past and reflected in his negative self-appraisal and absence of self-awareness. His chronic depressed mood levels were inextricably tied to his deep-seated Arabic, sociocultural determinants. Based on his emotionally scarred background that was marred by innumerable traumas since childhood, Sirhan carried multiple mental scars. How those scars influenced his life is a major issue in determining Sirhan's individual criminal responsibility.

Sergeant Mike Nielsen, a member of the Los Angeles Police Department's SUS, a Special Unit Senator set up to investigate RFK's assassina-

---

12   Trial Vol 24: 6987, March 21–26, 1969.

tion explains, "There was probably a tremendous amount of trauma when Sirhan was small. There were villages that were being wiped out. I could easily see why and how Sirhan would be affected by his early childhood upbringing and how this hatred between the Arabs and the Jews affected him."[13]

To a degree, Sirhan saw himself, even at age twenty-four, already as a failure in his life – different from other people who seemed able to achieve their goals. Sirhan remained frustrated because he did not achieve many successes. As a student at John Muir High School in Pasadena, he quickly discovered how different he was from the other students. Some came from wealthy families and drove the latest model sports cars to school. Students had an air of superiority that Sirhan alternatively envied and disliked. He felt out of his element. Day after day he went directly home after school to help his ailing sister, Aida, whose leukemia did not appear to be responding to medical treatment. Her death in 1965 represented another dark chapter in Sirhan's life.

After high school Sirhan enrolled in Pasadena City College, a two-year community college. Though he was an avid reader, because of his irregular attendance and nonacademic orientation, Sirhan dropped out before he flunked out. Dr. Diamond's testimony referred to Sirhan's poor self-concept and depression. "Yes, Sirhan was going to school, but this was an emotionally difficult period for him. His work in school was quite mediocre, and he saw himself largely as a failure, as a nothing; yet he was full of daydreams.…"[14]

Although Sirhan cultivated an active interest in many political viewpoints, his refugee status also factored into his positioning as a second class citizen, for instance, not being able to vote in US elections. Also reported was that, due to his "odd" looks and small stature, Sirhan was not attractive to women, though he fantasized himself to be somewhat of "a ladies man." He held a variety of low-paying jobs such as waiter, stock-boy, short-order cook, health food store clerk, landscaper, gas station attendant. Sirhan got a job in 1965 at the Santa Anita racetrack as an exercise boy and "hot walker," cooling down the horses after an intense workout or an actual race.

For a brief period, he worked at Hollywood Park Race Track in Corona. His small physical stature and body weight (approximately 115 pounds) seemed to qualify him to train as a jockey, but he lacked the nec-

---

13   Moldea. (2018).
14   Trial Vol 24: 6987, March 21–26, 1969.

essary coordination and physical skills for riding powerful and sometimes unpredictable racehorses. One employer noted his view that Sirhan was actually fearful of horses as well as lacking the nerve to become a real jockey. He was thrown from horses several times before he left Santa Anita the same year.

After his disappointment and thwarted goal to become a bona fide jockey and not merely a low status hot walker, Sirhan got another horse-stable related job at Granja Vista del Rio Thoroughbred Horse Farm not far from Corona, California, this time as an exercise boy and horse groom, earning $375 a month. Again, Sirhan was thrown from a horse in full gallop and sustained minor head injuries, requiring hospitalization and medical testing including X-rays. When he received $1,705 from the Argonaut Insurance Company for his injuries, this was the most cash Sirhan ever had at one time, but unfortunately his horse racing bets took care of most of the insurance settlement.

By late 1967, Sirhan landed another job with the same results. He was hired by Organic Pasadena, a local health food store, but terminated from the job based on his negative attitude and arguing with the store's boss. The Pasadena Police Department was called to sort things out, effectively ending Sirhan's foray into the vitamin business. Sirhan had no credit cards and little money, but he kept trying his hand at different jobs, which each ended badly, adding to his frustration and cumulative disappointment level.

This type of repetitive failure can contribute to the psychological condition known as "learned helplessness." This led to a question: Were Sirhan's efforts intentionally blocked by others as he believed, or was self-sabotage involved?

Sirhan's Rorschach responses suggested that his past painful life experiences would produce negative self-thoughts that often pervaded his consciousness, reinforcing his negative self-concept as a failure. On Rorschach card II, for example, Sirhan describes his perception of what he sees in the inkblot: [pointing to the card] "In here looks like blood smears around." On card IV he makes reference to "Very dark-serpents" [grimacing while viewing card]. Again on card IV he stated, "Now I feel like saving it, looks like a casket to me. It represents death!" These and additional Rorschach content responses are indicative of Sirhan's self-devaluation, depression, and perhaps suicidal ideation. Could his real motivation in the assassination plan be construed as a symbolic suicide gesture?

Dr. Meloy seems to confirm this self-destructive motif. He summed up Sirhan's depressive Rorschach responses: "The Comprehensive [Rorschach] System interpretive hypotheses suggest that Sirhan Sirhan, at the time of testing, was suicidal and profoundly dysphoric, confused by intense and painful affective disruptions. … His self-perception was negative, and although he maintained a rigid distance from others, he preferred dependency."[15]

4. ELEVATED ANXIETY LEVEL

Prior to the assassination, Sirhan's anxiety level was seen as elevated in the extreme, fueling his frustration and confusion. Certainly Sirhan was conflicted because of what he had planned and what he was about to do. Midmorning on June 4, Sirhan drove to the San Gabriel Valley Gun Club. He signed in as one of the first customers that day, immediately engaging in rapid firing, using his snub-nose, Iver Johnson .22 caliber eight-shot revolver. He stayed at the gun range until it closed at 5:00 p.m.

Was this rapid-fire session a rehearsal or a prelude to what he had planned later that day at the Ambassador Hotel? Presumably, Sirhan was highly anxious during the hours building up to the assassination and felt that the alcoholic drinks might serve to calm his nerves, or buttress his will to carry through on his plan, fully cognizant that he would shoot RFK later that night.

In 2008, Dr. Daniel Brown, an associate professor of clinical psychology at Harvard University Medical School and expert in hypnoanalysis (psychological treatment when the client is hypnotized), was hired by Sirhan's new attorneys to do an updated assessment of Sirhan's mental status. Dr. Brown's reassessment was not specifically designed to measure or guestimate Sirhan's anxiety level. After spending many hypnotic sessions with Sirhan, Dr. Brown realized that Sirhan was hyper-hypnotizable. Sirhan had practiced some form of self-hypnosis even as a child.

After conducting at least eight hypnotic sessions with Sirhan in 1969, Dr. Diamond also reported the same general finding and drew the same conclusion that Sirhan was a "perfect subject" for hypnosis. The doctors similarly agreed that, at times during the hypnotic sessions, Sirhan appeared to transcend into an almost automaton-like mental state of altered consciousness. Dr. Brown also noticed that when using a subtle hypnotic cue, he could get Sirhan to simulate firing a gun, molding his hand as a child might do when playing "cops and robbers," for instance.

---
15   Meloy. (1992).

Dr. Brown termed this hypnotically produced trance as "range mode," or the mental state Sirhan was often in when he practiced shooting at paper targets at a gun range. He further believes that on the night RFK was fatally wounded, Sirhan was probably in a similar range mode of altered consciousness and unable to distinguish being at a shooting range and his almost automatic actions, pulling the trigger in real time to kill Kennedy.

Was Sirhan's target practice (earlier that day at the San Gabriel Valley Gun Club), when he was obviously in range mode, somehow later triggered, putting him into a dissociated state where he may have conflated recreational target practice with the deadly shooting of RFK, as Dr. Brown opines?[16] It was also reported that Sirhan recalled "a memory of learning to shoot at vital organs and human [like] targets with a 'range master' at Corona Police Firing Range ... corroboration that the Corona Police Firing Range existed, and that [he] signed in the Saturday before the assassination to practice. ..."

Sirhan conveyed to the jury that on June 4, 1968, he signed in and practiced firing his gun at the Fish Canyon Range, perhaps another rehearsal to achieve range mode status.

Sirhan's ability to regulate his increasing anxiety levels progressively increased as the time approached for him to carry out his nefarious deed. His response to Rorschach card VIII exemplified his elevated anxiety level. As he viewed the card, Sirhan said, "I don't know. I feel very jittery – I can't hold still – it stirs me!"

Again, Sirhan painted a similar scene depicting anxiety on Rorschach card X when he said, "It is frightening – It frightens me – It frightens me. They [referring to the shape of the inkblot] all seem the same – wickedness – too many entanglements."

DR. RICHARDSON'S RESULTS

As noted previously, Dr. Richardson's testing results were based on the Rorschach and TAT as well as the WAIS, BVMGT, HVOT, MDS), and the MMPI. During his testimony, Dr. Richardson outlined why he used the Rorschach and commented on the importance of Sirhan's test results. When questioned by defense attorney, Mr. Berman, Dr. Richardson pointed out that his "approach to the Rorschach was somewhat different than Dr. Schorr's. Dr. Schorr had emphasized the quantitative features of the Rorschach. I have been in my practice more interested in what is called the 'content analysis' and 'sequence analysis.'"[17]

---

16   Brown, D. Exhibit H. to Petitioner's Reply Brief – Declaration of Daniel Brown, November 19, 2011.
17   Trial Vol 22: 6203–6502, March 17–19, 1969.

The HVOT and the BVMGT were both given by Dr. Richardson to help rule in or out the presence of brain damage or organic cerebral dysfunction as first suggested by Dr. Schorr as a possible mitigating factor due to the 1966 injuries Sirhan sustained when thrown from a horse twice. Medical and insurance records indicated that his injuries were not all that serious, but oftentimes the latent effects of a head injury do not immediately manifest themselves. In addition, Sirhan's brother Sharif noted that Sirhan had become obstinate, uncooperative, distant, uncommunicative, and isolated after the accidents.

Did the horse accidents in some way alter Sirhan's personality and reasoning ability? And if it did, was this a sufficient reason to reduce Sirhan's culpability for the crime? Lead defense attorney, Grant Cooper, of course, wanted to determine if Sirhan had some form of brain damage that could help predicate a defense against a first-degree murder charge.

Unlike the TAT and Rorschach tests, the BVMGT is specifically designed to measure potential for soft signs of brain damage. The client is not asked what they see, but after viewing the nine geometric figures on the stimulus cards, the patient is requested to replicate them on a sheet of blank paper. These figures are comprised of angular designs, lines intersecting and lines crossing drawings, the representation of dots, a semi-lunar-shaped figure, and various triangular representations. Sometimes a several-second memory delay during applications of the BVMGT, before the patient replicates the images, can help assess immediate recall function. The analysis of geometric figures opens up a new realm of valuable inquiry, however the test is not intended to be used as the sole basis for a diagnosis of brain injury, retardation, or other physical pathology.[18]

The test's value to a psychologist is to provide a reasonable guideline to differentially diagnose clients with or without signs of an organic brain condition. The BVMGT has been used to differentially diagnose brain damage, retardation, dementia, and additional organic brain-related issues since its inception in 1938. Moreover, it has proven utility in diagnosing certain psychiatric conditions: alcohol-related psychoses, dementia, some types of schizophrenia, and bipolar conditions. Of additional importance in Sirhan's case, this has a special forensic application in the diagnosis of malingering or faking behavior. A condition known as Ganser's syndrome, the act of presenting nonsensical answers to fairly simple questions, is sometimes associated with incarcerated individuals who may unwittingly manufacture false

---

18   Ogden, D.P. (2001) *Psychodiagnostics and Personality Assessment: A Handbook*, Third Edition, Los Angeles, CA: Western Psychological Services, 109.

psychiatric symptoms while in a dissociated state; (e.g., present incorrect information such as 2 times 2 equals 5).

In Sirhan's case, it was important to control for conscious faking behaviors especially memory faking. For the duration of his trial and even more than a half-century after the crime, Sirhan claims to have no memory of shooting Senator Kennedy.

Early into Sirhan's case, defense attorney Russell Parsons told a reporter from the *Los Angeles Herald Examiner* that the presence of organic brain damage could be introduced as evidence in behalf of Sirhan's defense.[19]

Oddly enough, Sirhan's results on the BVMGT were similar to the HVOT results, suggesting "unknown – probably mild to moderate – brain damage issue, organic disturbance or emotional dysfunction." This verification of an ongoing brain problem could have negatively impacted Sirhan's judgmental capacity, decision-making process, and supported the diminished capacity defense. But Dr. Richardson's testimony in this regard was apparently either mostly overlooked by the defense team, or considered to be unimportant, even though mild signs of organicity were verified on both tests that may have constituted mitigating factors regarding criminal intent, actual planning, and malice aforethought.

Dr. Richardson's testimony sparked a controversial exchange among the opposing legal counsels as he used the results of the BVMGT drawings to "ascribe social collision" to Sirhan's response patterns as a psychological factor impacting his life. This kind of psychological collision is symptomatic of severe psychiatric conditions. The results of Dr. Richardson's scoring tend to rule out significant signs of malingering and faking. He additionally contended that Sirhan's responses were more consistent with a psychotic patient than with a normal person.

As a corollary test, Dr. Richardson also gave testimony on Sirhan's HVOT results and testified when being examined by defense attorney, Mr. Berman. Regarding the HVOT, Dr. Richardson said, "That was negative for brain disease."

"In other words," Mr. Berman asked, "His problems were not in a disease process or from a blow, that is from the outside?"

Dr. Richardson answered that Sirhan "made nine errors out of thirty on this test," which placed him "within a range which is described as representing either severe emotional disturbance or mild brain disease." He further noted that the "indication of mild organic brain disease has to be checked out on the other tests. Since the other tests were negative,

---

19   "Sirhan's Defense? Brain Damage" *Los Angeles Hearld-Examiner*, June 20, 1968.

I concluded the meaning of the HVOT was that he was disturbed emotionally."

Lezak, et al. (2004) scoring guidelines for the HVOT may be generally contrasted with Dr. Richardson's conclusions when he scored Sirhan's HVOT results. Lezak stated: "Persons who make 7 to 10 failures comprise a 'borderline' group that includes emotionally disturbed or psychotic patients as well as those with mild to moderate brain disorders. Persons with scores in this range have a low to moderate likelihood of brain impairment. More than 11 failures usually indicates some degree of brain pathology."[20]

Sirhan's nine errors on the HVOT is suggestive of psychological dysfunction and mild-moderate brain pathology, quite possibly secondary to his horse riding accidents. Another area of critical importance is his unexplained behavior changes after the accident. His dramatic shift in his personality may be attributable to his head injury, although his condition was diagnosed medically as "mild trauma."

Did the head damage from the riding accidents cumulatively weaken Sirhan's cognitive abilities, lessening his specific capacity to make good behavioral or legal choices? And equally important, did the accident impair his mental functioning to meet the necessary elements to convict him of first-degree murder? It follows that the results from the HVOT could lend psychological support to Dr. Diamond's diminished capacity defense.

When Mr. Berman questioned Dr. Richardson, he also wanted to know the answer to this psychological defense issue. Dr. Richardson's answer seemed to buttress the defense's position regarding diminished capacity. Mr. Berman began the questioning.

> **Mr. Berman:** "Now, I want to ask your opinion as a doctor in psychology, could any such person as you have described have the mental capacity to maturely and meaningfully deliberate and reflect upon the gravity of his contemplated act, of a murder on June 5, 1968; and by 'murder' you may assume the unlawful killing of any human being with malice aforethought?"

> **Dr. Richardson:** "As I understand those terms, my answer would be that he is not able to maturely and meaningfully premeditate."

> **Mr. Berman:** "All right. Now, in that connection, assuming the same state of facts that I asked you in the last question, in your

20   Lezak, M.D., D.B. Howieson, D.W. Loring, with H.J. Hannay and J.S. Fischer. (2004). *Neuropsychological Assessment*, Fourth Edition. Oxford University Press. New York.

opinion, Doctor, could any such individual, particularly Sirhan, as described by you, have the mental capacity and ability to comprehend his duty to govern his actions in accord with the duty imposed by law, and thus have the mental capacity to act with malice aforethought?"

Dr. Richardson: "My general feeling is that at least for a year or two Mr. Sirhan couldn't be characterized as capable of maturely premeditating or of comprehending his duty as most of us would understand it. As I said in my report, his comprehension of his duty has been that of a kind of soldier and a representative of his nation. He goes beyond what we would consider our duty. His duty is defined on a highly personal, essentially psychotic basis. So in terms of that, I think my answer to your question is that he is not capable of malice as defined."[21]

At that juncture, defense attorney Mr. Berman inquired into a psychological assessment test not previously entered into evidence, The Menninger Diagnostic System (MDS) that was given to Sirhan by Dr. Richardson, but not explained. Throughout his testimony, Dr. Richardson spent a maximum amount of time presenting the biography of Dr. Karl Menninger, the test's author, to Mr. Berman, and minimal time presenting Sirhan's results on the MDS.

Dr. Richardson explained that the MDS categorizes psychiatric symptoms into five distinct levels according to the degree of mental dysfunction. Based on the results of the MDS (in Dr. Richardson's opinion), Sirhan's diagnosis of paranoid schizophrenia placed him into level IV, the more dysfunctional end of the psychiatric range of the scale.

However, these results were not presented as mitigating factors when Sirhan killed RFK (as they should have). Actual results of the MDS presented to Sirhan by Dr. Richardson were never even presented to the jury, nor commented on by any other researchers.

CHAPTER 7

A PARADE OF DOCTORS TESTIFY

After reviewing the many distinguished doctors who rendered psychiatric opinions as to Sirhan's mental status when he killed Senator Kennedy, I wanted to better understand why Sirhan's "dream" defense team lost focus, and lost the case in the process. I also wanted to know the roles played by the team of defense psychologists and the psychiatrist, Dr. Diamond, in Sirhan's conviction of first-degree murder and a date with the gas chamber.

From the beginning of the trial, Dr. Diamond's hope was for the defense doctors to somehow unify around the diminished capacity defense. However as the trial progressed, they strayed from that, putting forth testimony that only obfuscated the direction Dr. Diamond had envisioned. As the trial gained momentum, the doctors did not present a unifying, single psychiatric diagnosis, and at times alluded to a number of divergent opinions that seemed confusing to the ultimate triers of fact, the jury.

Even lead defense attorney, Grant Cooper, sensed that the jury was becoming saturated and worn down by the dueling doctors' conflicting psychiatric opinions. Oftentimes frustrated, and with a view to expediting the process, Cooper chose to conduct many of the interviews with the doctors himself.

The parade of defense psychologists/psychiatrists, several who served as diagnosticians and "review doctors" and helped to diagnosis Sirhan included: Bernard L. Diamond, MD; Eric Marcus, MD; Martin Schorr, PhD; Roderick Richardson, PhD; Steven Howard, PhD; and William Crain, PhD. The prosecution's team included Seymour Pollack, MD; Georgene Seward, PhD; George DeVos, PhD; and Leonard Olinger, PhD.

Reviewing the testimony presented by these doctors as they wove their way through Sirhan's uneven mental state, presenting their differing professional insights into the man who killed RFK, helped to put into perspective the complicated facets of Sirhan's case. The following describes each doctor's often conflicting diagnostic viewpoints that helped shaped the jury's final verdict.

ERIC HENRY MARCUS, MD

Shortly after Sirhan was charged with first-degree murder, pursuant to California Evidence Code 730, California Penal Code (CPC) 1368, Judge Arthur Alarcón appointed Dr. Eric Marcus to evaluate Sirhan's mental status. CPC 1368 required the judge presiding over a criminal case to consider whether the defendant understands the nature of the criminal proceeding being taken against them, and whether the defendant is capable of assisting legal counsel in the conduct of their defense in a rational manner.

More specifically, to make this determination, the court-appointed doctor (a licensed psychologist or psychiatrist) should address a number of psychological and judgmental factors clarifying CPC 1368 issues: if found guilty does the individual appreciate the range and nature of penalties; appraisal of available legal defenses; quality of relationship with defense counsel; planning of legal strategies; understanding of court procedures; and capacity to testify relevantly.

Dr. Marcus had consulted over the years with the Los Angeles Superior Court Criminal Division as a psychiatrist expert, assessing close to a hundred criminal defendants on issues associated with their ability to cooperate with his legal counsel, understand the nature of the criminal charges against him, and/or whether an insanity defense was applicable.

In keeping with the law, if a judge believes a defendant appearing before the court is not mentally competent, they must invoke that belief on the record and order a hearing to determine if the accused is, in fact, incompetent.

Surely Dr. Marcus could easily determine that Sirhan could meet the low-bar standards imposed by a court-ordered CPC 1368 assessment requiring that a defendant understood the criminal charges and could cooperate with consel. Thus it would seem that Sirhan was able to stand trial for murder (CPC 187). The next phase if a psychiatric defense was advanced by the defense would be to move to a CPC section 1017 – a plea of not guilty by reason of insanity assessment (NGRI). The use of this penal code section demands a higher level of psychiatric proof of a defendant's mental incompetence.

However, under California's insanity defense, a defendant is considered not responsible for their behaviors if they did not understand the nature of the criminal act or that they did not understand what they were doing was morally and legally wrong. For the insanity defense to be effective, it is necessary to prove that it is more likely than not that a state of insanity can be established at the time the crime was committed.

Even though Sirhan could easily satisfy the requirements of a CPC 1368 assessment, yet the second test (the CPC Section 1017, not guilty by reason of insanity, NGRI) was theoretically more troubling.

Dr. Marcus's forensic work for LA County was similar to my own decade of experience as a forensic psychologist for the San Jose and Santa Clara County Superior Court Forensic Panel. Dr. Marcus came to this assignment well qualified with BA and MD degrees from UCLA, an internship at the Los Angeles VA Hospital (LAVAH), a psychiatric residency at the UCLA Neuropsychiatric Institute, an assistant clinical professor of psychiatry at USC, the requisite psychiatric association memberships, and he was a past president of Southern California Society for Psychiatry.

Like most psychiatrists at the time, Dr. Marcus relied on his own clinical judgment and professional training and experience and felt at ease using an unstructured, open-ended interview process to gather what he considered essential clinical information used to make psychiatric decisions. Dr. Marcus assessed Sirhan's mental status, visiting him on four occasions between June and October 1968. And to get a more comprehensive perspective on Sirhan's psychiatric status, Dr. Marcus brought in Dr. Roderick Richardson, an experienced clinical psychologist with a forensic background who had all the psychometric tools (assessment tests) available in the late 1960s. Dr. Marcus reported back to the court subsequent to his examinations of Sirhan.

When defense attorney Parsons requested that Dr. Marcus draft a psychiatric report, the judge queried Parsons concerning the confidential nature of the report. Parsons said the results of the report would be "eyes only" for defense purposes. After making his motion in court to have Dr. Marcus evaluate Sirhan, Parsons informed the swarming press that he had "strong doubts that his client was in full possession of his faculties when he shot Senator Kennedy, hinting heavily that the defense for Sirhan would be psychiatric. The DA's office has already come to that conclusion."[1]

Starting on March 20, 1969, Dr. Marcus's *voir dire* (qualification of the witness) and the direct examination were conducted by Grant Cooper. During his testimony, Dr. Marcus told the court, "... [Sirhan] was mentally disturbed and became increasingly more disturbed during the spring of last year ... I feel that his mental disturbances were relevant and directly related to his political views and his feelings about Robert Kennedy; I feel therefore that he could not meaningfully and maturely think and deliberate on his actions."[2] This was positive feedback for the struggling defense team.

1   Klaber and Melanson. (1997).
2   Klaber and Melanson. (1997). 206.

Thus at least in Dr. Marcus's opinion, Sirhan based on a diagnosis of paranoid schizophrenia could be judged as meeting the requirements of the CPC 1017–NGRI. He clinically diagnosed Sirhan as experiencing a type of schizophrenia, quickly focusing on what he saw as Sirhan's split or perhaps dissociated personality as he stated, "It was as if two people or two personalities exist in him at the same time; a sick personality and a healthy personality. These are not watertight compartments. Sometimes one part, the sick part, may take over; sometimes they are both doing something at the same time." This "two personality opinion" rendered by Dr. Marcus supports my own later clinical diagnosis of Sirhan's mental condition – a dissociative identity disorder (DID).

Still this diagnosis could not help account for the relevant psychological fact that faced all the doctors who examined Sirhan – that he denied any recall of the actual shooting of RFK, or why he did it. Note that amnesia is an important element when making a dissociative diagnosis.

During cross-examination by prosecutor Fitts, Dr. Marcus defined "schizophrenic" as having a special meaning because it indicates that the patient has something wrong with the operation of their brain. He compared brain functioning affected with schizophrenia to a telephone switchboard dysfunction when wires become crossed, disallowing communication. He contended that such malfunction results in a disturbance in the way a person's thoughts are formed then tracked.

Was Sirhan lying about not recollecting the circumstances surrounding the assassination? Or was the impact of the crime itself so psychologically traumatic that he buried all memory of it deep into his unconscious unavailable for conscious retrieval?

Unfortunately, Sirhan's legal team seemed firmly convinced that his motive was simply politically driven, and they weren't interested to find out whether he acted alone or with others. Based on his memory lapse (and because his doctors and defense team lawyers told him so), Sirhan also became convinced that he killed RFK because of his support for Israel. Sirhan internalized this imposed belief system and continued to accept the conclusion as an established fact.

In her 2018 book, *A Lie Too Big to Fail*, Lisa Pease addressed the possibility of Sirhan's lying: "If Sirhan has been lying all this time, we have to ask fifty years later, 'What's the point?' He's already in jail for life with no likelihood of parole. Why keep up the charade, if that's all it is? Why not just tell what happened? … But if Sirhan were lying, that would also mean he was conscious of the plot.… If Sirhan is telling the truth about not remembering the shooting scene in the pantry, what prevents him from remembering?"[3]

Responding to Cooper's inquiries, Dr. Marcus said he had interviewed members of Sirhan's family (his brother Adel and his mother); reviewed notes written in Sirhan's diary, and interviewed Sirhan after he had consumed six ounces of alcohol and participated in a brain wave test in the county jail.

At that point, the questioning moved from a purely clinical direction into more of a political analysis, focusing on the assassinations of prominent political figures in history. Dr. Marcus produced a pamphlet titled, *The Violent Offender,* published by the US Department of Health, Education, and Welfare for the National Parole Institute. Dr. Marcus continued his political stream of thought referencing another psychiatrist who was also deeply interested in potentially violent persons who had made threats against the President of the United States. One key article was written by Dr. Edwin Weinstein, a Washington, DC, doctor commissioned by the US Secret Service to do an investigation of people who had made overt threats against the President, either in person or in writing. It seemed clear that Dr. Marcus had pegged Sirhan as a person whose killing of RFK was based substantially on political motives and not on some unknown psychological drivers yet to be determined.

Dr. Marcus testified that the main source of information he considered in his diagnosis of Sirhan were his notebooks and the psychological tests' results. He said the "more erratic, irrational ramblings in Sirhan's notebooks were 'typical and very similar' to notebooks, diaries, and letters written by insane people who threatened the President, and who are now hospitalized at [California's] Atascadero State Hospital." In this regard, he had brought with him a package of letters from such 'insane murderers' who had been hospitalized."

Fitts's cross-examination of Dr. Marcus addressed the issue of Sirhan's specific criminal intent, and Dr. Marcus acknowledged that in his professional opinion: Sirhan certainly could form the specific intent to commit murder. He said that "hypothetically" Sirhan had the capacity to form the specific intent to kill and specifically to kill RFK.

Dr. Marcus's testimony then drifted back to Sirhan's possible paranoid motivation for selecting RFK to be "taken out." He subscribed to the notion that Sirhan's homicidal impulse to kill RFK was based on his ardent belief in the Arab political cause. Marcus said, "…paranoid people,

---

3   Pease. (2018). 375–376.

especially paranoid schizophrenics, will pick some seemingly reasonable cause – they always do. Very few of them are so disturbed that their causes are obviously 'out,' [there] for example, the Martians! Most of them will pick up something reasonable that fits some life context that they have already been in. In Sirhan's case his relevancy goes back to the Arab thing, and broadens out."[4]

Fitts then directed Dr. Marcus's attention back to the night of the RFK assassination, wondering if, with Sirhan's brain switchboard crossed or short-circuited, could he have asked people around him if Senator Kennedy was about to pass through the pantry?

Dr. Marcus agreed that Sirhan might have gone to the Ambassador Hotel with specific intent to kill RFK, saying, "It could have been planned that way. But the planning was done within Sirhan's delusional, bizarre system."[5]

Fitts asked Dr. Marcus, "Sirhan told you he didn't remember the shooting, didn't he?"

To Dr. Marcus's "yes" answer, Fitts asked, "You don't believe it, do you?"

Dr. Marcus hesitated, as though pondering his answer, then said, "Yes, I believe it."

The point of this line of questioning was that neither the defense nor the prosecution could establish if Sirhan was telling the truth, especially during and after the killing. Fitts thought, since Dr. Marcus was supposedly a neutral witness, he might supply the answer that could undermine the defense's position that Sirhan really could not recall what happened.

Dr. Marcus added, "My experience in examining murderers and people who have committed murder, very serious crimes, many of them have an amnesia for those crimes."[6]

Dr. Marcus revealed that Sirhan's planning of the assassination was psychologically filtered through his evolving delusional system, meaning that the planning could have been done when he was in an altered state of consciousness. Dr. Marcus noted, "I imagine he may have been planning an assassination which was within the framework of his delusional system. That doesn't mean he can't plan logically to do the assassination."

Sirhan's capacity to preplan to murder RFK, if proven, would go a long way toward a conviction for first-degree murder.

---

4   Trial Vol 23: 6767, March 20–21, 1969.
5   Kaiser. (1970). 452.
6   Trial Vol 23: 6787, March 20–21, 1969.

Dr. Martin M. Schorr

As noted previously, Dr. Martin Schorr as a defense psychologist was without question the most controversial witness to provide expert defense testimony in Sirhan's uneven trial. During his cross examination by prosecution attorney John Howard, Schorr had clearly fallen into a trap carefully crafted to expose his unauthorized use of another doctor's materials he naively claimed as his own. And to make it worse, he then blended this purloined information into his psychological report he submitted and read in court. This was a huge mistake for Dr. Schorr and a severe blow to his credibility, and the defense team. Aside from this professional blunder, Dr. Schorr was actually a sophisticated diagnostician, giving a unique perspective into the psychodynamics of Sirhan not reached by the other defense experts.

During his testimony conducted by Mr. Berman, when describing Sirhan's clinical diagnosis, Dr. Schorr said, "Well, essentially I am referring back to the profile [Sirhan's] of the paranoid, psychologically paranoid state. At the level of the conscious mind, his own image of himself consciously, is that of a law-abiding, conforming individual who keeps fantasies, hostilities, and aggressions in check. The only way you can discharge the course of these aggressive hostile and assaultive fantasies is as he is not really aware that they exist. He doesn't really split off, but he does what we would call in the trade 'dissociate.'"

Dr. Schorr saw Sirhan's major diagnostic issues as paranoid plus a dissociative reaction later diagnosed here as dissociative identity disorder (DID). He alluded to Sirhan's Dr. Jekyll vs. Mr. Hyde syndrome, stating that Sirhan in fact had developed a second or an alter personality. When asked whether he was aware of the second Sirhan personality, Dr. Schorr said, "I don't believe that he is at all aware that the personality of the killer, the personality of the assaulter, the preying guy on society is his personality at all. He is not consciously aware of it ... I never said he was either Jekyll or Hyde except under dissociative states. I said he'd got two personalities in one, so to speak. One is not aware of the other, because the conscious Sirhan conceives of himself as a nice guy."

Dr. Schorr commented further on the paranoid features of Sirhan's personality, "The personality structure of this individual is essentially that of a paranoid state or paranoid psychosis, and the paranoid state itself doesn't matter whether he is in the dissociate reaction, or he is a paranoid psychotic, through psychotic disturbance, the paranoid state, personality structure, when in the dissociate or he is a paranoid psychotic."

Referring to the results of Sirhan's psychological tests in relation to Sirhan's diminished capacity defense, Dr. Schorr sums up his diagnostic impressions stating, "…these tests plus the facts, I said these tests suggest a paranoid psychosis, a paranoid state with fragmentation in the direction of veering toward a paranoid schizophrenia and a dissociate reaction potential under stress…. Adding to this the concept of diminished capacity is this man's complete lack of awareness of what has been happening."

When asked if Sirhan was in an altered state of awareness or in a dissociative state when he fired on RFK, Dr. Schorr's answer left open the questions of Sirhan's dissociative state: "Well, I think his mind is so clouded by his paranoid state that he is not with what is going on here, except in a partial state. I don't think he is in a dissociative state today, but I don't know."[7]

Dr. Schorr came very close to diagnosing Sirhan as experiencing a multiple personality disorder (MPD) or the current dissociative identity disorder (DID), but very similar to Dr. Diamond, he stopped just short, choosing to stay with a split or altered dissociative conception of Sirhan.

DR. RODERICK RICHARDSON

Dr. Richardson, as requested by court-ordered psychiatrist, Dr. Eric Marcus, did a comprehensive psychological assessment of Sirhan. Prior to Dr. Richardson's sessions with Sirhan, Dr. Marcus supplied Sirhan with a copy of the MMPI, a broad-spectrum personality test to be filled out by Sirhan and later scored by Dr. Richardson.

Sirhan was assessed by Dr. Richardson on July 20, 1968, in the LA County jail, and the results of Sirhan's raw testing data were distributed to two other psychologists – Dr. Georgene Seward and Dr. George DeVos – for their second-opinion viewpoints.

Similar to Dr. Schorr, and absent Dr. Schorr's plagiarized sections, Dr. Richardson also wrote a complete psychological report on Sirhan's testing results. His report, "The Psychological Evaluation of Sirhan Bishara Sirhan," began, "The psychological inferences drawn from the entire test battery of tests administered indicate the presence of vulnerability to ego states, in which Mr. Sirhan's thinking is markedly regressive, concrete, and paranoid to a psychotic degree."

Sirhan's distrust of others and leanings toward paranoia were also suggested: "From a personality standpoint and in terms of Mr. Sirhan's psychological reaction to his present situation, test evidence is of deep distrust of others.…"

---

7   Trial Vol 20: 5605–5904, March 10–12, 1969.

Sirhan's hatred of Jews played into his paranoia as seen when he developed this response to a Rorschach card: "I feel jittery. I can't hold still. I hate the Jews."

Dr. Richardson's Summary Diagnostic Statement in part read, "Psychological testing is indicative at this time of a very severe emotional and mental disturbance in a man of bright-normal to superior intellectual potential … his personality structure or organization is highly fragile, so that his best and most adequate level of functioning is not stable.… At such times, his behavior and thinking become psychotic and are characterized by paranoid, projective distortion.…"

Dr. Richardson also asserted that Sirhan's personality was negatively affected by his gloomy outlook on life, and self-rejection combined with chronic depressive episodes. His analysis of Sirhan's MMPI scales confirm Dr. Schorr's dissociative theory where Sirhan endorses these statements: "I have periods in which I carry on activities without knowing later what I have been doing," and "I often feel as though things were not real."

Dr. Richardson reported that on the MMPI paranoid scale, Sirhan endorsed statements indicative of paranoid thinking, i.e.,

"I'm sure I get a raw deal from life."

"If people had not had it in for me I would have been much more successful."

"I believe I am being plotted against."

"I know who is responsible for most of my troubles."

"I feel that I have been punished without cause."

And he answered *false* to the question: "I have no enemies who really wish to harm me," which means "real or perceived enemies were out there to do him harm."[8]

Dr. George DeVos

Dr. George DeVos and Dr. Diamond knew each other from the University of California Berkeley faculty. They appeared as antagonist witnesses during the course of the Sirhan trial.

Dr. DeVos was the one professor at Berkeley whose academic credentials could rival Dr. Diamond's, and he also maintained impressive memberships in a wide variety of professional associations. He held a bachelor's in sociology, a masters in anthropology, and a PhD in psychology from the University of Chicago. His academic background qualified him as a hybrid California licensed psychologist and cultural anthropologist.

8   Trial Vol 22: 6203–6502, March 18, 1969.

His professional training included an internship at the Illinois Neuropsychiatric Institute in Chicago and, as an extension of that training, an internship in diagnostic testing followed by Japanese language school at the University of Michigan, followed by a Fulbright scholarship in the neuropsychiatric center in Nagoya, Japan. He moved on to the UC Berkeley, and at the same time became a consultant to the Ministry of Planning for the Egyptian government.

Dr. DeVos's real strength and obvious contribution to the trial was his background in diverse, cross-cultural studies, especially his investigation of Arab sub-societies. Sirhan, as an Arab, held strong pro-Palestinian beliefs that were of anthropological and psychological interest to Dr. DeVos.

DeVos's interest in psychological testing formed the backdrop for a cross-cultural analysis of the Rorschach test between Americans and Japanese. He also published an article, "Algerian Culture and Personality in Change," followed by a study of Algerian Arabs. He was just what the prosecution needed – an expert in the cross-cultural interpretation of the Arab personality type – Sirhan's personality.

Similar to experts Howard, Crain, and Seward, Dr. DeVos conducted another blind analysis of Sirhan's testing results and found himself in an odd strategic position, because his testimony regarding Sirhan's mental state generally supported the diagnostic conclusions promulgated by the defense doctors – an important fact, particularly to Dr. Diamond.

Via his informal "intelligence-gathering network" on the Berkeley campus, Dr. Diamond had reported back to defense attorney Grant Cooper the good news that DeVos had come to a conclusion that "Sirhan was schizophrenic."[9] Dr. DeVos was also reported to have commented, "Many Arabs are indeed paranoid ... but Sirhan goes way beyond them!"

Armed with this new diagnostic impression, Dr. Diamond informed lead defense attorney Grant Cooper that a paranoid schizophrenic diagnosis would buttress his own clinical diagnosis that Sirhan was schizophrenic – an important element to support his theory of diminished capacity.

Cooper began his examination of Dr. DeVos, who seemed to straddle the line between being a defense versus a prosecution witness. Cooper asked Dr. DeVos if (when asked by Dr. Pollack to evaluate the raw psychological testing data from Richardson and Schorr), "Were you asked at that time to consider the cross-cultural influence, that is to say the fact that the individual whose test material you were to evaluate had been born

9   Kaiser. (1970). 422.

an Arab in Palestine and had lived in Palestine twelve years, and had then spent the remaining twelve, twelve and a half years in the United States, particularly in Pasadena?"

Dr. DeVos answered, "Dr. Pollack was aware of my work on Algerian Arabs and suggested I do an evaluation of the test results from that standpoint."

When Cooper asked if he came to any conclusion or opinion, Dr. DeVos said, "Yes, I considered the subject was a paranoid schizophrenic."

In further questioning, Dr. DeVos confirmed that he did not know what diagnoses had been made by Drs. Schorr or Richardson.

At this point in the questioning, Cooper began to focus on Sirhan's Palestinian, Arab background to determine if his Middle Eastern heritage played any role in Dr. DeVos's psychiatric evaluation and final diagnosis, and the possibility of cross-cultural differences engendering a bias regarding an Arab defendant like Sirhan taking these psychological tests. The important clinical issue at hand involved the appropriateness of the Rorschach test, essentially a central European-derived test, being used to diagnose a person with such a different cultural background.

Cooper raised another persistent psychological issue: Was Sirhan possibly faking his responses in particular on the Rorschach test?

Dr. DeVos confirmed that the testing experience and results were valid on all points.

During cross-examination by prosecutor Mr. Howard, Dr. DeVos said that his diagnosis was, at least in part, shaped by the results of the MMPI, and that there was at least a trend or an indication toward schizophrenia.

DR. SEYMOUR POLLACK

Dr. Seymour Pollack was to be the prosecution's counterbalance to the defense's star psychiatrist, Dr. Bernard Diamond. Like Dr. Diamond, Dr. Pollack was a highly trained professional MD, with many years of experience. He was based at the University of Southern California where he chaired the prestigious Institute on Psychiatry and the Law, a similar department to UC Berkeley's School of Criminology headed by Dr. Diamond.

Initially, Dr. Pollack's responsibility as a prosecution witness was only as an observer to carefully watch Sirhan's behavioral reactions during the trial proceedings, a role that dramatically changed, and perhaps changed the course of the trial as the case moved forward. Grant Cooper changed this restrictive no-contact policy for Dr. Pollack, allowing him to meet with and even hypnotize defendant Sirhan, which he did on two occasions.

Cooper was hoping that Dr. Pollack would be able to diagnose Sirhan with a severe psychiatric condition, perhaps a chronic psychosis, thereby buttressing the diminished capacity defense. The downside risk was that Dr. Pollack might not diagnose Sirhan in line with a diagnosis that would help the defense. For Cooper, the rewards to this strategy outweighed the attendant risks.

Cooper put forth another risk-reward strategic decision to convene all the defense doctors in his office, along with the prosecution's Dr. Seymour Pollack, to share and discuss their various diagnostic opinions. The meeting on February 2, 1969, included experts: Drs. Diamond, Richardson, Marcus, Schorr, and Pollack.

Prior to the meeting, Dr. Pollack was given the results of the psychological testing conducted by the two primary defense psychologists. Defense attorneys Berman and Cooper joined later to provide structure to the meeting and hopefully learn that Dr. Pollack's diagnostic opinion(s) of Sirhan were consistent with the defense team.

The problem was, Dr. Pollack's opinion of Sirhan's psychiatric status was shrouded by his own conflicting and, at times, confusing testimony when examined by prosecutor Howard. It was evident to Howard that Dr. Pollack had diagnosed Sirhan with a paranoid personality – not exactly what the defense wanted to hear.

Dr. Pollack explained, "The term, paranoid personality, has a number of meanings, and the term should be considered to be a shorthand phrase that has a number of characteristics. These are characteristics and thinking and attitudes and behavior and generally the individual ... is more guarded in his attitude, he is more suspicious, and distrustful. ... Now that personality can be but it doesn't have to be, and is often accompanied by the subconscious belief of being superior. ... These paranoids can be accompanied by different degrees or amounts of depression."

Howard then asked, "Now doctor, when you use the term then, 'paranoid personality,' you are describing a form of what we call mental illness, is that correct?"

Dr. Pollack said, "That is correct. It is a form of mental illness that is used by psychiatrists or termed by psychiatrists as, such an exaggeration of these personality traits."

Mr. Howard sought even more clarity on Dr. Pollack's paranoid personality description by referencing the *Diagnostic and Statistical Manual of Mental Disorders (DSM-II).*[10]

---

10   *DSM-II, Diagnostic and Statistical Manual of Mental Disorders, Second Edition* (1968).

Dr. Pollack quoted from the *DSM-II*, "Patients are described as psychotic when their mental functioning is sufficiently impaired to interfere grossly with their capacity to meet ordinary demands of life. The impairment may result from a serious distortion in their capacity to recognize reality. Hallucinations and delusions, for example, may distort their perception...."

His endorsement of Sirhan as experiencing a psychotic reaction as outlined in the *DSM-II* on the face of it seemed to lend support to the defense position, particularly Dr. Diamond's paranoid schizophrenia diagnosis of Sirhan all along. Then again, Sirhan's psychotic symptoms might fit nicely into the diminished capacity structure.

However, Dr. Pollack's diagnosis of psychosis appears to fall apart during his later testimony when he perhaps realized that he may have over-diagnosed Sirhan, and he negated his first diagnosis, saying "Now the reason that I am stressing this [Sirhan's real diagnosis] is that it is my very strong and clinical opinion that Sirhan Sirhan was not clinically psychotic."

This reversal in opinion raises the essential question for the prosecution: Was or is Sirhan experiencing a psychotic or a nonpsychotic disorder? It certainly seems Dr. Pollack tried to have it both ways, adding, "There was nothing whatever that was revealed to me by any material from his relatives nor any material from witnesses which indicated at any time that Sirhan was clinically psychotic."[11]

Oddly enough, as a prosecution witness, Dr. Pollack seemed to appreciate, and even develop an empathic bond with, the defendant as his jail sessions progressed.

In this sense, Dr. Pollack also seemed to equivocate, not diagnosing Sirhan as either a psychotic or as a nonpsychotic paranoid. During the doctors' conference (collective meeting between both defense and prosecution experts) held on February 2, his diagnostic perspective was key, but to everyone's dismay he was evasive, saying, "I haven't any firm opinions...."

When pressed by Dr. Diamond, Pollack said, "I haven't decided yet ... I have raised questions......"

Dr. Diamond was angry that Dr. Pollack had been given extended access to Sirhan, and was now saying he didn't have a professional opinion about the defendant.[12]

Washington, DC. American Psychiatric Association.
11   Trial Vol 27, 7713–8018. April 2–4, 1969.
12   Klaber and Melanson. (1997). 63.

As it turns out, although somewhat upset by the direction of the meeting, Dr. Diamond left early, not knowing of his unanticipated impact on Dr. Pollack's reasoning. All along, Dr. Diamond suspected that Dr. Pollack was ambivalent toward Sirhan, wanting to do his job as an advocate for the prosecution, yet perhaps appearing overly sympathetic to Sirhan's impossible plight.

Subsequent to the meetings of the opposite-side doctors, Dr. Pollack drafted a report, in essence an extended memorandum, to District Attorney Evelle Younger, expressing his opinion that more or less he agreed with the defense position – Sirhan was psychotic – not the news the DA wanted to hear, but also not a surprise given the conversation he had with Dr. Pollack after the meeting with the defense doctors.

Younger then casually strolled into Judge Herbert Walker's chambers along with the defense attorneys. Judge Walker posed this question to Grant Cooper: "I understand that the defendant is prepared to plead guilty and accept a life sentence. Is that right, Mr. Cooper?"

Cooper said yes, his defense team agreed this was the preferred course to take given all the psychological evidence at hand.

Younger nodded in agreement and said, "We favor it, Judge, and the law requires your approval. ... Now that we have gotten our psychiatrist's report, a man whom we have great confidence in, we are in a position where we can't conscientiously urge the death penalty, number one. Number two, we don't think under any circumstances we would get the death penalty even if we urged it, and number three, we don't think we can justify the trial under those circumstances. It appears that the result is a foregone conclusion. Our psychiatrist, in effect, said the defendant is psychotic, and his report would support the position of the defense because of diminished capacity. And the death penalty wouldn't be imposed. So the alternative ... are we justified going through the motions of a trial, a very traumatic and expensive trial, when we say we can't conscientiously ask for the death penalty anyway? I don't think we are."

Judge Walker apparently went to great lengths to show that he had given a lot of thought to Younger's proposal. However, upon reflection, the judge firmly stated his position: "I appreciate the cost. I appreciate the sensation. But I am sure it would just be opening us up to a lot of criticism, and criticism by the people who think the jury should determine this question. We have a jury. Whatever expenses we incur from here on would only be negligible with what I think would be incurred if we did otherwise."[13]

---

13   Klaber.

With no plea bargain deal in this case, and as agreed by the prosecution and defense team, the trial began on January 7, 1969. The State charged Sirhan Bishara Sirhan with California Penal Code Section 187, first-degree murder. However, to sustain a conviction for first-degree murder, the crime is reserved for especially heinous crimes involving premeditation, deliberation or deliberate planning, and a specific intent to kill. If none of these special circumstances are applicable, the prosecutor may charge a defendant with second-degree murder. The charging document in Sirhan's indictment for first-degree murder stated that "on or about the fifth day of June 1968 the defendant Sirhan Bishara Sirhan, did willfully, unlawfully, feloniously and with malice aforethought murder Robert Francis Kennedy, a human being."

Dr. Steven J. Howard

Dr. Howard, a clinical psychologist, participated in the Sirhan trial as a second opinion review doctor, who reassessed Dr. Richardson's testing results to affirm a psychiatric diagnosis of borderline psychosis. Dr. Howard acknowledged that his only role in the Sirhan case was to critically review the raw assessment data submitted to him by Dr. Richardson, and that he knew that the testing data he was presented was taken from Sirhan's jail testing session.

Fitts engaged Dr. Howard in a long dialogue during his cross examination, addressing Sirhan's known political activism, his suicide ideations (possibly having undertaken the assassination as a symbolic suicide mission), and whether Sirhan may have been a political terrorist fueling his homicidal rage.

Like all members of the prosecution team, Fitts never missed an opportunity to posit Sirhan's murderous intent to the deplorable conditions he experienced as a child in Palestine prior to relocating to America at age twelve. But Dr. Howard did not bite on Fitts's weak connection and Sirhan's homicidal act as being like the act of a suicide bomber. Sirhan was quite familiar with the devastation that could be caused by a single suicide bomber.

The defense's legal team also advanced the theory that Sirhan engaged in homicidal behavior because, as a child, he saw violent acts happen all around him to Arab people, his people. Psychologically, this represents a kind of modeling behavior where, in theory, if a young child is exposed to violent scenes, this increases the probability that they will engage in similar acting-out behaviors as an adult. Criminology research shows extensive evidence on the "modeling of violence" to support this theory.

Cooper's serious questioning centered on what conclusions Dr. Howard reached after he analyzed Sirhan's raw psychological test results. The defense team hoped to find any, even weak, clinical indication that Sirhan was suffering from some form of psychotic condition. Cooper wanted to fit Sirhan's psychopathology into a defense strategy that would convince the jury that in fact his compromised mental status played a major role in Sirhan's irrational (crazy?) decision to assassinate RFK.

He sought some solid psychological evidence that Sirhan was experiencing a psychotic condition when he killed a person he'd at one point held in high esteem, even praised. Cooper found the exact answer he was searching for when he asked for Dr. Howard's psychiatric conclusions.

> **Dr. Howard:** "My conclusions were that Mr. Sirhan, he is a very sick man who I diagnosed as a borderline psychotic person, but by this I meant, as an individual who can go in and out of psychosis, depending on the rather relative minor stresses which occur in his daily life."
>
> **Mr. Cooper:** "Anything else?"
>
> **Dr. Howard:** "I feel that his record was characterized also by a great deal of projection, the blame which paranoiac – and that he was quite suspicious of others – that he was also quite depressed, being very tired of the constant fight that he felt within himself, between, on the other hand, strong impulses and drives which were seeking to come out, and the defenses which were seeking to control this drive to inhibit it. I feel that was a chronic state that he'd probably been in for the most part of his life and that the defenses were definitely weakened, and were not sufficient any longer, and were simply inhibited through those impulses."

Referring to Dr. Richardson's report where he made the diagnosis of paranoid, obsessional and schizoid personality, Cooper continued questioning, and Dr. Howard testified that he agreed that Sirhan is "paranoid," and "schizoid." Dr. Howard explained also that "he has developed what we call obsessive-compulsive defenses ... turned him into the borderline personality, borderline psychosis with paranoid features," and "that there is a definite possibility for suicide in patients who present this kind of record," and "there is some possibility of homicidal acting out."

Cooper was able to achieve one of his important goals – to validate that Sirhan had some very serious psychiatric problems that contributed at least in part to the motivation for the assassination of RFK. Clearly, Dr.

Howard's findings were similar to Dr. Richardson's, although he blended in new diagnostic categories to Sirhan's composite psychiatric picture. The variety of psychiatric diagnoses was expanding, which further confused the defense's strategy.

The defense and the prosecution became interested in determining whether exposing Sirhan's multiple diagnoses was impacted by hearing so many conflicting psychiatric diagnoses. Cooper wanted to question as many of the doctors as possible to make his points, then excuse the witnesses. He also wondered whether the diminished capacity defense might be slowly losing focus. Above all, he asked, "What was actually wrong with Sirhan from a psychiatric viewpoint?"

DR. WILLIAM CRAIN

Dr. William Crain had also evaluated Dr. Richardson's raw psychological testing data. To see if Dr. Crain's results agreed with Dr. Howard's opinion, Cooper began his questioning using the usual expert witness qualifying questions, starting with the psychological tests that Dr. Crain was familiar with using. Cooper wanted to confirm that Dr. Crain was versed in the same tests Dr. Richardson presented to Sirhan. Once confirmed, Cooper asked Dr. Crain about his entrance into the Sirhan case, beginning with his communications with Dr. Richardson.

As a second review doctor, like Dr. Howard, Dr. Crain did not receive any prior psychodiagnostic feedback, clinical conclusions, or results of Sirhan's mental state. His assessment represented another "blind review," as neutral as possible, absent any information that would tip him off as to Dr. Howard's diagnostic findings. After his careful review, Dr. Crain told Cooper that he wrote up his independent findings in the report that Cooper carefully began to page through during questioning.

Dr. Crain also viewed Sirhan as a suicide risk, but did not concur with Dr. Howard's schizoid diagnosis. Cooper took a while to weave through Crain's testimony to get where he needed to go – to obtain yet another psychosis diagnosis that would signal to the jury that Sirhan was a deeply troubled man who, based on his mental illness, may be only guilty of the lessor crime of second-degree murder.

Again Cooper sensed the jury was feeling courtroom battle fatigue. With so much overwhelming psychological information, test scoring, results, analysis, and conclusions about Sirhan's mental state, the jury might perceive the entire defense position as simply an exercise in courtroom psychiatric jargon.

DR. GEORGENE SEWARD

Dr. Georgene Seward, a clinical psychologist and the first witness for the prosecution, appeared on Thursday, March 27, 1969. Because it was getting late in the trial proceedings, and feeling somewhat disheartened by the length of the trial process, Cooper wanted to know if Dr. Seward's professional opinions were principally in line with Drs. Richardson and Schorr's diagnostic view of Sirhan's mental status when he shot RFK.

Noticing that Dr. Seward appeared ill at ease as she took her seat in the witness chair, Cooper suggested that it might help to "sit back and relax." He went on to verify that Dr. Seward was a duly licensed California psychologist; a graduate of Barnard College and Columbia University where she earned a BA, master's, and PhD. Her internship at the New York Neurological Institute and postdoctoral work and specialized training was in the administration, scoring, and interpretation of the Rorschach, conducted under the direction of Dr. Bruno Klopfer, the master researcher himself, whose seminal book on the principles of the Rorschach is used in graduate psychology programs around the nation.[14]

Among her many achievements (a virtual *Who's Who* of professional women), Dr. Seward had published a study, "Clinical Studies in Cultural Conflict," an investigation into problems that people from different cultures encounter when they are acculturating to the American culture. This information could be very important when looking into Sirhan's adaptation or non-adaptation into the American sociocultural belief system.

Perhaps because Cooper felt the jury had had enough of the graphs, charts, psychodiagnostic diagrams, and polysyllabic diagnoses, he said, "And now I am not going to ask you to explain the Rorschach because these jurors have had the Rorschach coming out of their ears ..."[15]

He wanted to establish whether Dr. Seward's review opinion would substantiate the almost universal diagnosis that Sirhan was experiencing some sort of schizophrenic reaction, probably classified as a paranoid reaction. Her diagnosis was based at least in part on the results of Drs. Richardson and Schorr's Rorschach testing results.

She answered, "It was, in my opinion as a clinical psychologist, a clear case of schizophrenic reaction, paranoid type. There was no doubt about it ... I would not have any hesitancy in coming to such a diagnosis; in fact, I really could come to such a conclusion from the Rorschach...."[16]

14   Klopfer, B, M.D. Ainsworth, W. G. Klopfer, and R.R. Holt (1954). *Developments in the Rorschach Technique*. Harcourt, Brace & World, Inc.,New York.
15   Trial, Vol 25: 7235, March 27, 1969.
16   Trial Vol 25: 7235–7236, March 28, 1969.

Mr. Cooper said, "Now, you were introduced to this case sometime shortly after February 2, 1969. You were asked by someone to evaluate the raw data and psychological data and psychological findings of Dr. Schorr and Dr. Richardson, both psychologists who have testified in this case?"

Dr. Seward answered, "Yes, Sir, with one qualification. The raw data of Dr. Richardson came to me as it was originally given by Sirhan. In the case of the material from Dr. Schorr, it was not original data, but his summary of it."

Cooper followed up, "And from whom did you receive the request to make that evaluation?"

"From Dr. Seymour Pollack," Dr. Seward said.

Cooper asked, "And Dr. Pollack is the psychiatrist that has been engaged by the prosecution in this case?"

"Yes, Sir," responded Dr. Seward.

"And you were asked to make an honest evaluation?"

"That's correct, Sir."

When asked how she made her evaluation of the raw data of Drs. Richardson and Schorr, she answered, "I proceeded as if I were dealing with the patient in a hospital on whom I was asked to make a blind diagnosis. That means I examined each of the tests by each of the examiners and I compared them."

Dr. Seward conceded that the MMPI quite "clearly suggested a diagnosis of schizophrenic reaction, the paranoid type … raw data from both of the examiners showed that. There were some differences that were interesting … in Dr. Richardson's, which preceded that of Dr. Schorr's, there was an indication of a very extreme degree of anxiety which is so extreme that one seldom finds it … but is often found in a patient who is just about to have a psychotic break. That was not assumed on Dr. Schorr's, which came four or five months later."

During her cross examination, Dr. Seward addressed an important issue faced by all the doctors: Did Sirhan's confinement in isolation in the LA County jail in some way impact his testing results? And did this ultimately affect the psychiatric diagnoses made by the doctors?

In my own evaluations of defendants charged with capital crimes, as Sirhan was, who were confined for long periods of time before their trials on a no-bail basis, I have found that such confinement can negatively affect the results of their psychological testing and resultant diagnoses. Confinement in isolation can certainly affect certain "situational" variables such as reactive depression, suicidal thoughts, confusion, withdrawal, anger, alienation, and anxiety.

Many of the psychological tests I continue to use, especially the most current MMPI version (MMPI-2-RF), show elevations on the depression and anxiety scale for persons confined for long periods of time. When approaching such a case, I almost anticipate elevations of these key scales. Most often these reactive symptoms are transitory and not static over time. Defendants who are cast into isolated confinement can have their thoughts easily drift into the dark areas in their minds, fostering destructive thoughts: *Why bother to deal with this? I have no future, so what's the use? Maybe it's for the best to simply end all the pain. Maybe my life just isn't worth living.*

Due to the seriousness of the State's criminal charges against Sirhan if convicted (possibly facing the gas chamber or life in prison) depressive, self-destructive thoughts should not be ruled out.

Dr. Seward's analysis of Sirhan's testing results by Drs. Richardson and Schorr showed just the opposite of these situational variables often associated with confinement. She commented, "One thing that is interesting is the very high anxiety indicator was on the first examination, not the second. That was early in the period [of jail confinement]. I don't know where he was at the time when Dr. Richardson examined him; I presume he was in prison, but it was the earlier stages, wasn't it? July or August? And one might have thought that this would have worked in reverse, but to the contrary it was the first examination that showed it."[17]

The unanticipated finding that Sirhan's overall anxiety level dropped the longer he was in pretrial detention seemed to rest on the assumption that, the longer he was in custody, the more he accommodated to his situation – in spite of the fact that, in Dr. Seward's opinion, the longer Sirhan was in the county jail, the more his psychiatric symptoms seemed to worsen. This was especially the situation with his psychotic symptoms, as Dr. Seward noted during her cross-examination.

Specifically, when going over Sirhan's individual scales on the MMPI, Dr. Seward said, "The thing that impressed me more than anything else was the relationship between the SC [schizophrenic scale] to the PA [paranoid scale]. That is a nuclear function demonstration of a relationship of mental process that is very clearly diagnostic of schizophrenia.... And we also have the same relationship between the SC, the schizophrenic; and the PT, the psychasthenic, which suggests psychotic reaction. It certainly suggests confirmation of the diagnostic impression of schizophrenic reaction, paranoid type."

---

17   Trial Vol 25: 7712A–7397, March 26–28, 1969.

Dr. Seward also indicated that, from her analysis of the results given by Drs. Richardson and Schorr, Sirhan became more mentally impaired as time went on. She noticed that this psychological impairment increased from the time of Dr. Richardson's assessment in mid-July 1968, to Dr. Schorr's assessment at the end of 1968.

DR. LEONARD OLINGER

Dr. Leonard Olinger was a unique prosecution rebuttal witness not on the original list of experts. A licensed clinical psychologist, Dr. Olinger had a PhD from UCLA and did an internship at UCLA Psychological Clinic. He had expertise in the administration, scoring, an interpretation of the Rorschach test. He consulted within the court system, doing psychodiagnostic work for the LA Courts, and provided psychological consultative services to private attorneys and psychiatrists. In his testimony, he explained the nature of the research that culminated in his paper, "The Professional and Nonprofessional Skill and Interpretation in Proficiency with the Rorschach Test."

Dr. Olinger's tacit role was to challenge and cast doubt on Sirhan's schizophrenic diagnosis made by the defense psychologists. The prosecution was additionally interested in his professional opinion whether Sirhan could maturely and meaningfully premeditate and deliberate to commit murder. Dr. Olinger was also questioned about the effect of Sirhan's pretrial confinement on his test scores. Like experts, Drs. DeVos and Seward as second opinion doctors, Dr. Olinger had to rely on the psychological testing administered by Drs. Richardson and Schorr, and an earlier, court-ordered assessment by Dr. Marcus.

When asked about his unsolicited role in the Sirhan case when he was sworn in on Monday morning April 7, 1969, Dr. Olinger somewhat arrogantly responded, "I thought I could help justice." Dr. Olinger had an itch and he couldn't wait to scratch it as he pursued his concept of justice. It was as if he came right out of a Clint Eastwood film – maybe *The Good, Bad and Ugly,* where a stranger shows up nameless to save the town, but Dr. Olinger showed up to literally show up the defense doctors' diagnoses of Sirhan.

Olinger had volunteered his services, unsolicited, to the State prosecutors before seeing any of Sirhan's tests, but felt strongly that, from what he'd read in the newspapers about the case, the experts who diagnosed Sirhan as a paranoid schizophrenic with psychosis had erred. Despite "intense cross-examination" by Grant Cooper, Olinger did not waver in his view. He insisted that the other experts did not have "the same material that I had," thereby by inference not the same unassailable expertise; however, he did not specifically describe that material, or why he had some special insights into the Sirhan case he had gleened from reading news reports. He admitted that he knew the State needed someone to counteract the testimony by Drs. Schorr and Richardson. An article in *The New York Times* referred to his conceding to a personal bias.[18]

Dr. Olinger contended that "Sirhan has been mentally capable of planning and carrying out the fatal shooting of Robert F. Kennedy last June 5." He diagnosed Sirhan as "a borderline schizophrenic with primary neurotic features of the primary factors … frequently encountered but which is not listed in the American Psychiatric Association's group of diagnoses, namely a 'pseudo-neurotic schizophrenia.'" Dr. Olinger continued: "… A borderline schizophrenic with primary neurotic features. …" On direct examination from prosecutor Howard, Dr. Olinger was asked: "In your opinion could the individual showing this test pattern form a specific intent to commit murder?" Dr. Olinger answered, "Yes, Sir, he could." At one point during his testimony, he did attempt to clarify several of the psychological tests presented by Drs. Schorr and Richardson – that was helpful. However, at a certain point maybe based on his special insight he drifted into a strange interpretation of Greek mythology telling the tale of the "Procrustean fallacy" that had nothing to do with Sirhan's case leaving defense attorney, Mr. Cooper, scratching his head. Dr. Olinger tried to clarify the Procrustean fallacy: "… It's one where, as it is interpreted, instead of arriving at a diagnosis based on the actual data, you try to fit the data into the presonceived notion and then he is engaged in this fallacy!" Along with Mr. Cooper, this probably led the jury to do their own head scratching.

DR. GEORGE Y. ABE

Dr. George Abe, a well-respected psychiatrist and superintendent of the Norwalk State Hospital, served as the second court-appointed psychiatrist to examine Sirhan. Like Dr. Marcus, he was a member of the LA County Psychiatric Forensic Panel, who was asked from time to time to evaluate inmates or defendants regarding their ability to cooperate with legal counsel and determine whether they comprehended the criminal charges against them.

Dr. Abe also provided court testimony in the Bassett macabre parricide case (previously mentioned in Chapter 4). The California Supreme

---

18   "Both sides rest in Sirhan Trial: Summations may end on Friday," Douglas Robinson. *New York Times*, April 9, 1969.

Court decision in Bassett was issued at the same time as the Sirhan trial was beginning. The LA forensic panel members could also provide opinions related to NGRI pleas.

Dr. Abe was appointed by Judge Richard Schauer to replace Dr. Edward Stainbrook who turned down the court's appointment to interview Sirhan in the LA County jail. In his work at the Norwalk institution, Dr. Abe was well acquainted with various types of psychiatric patients including convicted felons and defendants in similar legal situations to Sirhan's. He was often called upon to diagnose patients where serious diagnoses like schizophrenia and paranoid psychosis were disputed. Dr. Abe's appointment entailed his making a diagnosis of Sirhan, then writing a report to include his psychiatric findings to be submitted back to Judge Schauer.

Specifically, in Sirhan's case, Dr. Abe provided his findings to the defense team to better allow them to make decisions based on the doctor's psychiatric diagnoses. In other words, whether Sirhan was experiencing any form of mental illness at the time of the killing of RFK (for instance, diminished capacity as Dr. Diamond had proposed throughout the trial) that could vitiate one or more required mental elements necessary to legally prove a charge of first-degree murder.

Although Dr. Abe was not called as an expert witness in the Sirhan trial for the defense or prosecution, he provided his assessment results in professional conferences with his colleagues who considered his opinions important. Notably, Dr. Pollack carefully weighed Dr. Abe's psychiatric opinions and insight into Sirhan's mental state when it was his turn to testify. Dr. Abe found that Sirhan's psychological tests indicated "an emotionally unstable individual, one test indicating a capacity to become schizophrenic and the other test a paranoid psychosis."

A further examination of Sirhan revealed paranoid tendencies in regard to his political beliefs, which were rather rigid, and a personality that was essentially pleasant. Sirhan's inappropriate emotional affect added to Dr. Abe's opinion that Sirhan is psychologically a fragile man who could easily become psychotic, although he was not psychotic at the time he assessed him.[19]

DR. EDUARD SIMSON-KALLAS

In my view, Dr. Simson-Kallas provided the most pre-post-trial insight into Sirhan's psychiatric condition, especially the absence of gross diagnosable symptoms supporting paranoid schizophrenia. He probably

---

19   Trial Vol 27, 7857, April 3, 1969.

came closest to rendering the most accurate diagnosis of Sirhan's personality during his thirty to forty hours of intense assessment when Sirhan was an inmate on San Quentin's death row. During his assessment of Sirhan, Dr. Simson-Kallas was initially surprised that Sirhan's presenting psychological status was nothing like the other murderers he had tested and assessed as the chief of the prison's psychological assessment team.

Dr. Simson-Kallas could not confirm the multiple psychiatric diagnoses made by Sirhan's team of defense or prosecution doctors, especially Dr. Diamond's.

The psychiatric symptoms of paranoid schizophrenia that the doctors who diagnosed Sirhan, pretrial, included the presence of persecutory or grandiose delusions, hallucinations, personality disorganization, and aggressive and hostile behaviors, as classified in the 1968 *DSM-II Edition*. (Sirhan did not present with the symptomology usually associated with what now diagnostically fall into the schizophrenia spectrum and other psychotic disorders in the 2022 *DSM-5-TR*.)[20]

Using 1968 psychotic diagnostic criteria, "this large category includes a group of disorders manifested by characteristic disturbances of thinking, mood, and behavior. Disturbances in thinking are marked by alterations of concept formation which may lead to misinterpretation of reality and sometimes to delusions and hallucinations...."

Dr. Simson-Kallas could not match these symptoms against Sirhan's current mental status when he interviewed and intensely tested him. He believed that Sirhan had been grossly misdiagnosed as a paranoid schizophrenic as an expedient way to align his supposed behaviors with the diminished capacity defense so strongly advanced by Dr. Diamond. It was clear to him that the man he spent time with in San Quentin was not the same man depicted in the many psychological reports written about him by the trial doctors, either defense or prosecution.

William Turner, coauthor with Jonn Christian of *The Assassination of Robert F. Kennedy: The Conspiracy and Coverup* (2006), had the benefit of personally interviewing Dr. Simson-Kallas in 1975 at his home in Monterrey, California. According to the authors, they characterized Dr. Simson-Kallas's belief about the psychiatric testimony provided at Sirhan's trial.

"Simson displayed equal indignation when he talked about Dr. Diamond's testimony and other psychiatrists at the Sirhan trial, which he emphatically labeled 'the psychiatric blunder of the century.'"[21]

20   *DSM 5-TR, Diagnostic and Statistical Manual of Mental Disorders, Fifth Edition*, Text Revision. American Psychiatric Association, Washington DC.
21   Turner, W. and J. Christian. (2006). *The Assassination of Robert F. Kennedy: The Conspiracy*

Dr. Simson-Kallas also took issue with Dr. Diamond's hypnotic trance theory that Sirhan was in a self-induced trance or alter state of awareness when he killed RFK, "pointing out that it is utterly impossible for a person to place himself in such a deep trance state that he suffers an amnesia block."

Dr. Simson-Kallas also questioned Dr. Diamond's diagnosis of Sirhan as a paranoid schizophrenic: "Nowhere in Sirhan's test responses was I able to find evidence that he is a 'paranoid schizophrenic' or psychotic as testified to by the doctors at the trial."

Were Sirhan's trance states self-programmed? Or were they, as Dr. Diamond asserts, part of a larger dissociative reaction, possibly indicating a multiple personality disorder?

Four years after the end of Sirhan's trial in March of 1973, Dr. Simson-Kallas appeared before a notary public in Salinas, California: "the purpose of his visit was to dictate a 23-page affidavit.... He did not swear the affidavit lightly. He specifically recorded his 'reluctance' to become involved in the case of a prisoner which was then attracting controversy, and one which had already cost him his job at San Quentin. But his conscience told him he had to speak out. 'I am appalled at the conduct of the mental health professionals involved in this case.'"[22]

Did the Sirhan trial and disappointing outcome represent a real travesty of psychiatric justice as claimed by Dr. Simson-Kallas, or merely a rush to judgment to spare Sirhan from an ultimate fate that came true anyway.

---

and Coverup. New York,: First Carroll & Graf Publishers: An Imprint of Avalon Publishing Group, Inc.

22   Tate, T. and B. Johnson.(2020) *The Assassination of Robert F. Kennedy: Crime, Conspiracy and Cover-Up – A New Investigation.* Lume Books, Borough, SE1 OHS, UK, 2020, 268.

CHAPTER 8

DR. BERNARD L. DIAMOND'S FOCUS

DR. DIAMOND TAKES THE WITNESS STAND

As one of the nation's leading forensic psychiatrists, Dr. Bernard Diamond knew that much was expected of him in his role as the chief defense psychiatrist. The major part of the defense team's strategy relied on his expertise to explain sometimes confusing psychiatric defenses that was offered into evidence on Sirhan's behalf.

Judge Walker was a former chief deputy district attorney for LA County, so he knew many of the players who would appear in his courtroom. Judge Walker also knew of Dr. Diamond's stellar track record, testifying in a variety of criminal cases and major contributions in facilitating California's adoption of the unique diminished capacity defense. He held Dr. Diamond in high regard.

When defense attorney Berman began to question Dr. Diamond, he made the mistake of immediately jumping into the direct examination instead of detailing Dr. Diamond's impressive listing of accomplishments. As far as the jury knew, Dr. Diamond was simply another defense "doctor for hire" who might have been selected by the defense attorneys from the *Yellow Pages*. Even worse, he could have been another "walk on" doctor hired by the prosecution, like the volunteer, Dr. Olinger, who seemed to have all the right answers (in his opinion) from the prosecution's viewpoint. Berman's *faux pas* in the proper qualification of Dr. Diamond's credentials to the jury can be added to the string of unforced errors committed throughout the trial by the defense team who should have known better.

Only later during the direct examination did Berman finally catch on that he had not exposed Dr. Diamond's impressive psychiatric and academic background, so he gave him an opportunity to describe his vitae as well as how he became involved in the Sirhan Sirhan case.

Dr. Diamond was a full professor of psychiatry in the University of California Medical School in San Francisco, a professor of Law and professor and associate dean in the School of Criminology. His many recognitions included the Royer Award from the Regents of the University of California for advancement in psychiatry, the Isaac Ray Award from the American Psychiatric Association for advancement in psychiatry and the law, Gold Metal Award from the Mt. Airy Foundation for distinction in psychiatry, the Gold Apple Award from the American Psychiatric Association and the law, Yochelson Memorial Lecturer in Criminology at Yale University School of Medicine, consultant in forensic psychiatry to the VA Hospital in San Francisco, and more.

Lead defense attorney Grant Cooper also knew Dr. Diamond by reputation, and because they had worked on a California Governor's Commission to make recommendations to the California legislature concerning the applicability of the insanity plea in State courts. Cooper was well aware that Dr. Diamond was almost singlehandedly responsible for the acceptance of the diminished capacity defense in California.

Dr. Diamond was the expert Cooper thought could save Sirhan's life. For Dr. Diamond, this case was another key opportunity to expand the reach of the diminished capacity defense; and winning such a high-profile case could help to solidify a wider use of this unique defense. He did not hesitate to accept Cooper's offer; and further he did the work pro bono, even paying his own expenses incurred flying back and forth from Berkeley to LA.

When I (as a doctoral student) met with Dr. Diamond at the UC Berkeley, his intentions from the outset of the trial were highly motivated to give Sirhan the best defense possible to avoid the death penalty. During half of an entire academic year, Dr. Diamond tried to define then elucidate the many legal nuances woven into California's vague not guilty by reason of insanity plea. Our graduate seminars were conducted concurrently with his multiple trips back and forth to LA to continue to examine Sirhan and ultimately provide trial testimony.

Dr. Diamond first interviewed Sirhan at the LA jail on December 23, 1968. He spent more than twenty-five hours during eight sessions (between December 23, 1968, and February 1, 1969) examining Sirhan. During eight of these sessions, Dr. Diamond used hypnosis to get Sirhan to possibly "open up" to gain a picture of his fractured personality unavailable in a totally conscious state. The information Dr. Diamond gleaned from these sessions, especially the hypnotically induced ones, helped him formulate his later theory of the crime and Sirhan's psychiatric diagnoses.

As a unifying figure for the defense, Dr. Diamond played a pivotal role in trying to uncover the personality defects of the "real" Sirhan. During his extensive testimony during direct (defense) and cross-examination (prosecution), Dr. Diamond examined Sirhan's biosocial, historical, and psychiatric history to search for what might explain his murderous behavior on June 5, 1968. All the doctors (defense or prosecution) had to struggle to identify Sirhan's hidden, psychological or criminal motives to commit murder in a crowded, public venue where escape was not possible.

During his extensive interviews with Sirhan, Dr. Diamond came to the conclusion that Sirhan was schizophrenic, paranoid type, and was also, at the time of the assassination, in a dissociated state of awareness. He acknowledged these diagnoses as he was questioned by defense attorney Mr. Berman.

When Berman asked if Dr. Diamond had formed an opinion concerning Sirhan's mental condition at the time he shot and killed Senator Kennedy, he said, "It is my opinion that Sirhan Sirhan was suffering from a chronic paranoid schizophrenia, a major psychosis at the time of the shooting. He was in a highly abnormal dissociated state of restricted consciousness as a direct consequence of this psychotic condition."[1]

Dr. Diamond summed up his characterization of Sirhan's mental state at the time of the crime, saying, "He was a sick person, and this was a sick crime! I feel Sirhan killed Kennedy while he was in a dissociated state. I don't think he knew what he was doing."[2]

The abstract reasoning to identify Sirhan's specific diagnosis was hard to empirically pin down. Were there times that Sirhan was in full contact with reality? And still other times when he was not in positive contact and couldn't remember select facts? And did this mean that he had some sort of a "personality split" when he went into a dissociated state of consciousness? Was Sirhan, in fact, becoming two distinct personalities? Or even more profoundly, had he over a period of time, perhaps since childhood, developed two differentiated personalities?

Dr. Diamond's theory seemed to move into an obscure psychological space referred to at the time as multiple personality disorder (MPD), a somewhat uncommon psychological disorder that attracted considerable attention and generated professional controversy among mental health specialists after the 1957 publication of *The Three Faces of Eve* by psychiatrists, Dr. Corbett Thigpen and Dr. Hervey Cleckley.[3] The well-publicized story of the three Eves, Eve White (the good Eve) versus Eve Black (the bad Eve), and the neutral Jane, was made into a fea-

1   Trial Vol 24: 6795–7112, March 21–26, 1969.

2   Kaiser. (1970).

3   Thigpen, C.H., and H. Cleckley. (1957). *The 3 Faces of Eve*. New York,: Popular Library.

ture-length film for which Joanne Woodward won an Academy Award for best actress in 1957.

If there were (as suggested by Dr. Diamond) indeed two Sirhans (split because of his abnormal dissociated personality), then Dr. Diamond was certainly plunging into the realm of the disputed MPD diagnosis; however, he did not acknowledge the full impact of this specific diagnosis when interpreting Sirhan's homicidal behavior. I wondered why.

Berman needed a lot of clarification about the dissociated state theory Dr. Diamond referred to – was Sirhan a kind of split personality, where one personality was unaware of the other? Was Sirhan a veritable Dr. Jekyll and Mr. Hyde, as defense psychologist, Dr. Schorr, believed? And if this is true, can this help explain Sirhan's scrambled writings in his damaging diary? Also, was one personality capable of doing good whereas the second was equally capable of doing bad?

Dr. Diamond's therapeutic work with Sirhan, using hypnosis and auto-suggestion, informed his professional opinion to embrace a cautioned diagnosis of dissociated disorder, but not quite reaching a definitive MPD diagnosis. However the MPD theory could help explain the incriminating messaging contained in Sirhan's diary. Dr. Diamond's theory was that three specific types of writings were represented in Sirhan's diary, "RFK Must Die!" He surmised that while some of the diary entries were written in a conscious state, others were done as Sirhan was in nonconscious state, or in a dissociated state of consciousness. Dr. Diamond was aware that applying this same psychological reasoning to Sirhan's memory lapse and his direct involvement at the time of the assassination was a diagnostic stretch that he was unwilling to make. Dr. Diamond noted a third type of writing that he couldn't quite identify.

I am certain that Dr. Diamond had sound, clinical reasons why he initially did not choose to diagnose Sirhan with the full MPD diagnosis, rather sticking with the primary and more accepted (at the time) paranoid schizophrenia diagnosis with dissociation diagnosis added as a secondary condition. Historically in psychiatry, the investigation of patients diagnosed with MPD had proven (at best) to be clinically controversial, and (at worst) a fraud entirely based on psychological junk science established in the bogus Sybil case deconstructed years later.

The controversial MPD diagnosis (if explained to the jury in language they could understand) could have theoretically been used to support Dr. Diamond's psycho-legal doctrine of diminished capacity.

Having the benefit of Dr. Diamond's guidance with his graduate students back at the university campus in Berkeley, hopefully we could comprehend his in-depth lectures explaining what was and was not Sirhan's dissociated psychological states. But could he achieve the same level of comprehension with a group of twelve ordinary LA citizen as jurors?

Dr. Diamond read as much about the case that was available to him and consulted additional sources, including extensive interviews with Sirhan's mother, brother, and the experts: Drs. Schorr, Richardson, Seward, DeVos, and Marcus; a report of an electroencephalogram done by Dr. P. H. Davis, "which was normal, as was a report of chromosomes done by the bioscientific laboratory; and investigator reports by McCowan and Kaiser."[4]

Dr. Diamond read transcripts of all interviews with Sirhan and law enforcement officials after his arrest, and personally inspected the crime scene. Of his first meeting with Sirhan, he shared his impression "that Sirhan was telling the truth about some things; that he was being very evasive about other things; and that he was lying to me about some third things; and it was very difficult for me to determine what was the truth, which were evasions, and which were lies."[5]

In his search to uncover Sirhan's background, Dr. Diamond visited Sirhan's home where he located then inspected a variety of items such as a mirror Sirhan often gazed into for self-induced, trancelike, dissociative states; and Sirhan's fishing weight pendulum he suspended from the ceiling of his room to test his powers of telekinesis (willing a physical object to move on command). The mirror and pendulum both figured into Sirhan's mind-control studies facilitated by his commitment to mystical Rosicrucian practices he engaged in to increase his ability to concentrate, focus, and control his physical milieu. In the search of Sirhan's bedroom, Dr. Diamond found an eclectic book collection, Rosicrucian pamphlets, information from correspondence courses, and other materials he thought impacted Sirhan's mental status and may have figured into the assassination of RFK.

Dr. Diamond derived considerable additional information while Sirhan was interviewed under hypnosis. He found Sirhan an excellent hypnotic subject, who went into a trance state easily, suggesting to Diamond that Sirhan had previously experienced equivalent altered states of consciousness achieved through hypnotic trances. Dr. Diamond attributed

4   Trial 6881–3.
5   Trial 6884.

this quite possibly to his dissociative disorder combined with Sirhan's immersion into the Rosicrucian methods and belief systems.

During Dr. Diamond's cross examination, Fitts directly challenged the relationship between hypnosis and truth seeking – or that the information obtained during an altered state could produce unassailable facts, justifying that Sirhan was telling the truth. As noted, Diamond admitted, Sirhan was not always presenting the real facts, therefore ample room for error and perhaps conscious lying were possible.

THE ELUSIVE GIRL IN THE POLKA DOT DRESS

The public was generously teased by the press's daily coverage of a phantom-like girl in a polka dot dress who they thought accompanied Sirhan only minutes before he opened fire on RFK. Her story continually gathered momentum when the press zeroed in, trying to locate her as a possible witness or even a coconspirator tied to the assassination. Some investigators believed this girl might have served as a human prompt or stimulus, impelling Sirhan, who was hypnotically programmed to commence his rapid firing at RFK. Her presence or nonexistence still lingers as an unresolved mystery.

However, at least twenty-five credible witnesses provided corroborative information that a girl wearing a polka dot dress was wandering around the Ambassador Hotel at the time of the assassination. Prior to the shooting, many eyewitnesses were sure they saw this girl accompanied by a short, dark man, fitting Sirhan's general physical description, immediately prior to hearing the gunfire.

Fitts was also interested to know whether Sirhan could under hypnosis remember encountering an attractive girl in a polka dot dress apparently sighted only minutes before he open fire on RFK.

Several newspapers circulated a story that maybe the elusive girl was part of a larger conspiracy where she may have helped direct Sirhan or trigger his criminal actions as an active accomplice to the RFK assassination. Investigative writer and historian, Mel Ayton, wrote, "For decades conspiracy theorists have posited that Sirhan was accompanied in the hotel by a pretty girl who wore a polka dot dress and who might have been Sirhan's 'controller' or 'co-conspirator.'"

"Judith Groves, a political consulting firm employee who was in the lobby when the shooting occurred, heard three shots and saw a woman splattered with blood run out of the ballroom and a wounded man being carried through the lobby. She described going into the Embassy Ballroom through the Lautrec Room with the help of a 'strange man.' She said that the man spoke to two women in a foreign language and that one of the women was wearing a polka dot dress."[6]

Every conspiracy theory seems to require a shadowy figure lurking somewhere in the background, behind the curtain, more or less pulling the invisible strings moving the plan forward toward an ultimate goal. The press's wide coverage about the unidentified girl quite naturally commanded the attention of prosecution and defense attorneys who were intent on verifying or debunking whether she existed at all, or whether this was a media-created sideshow, a fantasized element in the case, reinforced by the media's penchant for drama. Allegations also sprang up that this mysterious figure maintained some kind of a physical connection with Sirhan, a conclusion never established.

Controversy centered on the girl in the polka dot dress was not going away, and the prosecution seemed intent on assigning more importance to this girl than the facts merited. "Dozens of detectives – often aided by special agents from the FBI's LA Field Office and lawyers from the District Attorney's staff – dutifully logged every alleged sighting before LAPD abandoned the investigation and announced that the search for Sirhan's female accomplice had been a wild goose chase: nothing more than the invention of an 'overwrought' twenty-year-old campaign worker."[7]

In their book, *The Assassination of Robert F. Kennedy: Crime, Conspiracy and Cover-Up*, Tim Tate and Brad Johnson devoted a chapter to their belief that they finally tracked down the girl in the polka dot dress (Elayn Neal), and that her husband claimed to have worked for the CIA in mind-control experiments. "Neal died in 2012, the husband years earlier."

During his sessions with Sirhan, Dr. Diamond had also wanted to know if the mystery girl actually existed and, if so, what role she may have played in the RFK assassination; and was she, in fact, an important witness with a real set of facts that could affect Sirhan's fate?

The courtroom exchanges between Fitts and Dr. Diamond were marked by high-tension moments concerning the girl in the polka dot dress, and also whether Sirhan experienced Dr. Diamond's hypnotic sessions as merely "fun and games!"

Dr. Diamond took obvious offense at the characterization of his hypnotic sessions with Sirhan and anything less than a professional's inquiry to find the facts.

6   Ayton, M. (2019). *The Forgotten Terrorist: Sirhan Sirhan and the Assassination of Robert F. Kennedy,* Second Edition, Potomac Books: An imprint of The University of Nebraska, 147.
7   Tate and Johnson. (2020). 213.

Mr. Fitts: "Well, I am bringing this up [the girl in the polka dot dress] for a different purpose obviously."

Dr. Diamond: "Well, obviously you are. I am sorry I can't accommodate myself to this, but I will be very pleased to consult the original tape [tape recorded interview of Dr. Diamond and Sirhan] and then give you an answer."

Mr. Fitts: "Perhaps that can come up later. In any event at this conference you did say, well he [Sirhan] said, 'I don't remember what kind of dress she was wearing, but I read about the polka dot girl in the newspapers?'"

Dr. Diamond: "Yes."

Mr. Fitts: "I believe it was one of your earlier hypnotic episodes, Sirhan's hypnotic episodes, you were eliciting certain information about a girl at the coffee shop urn, is that right?"

Dr. Diamond: "Yes."

Mr. Fitts: "And Sirhan, under hypnosis, described the girl he met at the coffee urn in a certain way, she was dark, and she was buxom, she was pretty, but she was the sort of girl that might not have gone out with an Arab, and you remember that sort of thing? And you also described she was wearing a polka dot dress."

Dr. Diamond: "If I recall, I don't think he did under hypnosis. I am not absolutely sure, but he described her later as a girl with a polka dot dress, and explained that was incorrect when I questioned him about it, but I am not absolutely sure whether he was awake or asleep at the time this came up."

Mr. Fitts: "The question was whether or not Mr. Sirhan under hypnosis described the girl he met by the coffee urn as the polka dot dress girl, and that is all I am trying to elicit...."

Dr. Diamond: "What I would like to explain is my own conversation, if you are talking about the polka dot girl and Sirhan's way of talking, which I confess, as he told me further about the polka dot girl, and I am not prepared to say whether it first came up under hypnosis or not, but it came up under both probably or possibly, and there was a girl with a polka dot dress that was described in the newspapers. You don't understand, Mr. Fitts, that I would hypnotize him for a short period of time and make him awake and then we would discuss what went on under hypnosis, and then put him to sleep again. I would have to consult my original recording of my actual hypnotic discussions of the polka dot girl under hypnosis for a minute or two."

Mr. Fitts: "In any event you did say, he [Sirhan] said, 'I don't remember what kind of dress she was wearing, but I had read about the polka dot girl in the newspapers'"

Dr. Diamond: "Yes."

Mr. Fitts: "Now, so that we can be sure as to your state of recollection that under hypnosis, he described the girl at the coffee urn as the girl in the polka dot dress, that he was having fun and games with you under hypnosis."

Dr. Diamond: [with a CLEAR EMOTIONAL REACTION, Author's capitals] "No, Sirhan was not having fun and games with me! There was a very specific reason. Sirhan knew nothing about the real girl in the polka dot dress, so far as I can gather. He read about the polka dot girl in the newspaper, and it cut to his romantic fantasy, if you wish it labeled that way, that the other girl whom he talked to in a relationship, well in my mind that was the girl he was talking about, and I was confused, because I had not thought of any other one. If there was really a polka dot girl, and I asked him, 'Was there really a polka dot dress on this girl at the coffee urn?' And he said, 'No, there wasn't,' and I said, 'Why did you call her the polka dot girl?' And he said that he read it in the newspapers, and I said, 'The girl you are really talking about is the girl in the paper, as it turned out,' and he said, 'No, that was a different girl, quite different than the polka dot girl'; so my confusion was eventually straightened out, and whether Sirhan is or is not, I am not ready to say."

Mr. Fitts: "Well, in any event, under hypnosis if Sirhan introduced something that he has read in the newspaper that is just an example, is it not, of how imagination, fabrication, or fantasy can creep in to that which you are trying to elicit in a subject under hypnosis?"

Dr. Diamond: "A newspaper is not fabrication, fantasy, or what have you. As I have said, hypnosis reveals what is in a person's mind, and what is in their mind is not the world of reality. This is true for everybody. I wasn't administering the lie detector test."[8]

This exchange prompted Dr. Diamond to make it clear that during a defense doctors' conference that included the prosecution's psychiatrist, Dr. Pollack, he asked about this girl in the polka dot dress. Mr. Fitts continued his testy cross examination of Dr. Diamond.

Mr. Fitts: "You are aware of the fact, are you not, that when Sirhan talked to Eric Marcus – that is Dr. Marcus – that he [Sirhan] didn't

---

8   Trial Vol 25, 7180–7182. March 27, 1969.

have any recollection of anything from the time he left his car until he was being choked on the table? Isn't that right?"

Dr. Diamond: "I don't recall precisely what he told Dr. Marcus."

Mr. Fitts: "Well, in any event, was it necessary for you to use hypnosis to elicit from him this information that he had been to the coffee urn and had met this girl?"

Dr. Diamond: "I don't recall, Mr. Fitts, exactly the sequence. We talked about this girl so many times in and out of hypnosis that I'm not prepared to say that it was mentioned for the first time before or after [hypnosis]. I didn't attach the special significance to it which you did, so that I don't have this recollection."

The mystery girl in the polka dot dress, as it turns out, was also an enigma to Sirhan who accessed information about her, like millions of newspaper readers from the media coverage, and not from any personal contact with her. Nevertheless, the press continued to move in the direction that Sirhan had more knowledge of her and his relationship than he was willing to divulge either during hypnotic states or not under hypnosis.

The LAPD's conclusion did not deter the continued interest in finding this perhaps important missing part of the assassination story. In addition to the FBI and LAPD searches, interviews were conducted with witnesses who claimed to have seen a girl or two, or look-alikes, wearing a polka dot dress, meandering around the Ambassador Hotel, talking to Sirhan.

Pamela Russo, an administrative assistant to the press secretary for the Max Rafferty campaign (he was running for the US Senate) also hosted an open political party on the evening of June 4, 1968. She and several other eyewitnesses were interviewed by Fernando Faura, a reporter with *The Hollywood Citizen News.* Faura asked Russo to describe the "girl in the polka-dot dress you saw over there."

Russo said, "The girl I saw in the polka-dot dress, the reason I remember her is because I have a very similar dress.... The girl was maybe 5'5" or 5'6" – she wasn't real tall. I think she was a little taller than I am, but I, it is hard to tell with women, their hair. She had a kind of bouffant hairdo.... The girl had a long nose. It was almost when you looked at it – it looked a bit crooked ... I remember that nose. I saw the girl enter the Rafferty room. She had a drink in her hands."

According to Faura, "Russo's declarations were closing some of the gaps. The polka-dot girl had now been placed early in the evening at the

Rafferty party, the same place where Sirhan was later proven to be at just about the same time. Was the Rafferty party their rendezvous place?"[9]

In her book, *A Lie Too Big To Fail: The Real History of the Assassination of Robert F. Kennedy,* Lisa Pease fell into the camp of believers in the girl in the polka dot dress story, portraying this figure as an enabler or helper. She wrote, "Perhaps the most interesting of the helpers was a girl in a polka dot dress that pulled the focus of surprising number of witnesses. Inspector John Powers told the *Los Angeles Times* that, had the girl been found, 'she would have been considered a principal in the case.'"[10]

FORENSIC HYPNOSIS: WHAT IT IS AND ISN'T

Dr. Diamond relied heavily on the results of eight hypnotic sessions with Sirhan to complete his in-depth analysis and develop his diagnostic opinion of the man who, at times, admitted killing RFK, and at other times said he had no memory of the shooting. This was obviously a puzzling factor that was never completely resolved. The preponderance of his clinical data was obtained from Sirhan as he entered into deep hypnotic trances. He felt that the issue of Sirhan's spotty memory recall could be solved using hypnosis-induced age regression. Sirhan's memory of what happened on June 5, 1968, leading to the assassination of RFK, and why Sirhan allegedly had no memory of the actual shooting, puzzled Diamond and the entire defense team. Specifically, why did Sirhan actually not recall the most salient facts in the case, which continued to cloud his credibility?

Diamond knew it was necessary to reclaim Sirhan's lost memories, analyze them, try to solve the memory puzzle, and hopefully unmask the mind of a murderer. Probing Sirhan's inner self led to the discovery of hidden information otherwise unavailable in an ordinary waking state.

Because hypnosis played such a material role in Sirhan's case, his complete story can be better represented by presenting a brief history of hypnosis and its forensic application in criminal courts. The study and practice of hypnosis dates back to ancient Egyptians, Greeks, and Chinese societies when hypnotic states were identified as mysterious trances thought to be somewhere between a sleep state and wakefulness. Early adaptations of trance states were often associated with negative concepts suffused with magic, mysticism, superstition, occult practices, and even demonic rituals that were anti-scientific and unreligious.

9   Faura, Fernando (2016). *The Polka Dot File: On Killing Robert F. Kennedy.* Trine Day LLC, Walterville, OR 97489, 144–147.
10   Pease. (2018).

The modern history of hypnotic trance states is closely tied to the late eighteenth century work of Franz Anton Mesmer who struggled to gain even a modicum of scientific acceptance for his controversial work throughout Central Europe. Though he mostly failed in this effort, he helped set the stage for the modern era of hypnosis. His sometimes misguided seminal work is useful in reconstructing the foundation of the later forensic hypnosis movement.

After Mesmer completed his medical studies at the University of Vienna and cultivated a quasi-medical practice in Vienna, his new theory was based on the concept of "animal magnetism," which he defined as an energy source within all humans that needed to be rebalanced when physical illness struck. Placing his hands over the affected physical area of a patient, he effectuated a trancelike state, liberating the adverse effects of animal magnetism. That mind body fusion became known as "being mesmerized." Mesmer's fledgling work served as a springboard for the expansion of the European hypnosis movement, paving the way for early nineteenth century proponents such as British doctor, James Braid who officially brought the term hypnosis into popular usage.

The next big step in the field of hypnosis came from Dr. Hugo Munsterberg, who earned his PhD in psychology at the University of Leipzig and his MD at the University of Heidelberg. Unlike Mesmer, Dr. Munsterberg had the academic credentials to be a professor at any university he chose. He began his academic career teaching at the University of Freiberg. As an innovator in the psychology and criminology fields, he is often also referred to as the father of modern forensic psychology.

Based on his research, he tried to establish that key psychological factors could influence the outcomes of criminal court cases. He contended that these factors could be grouped into five areas: lie detection, jury deliberations, faulty eyewitness testimony, false confessions, and memory distortions.

Invited to teach at Harvard University in 1892, Munsterberg spent his remaining academic career at Harvard, save a brief return to Germany. In this recently republished 1908 treatise, *On the Witness Stand: Essays on Psychology and Crime,* he stated, "Those stubborn people who simply did not believe that such a thing as hypnotism existed have probably slowly died out; they might just as well have refused to believe that there are mental diseases. And those at the other extreme, those who saw in the hypnotic state a mythical revelation in which superhuman powers manifested themselves, have slowly lost their ground now; they might just as well call sleep or hysteria or epilepsy a supernatural mystery. No, science understands today that the facts of hypnotism are in no way more mysterious than all the other functions in the natural life of the mind."[11]

For Munsterberg and modern-day forensic psychologists, memory and the hypnotic experience are inextricably connected. The goal of memory recall is to produce accurate memories absent distortion and confabulation (making up missing information). In the courtroom, where forensic psychiatrists and psychologists fight it out with opposing legal counsel, the witness is constantly in a battle seeking legitimacy.

Munsterberg became the accepted leading researcher in eyewitness research and was an expert witness in many criminal trials. His controversial thesis, that a witness' memories might not be trusted as factual, meant juries needed the guidance of experts (like him) to guide them toward the truth. Juries needed witness testimony checked, evaluated, and analyzed. This was a radical and often misunderstood position that, even during the 1920s, appeared to directly challenge the underpinnings of what was admissible in the US court system.

The late 1960s and into the 1970s was marked by a resurgence in Munsterberg's suggestion to use psychiatrists and psychologists as screeners to help weigh the admissibility of witness testimony. This new class of professional truth screeners or proxy triers of fact would seriously diminish judges' historic discretion as the trial gatekeepers monitored what was admissible in a trial.

Authors Phyllis Amabile and Thomas Jobe stated, "It is reassuring to note that the courts have generally refused to admit into evidence pretrial statements made by the accused while hypnotized. The dangers of inaccuracy, confabulation, and simulation are exacerbated by the accused's urgent, personal stake in the outcome of the trial."

For a defendant like Sirhan to have his refreshed or hypnotically induced statements taken pretrial, two conditions had to be met. "First certain minimal safeguards must be employed during the hypnotic interview ... these include a hypnotist who is specially trained and has no role in the investigation, a videotaping of all contact between the hypnotist and the subject, and complete privacy during the hypnotic sessions. Additionally, there must be no coercion, intimidation, leading questions, or other undue influence."[12]

---

11   Munsterberg, H. (2009). *On The Witness Stand: Essays on Psychology and Crime. New Foreword* by Elizabeth Loftus. Greentop Academic Press, Greentop, MO.
12   Amabile, P.E. and T.H. Jobe. (1987)."Hypnosis in the Criminal Case: Facts and Fallacies." *Jefferson Journal of Psychiatry:* Vol 5: Iss, Article 3. DOI:https//doi.org/10.29046/jp.005.1.001, 12–13.

The new hypnosis movement in the 1960s rapidly spread to include not only professional psychiatrists and psychologists, but the general public was also exposed, even overexposed, to the benefits of the intriguing hypnosis models. The legal community quickly took up the mantle of the new forensic hypnosis, endorsing its practitioners who without much evidence guaranteed that the search for the truth was only a trance or two away. This resurgence and popularity of forensic hypnosis spread across the country.

The concerted efforts of an LA-based, self-taught hypnotist and MD, William J. Bryan, who had applied hypnotic techniques to US soldiers, reinforced the field of hypnosis in a 1957 criminal case where he introduced hypnosis as a process that could "open up the mind of an offender." Convinced that he had formulated a unique approach to accessing long-forgotten information from criminals, Dr. Bryan began advertising his memory retrieval system mainly to defense attorneys in Southern California. He promoted that he could use a specific form of hypnotic age regression to place a defendant back in time, i.e., to the scene of a crime for instance, and trace their actions, and specifically diagnose the defendant's mental state at the exact time a crime was committed. His self-promotion began to pay off as he created his own professional niche.

Noted attorney F. Lee Bailey became a "true believer" that Dr. Bryan was onto something big that could be of value in the defense of his clients. Bailey attended a convincing demonstration of Dr. Bryan's special hypnotic abilities sponsored by another legal eagle, Melvin Belli, the San Francisco-based high-profile lawyer to celebrities.

Duly impressed by Dr. Bryan's presentation in Belli's office, Bailey engaged him to work on the still controversial "Boston Strangler" case. Apparently, Dr. Bryan used his hypnotic skills to coax or extract what could be considered a false confession from the narcissistic but not-so-smart Albert DeSalvo, supplying him with abundant incriminating statements concerning his role in killing thirteen women in the Boston area. Dr. Bryan's selective application of forensic hypnosis, which probably included memory implanting, certainly was not in DeSalvo's best self-interest.

In 1961, during Dr. Bryan's first court appearance in a California case as a novice expert witness, he was involved in the particularly gruesome serial killer case of twenty-nine-year-old Henry Adolph Busch. Without any provocation, Busch stalked then strangled three elderly women. The LA news press labeled Busch the "Hollywood Strangler." Dr. Bryan testified his belief at trial, that under hypnosis, Busch was unable to form the

131

legal intent to kill necessitated by California law. One of the homicides (according to Busch) occurred after he and the victim watched the 1960 Hitchcock thriller *Psycho* together in a movie theater, which inexplicably triggered an accidental, but overwhelming trance state that fueled his rage to kill the victim.

A psychiatrist who also examined Busch diagnosed him as a schizoid personality with recurring schizophrenic episodes. The judge excluded Dr. Bryan's testimony from the trial record – a decision that was appealed ultimately, reaching The California Supreme Court, which upheld the lower court's decision based on Busch's obvious intent to kill, and denied the motion for a new trial.

The Court's ruling also addressed Busch's ability to deliberate and premeditate read, "Defendant conceded that he knew it was wrong to take the lives of all of his victims at the time of the homicides."[13]

Conspiracy theories in Sirhan's case were fueled by unfounded rumors that Dr. Bryan was somehow connected to the Sirhan case; perhaps even secretly hypnotizing him prior to the killing of RFK, and perhaps Sirhan was preprogrammed as a ready-made assassin directed by some outside agency or organization (CIA, FBI, Fidel Castro, the "mob," or even the Rosicrucians) to kill RFK. Dr. Bryan quickly tried to put that rumor to rest.

Dr. Bryan played a role in the 1971 Charles Manson case, helping Linda Kasabian's defense attorney to structure a defense for why she became of member of the Manson family, and specifically how she became involved in the murder of Rosemary and Leno LaBianca. Dr. Bryan commented that hypnosis is a powerful mind control technique and was certainly part of the psychological menu used by Manson, "but there is another, far more powerful influence which may be seen here – brainwashing. Under long-term confinement, deprivation, and brutality ... suggestive influence may be brought to bear which will completely change a personality."[14]

Eventually, after having his medical license suspended by the California State Board of Medical Examiners for having sex with four women he seduced using hypnosis, Dr. Bryan's career ended, and he died under suspicious circumstances in a Las Vegas hotel room in 1977.

Though his work in forensic hypnosis was filled with serious errors in professional judgment, avoidable missteps, and hubris, he inadvertently

13   United States Supreme Court (California). *People of the State of California, Plaintiff and Respondent v. Henry Adolph Busch*, Defendant and Appellant, Nov. 22, 1961, 16 Cal. Rptr. 898, 56 Cal. 2nd 868, 366.2nd 314.
14   Pease. (2018).

inspired many ethical forensic psychiatrists and psychologists to enter the field to quite possibly help rehabilitate the tattered image of hypnosis.

On the East Coast, Henry Arons, an experienced lay hypnotist developed his own hypnotic institute in New Jersey. Similar to Dr. Bryan, he believed the brain was hardwired to record memories like a giant tape recorder that could be played back verbatim once the correct "button" was pressed. This concept was presented in court cases as representative of true memories called up using a free recall method.

This sparked the so called "memory wars," challenging the tape recorder model in support of the notion that all memories are transient, imperfect, and often simply lost forever. In a conscious, waking state, these memories remained obscured, but with the facilitation of a professional the fog of long-forgotten memories could be lifted. There are at lease 110 documented studies that confirmed the authenticity of victims' completely forgotten childhood sexual abuse.[15]

Arons and Dr. Bryan were brought in by F. Lee Bailey to consult on a high-profile murder case held in Freehold, New Jersey, in 1966. Dr. Carl Coppolino was accused of killing his friend and neighbor, Col. William Farber, with the assistance of his lover, Mrs. Farber, by hypnotizing her to administer a fatal injection to her husband. The chief issue at trial was Mrs. Farber's contention that Dr. Coppolino had hypnotized her against her will to assist in her husband's murder. She provided testimony that she and Dr. Coppolino had an ongoing sexual tryst, and she also claimed the sexual liaison was induced via Dr. Coppolino's clever hypnotic suggestion.

The jury's charge was to determine if Mrs. Farber could be forced under hypnosis to kill her husband contrary to her freewill. Arons told Bailey that, although she had been hypnotized to stop smoking, the other claims were not true. He said that any hypnotist who was trying to force a person to commit a crime "would be certain to cover his tracks by giving his patient posthypnotic instructions for pretending amnesia." Dr. Coppolino was found not guilty.[16] But he faced another jury in a second murder trial for the murder of his first wife, Carmela, and this time a Florida jury saw the facts differently and convicted him.

Arons's contribution to the field of forensic hypnosis, established during the Coppolino trial, strengthened the fact that a hypnotized per-

15   Wester, C. W. and D.C. Hammond. (2010). "Solving Crimes With Hypnosis." *American Journal of Clinical Hypnosis*, 53:4, 250, April 2011.

16   Block, E.B. (1976). *Hypnosis: A New Tool in Crime Detection*. David McKay Co. New York, 113.

son is not a robot who can be programmed to act against their moral principles. A century before, Munsterberg was confronted with the same issue. He received many inquiries from lawyers asking if there was any basis for a defense that the crime was done in a hypnotic or posthypnotic state. He always insisted that hypnotic suggestion is "unable to break down the inner resistance ... the frequent claim of defendants that they must have been hypnotized is, nevertheless, mostly no conscious invention. It is rather the outcome of the fact that the criminal impulse comes to the unbalanced diseased mind often like a foreign intruder...."[17]

WAS SIRHAN A HYPNOTIZED KILLING MACHINE?

Certain conspiracy writers have characterized Sirhan as being kind of a dupe who could have been hypno-programmed, having his volition and free will compromised via a mind control method to kill RFK. Early in the investigation, April 19, 1969, Robert Blair Kaiser (the defense team investigator commissioned to write a book about the Sirhan trial) had second thoughts about Sirhan's single-shooter involvement in the planning and implementation of the assassination of RFK. He consulted the FBI, which had done an exhaustive investigation into the murder to find out if that agency had any relevant information they could share with him. FBI Director J. Edgar Hoover answered tersely, "No!" If the FBI knew anything on this subject, the agency was not telling.

The desire to create a human robot using hypnosis to kill against their will has tantalized the dark imaginations of military doctors since the Korean War. Moreover, fantasies of mind control have taken up space in the heads of some doctors, providing external, motivational patterning to unsuspecting patients to engage in behaviors not in their best interest. This same group of operatives, doctors (mostly psychiatrists), and shadowy governmental operatives pooled their resources, creating clever schemes to be able to mold a person into an unwitting instrument of evil intent.

According to John Marks, author of *The Search for the Manchurian Candidate*, "No mind-control technique has more captured popular imagination – and kindled fears – than hypnosis. Specifically, the field of psychiatry has long dreamed they could use overwhelming hypnotic powers to compel others to do their bidding. And when the CIA officials institutionalized that dream in the early Cold War Days, they tried like

---

17   Munsterberg. (2009). 141.

modern-day Svengalis, to use hypnosis to force their favors on unwilling victims."[18]

And an attempt to create a real "Manchurian Candidate" during the 1950s is what the CIA covertly set out to do. Financed with a ten-million-dollar ($100m in 2024 dollars) budget CIA operatives set in motion the master project codenamed, MK-ULTRA, that began in 1953. CIA Director Allen Dulles set the secret project in motion. Tightly focused on mind control, the research gained momentum supported by CIA intelligence that the Chinese, North Koreans, and Soviet governments were already engaging in multiple brainwashing experiments.

The existential danger posed by the Cold War between the US and the Soviets was greatly exaggerated by the CIA to demonstrate how necessary a project like MK-ULTRA was necessary to preserve US security. "If our enemies were doing it we'd better jump in!" In addition to MK-ULTRA, the fear of foreign enemies gaining an advantage in the brainwashing business contributed to the development of additional MK-ULTRA sub-projects codenamed Paperclip, Chatter, Bluebeard, and ARTICHOKE. The experiments maintained three primary goals: "to induce hypnosis very rapidly in unwitting subjects; to create durable amnesia; and implant durable and operationally useful posthypnotic suggestions."[19]

These ethically challenged CIA hypnotic mind control experiments were allowed to operate with little or no governmental oversight. If questions arose for instance by a congressional budget committee came up, the CIA denied that the brainwashing projects ever existed. The recruitment of teams of psychologists and medical doctors constituted the first link in the nefarious chain. Underpaid university professors supplemented their incomes to set up what they had to realize were unethical, perhaps illegal, and dangerous psychological experiments using sensory deprivation, electroconvulsive therapy (ECT), powerful drugs including LSD, hallucinogenic agents, and enhanced hypnotic techniques.

Additional researchers concluded that the process of hypnosis can enhance certain memory recall, particularly for personal information (autobiographical memory) that was negatively influenced by trauma or extreme emotional factors. Other researchers suggested that under hypnosis, a subject may in fact recall more information, but that in certain

18   Marks, J. (1979). *The Search for the Manchurian Candidate*. W.W. Norton & Company, New York, 194.
19   Ventura, J. and D. Russell. (2010). *American Conspiracies*. Skyhorse Publishing. New York 71.

cases, such memories are characterized by confabulation (filling in blank spots) and yielding altogether false recollections or pure fantasies.[20]

According to Winter, "It was easy to take the first steps to pursue an interest in inculcating hypnosis into a defense attorney's practice by simply attending a lecture, demonstration, conference, or even extended training course...."[21]

Some evidence suggests that Sirhan had knowledge of the Boston Strangler's trial held in Cambridge, Massachusetts two years before his trial. Coverage of the DeSalvo case attracted nationwide headlines and, as demonstrated throughout Sirhan's trial, he was an avid newspaper reader. According to Pease, "On one page in Sirhan's notebook can be found the phrase 'God help me' followed by 'SalvoDi Di Salvo Die S Salvo.'"

"In the middle of the 'long live Nasser' scribblings on another page, 'Die Sovo' in quotes appears between phrases."[22]

In a conversation Sirhan had with police shortly after he was taken into custody in the early hours of June 5, 1968, he referred to the Boston Strangler case. During casual conversation "with policeman Frank Foster in a session at the jail, which he did not know was being taped, Sirhan talked about Albert di Salvo [sic], the Boston Strangler. Sirhan said 'the sex killer's method of operation was 'really cool.' He expressed surprise that most of DeSalvo's victims were old women. 'Gee, man, that's something ... I wonder often what provokes or causes such a man to do that.'"

"Foster said, 'The way they feel ... is that it's a younger person, and he has a psychological factor that he should kill his mother.'"

"Oh," said Sirhan.

Foster continued, "This is the way the psychologists have been setting up the pattern."[23]

Foster believed that Sirhan had indeed read about the DeSalvo case, especially that the sexual assaults were supposedly committed by DeSalvo when he was in an undefined dissociated state. Foster wondered if this was connected to Sirhan's own state of mind when he shot RFK.

Perhaps Sirhan was considering his own defense, refining his strategy, then improving on DeSalvo's failed attempt to fake insanity, and not confessing to a crime that was simply outside his awareness. Though vociferous in asserting that he was not insane or crazy, was Sirhan setting

20   Wester and Hammond (2010).
21   Winter, A. (2012) "The Rise and Fall of Forensic Hypnosis." DOI10.1016/j.shasc.20012.39.011, https://doi.org/10.106/j.shasc.2012.09.011, 7.
22   Pease. (2018). 445–446.
23   Seigenthaler, J. (1971). A Search for Justice. Aurora Publishers Incorporated, Nashville, TN, 276.

the stage for Dr. Diamond's diminished capacity defense? Was he playing into the defense doctors' hands, subtly acknowledging that, although he might be somewhat limited in his compromised mental capacity, he was not legally insane, nor would he accept a complete insanity defense?

Could Dr. Diamond's revelations of Sirhan's personality, achieved through many hypnotic states, yield admissible evidence to support a contention that, because he had been diagnosed with serious psychiatric diagnoses, he was less responsible for the assassination? More important, and setting aside the insanity cloud that hung over his head, was Sirhan afraid that Dr. Diamond could use future hypnotic sessions (as Bailey had with DeSalvo) to make him confess to a murder he steadfastly denied recalling?

In any case, in the real criminal trial arena, the question arises, what kind of hypnotic evidence is admissible and what is not? The answer to this question has remained persistent throughout the history of the use of hypnotic-induced testimony in the courtroom. The generally accepted guidelines established by the Society of Professional Hypnosis indicate that when a patient's lost or repressed memories are recovered using a variety of hypnotic methods, such information may be admissible at trial only when four criteria are met: 1) "the hypnotic procedure is fully exposed in evidence and fully explained either to the judge or the jury or both; 2) the person offering the witness must show that the witness on the stand now remembers the actual incident; 3) the person offering the hypnotic procedure must show during testimony ... that at no time were any improper suggestions made to [the hypnotic subject] and that he is fully testifying from his own recollection and not from any suggestion that was given to him [implanted]; and 4) the person offering the testimony must show that the psychiatrist, doctor, or psychologist in the case is a properly trained expert.... Naturally all other necessities to prove the case must, in fact, be proven under the technical rules of testimony and evidence."[24]

In the late 1960s, many defense attorneys flocked to the forensic hypnosis seminars offered on both US coasts, demonstrating how the "new hypnosis" might help give them an edge in the defense of their clients. From my viewpoint, the era could aptly be labeled "hypnosis mania," and many attorneys seemed eager to catch it.

The theory that Sirhan was given a triggering, posthypnotic suggestion (under hypnosis) by certain unknown handlers, such as Dr. Bryan, to kill RFK is ongoing. Without much evidence, these writers have advanced

24   Block, E.B. (1976). *Hypnosis: A New Tool in Crime Detection.* David McKay Co., New York. 20.

the possibility that in order to achieve this end, Sirhan may have been abducted by people who were connected to the CIA or its operatives after he was thrown from a horse at the Corona Race Track. There is further speculation that he could have been readmitted to a different unidentified medical facility, possibly operated by the CIA, for a period of two weeks to more or less hypno-program him beyond his conscious awareness, psychologically conditioning him to assassinate RFK.

Testimonials from his friends and family after the riding accident combined with whatever psychiatric mind control he experienced at the mystery hospital were said to have produced a marked alteration in Sirhan's personality. "Moreover, it appears that LAPD detectives knew Sirhan had indeed disappeared for a significant period immediately after his accident. In 2005, Bill Jordan, a sergeant who had worked within Special Unit Senator [SUS unit established to investigate RFK's assassination], told *The Independent* (UK) newspaper that he and his colleagues had questioned Sirhan extensively about the missing period.... 'We took him back for more than a year with some intensity – where he'd been, what he'd been doing, who he'd been seeing. But there was this ten or twelve-week gap ... we could never penetrate.'"[25] The fact remains that this information, pertaining to Sirhan being swept away and sequestered against his will in a "Clockwork Orange" brainwashing lab, was mostly developed many years after Sirhan had his day in court.

Dr. Diamond felt strongly that Sirhan was indeed in an altered state of awareness when he committed the murder, stating, "With absolutely no knowledge or awareness of what was happening in his Rosicrucian and occult experiments, he was gradually programing himself, exactly like a computer is programmed by its magnetic tape, programming himself for the coming assassination. In his subconscious mind there existed a plan for the total fulfillment of his sick, paranoid hatred of Kennedy.... In his conscious mind there was no awareness of such a plan or that he, Sirhan, was to be the instrument of assassination. It is my opinion that through chance circumstances, and a succession of unrelated events, Sirhan found himself in the physical situation in which the assassination occurred. I am satisfied that he had not consciously planned to be in that situation. I am satisfied that if he had been fully conscious and in his usual mental state [non-dissociative], he would have been quite harmless, despite his paranoid hatred and his loaded gun."

---

25   Tate and Johnson. (2018). 279.

Dr. Herbert Spiegel, a recognized authority on the use of forensic hypnosis, particularly with dissociative patients, retrospectively approached Sirhan's case from a different angle. He believed that at the time of the assassination, Sirhan could have been in a programmed hypnotic trance effectuated by outside co-conspirators to unwittingly encourage Sirhan to engage in a violent act that he later could not recall, based on an amnesic posthypnotic suggestion.

Describing Sirhan's demeanor shortly after he was arrested and taken to the Rampart Street Police Station in Los Angeles for interrogation, Dr. Spiegel stated, "He does not have an emotional knowledge that he committed a crime, so in that sense, he's an honest liar. So he could easily feel at ease and sharp and alert, because he doesn't feel guilty about anything. The last thing he knows, he was having coffee with this woman and then to be in a police station – he has no knowledge of what happened, so why am I here? He had a total blank because he's totally dissociated from it."[26]

Dr. Diamond alluded to the possibility that an alternate Sirhan personality could have been aware of his malevolent intentions to take a human life when he was in his "non-usual" (dissociated state) conscious state as opposed to when he was in the "usual Sirhan" (ordinary conscious state) mental state. This presented a perplexing psychological conundrum for Dr. Diamond, alluding to the fact that most likely he was dealing with two of Sirhan's separate and independently operating personalities. How could he articulate this perspective to an already-doubting jury?

If there was any credible evidence lending support to the novel belief that there were certain unnamed co-conspirators pulling the strings behind the curtain who turned Sirhan into a "killing machine," an active shooter, in a quasi-military CIA plot to kill RFK, this information would have been equally relevant to the defense lawyers and the prosecutors. Before determining Sirhan's fate, it seems only logical and good lawyering to bring evidence of Sirhan's hypno-programming and Manchurian Candidate status to the jury's attention.

Dr. Diamond addressed this issue, whether Sirhan acted alone or in concert with other possible co-conspirators, and a second assassin, with Sirhan twice under hypnosis. He asked, "Sirhan, did anyone pay you to shoot Kennedy? Did anyone pay you to shoot Kennedy, yes or no?"

Sirhan responded in a quiet but understandable voice, prompting Dr. Diamond to admonish, "Sirhan, speak clearly!"

---

26   O'Sullivan, S. (2008). *Who Killed Bobby: The Unsolved Murder of Robert F. Kennedy.* Sterling Publishing Co., Inc. New York, 382.

In a more audible voice Sirhan said, "No."

Dr. Diamond followed, "No? No one paid you to shoot Kennedy? Did anybody know ahead of time that you were going to do it, Sirhan? And did anybody from the Arabs tell you to shoot Kennedy? Did any of your Arab friends? Did the Arab government have anything to do with it?"

Sirhan again said, "No."

Dr. Diamond asked, "Did you think all this up by yourself?"

Sirhan took a four-second pause and said, "Yes!"[27]

Paradoxically, five years after Sirhan was tried, proved guilty, and sentenced to death, Dr. Diamond told reporter Betsy Langman, who had closely followed Sirhan's saga, "Let me immediately state that it was immediately apparent that Sirhan had been programmed.... His response to hypnosis was very different ... strange, in many respects. And he showed this phenomenon of automatic writing, which is something that can be done only when one is pretty well trained."[28]

After the guilty verdict came in, Dr. Diamond did not dwell much or reminisce on the Sirhan case and granted very few interviews to the press. Yet I felt that, in the back of his mind, he had the lingering feeling that perhaps he could have presented his psychiatric evidence a little differently. The introduction of the diminished capacity defense connoting that Sirhan was kind of guilty, but perhaps only to a lesser charge, for second-degree murder, thus sparing Sirhan the gas chamber became a contentious point for the defense.

Obvious to us graduate students at Berkeley was that Dr. Diamond perceived the negative outcome as a professional setback. After all, he went into the case with a series of impressive defense court victories that helped extend the applicability of the diminished capacity defense. It is an understatement to say that Dr. Diamond was disappointed and crestfallen because of the jury's decision to convict Sirhan on first-degree murder and recommend the death sentence.

---

27   Trial Vol 24, 6932, March 24, 1969.
28   O'Sullivan. (2008). 382.

CHAPTER 9

SIRHAN'S IDENTITY TRANSFORMATION

PHASE I: EROTOMANIA-MOTIVATED MURDER

In an exhaustive analysis of Sirhan's collective personality factors and history, I looked for and then isolated the more-hidden psychological factors that so profoundly affected his life and led him to make a series of terrible mistakes that culminated in shooting RFK. The transformational identity factors that completely changed Sirhan's life represent a confluence of established psychiatric factors and a newly conceptualized criminological disorder that had been forming in his unconscious for years prior to the assassination.

I have diagnosed and treated many criminal clients over the years, who (like Sirhan) committed shocking offenses such as cold-blooded murder; yet for reasons unknown to them in their ordinary state of consciousness, they did not comprehend exactly why they deviated from society's accepted moral code and prevailing laws. Simple attribution to weak impulse control system as measured on a series of psychological tests like those given to Sirhan seemed descriptive enough on the surface, but begged the real question: Why did these usually law-abiding individuals turn to crime, even to commit a single homicidal crime as Sirhan did?

From my concerted probing in support of retrospective analyses, it became evident to me that many of these offenders underwent a type of identity transformation that resulted in the surrender of their lawful noncriminal identities, and caused them to drift into an unknown "space" where their thoughts were suddenly overtaken with intrusive, antisocial ideations that were beyond their ordinary control. The phase I identity transformation, the process that turned Sirhan into a killer, formed the foundation in support of his actual motivation as he stated many times, "RFK Must Die"!

SIRHAN'S FIVE PHASES OF IDENTITY TRANSFORMATION

Among the many thousands of anecdotal or self-reported accounts of criminals' states of mind, few criminologists have addressed the subjective experiences prior to, during, and after the commission of a criminal act: What were the person's thoughts during the commission of their crimes? How did they feel after the offenses? How were their psychological states altered by the crime experience?[1]

I recognized five phases of criminal identity transformation, or surrender, enhanced by the investigative concept of psychological DNA that can better explain why Sirhan committed a single, homicidal act. These five transformative identity phases impacted Sirhan's reasoning and help to underscore the motivation for his crime:

> Phase I. *Erotomania-motivated murder*, based on his vicarious pathological and deadly love-hate connection to RFK.
>
> Phase II. *Split or dissociative second personality*, central as his "alternative self" shot RFK.
>
> Phase III. *Co-occurring complex post-traumatic stress disorder* (C-PTSD), influenced by his well-documented early childhood traumas.
>
> Phase IV. *Trauma-induced paradox* (aka Stockholm syndrome), derived from his vicarious connection to his perceived captors.
>
> Phase V. *Learned helplessness*, operating on an unconscious level, impacting Sirhan to the extent that, in his mind, whatever he did he was doomed to fail. As he said, "The cards were always stacked against me!"

We can reasonably assume that Sirhan did not wake up on the morning of June 4, 1968, happily smiling and then deciding, *Today after I go to the shooting range seems like a good time to murder RFK.*

He was instead driven to that point of no return because of the five powerful criminal psychological forces that he struggled with yet failed to comprehend. At that point, his "transformational antisocial identity" was complete; and his uncontrolled, violent rage took executive control over him.

In keeping with my analysis of the identity transformation phases, the compromised reasoning Sirhan used to enable him to commit this crime originated somewhere hidden deep in his mind that was not immediately available to his ordinary state of consciousness. Sirhan's criminogenic thoughts had been percolating, even seething below the surface for a period of time prior to the assassination as he became more impacted, or even directed, by those negative forces, insuring his complete identi-

---

1   Brady, J.C. (2017). *Men of Steal: Is Crime Addictive? Three Men Who Found Out.* Western Psych Press, San Jose, CA..

ty makeover. My assertion is that the collective impact of each of these psychological phases, working in unison, finally contributed to Sirhan's departure from ordinary reality as he previously experienced it.

My further contention is that Sirhan's entry into, and processing through, each of these nonsequential phases, represented a step-by-step process of identity transformation that remained beyond his level of awareness. This resulted in his moral erosion, thereby allowing him to engage in a homicidal act, which in his unconscious mind seemed justified, or that he believed was somehow permissible. This moral compromise pushed Sirhan to where he didn't consciously want to be; nevertheless he got there – almost unwittingly neutralizing his moral resistance to committing the assassination.

While several of these phases can be reduced to newly verified psychiatric diagnoses (provisional)(i.e., complex-post-traumatic stress disorder and dissociative identity disorder) not made at the time of Sirhan's trial, other phases are identified as transitional psychological conditions (i.e., learned helplessness and the trauma-induced paradox, aka Stockholm syndrome). In examining these collective phases, each of these combined conditions played a significant role that led to Sirhan's subsequent criminality.

We begin with a description of the unique homicidal condition identified as erotomania-motivated murder.

PHASE I:
EROTOMANIA-MOTIVATED MURDER

Sirhan's illogical reasoning underlying the killing of RFK was far more complex than presented during the trial or described by reporters, journalists, or researchers years after Sirhan's conviction and death sentence. Immediately after his arrest and during ongoing investigations conducted by the FBI and the LAPD, the assumptions were that he committed the assassination alone, and that his motive was solely driven by festering political hatred for RFK because of his support for Israel.

Contrary to this "rush to judgment" thesis, my interpretation of Sirhan's crime goes further, more deeply evidencing multilayered psychological and criminological determinants.

Sirhan's single, felonious act was partially driven by a subset of what is now identified as "personal cause homicide," specifically the subsection labeled erotomania-motivated murder. This disorder involves an offender's delusional fixation that goes far beyond mere identification or obsession with the selected victim. In a pathological sense, the offender blends or merges his or her personality into the victim's in a fantasy based on idealized romantic love or a spiritual union with a selected person."[2]

In Sirhan's case, this erotomania-motivated murder disorder is closely associated with his identification and delusional connection with RFK, a person he never actually met, but was adored vicariously from afar. Throughout the trial and specifically during his testimony, Sirhan made many conflicting statements concerning his "love-hate" feelings for his target, RFK. His psychological identification patterning went far beyond mere idol worship for a respected political figure or celebrity. His feelings for RFK were profound and fluctuated wildly over time from love to hate and vice versa.

For example, Sirhan told Dr. Diamond about seeing RFK during a TV appearance, and he was unexpectedly impressed, stating enthusiastically, "It was a thrill to see him. Shit yes, really. Really. Hell, you know a presidential candidate, my first time."

During a 1989 TV interview with British journalist David Frost, Sirhan went so far as to praise RFK: "I thought he was the prince, Sir. He was the hope of all the poor people of this country, the minorities; to me he was my hope, he was my champion."[3,4]

As time passed, Sirhan attached a type of fantasy relationship and worship for RFK, who he initially strongly identified with his hero, until the point that RFK did something to anger (betray) him. And over time, Sirhan's negative statements become more intense, more puzzling, and progressively negative. He acknowledged this preoccupation in writing: "My determination to eliminate RFK is becoming more of an unshakeable obsession."

In line with the erotomania-motivated murder diagnosis, such a false, almost delusional, and total identification patterning with a powerful person continues until it becomes psychologically twisted and converted into a homicidal delusion, for instance, if the powerful person does something to destabilize the perceived balance in the relationship, this can result in unexplained feelings of abandonment and betrayal. Suddenly, Sirhan perceived that his world had turned upside-down, and RFK was responsible.

---

2   Douglas, J.E., A.W. Burgess, A.G. Burgess, and R.K. Ressler (2013). *Crime Classification Manual: A Standard System for Investigating and Classifying Violent Crime.* Third Edition. John Wiley & Sons, Inc., Hoboken, New Jersey, 165–166.

3   *Reach for Your Gun, Sirhan Transcript,* http://rfktapes.com.

4   Ibid.

Sirhan went from an almost love-driven conceptualization of RFK to a hateful, murderous characterization. Perversely, he formulated a final solution to eliminate the potential traitor, "RFK Must Die," as he ruminated and scribbled in his diary over and over.

Sirhan's erotomania-motivated murder theme was well evidenced, yet not diagnosed during his many clinical sessions with the team of forensic psychologists and psychiatrists. For example, Sirhan told Dr. Diamond that he was drawn to RFK, though reflecting contradictory viewpoints – "like a magnet. I loved the man, I hated him."

Sirhan also voiced his strong, conflicting feelings for RFK to Dr. Pollack, who reported, "He loved Senator Kennedy … had formed a strong attachment [though vicarious] for him in a personal way, just as he had loved President Kennedy. But then (learning Kennedy's support for Israel) he hated Senator Kennedy … wanted him dead. His love actually turned to hate."[5]

During his testimony under cross-examination by Mr. Lynn "Buck" Compton, Sirhan was questioned repeatedly regarding his feelings for RFK before and after he watched a TV show where RFK voiced a definite leaning toward Israel and by extension against Sirhan's people, the Palestinians. The attorney pointed out that Sirhan made a troubling statement in his writing to the effect that he maintained a strong determination to eliminate RFK and that this feeling was a force beyond his control

Sirhan said, "I felt that he had betrayed me, and he was for Israel."

This emotional rollercoaster ride, fluctuating from positive to negative, is a key characteristic of the erotomania-motivated murderer. This switching process, from affection and love to rejection and hate, and back again, as in Sirhan's case, can have devastating consequences.

THE CRIMINAL CONCEPT OF EROTOMANIA-MOTIVATED MURDER

Erotomania-motivated murder is a sub-diagnosis of personal-cause homicide as defined in the *Crime Classification Manual III (CCM-III)*.[6] The diagnosis derives from the psychological research conducted by French psychiatrist, Dr. Gaëtan de Clerambault, who first identified the condition in 1885. More recently Douglas, et al., assembled a criminological task force at the FBI's National Center for the Analysis of Violent Crime and refined the criminal classification system (the *CCM-III*),

---

5   Seigenthaler, J. (1971). *A Search for Justice*. Aurora Publishing, Inc., Nashville, TN, 300.

6   Douglas, et al. (2013).

which defines the condition: "In erotomania-motivated murder, the murderer is motivated by an offender-victim relationship based on the offender's fixation. This fantasy is commonly expressed in such forms as fusion (the offender blends his personality into victims) or erotomania (a fantasy based on idealized romantic love or spiritual union of a person, rather than sexual). This preoccupation with the victim becomes consuming and ultimately leads to his or her death. The drive to kill arises from a variety of motives, ranging from rebuffed advances to internal conflicts stemming from the offender's fusion of identity with the victim."

After many years of clinical research, the *CCM-III* was developed to better enable forensic psychologists and psychiatrists, criminologists, and other mental health professionals who struggle to understand some perplexing criminological factors that support certain types of deviant behavior. The FBI research team had found little comprehension of why people engage in most criminal behaviors, especially homicide, by consulting the standard manual developed by the American Psychiatric Association (*DSM-5-TR*).[7]

Extending back to its origin, the erotomania-motivated murder diagnosis was rarely made until criminologists began to notice an increase in the frequency of homicide cases that fell into this category where personal-cause homicide played a central role. Those professional criminologists (like me), who desired to broaden the criminological understanding of homicide offenders, found that the *DSM-5-TR* and its predecessor manuals failed to provide almost any guidance into offenders' motives, especially for committing murder.

Although the *DSM-5-TR* does not specifically define erotomania-motivated murder, it discusses the psychological characteristics used to identify and diagnose less-complicated erotomania, grouping it in the schizophrenia spectrum and other disorders subdivided as delusional conditions. This differentiation reduces its usefulness for those of us charged with the daunting task of explaining why a person like Sirhan makes the irreversible decision to commit a murder. It is well understood by forensic psychologists and criminologists that the *DSM-5-TR* was never intended to diagnose most criminal behaviors or other serious criminal psychopathology, therefore erotomania-motivated murder was not classified.

---

7   *American Psychiatric Association: Diagnostic and Statistical Manual of Mental Disorders,* Fifth Edition, Text Revision (DSM-5-TR). Washington, DC Arlington, VA, American Psychiatric Association, 2022.

FOUR EROTOMANIA SUBCATEGORIES AND CASE STUDIES

The erotomania-motivated murder diagnosis facilitates the understanding of four high-profile murder cases that I will describe here. To provide background for Sirhan's reasoning for assassinating RFK, and for diagnostic classification purposes, I have subdivided and extended the original erotomania-motivated murder diagnosis as given in the *CCM-III* into four, sometimes overlapping criminal categories: 1) anger-vengeance, 2) fatal identification, 3) pathological fusion; and 4) ally assisted. Each subcategory is supplemented with a sample criminal case. I acknowledge that there may well be subclassifications of erotomania-motivated murder defined differently by other criminologists or forensic psychologists interpretating this relatively newly formulated condition.

These case studies are not simple "love gone bad" situations where anyone familiar with the facts could anticipate that a bad ending was unavoidable. The multilayered psychodynamics of erotomania-motivated murder are infinitely more complicated when, for instance, compared to a romantic lover's falling out over a financial issue, substance abuse, infidelity, spousal abuse, emotional instability, or another issue resulting in impassioned friction between two people.

1. ANGER-VENGEANCE:
THE CHARLES MANSON CASE

Four months after the jury convicted Sirhan of first-degree murder, Los Angeles was shocked again by the Manson serial murders. Sharon Tate, eight-and-a-half months pregnant, and the star of the film, *Valley of the Dolls,* was one of seven well-to-do victims who were brutally slaughtered during a two-night killing spree. A fictionalized account of these murders in the film, *Once Upon a Time in Hollywood,* written and directed by Quentin Tarantino, was released in 2019.

It has been hypothesized that Manson mentally conditioned (effectively brainwashed) his cult followers to commit the carnage while he remained at his squalid, remote ranch in the southern California desert. An in-depth psychological analysis of Manson's personality convinced me that his behavior was consistent with the characteristics of erotomania-motivated murder, subtype anger-vengeance. In some cases, the victims become largely symbolic, sometimes anonymous, faceless persons who represent an institution, a higher-societal strata or a way of life – the privileged versus the underprivileged. Anger-vengeance erotomania-motivated murder is not influenced by personal or financial gain.

When examined carefully, the motivation in the Manson-directed killings stems from his real or perceived rejection and humiliation by Hollywood elites in the music industry, initially supporting Manson's recording career, then rejecting him – a change he couldn't accept. Early on, his music industry connections included tacit support from The Beach Boys' Dennis Wilson who later recorded Manson's song "Cease to Exist," changing the title to "Never Learn Not to Love," then denied him writing credit. Manson's immediate response was to threaten to kill Wilson. An additional blow to Manson's identity came when Terry Melcher (record producer and son of Doris Day) informed Manson that there would not be a record deal in his future.

When Melcher lived with actress Candice Bergen at the now infamous address, 10050 Cielo Drive, in Los Angeles, Manson visited the house to discuss a recording contract. Later the house was rented by film director Roman Polanski and his wife Sharon Tate. Manson internalized and magnified his rejection by the Hollywood recording industry as a personal attack, and he needed to even the score.

In criminology research, a crime model developed by Gresham Sykes and David Matza facilitates our understanding of why people commit crimes based on the reasoning that the erosion of a person's moral controls leads to deviance. To commit crimes, the perpetrator needs to neutralize their moral, judgmental reasoning prior to the violation of prevailing laws by rationalizing or justifying their untoward behaviors. Sykes and Matza generally called these rationalizations techniques of neutralization. Specifically, one such technique is to reject the potential rejecters or the condemnation of the condemners before they reject you. In the Manson case, he clearly rejected the same people who rejected him, as part of a paranoid delusional system that, in his mind, determined that they deserved to be punished before they could hurt him again.[8]

Always boiling to the surface, Manson's anger uncontrollably boiled over, culminating in a conflagration of evil rage. He needed to strike back at the privileged members of society who cast him off like human garbage – a slice of high-society, in his view, that he was unfairly denied entry to. A paranoid delusion, *They were out to get me, so I'll make them pay first!* pervaded his thoughts. The result: seven people dead, including a well-known Hollywood actress.

---

8   Sykes, G. and D. Matza. (1957). *"Techniques of Neutralization: A Theory of Delinquency."* *American Sociological Review.* 22: (Dec).

Sirhan developed similar focused feelings of vengeance and retaliation directed at RFK who, he perceived, had somehow betrayed him by turning against his beloved Palestinian people. However, because his anger was specifically aimed at RFK, I found minimal clinical indication that Sirhan would displace his specific anger to others and become a serial killer (for example, like Manson).

Manson had a love-hate relationship as well, but not with a person; he created a perverse image of Hollywood itself as the enemy. Manson's delusional paranoid thoughts, dissimilar to Sirhan's, were diffuse, generalized, and indirectly focused on society's power elite. He needed to strike back at his delusional rejectors, and he did.

2. *FATAL IDENTIFICATION:* *THE SELENA PEREZ CASE*

The murder of up-and-coming Latina singer, Selena Quintanilla Perez, provides a good example of the psychodynamics involved in the fatal identification murder subcategory. Selena's death in 1995 at age twenty-three was front-page news that shocked her worldwide, cult-like, Latino followers. Many unanswered questions remain concerning what really happened in her murder case. Actress Jennifer Lopez played Selena in the 1997 biopic film, *Selena*.

Shortly after the singer was gunned down in a seedy Days Inn motel in Corpus Christi, Texas, her assassin, Yolanda Saldivar, was immediately taken into custody, tried, and convicted of Selena's murder. Since 1991, Saldivar had served as president of the Selena fan club, and later she was accused of embezzling $60,000 from the fan club and from other Selena business interests.

Immediately, the ostensive motive for the killing was that Selena discovered the theft and confronted Saldivar, who shot the singer. Police investigators linked the theft motive to Selena's murder, and Saldivar's abnormal, erotomaniac attachment to her idol was not even considered as fueling her real sinister motivation.

Saldivar had claimed that she truly loved the singer, a determinant factor in all erotomania-motivated murder cases. So how and why did this extreme emotional attachment sour and lead ultimately to Selena's murder? The simple motive that Ms. Saldivar's exposure as an embezzler was the prime motive for her killing Selena, a woman Saldivar idolized as her hero, may be descriptive, but is not criminologically explanatory.

A deeper analysis into Ms. Saldivar's antisocial personality psychodynamics revealed several dark themes. Many of her personality characteristics fit into the fatal identification murder syndrome. Observers of the relationship between Selena and Saldivar remember that Saldivar was obsessed with Selena's success, her bedroom was covered with posters and photos of the singer, and she burned votive candles at a kind of star-shrine to her heroine. At her parties, she entertained guests by playing CDs and videos of Selena performing.

Her envy and jealousy of Selena led to her psychopathological identification with the singer. She mimicked her speech and dressed like Selena, wearing her hair in a similar style.

In most ways, Saldivar was totally unlike her heroine in body shape, size, hair, facial characteristics, and especially in the area of talent. If Selena was the complete package – beautiful and famous – a winner in every sense, Saldivar was a far second or third. In her obsessive adoption of Selena's identity, she wanted to be like Selena, to be somebody, or to actually be Selena.

Saldivar's fatal identification with Selena was almost complete until Selena terminated her coveted position as president of the Senena fan club and personal assistant. So too ended Saldivar's delusional fantasy that she was as important as her fantasized queen. Feeling betrayed and rejected, she suddenly became an insignificant outsider who was mentally crushed by the woman she so desperately want to be. Based on this very deep, personal rejection, Saldivar determined out of desperation that, in the end, her false goddess misplaced high on a pedestal was no different than the other people in her life who had relegated her to a secondary status. Saldivar chose to eliminate the woman she initially worshiped.

Identifiable crossover psychological features are seen between Yolanda Saldivar's delusional identification with Selena, and Sirhan's vicarious and dangerous identification with RFK. Several times during his court testimony, Sirhan voiced his admiration for RFK as if they had some type of personal relationship.

In fact, Sirhan's connection to RFK, unlike Saldivar's connection to Selena, was entirely predicated on a delusional or vicarious fantasy. His delusion that he was somehow connected to RFK was driven by his sense of emptiness and need to identify with a powerful person. Like Saldivar and Manson, Sirhan believed he was always consigned as an outsider, denied access to the people who really made the decisions that made the world either a place of material success or, conversely, one marked by continuous strife, fostering greater alienation.

At age twenty-four, Sirhan had already experienced personal rejection stemming from his Middle Eastern heritage and small physical stature. He felt that he was a failure, and he compensated by trying to improve his mind using mystical Rosicrucian techniques and self-hypnosis. He was clearly not going in a direction he desired; first as a jockey, where he failed, or then oddly enough as a foreign diplomat. His self-loathing added to his ambivalence over his relationship with RFK.

In Dr. Diamond's view, "In Sirhan, this ambivalence took the form of extreme love and hate reactions. The more he felt like a failure [the more] he hated himself, the more also investment he would make in his inner fantasies of being a hero ... he thought that Senator Kennedy would be the savior of his people, all emotions which he had invested in President Kennedy were now shifted over to Senator Kennedy."[9]

At a certain point, Sirhan realized that his connection to RFK was a false one, and his investment into this vicarious relationship was terribly misplaced, i.e., no longer providing emotional payoffs for him. In his revised thinking, Sirhan again felt rejected, and now RFK represented an imminent threat who had to be eliminated. As a result of RFK's ongoing support for Israel, Sirhan's personal identity took another hit, and the road before him was now irreversible. In his distorted thought processes, he believed the man he had so closely aligned himself with had suddenly turned against him.

When Yolanda Saldivar was rejected, she selected a devastating course of action that ended Selena's life and confined her to a Texas prison for life. Likewise, when Sirhan felt alienated and abandoned by RFK, he pursued homicide as his selected retaliatory method.

Commensurate with Sykes and Matza's reasoning (techniques of neutralization: rejection of the rejecters), Sirhan desperately needed to reject RFK and, again in his delusional view, so he could not make Sirhan even more insignificant.

Sirhan psychologically switched his prior love attachment to RFK into a hate/homicidal motif. His descent into the fatal identification like Saldivar's came quickly as opposed to Manson's, which took literally years of brooding and delusional self-humiliation before he instructed four of his cult followers to strike out with deadly force.

For reasons not particularly clear to him, Sirhan's sense of indignation, tied to his delusional fatal and vicarious identification with RFK, reached a point of no return when he entered the Ambassador Hotel's small pantry,

---

9   Trial Vol 24, 6909, March 24, 1969.

carrying a loaded .22 revolver. He heard the echoing cheers for his fallen hero as RFK acknowledged his victory in the California Democratic Primary election. This palpable adulation for the man Sirhan once admired, but now hated, may have been the final trigger in a murderous sequence of events ending with Sirhan firing all eight rounds from his gun at close range. The strange truth for Sirhan is that nobody ever cheered for him.

Analyzing the murder scene at the Ambassador Hotel, Sirhan's plan had one major flaw – he made no provision for his escape. After the shooting, he was immediately subdued by RFK's supporters and taken into custody. He was taken to the LAPD's Ramparts Division Police Station where police booked into evidence the contents of the pockets of his clothing. Among these was a typed song sheet with lyrics extolling RFK's compassion for humanity and good will toward all people, "This Man is Your Man, This Man is My Man." The first two verses each end with, "That Man is ROBERT KENNEDY." The third verse also ends, "THE MAN IS ROBERT KENNEDY."[10]

How strange that when Sirhan was on his way to assassinate RFK, he stuffed into his pocket a piece of paper with the song lyrics praising the man he was about the murder. Was this a symbolic send-off in death to the man he once so ardently supported in life?

3. PATHOLOGICAL-FUSION: THE JOHN LENNON CASE

This subcategory goes several steps beyond, and manifests increased psychological intensity when compared with the fatal identification category, and there are also important differences between the two conditions. On December 8, 1980, Mark David Chapman, a crazed John Lennon fan, shot the music icon five times in the back as he and his wife, Yoko Ono, entered their upscale Manhattan apartment building, The Dakota. Shocked by the shooting, Ono was helpless to stop the murder or assist her fatally wounded husband. She too could have been a target. Fortunately, Chapman's hollow point .38 caliber bullets just missed her.

Chapman and Sirhan seemed to share certain clearly delusional, psychological commonalities that needed to be contrasted to understand why Mark David Chapman assassinated John Lennon. Chapman, the twenty-five-year-old killer had a history of collecting everything "Beatles," in particular anything connected to Lennon. His obsession with the singer-songwriter as well as his devotion knew no limits. His commitment to

---

10   L.A.F.O. #56–156: sub file X-1, Vol 2.

Lennon was similar to Sirhan's professed love and admiration for RFK, yet in both cases something psychologically tragic happened to turn love into hate, and erotomania murder.

Only a few hours before Chapman pumped the deadly bullets into Lennon, the singer gladly signed Chapman's copy of the newly released album, *Double Fantasy*. Chapman said Lennon was very cordial and accommodating when he solicited the autograph, yet this outward sign of goodwill did not alter Chapman's modus operandi to kill his onetime hero.

After Chapman shot Lennon, he made no attempt to flee the crime scene; and apparently like Sirhan, he had no intention of running or seeking escape. When confronted by a shocked doorman from The Dakota, Chapman waited quietly for the arrival of the police. Reportedly, he seemed very calm, definitely not anxious while casually reading J.D. Salinger's novel, *The Catcher in the Rye*, written from the narrative view of a disturbed seventeen-year-old boy, Holden Caufield, who is alienated, depressed, and cut off from most of society. Apparently transfixed in his reading, Chapman was startled by the arrival of several New York Police Department cruisers as the officers poured out, surrounded him and made the arrest.

The origin of Chapman's pathological, homicidal fusion may have begun when he completely identified with Holden Caulfield, a misfit and societal castaway. Chapman was so enamored with the Caulfield character, he wanted to change his name to Holden Caulfield, and sometimes signed his name Holden Caulfield. As time went on, Chapman assumed the alter identity, Holden Caufield. This dissociative aspect of Chapman's identity, in my view, was strikingly similar to Sirhan's alter personality identity when he killed RFK.

As Chapman became more immersed in the Lennon identification delusion, he was slowly switching his real identity to one more consistent with Salinger's fictionalized character. He wanted a more complete psychological, identity makeover, discarding his former one and reshaping his new self-identity. It appears that Chapman later switched his identity formation from the fictionalized Holden Caulfield to a real-life figure, John Lennon (a similar transformation experienced by Sirhan when switching his pathological identity from RFK's beloved brother, President John Fitzgerald Kennedy).

Chapman's obsession, to make all aspects of his life congruent with John Lennon's, launched his pathological fusion with Lennon. To emulate Lennon, Chapman began playing the guitar, joined a rock band, and married a woman of Japanese heritage (like Yoko Ono). Chapman surrounded himself with everything Beatles: recordings, posters, photos, and magazine articles describing the "Fab Four."

During a CNN interview, Chapman stated, "I always wanted to be a Beatle; I always think, *man, what would it be like to be a Beatle?*"

Recalling a particularly intense acid trip, he told a friend he thought he had become the former Beatle. However, his affection for Lennon eventually waned.[11]

"Chapman had apparently been building a fantasy life for several years centered on John Lennon.... An explanation for his motive [in the assassination] may be found in the testimony of a psychiatrist during the trial: the more that Chapman imitated Lennon, the more he came to believe he was John Lennon."[12]

The moment Chapman traveled down an irreversible path into pathological fusion with Lennon, he began to show clinical signs of delusional attachment and psychotic, cognitive associations departing from reality and tied directly to becoming John Lennon. In killing Lennon, Chapman was symbolically killing that part of himself that was so unacceptable to society. Maybe this was his second chance, maybe his only chance to reconstitute himself and finally be accepted and, like Sirhan, finally "be somebody." By eliminating his flawed, weak, and powerless persona, and replacing it with Lennon's almost perfect, strong, and powerful identity, Chapman wanted to make real an impossible psychological rebirth as a distinctly new person – a dissociated second personality.

Chapman's Lennon fixation abruptly ended in 1971 when Lennon made a statement (probably tongue-in-cheek) that now the Beatles (especially John Lennon) were "more popular than Jesus." Chapman had by then experienced an extreme religious conversion, and he likened Lennon's boasting to blasphemy, saying, "How dare Lennon elevate his status to the spiritual level of the Lord?" He considered Lennon's statement heresy, and now he questioned whether his devotion to Lennon was terribly misplaced. He began to seek out additional flaws in Lennon's life, especially his opulent lifestyle, though his song lyrics extolled compassion for the poor and disadvantaged. His resentment was mixed with a sense of jealousy that John Lennon and Yoko Ono maintained a hypocritical, lavish lifestyle while he barely survived; it simply wasn't fair.

11   Sloane, D. *Inside the Mind of John Lennon's Killer.* CNN Special Report. https://www.cnn.com/2015/us/mark-david-chapman-lennon-interview/index.html
12   Douglas, et al. (2013).

Chapman's wife Gloria said this about her husband, "He was angry that Lennon would preach love and peace but yet have millions."

She added that Chapman had said of Lennon, "He told us to imagine no possessions and there he was, with millions of dollars and yachts and farms and country estates, laughing at people like me who had believed the lies and bought the records and built a big part of their lives around his music."[13]

Chapman claimed since childhood, whenever his psychosocial functioning level dropped into a nonfunctioning zone, that an evil or demonic force in his head, "the [dissociative] little people," his alter personality took executive control over him, encouraging him to engage in nefarious behaviors. This included the planning of John Lennon's murder. Obviously, this thought process was tied to a nonspecific, ongoing delusional process or even the presence of a dissociative second personality. Based on the "little people" controllers and other delusional thoughts that Chapman manifested, he was obviously a suitable candidate for the insanity defense, NGRI.

But instead of taking the reasonable NGRI defense based on his dissociative states, he wanted his attorneys to withdraw his original insanity plea and plead him guilty to second-degree murder because, in his words, "That's what the Lord wanted."

Regardless, the judge handed down a twenty-years-to-life sentence, resulting in Chapman's incarceration for the forty-two years and counting as of 2024.

In a similar way, Sirhan also constructed a twisted sense of retributive justice, applying it to RFK: as long as he continued to conform his behavior to his personal code, he was in the safe zone. But when Sirhan proved to himself that RFK violated his own twisted personal moral rules, Sirhan had to retaliate – RFK must be condemned for his actions.

To achieve their ultimate assassination goals, physical stalking was another commonality Chapman and Sirhan shared. When Chapman convinced himself that John Lennon was not the hero he had envisioned and fantasized about, he had to stalk Lennon's moves to carry out his assassination plan. On his arrival in New York from Hawaii, Chapman began tracking Lennon's movements in and out of the upscale Dakota apartments.

Likewise, Sirhan stalked RFK around southern California prior to the actual killing between May 20 and the night of the crime, June 4, 1968, on

---

13   "Who Shot John Lennon and Why? Mark Davis Chapman's Motive for Killing Beatles Icon."   https://www.newsweek.com/john-lennon-death-mark-david-chapman-motive-killing-40anniversary-1553156

at least four occasions. Whether he had planned to kill RFK during those shadowing experiences is not known.

4. ALLY ASSISTED-MOTIVATED MURDER: THE MAURIZIO GUCCI CASE

The psychological drivers underpinning the fourth subcategory, ally assisted-motivated murder, derives from fixated self-involvement, personal aggrandizement, clinical depression, narcissism, and low impulse control that drives the perpetrator to commit an irrational, murderous act facilitated by others. This form of erotomania-motivated murder necessitates the use of paid allies to commit a directed homicide, and may be criminologically the most complicated.

Usually, the ally-assisted-motivated murderer can have unfettered access to the potential victim. Though divorced from Maurizio Gucci, a fabulously wealthy aristocrat and one of the heirs to the House of Gucci fashion fortune, Patrizia Reggiani still had almost unlimited access to his life and the people in it, allowing her and her murder allies to monitor his daily routine – a form of pre-homicide stalking we also see in the Mark David Chapman and Sirhan cases.

On Monday March 27, 1995, Patrizia's "off-the-shelf" hired hit man fired the fatal shots at Maurizio as he climbed the stairs to enter his Gucci offices in Milano, Italy. The tragic ending of Maurizio's life story and untimely demise was portrayed in the 2022 film, *The House of Gucci* with Lady Gaga in the role of Patrizia Gucci (née Reggiani), whose homicidal impulse was triggered by a delusional, self-generated compulsion for revenge, a key component in an ally assisted killer.

Patricia Gucci's murder trial was to Italy what the O.J. Simpson trial was to the US – huge news. The Gucci's murder saga, like an episode from the TV series, *Breaking Bad,* or *Dexter* was populated with some of society's most dangerous people, but it came with a tragic ending more like one of Tony's hit jobs in *The Sopranos,* the long-running TV-mob series.

Patrizia Gucci's self-serving crime involved her uncontrolled delusional eruptions that became a singular thought: her ex-husband had to be punished and killed for rejecting her. She put together a rag-tag team of would-be assassins to carry out her plan.

Even before she married into serious Gucci money, Patrizia was possessed by ungoverned, omnipotent impulses compelling her to do whatever it takes to ascend to the top of upper Italian society. She always wanted to be like the diva in Italian opera, performing on center stage. Charles

Manson possessed the same delusional trait, wanting to look up and see his name in lights.

When Maurizio first began dating Patrizia, his father, Rudolfo, disliked her even before meeting her, hearing that "she was an uncouth social climber, a party girl who came to class wearing tiny cocktail dresses and fur coats from the night before."[14]

Rudolfo's first instinct about the woman his only son would ultimately marry was accurate. Patrizia wanted a new transformational persona – a figure of high social standing, with all the trappings money could buy, and buy she did.

ALLY ASSISTED-MOTIVATED MURDER FACTORS

The factors that identify this ally assisted-motivated murder subcategory of homicide are at times divergent from and more complex than the homicidal factors identified in the other three categories.

Patrizia was influenced by a set of maladaptive criminal factors underscored by an unforgiving, callous, and psychopathic attitude. Callousness was systemic in her personality long before she married into the Gucci empire.

The ally assisted-motivated murderer necessitates delegation of assigned duties to accomplish the criminal mission. Patrizia probably realized deep down that she was a coward, incapable of carrying out her plan alone, so she ingratiated herself to four easily persuaded accomplices, including the trigger man, to do her "dirty work." When asked by a reporter why she did not choose to shoot Maurizio herself, Patrizia flippantly responded, "My eyesight is not so good. I didn't want to miss!"

The Italian press labeled Patrizia, "La Verdova Nera" – the black widow. Another indicator of her almost irreversible callousness was evidenced when Patrizia was offered an early parole after spending sixteen-years of her twenty-nine-year sentence for murder. To gain this early release in 2011, she had to fulfill a single requirement – find a job on the outside. She refused the offer, telling her lawyer, "I've never worked in my life, and I don't want to start now."

She served eighteen-years in Milan's dark San Vittore prison prior to being released in 2016. She sneeringly referred to that time as "my stay at

---

14   Menza, K. (2018) "How Patrizia Reggiani Became La Vendova Nera – The Black Widow and Had Maurizio Gucci Killed." *Town and Country Magazine*. https://www.townandcountrymag.co/leisure/arts-and-culture/a38305993/who-was-Patrizia-reggiani-house-of-gucci/

the Vittore Residence," a reference to a comfortable stay in an Italian villa rather than in a dingy prison.[15]

In the Manson and Chapman cases, the victims had little forewarning that they were in danger or could be the victim of a murder attempt. For Maurizio Gucci, the opposite was true – he had hundreds of confrontational encounters with his ex-wife Patrizia. This up-close and personal aspect of the Gucci case is often associated with ally assisted murder.

Maurizio Gucci knew that the ongoing hostilities between him and the volatile Patrizia focused mostly on escalating money matters. "When Maurizio refused to take her calls, she would send him tape recordings calling him a 'monster' for not taking care of their daughters and warning, 'the inferno for you is yet to come.'"[16]

Patrizia's anger toward her ex-husband escalated. A typical example concerned Maurizio's absence at his daughter's debutante ball. Patrizia and her daughter's godfather were left to greet four hundred of her closest friends at a huge villa outside Milan as the popular group the Gipsy Kings played.

Patrizia had taken over the planning for the occasion. "To look best for the event," she even arranged plastic surgery on her nose and on her daughter's breasts.

When Maurizio did not show up, Patrizia was bubbling with seething rage, and asked her lawyer, Mr. Auletto, "What would happen if I decided to teach Maurizio a lesson?"

"What do you mean 'teach Maurizio a lesson?'" Auletto asked, startled.

"I mean, what would happen to me if I got rid of him?"

Some weeks later, when she asked him the same question again, Auletta refused to continue representing her.[17]

Over the years, Patrizia maintained a diary in which she frequently expressed her progressive hatred for Maurizio. Her diary entries offer added insight into her dysfunctional personality, her building hostility, and her murderous impulses directed at one person. Like in Sirhan's "RFK Must Die" diary, she memorialized her angst, listing her growing grievances against the man she later paid assassins to murder.

In addition to angry writings, Patrizia dictated many disturbing tape recordings she vindictively gave to Maurizio, who quietly listened to the

15   Ibid. https://www.theguardian.com/fashion/2016/jul24/the-gucci-wife-and-the-fashion-darkest-tale

16   How Patrizia Reggiani Plotted to Kill Her Ex-Husband Maurizio Gucci. https://www.biography.com/news/Patrizia-reggiani-maurizion-gucci-ex-husband-murder

17   Forden, S.G. (2001). *The House of Gucci: A Sensational Story of Murder, Madness, Glamour, and Greed*. HarperCollins Publishers, New York, NY, 237–238.

vitriol she spewed until he simply had enough and threw the tape recorder across the room, smashing it to pieces.

Their pathological writings are evidence that Patrizia and Sirhan both felt profound rejection by powerful figures and, even more important, rejection and exclusion from entering the upper strata of society. Perceiving themselves as societal misfits, Patrizia and Sirhan entered into what I call a "criminal killing zone," offering no opportunity for retreat or escape. This homicidal-addictive zone forms the psychopathological undercurrent fueling ally assisted-motivated murder.

When a side-by-side comparison is made of the two sets of diaries (Sirhan's "RFK Must Die" document and Patrizia's tapes and diary), we can see a striking similarity, psychologically anchoring Sirhan and Patrizia's malevolent intentions toward their selected prey, portending the bad endings to come.

After Patrizia had a benign brain tumor successfully removed, she quickly attributed the tumor's origin to stress caused by Maurizio. She wrote that she wanted to "destroy everything." Days later, one of her entries read, "As soon as I am fit to talk to the press, if my doctors will allow it, I want everyone to know who you really are. I will go on television, I will persecute you until death, until I have ruined you."

In a tape recording at about the same time, Patrizia barked, "Maurizio, I am not going to give you a minute of peace.... You tried to crush me, but you couldn't.... You are a painful appendage that we all want to forget ... Maurizio, the inferno for you is yet to come."

Despite generous revisions to her financial arrangement with Maurizio, Patrizia "invited journalists to her luxurious Galleria Passarella apartment for interviews in which she smeared Maurizio as a businessman, husband, and father."[18]

In addition to her alleged material losses in her divorce decree, Patrizia was even more infuriated that Maurizio blocked her from further referring to herself by using the surname Gucci. Her grandiosity and self-aggrandizement liberally poured out in her diary writings (and in statements made to the press and to others) fits the diagnostic symptoms of the ally assisted-motivated-murder pattern.

Patrizia and Sirhan each directed their concerted attacks against wealthy and powerful people in society. Both appeared to have acute episodes of jealous rage against their respective social systems, from which they felt excluded.

---

18   Ibid. 232–233.

THE CHOSEN ALLIES

In two of the sample cases presented here, the Charles Manson case and the Patrizia Gucci case, the killer used allies or co-conspirators to accomplish their respective homicides, leaving the untidy murders to their hired underlings. The Manson case is an extreme example of how using allies can also achieve evil ends. Manson, as the Machiavellian leader of the Manson family – really a cult – used multiple forms of drug-induced hypnosis, radical political ideology, racist dogma (Black vs. White revolution), sex, violence, and additional mind control techniques to convince his "family members" to brutally slaughter seven people on two consecutive nights in Los Angeles as he remained sequestered at his run-down, communal ranch. But there was little doubt that he was calling the shots.

In a less-perverse sense than Manson, Patrizia chose a more traditional form of human reinforcement to cajole her four allies to murder her ex-husband – money. Based on what she considered to be a perfect murder plan, Patrizia realized that she could easily abdicate the more odious part of the crime she planned to the "paid help." However, similar to Manson's absence at the two murder scenes he set up, Patrizia was not present at the time the triggerman she hired pumped three nonfatal bullets into Maurizio, and a fourth execution-style into his right temple.

Carrying through with her well-devised plan to kill her ex-husband, Patrizia continued to remain in firm control, just the way she liked it. Her behavior is emblematic of the modus operandi used by a pathological, control-contact killer. A good deal of Patrizia's behavior prior to her divorce from Maurizio was marked by her continuous efforts to control him. She had attempted to manage every aspect of Maurizio's personal and business affairs. Her sense of grandiosity and omnipotence was constantly on full display as she alleged that she knew more about how to run The House of Gucci than the Guccis did, and she couldn't comprehend how the company could continue to function without her guiding hand.

Patrizia even claimed that if she were in put in control of the fashion house that Maurizio's grandfather, Guccio Gucci, founded in the late nineteenth century, the Guccis would continue to own and operate the company; naturally with her as president, or at least in a special seat on the Gucci Board of Directors, perhaps even as a major stockholder. As this illusion occupied more space in her mind, she often fantasized, *Given the chance that I deserve, I could show them all who is really capable of controlling things – running Gucci. They just won't pay attention to me. They don't think I know anything. I know a lot! How can they be so stupid?*

Perhaps easily forgotten is that Patrizia Reggiani had minimal formal education, zero business acumen, and her knowledge of Gucci *haute couture* was mostly limited to the expensive Gucci handbags she carried at high-society, social galas. Conversely, Sirhan's psychological control emanated from his ongoing illusion that, like Patrizia's fantasy of saving an elite fashion house, he could be capable of saving the entire Middle East from further bloodshed or, not achieving that goal, he would become a famous diplomat, an ambassador commanding respect for all to see. Sirhan's sense of self-importance and quest for recognition figured largely into his personal rage as he fantasized that he was a self-taught Middle East political guru equipped to solve complex geopolitical questions providing simple solutions. There is, of course, a remote chance that, unlike Patrizia, Sirhan could have a few of the answers.

Under cross-examination by the prosecutor, Mr. Compton, when Sirhan took the witness stand, his inflated self-image and even more troubling criminal intentions were revealed to the jury involving a plan to assassinate the US Ambassador to the United Nations. He fantasized that he could become a great diplomat in support of the Palestinian cause.

Responding to a prior area of inquiry pertaining to the Middle East put to him by Compton, Sirhan's answers provided ample context to his cultivating his personal illusion, telling the jury that from his study of the violence-torn condition in the Middle East, he was ready with some of the answers to the simmering unrest. His dissatisfaction with US handling of the tensions in his homeland spilled over to a hatred for not only RFK, but to the US ambassador to the United Nations, Arthur Goldberg.

During later testimony, Sirhan contradicted himself when he definitively acknowledged that to eliminate the ambassador, he could choose to use deadly force against him. This provides us with further validation that Sirhan, like Patrizia, shared certain elements associated with pathological, control-contact-motivated murder.

When analyzing Sirhan and Patrizia's homicidal actions, four identifiable, criminogenic factors are evident: callousness, disregard for human life, poor judgment, and weak impulse controls – the modus operandi of both killers.

Sirhan believed he had a few reasons for hating Ambassador Goldberg: primarily he was a Jew, and he supported UN Resolution 242. This resolution passed in 1967 generally held that any and all Arab land captured by Israel during the 1967 Six-Day War did not obligate them to return any captured territories to the Palestinians.

Like his perceived rebuff from RFK, Sirhan personalized this ruling, because he once lived in mostly Arab-populated Jerusalem – annexed by Jordan. Sirhan feared that enactment of Resolution 242 would further endanger his remaining family there. Once again, Sirhan said he was "burned up," meaning he needed to take action to prevent Goldberg from further disenfranchising his persecuted people. Because as Sirhan impulsively put it, "I did not like his words," therefore maybe he should die.

During an interview conducted with Sirhan by the FBI dated June 10, 1969, he made additional statements similar to his declaration to kill Ambassador Goldberg, which suggested that he agreed to financially support a plan to assassinate RFK. The report quoted a statement by Sirhan some weeks before, when he "pledged" two thousand dollars toward a large "contract" to kill RFK "in the event it appeared he could receive the Democratic nomination for the Presidency of the United States.... He added he was actually sorry he had uttered this. He described Senator KENNEDY as a brilliant young man, and added ... he certainly had no desire to see Senator KENNEDY harmed."[19]

While Sirhan was sequestered in a cell in the LA County jail, he was examined by an apparently well-qualified team of defense psychologists and psychiatrists as well as one prosecution psychiatrist who collectively held that Sirhan was suffering from a psychotic condition, probably a variant of paranoid schizophrenia, or a hysterical disorder, and no attempt was made to search for alternative diagnoses. I believe this was a significant shortcoming made by these diagnosticians. The diagnosis of erotomania, as well as DID and C-PTSD, and two accompanying new, criminal conditions can better help us determine the constellation of criminally oriented factors that supported Sirhan's irrational and inexplicable act of killing Robert Kennedy.

However, at the time of Sirhan's trial more than a half-century ago, there was no definitive, criminalological classification or diagnosis for erotomania, or for erotomania-motivated murder. The defense had to substantiate a psychiatric diagnosis somewhere within the psychosis spectrum, thereby allowing Dr. Diamond to introduce the legal/psychiatric elements of diminished capacity to the jury.

---

19   Federal Bureau of Investigation Report, #56-156–2801, June 10, 1969.

CHAPTER 10

SIRHAN'S PSYCH TEST RESULTS
Thematic Apperception Test (TAT)
Minnesota Multiphasic Personality Inventory (MMPI)

AN ANALYSIS OF SIRHAN'S THEMATIC APPERCEPTION TEST (TAT)

Though the Rorschach test given to Sirhan was exhaustively explored, the results from his two TAT administrations were only fragmentary at best and not scored using a professionally recognized classification system. This presented a clear methodological problem for his defense doctors. Apparently neither the defense nor the prosecution expressed much concern about why there was no reliable record or scoring of Sirhan's performance on the TAT, either in preparation for or during Sirhan's trial. Understandably, the prosecutors probably weren't concerned with any psychological assessment results that might help with the defense in Sirhan's case. But the defense team should have cared.

During Sirhan's trial, almost zero attention was given to the essential insights that might have been clearly evident to the court and jurors if only the doctors had conducted their professional work and were able to construct a cohesive analysis of Sirhan's TAT results. Like so many other aspects of the defense team's strategy, this just did not happen, and the trial was bereft of essential psychological information that could have been beneficial, or at least informative, to the jury. This blunder by the defense attorneys denied the jury informed psychological information that could have contributed to their reasoning about Sirhan's mental state when he killed RFK. Instead they were given filtered psychological evidence based on a poorly constructed psychiatric defense that no one, especially Sirhan, could seem to figure out.

To remedy this situation herein, I have analyzed Sirhan's TAT responses in retrospect using a validated scoring system that represents a kind of "blind scoring methodology" or retrospective analysis of Sirhan's TAT responses.[1]

---

1   The blind scoring technique used by the review doctors who rendered second opinions to validate in particular the assessments (as conducted by Schorr and Richardson presented in Chapter 7).

The TAT is similar to the Rorschach in some methodological ways, but with some important differences. For example, the TAT provides clients – or defendants in Sirhan's case – with an unusually immersive experience where the client is able to project their hidden wishes, fantasies, desires, fears, sadness, joys, and unconscious criminality into a preset series of pictures presented by and then scored by a psychologist. The results of the TAT can be used to tap into a client's thought process otherwise unavailable using traditional "talk" interview methods. The client may be given up to thirty photos (usually about twenty) of realistic-looking people, objects, and environments, and several abstract photos, drawings, or scenes requiring their imagination to interpret their meanings.

The TAT images are presented on 8.5 x 11 cards, one at a time, for the client to respond to and with no time limit to develop responses. The client may generate as many responses as they desire. The psychologist records each response verbatim, as best as possible.

As a psychodiagnostic tool, the TAT was developed about a decade after Dr. Herman Rorschach pioneered his eponymous test. Both tests have enjoyed continuous usage by psychologists since their inception. The TAT was developed at the Harvard Psychological Clinic (HPC), by Dr. Henry Murray, the HPC director; and Ms. Christiana Morgan, a staff member at HPC.

Dr. Murray originally trained as an MD and surgeon who later added a PhD in biochemistry to his resume as well as psychological studies. He interpreted the basis of Freudian psychoanalysis, using the theory developed by his mentor, Dr. Carl Jung. "Murray devoted himself to furthering their investigation of dreams, fantasies, creative production – and projection – all which are primarily emotional and dramatic, such stuff as myths are made of. After much experimentation with evocative images, Murray, along with Christiana Morgan and their clinic staff, fashioned the neo-classic Thematic Apperception Test (TAT)."[2]

Murray was also influenced by Jung's teachings that human imagination and fantasy ideations are more fundamental to understanding of an individual than actual perception. Murray challenged himself as to how to best access imagination and fantasy as a route into a patient's unconscious mind. The TAT validates two of his essential hypotheses: 1) that people reveal their personalities and problems in talking about others, and in unstructured situations, and 2) that the same principles utilized to analyze and interpret daily behavior can be used in work with TAT material.[3]

2   Gieser, L. and M.I. Stein (Eds.)(1999). *Evocative Images*. American Psychological Association, Washington, DC. 3.

3   Stein, M.I. (1950). *Thematic Apperception Test: An Introductory Manual for Its Use With*

After its publication for commercial distribution to the psychological community, the TAT began to rapidly fill the clinical void as "the next big thing" in psychological testing. As a projective method, the client is urged to project their thoughts into the TAT images, which reveal their motivations, needs, goals, and problem-solving style. Of special interest in a forensic psychological application, such as with Sirhan, is the identification of aggression and potential violence patterning.

During my practice, I have used the TAT to assess criminal defendants, with a special focus on looking for criminal-oriented themes, i.e., "Both people were shot;" "She ended up stabbing him;" or "He simply pushed the other man off the bridge."

When analyzing Sirhan using appropriate psychological assessment tools, it was beneficial to be able to identify and track any trending toward these kinds of violent themes, weak impulse controls, or any additional markers associated with a criminological potential. In this sense, the TAT serves as a violence risk assessment tool as well as a psychiatric diagnostic aid.

In Sirhan's case, this violence risk component quite naturally looks back in time (retrospectively) to quantify those themes he developed (on the TAT) that can establish Sirhan's overt acting out and aggressiveness. To globally evaluate his possible aggressive or violent themes requires the psychologist to be aware of themes related to potential violence that are embedded in the TAT.

With most serious felonies, including murder, that I have been called upon to evaluate defendants, I found that the analysis of TAT responses focused on the number of aggressive themes and uncovered antisocial attitudes that were very helpful in determining a defendant's aggression history and potential for violence. Recall how Sirhan's aggression seemed to spill over and be displaced (from RFK) when he was questioned about an entry in his diary about UN Ambassador Arthur Goldberg. Sirhan wrote in his diary, "Goldberg must die," followed with a threat that, "Goldberg must be eliminated – Sirhan is an Arab."

The TAT can isolate overt and covert manifestations of aggression as well as additional critical personality components associated with uncontrolled extra-punitive aggression. In Sirhan's case, the aggression dimension is probably the most critical area needing assessment. Psychological factors connected to overt aggression were continuously evidenced as I analyzed the four subcategories of erotomania-motivated murder. The anger-vengeance subcategory, representing extreme violence, is charac-

Adult Males. Addison-Wesley Press, Inc. Cambridge 42, Mass.,viii.

165

terized, for example, by the overt aggression and murder of seven people as orchestrated by Charles Manson. Overtly expressed aggression (like Manson's rage) paves the way for the breakdown of impulse control, leading to physical violence.

For obvious reasons, offenders who experience chronic problems with aggression have difficulty interacting with members of society in non-offending ways. This group is also marked with a history of repeated irresponsible actions such as sexual acting out. When Sirhan's socio-psychological background is put into perspective, identifiable, violent markers can be reflected using the psychological analysis provide by the TAT.

Sirhan's manifestations of aggression appeared to be unconsciously buried or suppressed, thus remaining hidden. Because Dr. Murray designed the TAT to scrub a patient's perceptions, including self-perceptions, looking for motivational factors that could lead to violence, the test was a good fit for Sirhan.

Shneidman adds clarity to the advantage of the TAT, saying, "It has to do with stories, narratives, plot lines, threads, scenarios, themes, scripts, and imaginal productions – almost like short stories and close to literature. If the Rorschach is a paradigm of the individual's perceptual styles, then the TAT is a paradise of the individual's psychodynamics – the strengths and coping capacities as well as interpersonal neurosis and other possible pathologies; indeed, the complexities of human personality that psychologists are supposed to assess."[4]

The analysis of Sirhan's TAT responses are very much in concert with what Shneidman characterizes as the critical aspects of the TAT in that, "People's lives are composed of stories as they continuously give meaning to their experiences and inner selves. They communicate with one another primarily by telling stories."[5]

A probe into Sirhan's TAT responses, using data from his eleven available cards, is presented here to facilitate the psychological exploration deep into his thought process and provide some missing explanatory pieces in his case. When analyzing Sirhan's TAT responses, it became clear that telling his stories did in fact provide some key insights into the mind of a killer, which were not previously revealed. Sirhan's TAT results provided me with a new, after-the-fact psychological understanding of an

---

4   Shneidman, E.S. *The Thematic Apperception Test: A Paradise of Psychodynamics*. In Gieser, L. and Stein, M.I. (Eds.)(1999). *Evocative Images*. American Psychological Association, Washington, DC. 87.

5   Gieser and Stein. A View to the Future. In L. Gieser and M.I. Stein (Eds.).(1999). *Evocative Images*. American Psychological Association, Washington, DC. 215.

assassin who in a clear, conscious state of awareness had no idea why or that he murdered RFK.

The physical administration of TAT cards is usually quite easy. A defendant like Sirhan is presented with the first card, and the examiner simply states word to the effect, "I'm going to show you some pictures, one at a time, and your task will be to make up as dramatic a story as you can for each. Tell me what has led up to the scene shown in the picture, describe what is happening at the moment, what the people are feeling and thinking, and then give the outcome."

After viewing each picture, the psychologist can encourage the test taker by asking probing or linking questions that help move their story forward, i.e., "Tell me what happened. How did the event start? Who was involved? What was the thought? Who thought this? How did this make you feel? How did it turn out – happy or sad?"

The TAT offers the chance for the patient to expand on the face content of each story told, tapping into their reservoir of hidden or guarded information. By using this probing manner, the TAT provides innumerable stimulus triggers or mental stimuli that can enhance recall of provocative areas patients often defend against exposure during the interview process. These triggers can expand the understanding of a patient's innermost thoughts in a productive yet unobtrusive manner. Sirhan's TAT scoring protocol, as given here, provided useful psychological information, yielding insight into his personality structure. Naturally additional methods can be employed to tap into a person's buried thought structure.

At an early point in preparation for Sirhan's trial, Dr. Diamond suggested that Sirhan undergo a sodium amytal or sodium pentothal (so-called truth serum) interview to discover missing pieces to Sirhan's story, especially what took place in the early morning of June 5, 1968. However, Judge Walker, on the advice of the LA County sheriff, ruled out the use of any drug-induced interviews as too dangerous, considering the possible, adverse medical side effects. A drug-induced interview would have required a hospital medical setting far beyond what was available in the county jail. However, psychological testing – projective assessment, using the Rorschach and TAT tests is believed to be capable of accessing at least some hidden aspects of Sirhan's personality dynamics.

When scoring Sirhan's TAT protocol, an important task was to identify the hero figure in each card – the focal character as portrayed in the story. With no prior TAT scoring analysis conducted by Drs. Schorr or Richardson, this analysis was created and pieced together based on my own extensive search through the two doctors' information as presented in trial testimony.

Over the years, psychologists have relied on a variety of TAT-accepted scoring systems that can be combined in some situations to maximize their overlap. The first step in each case is an overall evaluation of the stories' content that the patient develops. Since Sirhan's TAT responses were not subjected to any accepted, uniform scoring system, I selected a professionally accepted scoring system to properly categorize them. I used the Bellak scoring system (one of the original systems and the one I most prefer), which relies on ten scorable categories of psychological analysis: 1) main theme; 2) identity and functioning of the main hero (male/female); 3) main needs of the hero; 4) conception of the world; 5) the main hero's relationship to peers and junior figures; 6) significant conflicts; 7) nature of fears, insecurities, and anxieties; 8) main defense and coping mechanisms; 9) moral functioning; and 10) outcomes.[6]

Once I had the requisite TAT information in hand, I scored each card using the Bellak system. This effort hopefully serves to fill an important clinical void in Sirhan's case that might have proved helpful back then in clarifying certain psychiatric and criminal issues that continue to be enigmatic more than fifty years later.

To better develop the clinical picture, Sirhan had been given the TAT on two occasions (once by Dr. Schorr and once by Dr. Richardson). Their use of the TAT, especially regarding its scoring, was limited in scope. Unfortunately, as pointed out regarding Dr. Schorr's recorded responses made by Sirhan on the TAT, information is only available for two cards – card 18BM and card 16. As mentioned, no documented clinical scoring record was kept of how Sirhan responded to any other TAT pictures. This is very different from the results of Sirhan's recorded Rorschach responses, because a reliable record of all Sirhan's responses are preserved and accurate, with a verbatim record.[7]

Card 18BM was given by Dr. Schorr to Sirhan and subsequently interpreted by consulting-review psychologist, Dr. Leonard Olinger, who was engaged by the prosecution to recheck Dr. Schorr's work. So we have a rather complete record of Sirhan's responses to 18BM.

Dr. Schorr also described Sirhan's responses to card 16, a blank card, in considerable detail, so that part of the record is available. Presenting the

---

6   Stein. (1950). 146.
7   Kaiser. (1970).

blank card gave Sirhan the opportunity to make up or create a story using his imagination and fantasy ideation.

No further information is available as to what additional TAT pictures were presented by Dr. Schorr, nor do we know what role the TAT results played in his diagnosing Sirhan as experiencing "a paranoid psychotic condition with the capacity for dissociate reaction under stress." It appears that Dr. Schorr did inform his psychiatric opinion using all the psychological tests, including the TAT.

When Dr. Schorr testified, he said, "These tests, plus the facts I said, suggest a paranoid psychosis, a paranoid state with fragmentation in the direction of veering toward paranoid schizophrenia."

For Dr. Richardson's presentation of the TAT to Sirhan (again relying on his court testimony as an informational guide), we have a clear record of him presenting at least nine TAT cards in his analysis. Dr. Richardson may have given Sirhan additional TAT cards, but we have no survivable information to establish that as fact. No other analysis of Sirhan's TAT responses is available from any source. The information retrieved from the surviving eleven cards constituting Sirhan's TAT protocols form the basis of this reanalysis of Sirhan's performance on the TAT as presented by both psychologists.

So why is this first real analysis of his TAT scoring results so important in order to better understand the psychological picture that has emerged of Sirhan? Because this analysis provides better overall understanding of Sirhan's life, and this understanding yields valuable information that was simply not available via other psychodiagnostic methods at the time, such as the MMPI and the Rorschach, used to develop a composite psychological picture of the man who killed RFK.

Most often, when defendants are criminally charged, they are reluctant to reveal their innermost thoughts, fantasies, and motivational patterns when directly questioned even by their own defense doctors or attorneys; quite frankly they become suspicious of how their answers might be used against them in a later trial. Thus during the interview process, they tend to give answers they perceive the examiner wants to hear, and ones where they tend to deny certain aspects of their behavior they prefer to keep private.

In other words, defendants tend to distort or manufacture faked responses, tending to cast themselves in a favorable light. They do this to protect themselves – a classic form of deception. In the analysis of Sirhan's TAT responses, the focus is not so much on what he said, but looking beyond simple content to reveal deeper unconscious material that flows naturally from his unguarded responses.

Throughout his short twenty-four-year history (at the time the murder and additional charges were filed), Sirhan often alluded to powerful factors beyond his control (societal issues) that disadvantaged him in the pursuit of his goals, thus leaving him unhappy with himself and with society in general for being against him. In his view, these environmental forces played a considerable role in his destiny.

As we carefully traversed through Sirhan's eleven available TAT cards for the first time in an organized way, the importance of this information in shaping his behavior and his world view became evident. Omitting this important TAT analysis as evidence during the trial was certainly not to Sirhan's defense team's advantage, and from my perspective, represents a serious misstep in a trial where all the facts were not presented.

SIRHAN'S TAT CARD-BY-CARD ANALYSIS AND SCORING

These reconstituted TAT stories, interpreted from trial testimony of the two doctors as well as from other reliable, secondary reviewer sources, are not arranged in any particular order. Note that Sirhan's responses to card 16, originally given to Sirhan by Dr. Schorr, is unique, because they are based only on Dr. Olinger's reportage of what Sirhan told Dr. Schorr. Dr. Olinger's is the only record of how Sirhan responded. Sirhan's responses to this card are also of special interest, because, as point out, card 16 is the blank TAT card. Sirhan's controversial responses to this card provided new insight into his inner antisocial thought formation.

TAT CARD 1. "Boy Contemplates Violin" was the first TAT card presented by Dr. Richardson for Sirhan to view. The card, showing a little boy contemplating a violin on a tabletop in front of him, is a drawing of a photograph taken of violinist Yehudi Menuhin when he was six years old. Sirhan named this card, "A Master in the Making," then renamed it "A Master Musician."

Dr. Richardson described what Sirhan said it represented to him: "He sees a man and the boy thinking of Beethoven and even looking at a Beethoven instrument, admiring it and contemplating that he would never be able to play as well as Beethoven, who is a master, a musician, a master musician. Well, he may be playing it; he may be looking at it and studying it, or whatever you might think he is doing."

Dr. Richardson stated, "Another interpretative implication of this story has to do with, well, it begins with the identification of the figure of great renown, and he identifies the master and then someone who is the best, and that would be one cue in the direction of his particular attitude toward the self and the demands on the self and, if we take a look there, there is a reasoning, a part of Mr. Sirhan's feelings about himself."[8]

BELLAK SCORING SUMMARY OF CARD 1

Sirhan's hero analysis on card 1 shows that he identifies with the older man who he respects, a master musician, reflecting his sense of potential importance. Sirhan strongly desired to be a powerful person in a grandiose way, capable of changing the world, or at least altering the US position toward Palestine. Maybe he could become a diplomat, ambassador, or other high public official helping to represent an Arab country he identified with. The functioning of the hero indicates success, achievement, and wealth areas where Sirhan had so far failed. As he put it, "just to feel what it would be like to be rich." His response supports a life script marked by struggle and failure, not the riches he dreamt of. His worldview is characterized by despair and sadness. His grandiosity is evidenced as the hero strives to be more than he is, always wanting more. The outcome: the hero is left frustrated and defeated.

TAT Card 18BM. "Man Held From Behind" was given by Dr. Schorr to Sirhan and interpreted by Dr. Olinger. The general content of this card shows a man being clutched from behind by three separate hands, indicating more than one person is an antagonist. The images of the antagonists are not visible, leaving this interpretation to the test taker. Dr. Olinger explained his scoring of Dr. Schorr's presentation of card 18BM, where Sirhan responded, "I can't figure it out. Why are there three hands? I haven't seen anybody with three hands before. This is weird. He's being assaulted. Somebody poisoned (pause) no, fixed his drink, and he looks drunk, but he doesn't drink. I don't like this card. And if he does drink, he can't handle it. He looks unconscious."

In Dr. Olinger's clinical view, "This is similar to his [Sirhan] not wanting to take coffee or something before the guard [LA County sheriff's deputy] drank it. Always wondering what is going to happen."

Dr. Olinger continued, "Whereas most people would make a story out of that, where they could find justification for what two hands belong to, and what the third belongs to, he gets hung up. Then he says, 'he's being assaulted,' which is his own projection and his own feelings about the individual in society. Individuals are victims of an aggressive assaultive society. 'They are out to get me....'"

---

8   Trial Vol 22: 6391–6393, March 18, 1969.

Dr. Olinger commented on the conclusions drawn by Dr. Schorr challenging the accuracy of his reporting: "I'm not sure how serious the designation 'hung up' is here as intended to indicate a degree of pathology. I don't know whether this is what actually was said by Mr. Sirhan ... I don't believe he does. 'They are out to get me,' and he goes further and says, 'somebody poisoned,' and then he stops, so he breaks into the paranoid theme again – suspiciousness."

Assistant DA John Howard then asked, "Now before leaving the TAT cards submitted by Dr. Schorr to Mr. Sirhan, did you form any opinion as to the cards used?"

Dr. Olinger answered, "I noticed that there was not the usual distribution of cards that are given for an average test battery. That they tend to provide stimulus material of a realistic depressive evocativeness. That is to say that the normal individual who looks at these cards would be apt to describe a depressive story."

Mr. Howard asked, "Would it be any indication per se, standing alone, to you of ambivalence or any symptom of schizophrenia?"

Dr. Olinger said, "No, it is not. He's reacting to a card which suggests something weird, the three hands, and he doesn't like anything that suggests mental illness, so he doesn't like this card."[9]

Bellak Scoring Summary of Card 18BM

Initially Sirhan showed signs of confusion, stating, "I can't figure it out." He projected an atmosphere of suspicion and fear and paranoia, referencing that the hero had perhaps been poisoned, yet there was no visual evidence from the card that this was true. Sirhan conveyed the thought that the main character was the victim of foul play rather than a person who is being helped or rescued by the person or persons behind him. This outcome lends support to Dr. Schorr's diagnosis of Sirhan as paranoid.

Sirhan also commented, "...fixed his drink, and he looks drunk." This connected to Sirhan's allegation that on the night of the RFK assassination that he was somewhat intoxicated. Sirhan then added, "He looks drunk, but he doesn't drink, and can't handle it."

Again this comment mirrored his statement that, on the night of the murder, he was inebriated. He seemed to be reinforcing his belief told to the doctors that his consumption of four Tom Collins drinks just prior to the shooting impacted his recall of the entire event. Sirhan's statement to Dr. Schorr that, "individuals are victims of an aggressive assaultive society" and, as his statement trailed off, he added, "they are out to get me," reinforces his conception of society as fraught with conflicts, and fuels his paranoid thoughts, fears, and suspicions of others. Dr. Olinger captured Sirhan's projection that "society is a dangerous place, so you need to be careful."

It is obvious that Sirhan identified with the hero figure who had become a societal victim. Sirhan's response to card 18BM pointed out his chief defense mechanism (projection) as a way out of personal responsibility, because no matter how hard you try, "they are out to get me." At this point, Sirhan's responses here were reflective of his sense of learned helplessness he acquired as a child during a war-torn Palestine: "No matter what I can do, it still won't matter. It won't change anything." Sirhan's summary of his responses on card 18BM indicated paranoid ideations, personal conflicts, alienation, and indications of extra-punitive aggression.

TAT Card 2. "The Country Scene" depicts three main characters: an older woman, a shirtless man working in a farm field, and a younger girl carrying books and gazing away. Sirhan named this card, "The rich and the poor." His response to this card began, "Well, I don't like it. It's the girl that has the books and not the man. Although I can understand the man has to do the harder farm work – there is more sadness, the girl is not indigenous to this atmosphere. Actually, the books don't blend in with that condition of the mother – and the plowman – desperate impoverishment. They are trying the best they can, but they still can't make it."

Dr. Richardson interpreted Sirhan's response to viewing the scene as exhibiting some tension and anxiety. He imputed this anxiety as tied to Sirhan's perceived sex role reversal where the young woman instead of the man appeared to be improving herself through reading.

Fitts challenged Dr. Richardson's interpretation of Sirhan's response as demonstrating a sex role reversal, asking, "Wasn't Sirhan influenced by his Arab culture?"

Sirhan seemed to be taken aback by this comment, but Issa Nakhleh, director of Palestinian Delegation at the UN, protested. As an international concession, Sirhan's legal team allowed Nakhleh to attend the trial on an ad hoc basis when he felt Sirhan needed him. Nakhleh did not want any Arab cultural misappropriation imputed to Sirhan's TAT responses. "Issa Nakhleh rose at his end of the counsel table and objected. 'Not any more,' shouted Nakhleh. 'Now women, too, become educated.'"[10]

---

10   Kaiser. (1970).

BELLAK SCORING SUMMARY OF CARD 2

Interestingly, Sirhan identified with the younger woman he referred to as "the girl." Her dominant role as the hero figure is apparent. Sirhan interjected his own sense of conflict, even though the picture does not portray any obvious tension among the three figures. Sexual bias is prevalent, exposing Sirhan's attitude toward women as well as male-female gender relationship in general. Sirhan alluded to his conflict over status, power, and money by labeling card 2, "The Rich and the Poor," a pervasive theme of Sirhan being chronically poor and from a poor family; his father abandoned the family, and his mother having to work part time at a Christian nursery school. He expressed his jealousy of the younger woman as he projected himself into the scene as a reluctant victim.

Dr. Richardson accurately pointed out the sex bias, that the younger man, not the young woman, should be holding the books in order to become educated. There seemed to be a natural cultural bias that women need to be domesticated, not educated, prompting the reaction from the UN representative. Although the young woman carrying the books does not seem unhappy, Sirhan ascribed a feeling of sadness to her. Sirhan projected his personal depression onto her.

His comment, "But they still can't make it," tied to his own life script as a person who is struggling, connecting this comment to the response he gave on card 18BM where a man saw himself held back in life. This theme was a dominant force, pervading his responses to several TAT cards. In this process, it became evident that Sirhan developed a number of irrational beliefs that supported his multiple diagnoses: paranoid schizophrenia, possible organic brain pathology, and suicidal ideation. Sirhan was progressively developing many irrational, messianic thoughts, for instance, that he could save the Arab people. The results of card 18BM support Dr. Richardson's diagnoses as well as Sirhan's sex role confusion, mental conflicts, and a worldview that casts women into secondary roles.

TAT Card 3BM. "Figure on the Floor," given by Dr. Richardson, shows a boy crouched on the floor with his head cradled in his bent right arm. He is slouched, clinging to a bench or short side table. To his left on the floor is what appears to be a revolver. Sirhan's response involved anxiety and depression, leading to a suicidal scene where the figure [depicted as a woman] apparently killed herself out of some kind of despair. Sirhan was somewhat shocked by the image's emotive content and stated that he wanted to "come back to this one." Nevertheless Sirhan went on to describe what he saw: "She must have killed herself, or she's doped up. Or cowardly. She can't face it."

Realizing that this card represented a young male figure, Dr. Richardson probed, "It's a girl?"

Sirhan's answer portended feelings of anger and abandonment. "Yes, maybe her boyfriend ran out on her. She's depressive, melancholic, thinking, *Should I or shouldn't I?* She's thinking, *The hell with it.* She's tired, you know."

The obvious interpretation of this card reflects a pattern of depression accompanied with self-destructive thoughts. According to Dr. Richardson, "People will see the figure as in despair, possibly contemplating suicide. There is an object over here in the corner which could be almost anything, but it tends to suggest a weapon if the person is suicidally inclined, and it is often described as a weapon, usually a pistol. My interpretation here of Mr. Sirhan's story is a summary of his feelings of exhaustion, feelings of depression, tendency to give up, to be let down, to give in to a side of himself which he ordinarily fights very hard – that's the passive, dependent, more receptive side of his personality."

When I see a TAT response like Sirhan's on card 3BM or on another card, suggesting profound loneliness or depression, and I am ordered by the court to do a psychological assessment of an in-custody defendant, including a report, my first clinical thought is to note that the inmate be put on a suicide watch. After an inmate voices suicidal threats, there is a heightened probability, although certainly not in every case, that they will carry through on their verbalizations.

Further commenting on this suicidal probability risk factor in Sirhan's situation, Dr. Richardson stated, "I'm saying that this is likely to be Mr. Sirhan's mood at this time, particularly since there were indications from the Rorschach of depressive feelings of great loneliness, being on lonely heights and completely isolated, that sort of thing."[11]

BELLAK SCORING SUMMARY ON CARD 3BM

Sirhan's response to this card involved his impression that there could be a gun on the floor near the figure. Sirhan's hero identification was with a central character he perceived as female. He went on to develop themes that reflected despair, conflict, depression, and suicidal tendency. Sirhan then appeared to model the female's depression, adapting it to his own situation of confinement. Sirhan manifested self-destructive

---

11   Trial Vol 22: 6404–6406, March 18, 1969.

thoughts that were also seen on his Rorschach responses. His profound sense of alienation and separation from others was developed in his responses. His conception of the world was bleak and pessimistic.

Most patients viewing this card who identify with the picture's hero see a male figure, not a female. This is contrasted with his identification of the female figure in card 2. In both situations, the women were seen as weak, conflicted, unhappy, almost as secondary citizens. This broad theme can be found on Sirhan's brief history of being rejected by the women he approached. His reference to the gun is suggestive of an acting-out motif where his aggression was not far from the surface.

TAT Card 12M. "The Controller" shows a younger man lying on what could be a couch with a gaunt-looking older man with one leg bent at the knee, bending over him. The older man's right hand is outstretched over the younger man's head in a manner that looks like he's casting a spell on him. This is one of the TAT cards that leads to clients' interpretations of mysticism and perhaps mind control. Sirhan commented, "This is really odd. It's the story of Edgar Cayce psychic readings, a man who controlled his subconscious. I don't know if it's a good or bad man here. It's the graphic interest of how the book describes, magic, medieval knowledge … may be a priest saying a prayer. He looks oriental though, I wonder if he's kneeling, then he's trying to heal the sick; I wish he were praying for me; I wish that patient good luck; but there's a little mysticism in here; it's dark, and a man with his hand out to put him into a trance. I'm reading a book now, and you call it *There is a River.* I think the man's name is Sugrue."

Dr. Richardson stated, "It was of interest that Sirhan worried about the man in the picture, if he was a good or bad man, and is he going to help me?; and certainly he is a man who is going to control; he's controlling us with his hands out, as if to put someone in a trance. He may be doing that for good or for evil, and there seems to be some doubt about that, so there is some oscillation back and forth between; he is suspicious … going into hypnosis, having something to do with the supernatural influence and extra-human influences on thinking and on personality, and so forth."

BELLAK SCORING SUMMARY OF CARD 12M

Sirhan chose the hero in 12M as the ominous man who appeared to be the controller figure. It is of import that Sirhan did not identify with the younger man who seemingly was being put into some type of spell. Sirhan wants to be in control of the situation. He felt that for too long society had a heavy hand in determining his fate, and to use his words, "he is fed up."

Sirhan's dominant script was to even the score and get back at the societal system that caused him so much grief. Unfortunately, he cast RFK as one of those powerful members of society who contributed to his misery. He saw RFK as one of the controllers and expressed this feeling in his diary, "RFK Must Die." This characterization of RFK as the persecutor points out Sirhan's paranoia that ran through many of his TAT themes. His venturing into the world of mysticism, self-hypnosis, black magic, and the occult, including affiliation with Rosicrucians, suggested that he was desperately trying to wrest back control over his life that he saw as being controlled by external agencies. He used these alternative methods as a pathway of escape, to seek a safe place as refuge.

This also provided a convenient escape from his early life traumas related to beatings by his cruel father, who he saw as one of the controllers. Sirhan's childhood abuse, combined with a war-torn history of violence when he lived in Palestine, contributed to his early onset stress syndrome, fully characterized by a dissociative reaction with the symptoms associated with complex-post-traumatic stress disorder (C-PTSD). Often patients faced with overwhelming traumas unconsciously alter their mental state so they can live in a world absent continued traumas.

TAT Card 11. "The Dragon and the Cliff" shows an elevated road rising up from a deep canyon between two steep cliffs with obscure figures in the distance. Emerging from a rocky wall on one side of the cliff appears to be the grotesque body and head of an ominous dragon-like creature.

Sirhan's response to the card: "I had some dreams about this once, an old Arab legend; there's a big valley and two cliffs all of gold and the only way to get the gold is to throw meat down. The birds eat the meat and fly up with gold sticking to the meat. It's called 'The Roc, R-o-c.'"

Because of the abstract nature of this card's content, Dr. Richardson consulted with another psychologist and said, "This is one of the ambiguous, amorphous cards here and, if you look at it very closely, you can see some sort of long serpent creature coming out of the cliff.... It's weird. Did you ever see the *Phantom of the Opera*?"

BELLAK SCORING SUMMARY OF CARD 11

The purely abstract nature of card 11 caught Sirhan somewhat off guard because there were no human figures represented for hero identification. His initial reaction to the presentation of this image led him into a surrealistic venture, referencing the arcane Arab legend he described. Sirhan turned this rather abstract, strange stimulus into a theme somehow involving the acquisition of gold. Symbolically, gold represented Sirhan's continuous desire for wealth so he could be equal to those societal members who have it. In his estimation, it was unfair that he remained poor when others became rich, a constant theme of envy and jealousy that pervaded many of his TAT responses. At one point, he voiced wanting, "just to feel how it would be like to be rich."

The bizarre way he described how to get the gold is puzzling: "The birds eating meat, that is the vehicle to getting the gold."

Sirhan then said, "I had some dreams about this one," meaning he dreamt of possessing great wealth. His drifting into this dreamlike fantasy is supportive of his delusional thought process.

Historically, the serpent can be symbolically interpreted as the obstacle for Sirhan to getting the gold he deserves. This reflects his use of overcompensation as a defense mechanism deployed when he didn't get what he believed he was entitled to.

TAT 7BM. "Wisdom and Insight" depicts two faces: an older man with gray hair with his eyes downcast toward a younger man who appears to be intently listening to him. Both men have stern looks on their faces as Dr. Richardson characterized it: "And this is an older man and a younger man, and it seems like a lawyer and a defendant or a father and a son ... or a business man and a younger business man."

Dr. Richardson described the following exchange with Sirhan: "He [Sirhan] said, 'Oh, what do you say, Doc?' And I have to say, 'Well, I am not taking ... the test.' Then he says, 'He's [younger man] seeking advice from an old man. The old man seems more understanding.' I said, 'How about the story on this one?' And he says, 'I don't know. I can't think of a story....'"

Dr. Richardson interpreted this card as involving "a dependent passive relationship to the older man in which he is looking as a kind of father in a hopeful way. The other man is understanding."[12]

BELLAK SCORING SUMMARY OF CARD 7BM

TAT card 7BM shows a rather old man and a younger man engaging in some dialogue, not establishing eye contact. Sirhan chose the older man as the hero. It is no coincidence that Sirhan designated the hero fig-

---

12   Ibid. 6414.

ure as being an attorney and the younger man as his client, perhaps Sirhan himself. At the time that Dr. Richardson gave Sirhan the TAT as part of his more extensive test battery in the LA County jail, Sirhan was inundated with defense attorneys. Lawyers formed a large part of his confinement routine. His response on this card suggests that, on some level, Sirhan realized that he needed legal guidance; after all, he was fighting for his life and, if convicted for first-degree murder, he could be sentenced to the gas chamber.

Sirhan also identified the older man as a father figure, bringing up his own adverse relationship with his abusive father. Sirhan wanted the hero figure to be someone he could trust not to betray him. His feelings toward the older man were conflicted. On the one hand, he wanted a person he could rely on, and on the other hand he was afraid that the father figure would punish him just as his father did. Because of this ambivalence, he found it difficult to repress his continuing hostility against his own father who abandoned his family, taking all their life savings with him. Still demonstrating ambivalence, Sirhan wanted the hero to provide guidance during his time of need, though he feared rejection if he invested too much energy in a figure who had already punished him.

Initially, Sirhan told Dr. Richardson that the content on this card confused him: "I can't think of a story." Then he softened his approach: that the acceptance of guidance from either the father figure or the attorney could in the long run prove beneficial to his situation. Sirhan's tacit acceptance was set off against his suspiciousness and paranoid themes evidenced throughout his TAT responses, i.e., on card 12M, where he was concerned over control. Sirhan projected a sense of understanding onto the hero but, whether the younger man accepted it, was not known. The Bellak summary reveals that Sirhan's psychological themes indicated a higher sense of intellectual functioning, potential resolution to conflict, and a decrease in his distrust.

TAT 8BM. "The Medical Operation" shows an adolescent boy standing, facing straight ahead, and what could be the barrel of a rifle is visible to one side; in the dimly lighted background, there appears to be a surgical theatre with an operation in progress, perhaps on an emergency basis. The doctor figure appears to be hovering over the injured patient, trying to help him.

Dr. Richardson described the photo: "There is a boy in the foreground with a rather neutral or unemotional expression on his face ... and in the background a rather ambiguous, vague material, and you see a man apparently operating or using a knife on the stomach of another man who is lying with his face contorted in some way. Another man is standing alongside this man with a knife, holding, well, it looks like a gun in this side of what – well, looks like it is a rifle in the side of the picture. So to this one, Mr. Sirhan says, 'Boy' (long pause) and he says, 'Oh, I see, the background is just fantasy of this boy's – I don't like it. He is maybe dreaming of shooting this guy or somebody else – and they are operating.'"

Dr. Richardson continued, noting that Sirhan looked rueful, "And at this point Mr. Sirhan trails off, ceasing verbalizing. He paused again, suggesting he couldn't (or didn't want to) verbalize any more about what he saw in the picture. He is now – whereas this is in the past, just maybe imagining more...."

Dr. Richardson adds, "This is rather difficult to interpret and I didn't make a great deal of it in my report [to the defense team] because it offers a great many possibilities for interpretation. There is an obvious analogous connection with the assassination and what the purpose is, the significance is, is rather disrupted, an unconnected style of expression here in the sense he is pulled in, he is involved in it, but that he is holding back, that he is disrupted and he is concerned, but there is the expression of a fantasy of shooting someone, which is very unusual in a normal personality who is in good control of his aggressive impulses will say this is a great story – such that – that boy is waiting outside an operating room for a good friend or his father, who is being operated on because of a hunting accident or he could go another way – a beautiful way of handling someone's aggression and one's hostile impulses – this is the normal way, which would be to say, 'this is the boy dreaming of becoming a surgeon in his later life.' The gun means that is the battlefield scene and they are operating on him under battlefield conditions and the boy or principal character, he is dreaming of this in this situation. The boy has nothing to do with the gun. He has to do with saving a man's life." [13]

BELLAK SCORING SUMMARY OF CARD 8BM

This scene depicted in the card is highly complex. A popular response is to characterize the two men being an older father, a country doctor, and the younger figure is his son. The doctor is Sirhan; he identified the hero figure as a surgeon performing surgery on a young person on the operating table. He contends that the man standing next to the operating table is holding a gun to maybe shoot someone. This image portends a theme of aggression and violence. This is probably a latent, unconscious or dissociative thought pattern that Sirhan had for a long period of time.

As an experienced marksman, understandably Sirhan knew his way around firearms, especially the snub-nosed .22 caliber revolver he used to kill RFK. Because of his allusion to violence, Sirhan was initially reluctant to discuss the picture with Dr. Richardson, because his memories of aggression quite possibly began floating to the surface. When his speech began to trail off as he described the scene, he was defending himself against further intrusive, negative thoughts associated with what he did – kill RFK. His secondary reference that this scene was a "pure fantasy" removed its impact from the reality that he actually did it. The bothersome gun image in the picture also brought into focus his bad memories associated with the Israeli-Palestinian conflict when he experienced bombs exploded close to him. During the reverie, Sirhan's thoughts may have also drifted back to the many scenes of violence he witnessed while residing in Palestine.

Sirhan defended himself against the nature of what he was accused of and attempted to relegate it to the fantasy aspect of the picture, an illusion, and something he desired to keep buried and distant from his consciousness. In this sense, psychological denial emerged as his master defense mechanism, yet in reality he continued to be the one locked in a dingy jail cell, accused of first-degree murder.

TAT 13MF. "The Sexual Bedroom Scene" involves a young man standing with his head downcast buried in his arm, seemingly sad. Behind him is a partially clothed woman lying in bed. Provocative and sexual themes are often told concerning this picture. Sirhan's response was no different, and generally reflected his attitude toward women.

Dr. Richardson described the content of the picture, "It shows a man turning away from a bed with his head down, like so [gesturing]; the woman is lying nude from the waist up in the bed."

Sirhan said, "I don't know. It's in a bedroom. Did he strangle her or rape her? He doesn't seem to be satisfied. He's hiding his face. I don't know why (laughs). I saw a movie where a detective tried to catch a guy with this woman. When he was leaving her bed, they snapped a picture of him. The girl is not too lively in this one."

Dr. Richardson inquired, "How does that appear?"

Sirhan answered, "I think that's my question – how does she appear? It's my question. Obviously she must have had intercourse with him. Her bosom is bare. It's a mystery though, because he's dressed."

Dr. Richardson's commentary: "There are a number of possible interpretations to the story. To be on the conservative side, I'd say the emphasis on aggression and hostility in association with sex is consistent with other implications from the test material in the Rorschach and other sources of a sexual problem, that is a conflict between sexual feelings and hostile or aggressive feelings, which makes the whole sexual role and the sexual act a frightening thing, a difficult thing, as opposed to an easy, accepted thing. The comment, the snapping of the man [meaning a breakdown] as he is leaving the girl in bed, is extremely unusual. I have never seen that in seven or eight thousand TATs, and it has a highly personal significance. It comes under the heading of highly personal fantasies which are very difficult to understand."[14]

BELLAK SCORING SUMMARY OF CARD 13MF

As stated, the scene involving the two figures is quite provocative in nature; the woman being half-naked can elicit sexually oriented material and responses. Sirhan's story describing this scene included the notion that the woman was raped and the man is covering his eyes to expiate his guilt over what he did to her. Sirhan identified the hero as the guilt-ridden man who tried to hide his face because of his actions.

This points out that, on an antisocial level, he knew what he did was both morally and legally wrong (maybe he murdered RFK?), so it became easy for him to connect with the hero. Sirhan putting himself into the bedroom scene, viewing the motionless woman as "not too lively" is an admission that the hero has indeed raped, and then killed the woman, therefore he is justified in feeling guilt for a commission of a heinous act. The snapping of the picture of the scene memorializes what is now a crime scene, and leads to his arrest, so there is little doubt that he'll pay for his crime.

Similar to Sirhan's assassination of RFK, there was no escape. The main script in Sirhan's responses centers on his personal rejection, sexual frustration, and displaced anger directed toward the victim for somehow causing the man to kill her. This juxtaposition or projection away from responsibility is wrapped up in a denial defense mechanism.

After Sirhan gives his interpretation of the bedroom scene to Dr. Richardson, he jovially transitions into a non-sequitur story involving a detective, a woman, and a man. This defensive departure represents his flight away from the fact that the hero had, like himself, committed a

---

14   Ibid. 6406–6408.

cold-blooded murder; although the hero's crime was sparked by sexual passion as evidenced by the woman's lifeless body lying in the bed.

TAT 6BM. "The Conversation," which Dr. Richardson also labeled "The Mother-Son" card, involves a short, mature woman with gray hair who stands with her back turned away from a younger man, who is holding a hat and whose eyes are fixed, looking downward. Both have serious facial expressions, and neither appear particularly happy. The son may be asking the mother's permission to do something he had planned for a long time. Most stories developed about this card have an obvious emotional conflict that may or may not be resolved. Sirhan smiles then tells this story: "Maybe he is asking her for money. Or he's going to get married, and she doesn't respect his wife-to-be. The mother seems negative toward his request, he wants what he wants, but doesn't want to hurt her feelings. That's about all. She is maybe the grandmother, looks a lot older, he's making a request of some sort."

Dr. Richardson gave his interpretation of that card as having to do with "the dependence relationship of the man to the older woman in the picture who is making a request; meaning money from the older woman." He said that is found in personalities who have remained in a conflicting role in a relationship with a female. "The man continues with the mother or, if by chance a married man, it might suggest a dependence relationship to the wife and an unemancipated role in which the man needs a woman for basic supplies, money, support, protection and so forth." Sirhan said that the "mother here is refusing the request," which he saw as rejecting his ability to fulfill his needs.[15]

BELLAK SCORING SUMMARY OF CARD 6BM

Sirhan identified the picture's hero as a younger man who appeared to be rejected by an older woman. The hero does not want this outcome; he wanted to be accepted by the woman, but it seems that no matter what he does, he faces rejection. Sirhan wanted the hero protected by the mother figure just as his own mother always protected him, especially from his abusive father and the dangers of war lurking near their home.

Mary Sirhan commented to Dr. Diamond about Sirhan's fears and how she tried to provide comfort to him during the street bombings.

When Dr. Diamond asked her, "How did this affect Sirhan?" she said, "He wouldn't move for some time, and he was pale for some time."

---

15   Ibid. 6408–6409.

She continued to describe a bomb or mortar shell exploding near their house, killing the owner, which Sirhan witnessed. She related one scene after a bomb blast when Sirhan saw a soldier's foot dismembered. She attempted to help him through these war-related traumas.[16]

The rejection of the hero caused Sirhan conflict because he was still traumatized by his father's rejection and by his wartime memories. Almost irrationally, he sometimes dreamt that he could do something to repair his damaged relationship with his cruel father. He also had thoughts of killing his father, reminiscent of a Sophocles tragedy, *Oedipus Rex*. This paradoxical confusion probably reentered his thoughts as he further described card 6BM, saying that maybe it was his rebelliousness that drove his father away. At the same time, he held two very different conceptions of his estranged father: a wish to reunite with him and the evil intent to kill him.

Sirhan was in a no-win situation marked by both sympathy and hostility toward his father. Based on his father's abuse, there seemed little doubt that seeds of a childhood abuse syndrome emerged, establishing his later Complex Post Traumatic Stress Disorder – C-PTSD. Quite naturally as pointed out in card 6BM, Sirhan (like the hero) in real life turned to the mother figure to be rescued and ultimately saved.

TAT 16. "The Blank Card" was presented Sirhan by Dr. Schorr, absent any content (no pictures or images), to elicit his response when given the task of creating a unique story that is made up or is perhaps reflective of some fantasized aspect in his history. And Sirhan had plenty of vivid and negative fantasies to draw from. Because he was free to create his own picture, there were countless directions his responses could have taken, however he selected one that related to his wild fantasy in a graphic way concerning the strife he experienced in the Middle East as a child. Sirhan told Dr. Schorr that he "saw the face of Moshe Dayan [then Israeli defense minister during the critical Six-Day War in Israel began against Sirhan's Arab brothers/sisters] looking down at people. 'But there's a bullet that's crashing through his brain at the height of his glory.'" Sirhan added that he was not "part of the scene, he was the scene." He said, "I'm the one killing him!" [17]

BELLAK SCORING SUMMARY OF CARD 16

This is the only completely blank card in the TAT presentation set. Dr. Schorr gave it to Sirhan, requesting that he create a story using only his fantasies and imagination. Sirhan dutifully complied, creating an

16   Kaiser. (1970). 306.
17   Ibid. 441.

abstract antihero hero, Sirhan himself. The antagonist in the scene was the Israeli Defense Minister Moshe Dayan, who fought against the Palestinian people, insuring the preservation of the Israeli State.

The central theme in Sirhan's created vignette on card 16 was molded around a plot to assassinate Dayan as an enemy of the Arab people. More startling is the fact that Sirhan informed Dr. Schorr that he was the assassin in the scene! As he stated, "I'm the one killing him." It is not a quantum leap to link Sirhan's hatred for Dayan to the hostility he heaped onto RFK who also had "to be eliminated," as he wrote in his diary, "RFK Must Die." Sirhan was expressing his generalized hatred for everything Jewish or to anyone who supported the Israeli State. His results on this card strongly reinforced Sirhan's latent homicidal drive that, when further probed, was uncovered.

This aggression theme is the same when discussing the assassination of the US Ambassador to the UN, when questioned about Arthur Goldberg's name he entered in his diary. After all, Goldberg was a Jew and staunch supporter of Israel, so why not eliminate him too? Sirhan's unguarded anger and potential for violence as expressed on this card was palpable. He made no attempt to disguise his murderous ideations when he created the fantasized story to card 16. In Sirhan's comment that the defense minister, "is looking down at people," he characterized the looking-down part as Dayan – as representative of the controller class – peering down at Sirhan as a Palestinian, clearly a second-class citizen.

Perhaps Sirhan's fantasy production on card 16, as he described to Dr. Schorr, was not so much a creation of his synthetic reasoning as it was of his actual homicidal impulses to do harm, which he did. It would be almost impossible to tap into Sirhan's realm of extra-punitive thinking using a simple question-answer format, however his open-ended responses to the TAT cards allowed him to inform Dr. Schorr of thoughts, feelings, and attitudes that he may have preferred to obscure if questioned directly.

Although the TAT results presented here, in my professional view, could have filled in many of the obvious psychological gaps in Sirhan's life, defense lawyers apparently did not feel the same. In addition to the informational aspects provided by the analysis presented here, Sirhan's responses to the eleven stimulus cards impacted his diagnostic patterning, leading me to formulate five new psychological conditions not addressed by Sirhan's psychologists and psychiatrists fifty-plus years ago.

SIRHAN'S TAT: TRAUMA-RELATED THEMES

In addition to the traumatic symptoms that indelibly stained Sirhan's early developmental years, resulting in a variety of psychiatric symptoms with hysterical features. His hysterical neuroticism, as categorized in the 1968 *DSM-II*, ties into his long history of stress and trauma-related incidents and events that contributed to the emergence of multiple conditions not previously diagnosed. One of those trauma-based psychiatric conditions diagnosed here for the first time is complex post-traumatic stress disorder (C-PTSD).

C-PTSD and additional conditions were evidenced during his assessment (using his TAT results), where critical areas were identified on at least seven of the TAT card responses Sirhan provided to the two examiners. The most impactful responses included and my rescoring analysis are described here.

Sirhan's responses on card 18BM strongly supported his paranoid ideations and fears of control because someone has "fixed" that drink (perhaps added a drug to his drink to render him semi-conscious), and he could lose control. People became victims of an aggressive and assaultive society that is "dangerous, so you have to be careful."

Sirhan's psychological themes on card 3BM demonstrated his paranoid thinking, self-defeating behavior, rejection and abandonment ("Her boyfriend ran out on her."). Depression and notions of suicide were also present. On card 12M, Sirhan invented an odd story that this was about the mystic, Edgar Cayce who made predictions about the future: "I don't know if it's a good or bad man who has his subconscious controlled.... He looks oriental. I wish he was praying for me. It's dark, and a man with his hand out to put him into a trance."

One supposition is that Sirhan was referring to the self-induced trance states he achieved during multiple, hypnotic sessions using Rosicrucian methods. The trance issue raised his conflict level: *Is this man doing good or evil?* Sirhan felt that for too long, society has played a heavy hand in the determination of his fate, and he said frankly, "He's fed up." This response reflected his life, the frustrating way things are, therefore he sought an alternative way to see his life, a new direction. He saw powerful people like RFK as controlling society, and himself as he becomes the victim of forces he could not control. Sirhan's venturing into the misty occult world of black magic and self-induced trances helped solidify the foundation of his total escape, creating an alternate existence as a dissociated, second personality.

Sirhan's responses to card 7BM are particularly revealing about his relationship with his abusive father who often meted out corporeal punishment to Sirhan for the slightest childhood transgressions. The content theme of this card depicts an older man talking to a younger man. Sirhan's reaction to this scene churned up bad memories of himself and his father, fostering the Oedipus complex to seek the safety provided by his mother after he eliminates his cruel father. For his own reasons, Sirhan connected with the older man in the picture who he perceived as the father figure. There was tension here based on Sirhan's recollection of his mistreatment as he reversed roles, hoping to create a sympathetic father who will listen and not punish the younger man. Sirhan wanted the father figure to provide comfort and guidance, but that was not the course of his relationship with his own rejecting father. Sirhan's troubled relationship with his father became a major traumatic factor influencing his flight into dissociation, contributing to his C-PTSD and to his multiple personality disorder.

In Sirhan's responses to card 8BM, a photo of what appears to be an operating room where a surgical operation is apparently in progress, he interprets a number of ambivalent items in this room as being instruments of aggression and potential violence: a gun, a knife, and a rifle. He said, "Boy, I see the background is just fantasy of this boy's (probably Sirhan was projecting himself into the scene) I don't like it. He's maybe dreaming of shooting this guy or somebody else...." The symbolism in the scene was interpreted by Dr. Richardson: "The gun means the battlefield scene, and they are operating on him under battlefield conditions...."

Of course, the picture painted by Sirhan had historic roots in his own childhood experience when he saw many military fighters with guns, rifles, and probably knives to be used in the Arab-Israeli war. These negative and intrusive thoughts formed still another component in his history of traumatic experiences that he wanted to mentally escape from, thereby forming an alternative reality, a violence-prone one, where retaliation was inevitable.

The scene depicted on card 13MF, "The Bedroom Scene," presents more trauma-related stimulus material as Sirhan responded to it – sexual tension was implicit in the scene. The scene showed a man with his head down who turned away from a bed where a woman was lying naked from the waist up. There is a wide range of possible interpretations to the scene: maybe the woman was just sleeping, maybe too tired to get up, simply lazy, or perhaps inebriated. Instead, Sirhan chose the violent options, rape or murder, stating, "It's in a bedroom. Did he strangle her or rape her? He doesn't seem to be satisfied. He's hiding his face. I don't know why (laughs)."

Sirhan then alluded to an oblique film reference, trying to connect the scene to his personal experience: "I saw a movie where a detective tried to catch a guy with this woman. When he was leaving her bed, they snapped a picture of him. The girl is not too lively in this one." Aggression and hostility toward the female figure was implicit in Sirhan's answer.

The minor yet important reference to taking pictures of the man fleeing the bedroom scene was reminiscent of his situation when he killed RFK, assuring that there was no doubt who did it, as memorialized by the multiple witnesses who mentally photographed him with "the smoking gun" still in his hand. A secondary theme emerged that, because of his homicidal act, Sirhan like the man in the TAT scene, must be punished. Sirhan mentally connecting this scene to the RFK killing was psychologically recorded as one more stressful event in his life.

Abstractly, the fantasized murder of a high-status, Israeli military official spelled out by Sirhan did not require a quantum leap to connect this fatal moment to the prior killing of RFK. In Sirhan's thinking, he was against all people who were politically against the Arab people and, in some cases, as part of his distorted reasoning, they had to be eliminated. Unfortunately for RFK, he was added to Sirhan's enemies list. Now fighting for his life, represented by what he perceived to be a Jewish-dominated defense team (mostly Jewish lawyers and doctors), Sirhan's unguarded homicidal impulses bubbled to the surface when he discussed the graphic details of Mr. Dayan's violent death, with him as the unrepentant triggerman.

Sirhan's Minnesota Multiphasic Personality Inventory (MMPI)
Dr. Richardson's Viewpoint

Sirhan's complex psychological responses on the eleven TAT cards confirmed his mental conflicts and potential for aggression. Now turning to an analysis of his MMPI results, Dr. Richardson gave Sirhan the MMPI as part of his testing battery during his consultations with the defendant in July 1968. In Sirhan's cell, Dr. Eric Marcus left a copy of the MMPI for Sirhan to fill out. During the uneventful visit with Sirhan, Dr. Marcus judged him to be competent to stand trial, thus the issue of a NGRI was set aside for the moment.

Dr. Schorr also included the MMPI in his assessment of Sirhan. This test has been the most reliable assessment tool to assess a person's personality components for both nonpatients and patients, including criminal defendants, since its inception, based on a research article appearing in 1940. At that time it was called the Minnesota Personality Schedule.

Writing in that article, Hathaway and McKinley summarized the research process they followed in the development of the items included in the preliminary test.[18]

These items totaled 550 items, and some versions used 566 items. The completed project was first published in 1942 when the authors provided three indexes of validity to determine whether it measures what it purports to. "After 1950 the basic format of the MMPI was set. Acceptance of the new test grew steadily in the United States and in translation throughout the world."[19]

The original MMPI was used until its revision in 1980 when the MMPI-2 was developed as an improved test. The most recent version of the MMPI that I use in my forensic practice is the MMPI-2-RF (2008), which brings sensitivity and specificity to the diagnosis of certain criminal populations. "The forensic comparison group for the MMPI-2-RF includes individuals charged primarily with serious felonies, ranging from first-degree murder, with the death penalty specifications, to theft. All were undergoing evaluations in connections with questions regarding offenders' competence to stand trial, or insanity pleas. Individuals charged with sexual offenses, including assaults against adults and children, are also included."[20]

Essential to this discussion of Sirhan's personality is to determine just what exactly the MMPI measures and how the results can provide insight into the mind of an assassin.

Dr. Richardson stated, "Here we have a clinical personality profile representing the results of the MMPI of the answers of the 560-odd items. These clinical scales to be looked at are hypochondriasis, depression, hysteria, psychopathic deviants or sociopathy, masculinity and femininity of interests, paranoia, psychasthenia, schizophrenia and hypomania."

When analyzing Sirhan's answers to the MMPI, Dr. Richardson said, "There was a clinical depression state, a gloomy, below self-rejecting mood. The other scale which is into the pathological range, the paranoid scale, tending to some findings from other tests of what we called, well, the use of the projection mechanism, that is a tendency to handle various unacceptable feelings and wishes and emotions ... and there is a very

18   Hathaway, S.R. and J.C. McKinley. (1940). "A Multiphasic Personality Schedule (Minnesota): 1. Construction of the Schedule." *Journal of Psychology*, 10, 249–254.
19   Butcher, J.N., J.R. Graham, Y.S. Ben-Porath, A. Tellegen, W.G. Dalstrom, and Kaemmer. (2001). B. *MMPI-2, Minnesota Multiphasic Personality Inventory-2*. University of Minnesota Press, Minneapolis, MN.
20   Personal correspondence with one of the MMPI-2-RF principal authors Yossef Ben-Porath, October 1, 2010.

strong trend to test in a depressive suspicious, hypersensitive in the sense of challenging an angry mood. The profile was a paranoid schizophrenic … we look at the Rorschach, well, that is the paranoid here and amplified and conforms in a single example; there is a play back and forth between the tests [Rorschach and MMPI].… As to the MMPI, you will note that there were some 560-odd items and there were certain critical items, certain items that we want to know about [that are reflective of an entire diagnostic category, to wit: schizophrenia or depression] – what did he answer of such-and-such, so I would like to read you the critical items and the way Mr. Sirhan answered them."

The MMPI also contains four validity scales to check the veracity of the respondent's answers to determine if they are faking and/or not telling the truth. About Sirhan's responses, Dr. Richardson says, "The following critical items are checked in the pathological direction: 'Evil spirits possess me at times;' 'I have strange and peculiar thoughts;' 'When I am with people, I am bothered by hearing very queer things.' He answers, 'Yes,' to 'I believe I am being plotted against.' He answers, 'Yes, I have wanderlust and am never happy unless I am roaming or traveling' … 'I have periods in which I carry on activities without knowing later what I have been doing;' 'I'm afraid of losing my mind' is left blank. 'Most of the time I wish I were dead;' 'I often feel as though things were not real;' I have strange and peculiar thoughts.' In addition, the following items were left blank, or simply not answered: 'At one or more times in my life, I felt that someone was making me do things by hypnotizing me.' Also he left blank: 'Someone has been trying to influence my mind.' Then he says, 'I feel anxiety about something or someone almost all the time.'" He also did not answer the question: 'I see things or animals or people around me that others do not see.'"

A review of Sirhan's endorsed critical MMPI items revealed more than purely diagnostic categories – paranoid thoughts and depressive ideations – but additionally his odd perception and belief in strange experiences. It's as if part of his life is lived as he wandered in a psychological fog or inexplicable mental state he couldn't quite escape from. This confusing state I identify as Sirhan's alter state of awareness (his second personality), representing a dissociated state of alternative consciousness. It is further my view, that he had drifted in and out of this unconscious, alternative reality state for years prior to and at the time he murdered RFK. This set of experiences is reflected on his MMPI responses reported in Dr. Richardson's results.

Dr. Richardson continued to analyze Sirhan's MMPI responses: "Then the paranoid scale was analyzed and because, within the paranoid scale are subscales and these subscales are called paranoia, a subtle, paranoia, obvious paranoia, persecutory ideas, paranoid poignancy, and paranoia, naiveté. The patient [Sirhan] checked the following items under the heading paranoia, persecutory ideas: 'I am sure I get a raw deal from life;' 'If people had not had it in for me I would have been much more successful; ' I believe I am being plotted against;' 'I know who is responsible for my troubles;' and 'I feel that I have been punished without cause.' He also endorsed, 'I have certainly had more than my share of things to worry about.' The question, 'I have no enemies who really wish to harm me,' is answered, false – that is, there are enemies who really wish to harm him."

Dr. Richardson's characterization of Sirhan's paranoia tendency appears somewhat paradoxical in that at one point he is seen as extremely suspicious and evidencing all the symptoms that could warrant a paranoid schizophrenic diagnosis. There is no doubt that Sirhan's ardent political beliefs fueled his sense of hypervigilance over the years because, like his Arab people, he too could be attacked as he was when he was a child.

Although the original version of the MMPI presented to Sirhan by Dr. Richardson was less standardized, using a criminal comparison population, it nevertheless provided a valuable psychopathic deviation scale (PD scale, scale 4) sensitive to those persons who may fall into the range of psychopathic behavior. These individuals were usually referred to a psychiatric service for classification of why they had continuing difficulties with the law even though they suffered no cultural deprivation, and despite their possessing normal intelligence and freedom from serious neurotic or psychotic symptoms. Items on the PD scale reflect a lack of concern about most social and moral standards of conduct, the presence of family problems, and an absence of life satisfaction.[21]

Assuredly, Dr. Richardson was well aware of the MMPI PD scale, and how it might help to determine if Sirhan endorsed items on this scale. If this was the case, Dr. Richardson would have delved into this important area during his testimony. Completing a forensic assessment of a defendant like Sirhan, back then or now, would be difficult absent an evaluation of the PD Scale. I have used both versions of MMPI, the original MMPI, the MMPI-2 and the 2008 MMPI-2-RF with hundreds of criminal offenders, and the PD scale number 4 is the first scale that gets my immediate attention. That Dr. Richardson did not mention that Sirhan's MMPI profile

21   Butcher, et al. (2001), 26.

showed an elevation on the PD scale means he paid less attention to this critical marker, consistent with a psychopathic index, often attributed to a suspect or defendant accused of a first-degree murder charge.

THE MINNESOTA MULTIPHASIC PERSONALITY IN-VENTORY (MMPI)

DR. SCHORR'S VIEWPOINT

During visits with Sirhan on November 25 and 26, 1968, Dr. Schorr administered the MMPI to Sirhan in his jail cell. On March 10, 1969, Dr. Schorr was sworn in as a defense expert. The principal focus of his reporting was to go over the results on the MMPI in contrast to Dr. Richardson's results and comments. Dr. Schorr began his direct testimony to Mr. Berman by discussing his disorientation in the large Hall of Justice Building where Sirhan was housed in a private room cell on the thirteenth floor, isolated from other inmates: "I'm not too well oriented today, but I think it's this building, yes?"[22]

Dr. Schorr was asked to review the 566 items of raw data from the MMPI, an inventory that he described as having "ten psychiatric scales and categories, four validating scales, a built-in lie scale, and three other scales that relate to the possibility that the person taking the test may be malingering or distorting the material – not telling the truth."

Dr. Schorr was asked to explain the scoring process and noted that on the lying scale for the whole test, Sirhan only lied in two responses, to which Dr. Schorr said, "Speaking on the basis of normal population distribution, for example, this is actually lower than the average individual would give in telling the truth, that is more people will give more lies on the average than Mr. Sirhan did."

Dr. Schorr explained the positioning of Sirhan's results on the MMPI that showed significantly higher scores in two areas (called non-abnormal personality or so called normal personality): paranoia and hypomania.

Dr. Schorr explained that, in hypomania, such an individual is "apt to be very aggressive, very restless, constantly on the go, in a state of flux, in a state of constant turmoil, sort of like a roadrunner if you are thinking of an image, but unable to relax, and constantly on the push. There is something driving this man."

Dr. Schorr's explanation for paranoia included that "an individual takes the position 'I'm okay, everybody else isn't,' or put another way, 'There is

---

22   Deeper into his testimony, Dr. Schorr's personal psychological disorientation ramped up and he departed the courtroom holding his head down.

nothing wrong with me because I have so much understanding of every-body else around me so I am the authority...' This score, the paranoia and hypomania scale exceed the point beyond which the so-called normal per-sonality goes, so they have to be viewed as pathologically significant..."[23]

Dr. Schorr's interpretation of Sirhan's MMPI results emphasized the validity aspects of the test: whether Sirhan was lying, attempting to dis-tort the truth, malingering by presenting himself in an unfavorable light to appear mentally ill, or whether he was consciously presenting a distorted picture of himself as not mentally ill.

Dr. Schorr's results on Sirhan's MMPI appeared tightly focused on the four validation scales as if he were more interested in the veracity of the responses than stressing the essential information conveyed from the ten clinical scales, which had been the focus of Dr. Richardson's approach.

Dr. Schorr's concentration on the truthfulness of Sirhan's responses was warranted because there were issues pertaining to Sirhan's credibility as well as the accuracy of many statements he made to his doctors and defense attorneys. He persistently argued that his memory of the events around the actual shooting of RFK was especially suspect. The question remained: *Why does Sirhan continue to deny any memory of the murder scene?* Dr. Schorr chose appropriately to look carefully at the MMPI valid-ity scales for guidance in his pursuit for the truth.

I have found the results of these four scales to be helpful, though not a lie detector, when assessing the truthfulness of what a defendant tells me during the non-testing part of a psychological assessment. As essential, I have found that conscious distortion of the picture a defendant pres-ents is not uncommon, and thus must be ruled out. Consistent with my perspective on Sirhan's memory deficits is my belief that he cannot recall certain events in his life because he was in an altered state of conscious-ness during some periods, therefore those memories of events, i.e., killing RFK, were not recorded.

Sirhan's absence of recall to this key event is not the only memory he was unable to retrieve. If I was to reassess Sirhan today (in addition to the MMPI validity scales), an accepted malingering test such as the Struc-tured Inventory of Malingered Symptomology (SIMS) or a similar faking instrument could prove valuable. The *DSM-5-TR* notes the symptoms of malingering as the "the intentional reporting of symptoms for personal gain (e.g., money, time off work)." Easily added to these would be a defen-dant's manufacturing of psychiatric symptoms to avoid prosecution using

---

a NGRI plea, or a lesser defense consciously formed to avoid personal responsibility for illegal acts.[24]

At the time Sirhan was assessed by Drs. Richardson and Schorr, the SIMS was not available, therefore they relied on MMPI validity scales to conduct their evidenced-based forensic evaluation to establish Sirhan's truthfulness. Widows and Smith state, "In response to the limitations of the *DSM-IV* criteria in the assessment of malingering, alternate models have been proposed that specifically emphasize the examination of the test data and the gathering of background information.... There have been three types of instruments used in the detection of malingering: 1) structured interviews, 2) general psychological or cognitive instruments, and 3) tests specifically designed for the detection of malingering."[25]

Challenging Sirhan's truthfulness was a reasonable pursuit in that he conveyed conflicting stories leading up to and during his actions at the exact moment RFK was fatally wounded. During questioning on March 4, 1969, Grant Cooper retraced Sirhan's movements on June 4, 1968, prior to going to the Ambassador Hotel, and he caught Sirhan in a lie about the order of events, and whether he had a gun.

But why would Sirhan attempt to obscure information that was so easily verifiable?

Sirhan described several blackout periods during which he experienced a total lack of recall before and after the assassination. Sirhan also told crime researcher, Dan Moldea, that when he arrived at the Ambassador Hotel after he attended a campaign rally for Senator Thomas Kuchel, "a Republican who was running for reelection to the US Senate. I crashed the party, but there wasn't very much going on. I struck up a conversation with someone who suggested that the better party was going on for Max Rafferty, another Republican, at the Ambassador Hotel across the street."

Sirhan said, "So I left the Kuchel party without even having a drink. I walked across the street to the Ambassador, I saw the Rafferty banner.... It was a hot night. There was a big party, and I wanted to fit in. I arrived there about 8:00. I drank four Tom Collins. It was like drinking lemonade. I guzzled them. My body is small. It was hot in there, and I wasn't used to it. I was feeling it, and I got sleepy. So I wanted to go home. It was late."[26]

Sirhan then recounted that because he was feeling intoxicated before he attended the Kennedy rally, he returned to his car, too impaired to

---

24   Ibid. DSM-5-TR.
25   Widows, M.R. and G.P. Smith (2005). *SIMS: Structured Inventory of Malingered Symptomology-Professional Manual.* Psychological Resources, Inc. Lutz, FL, 2–3.
26   Moldea. (2018)., 7.

drive, and he got his gun which he placed in his waistband. At this point, Sirhan said his thoughts became cloudy and his memory challenged.

As RFK arrived, and Sirhan first saw him, he was overwhelmed as he told Grant Cooper: "The first time, Sir, yes, Sir. And my whole attitude toward him changed, because every time I heard him before, I associated him with the Phantom jet bombers that he was going to send to Israel, and I pictured him as a villain every time I heard him, in relation to the Zionists and his support for Israel."

"When I saw him, Sir, that day, that night, he looked like a saint to me."[27] Shortly after this beatific scene, Sirhan inexplicably murdered RFK.

At about 10:00 P.M., "Sirhan asked hotel waiter Gonzalo Carrillo-Centa to hold his drink while he took a folding chair. After Sirhan sat down, the waiter returned his drink and walked away. Claiming to have had lapses in and out of consciousness, Sirhan next remembered standing in front of a teletype machine cranking away in the Colonial Room. He just stared at it, somewhat transfixed. 'I was mesmerized,' he says. 'I had never seen anything like that before.' Mary Grohs, a Western Union Telex operator, spotted Sirhan and described him as 'glassy-eyed.' 'I was shit-faced drunk,' Sirhan added."[28]

Sirhan did not have a clear recollection of events much after that but, because of his state of intoxication, he wanted a cup of coffee. "Sirhan remembers, 'the coffee was in a shiny urn. I remember standing there, saying, 'I like my coffee with cream and lots of sugar.' An attractive brunette was standing next to me, and she said that she liked her coffee the same way. I remember that she was wearing a plain white dress. We had a brief conversation, and I don't remember anything more than that."[29]

When Sirhan told investigative reporter, Dan Moldea, that his recall just abruptly stopped, was he being truthful? Or was he once again distorting the facts to align with his own self-interest?

Prosecution review psychologist, Dr. George DeVos was also interested in determining if there was any pattern of deception that suggested that Sirhan was attempting to fake or malinger his assessment results to appear either more pathological or less psychiatrically involved. If he tested as experiencing a serious mental disorder, this would lend credence to Dr. Diamond's conception of the diminished capacity defense that maybe Sirhan was not 100 percent insane, but just enough to meet the diminished capacity criteria, thereby reducing the first-degree murder charge to second-degree, sparing him the death penalty.

27   Trial Vol 17, 5143. March 4, 1969.
28   Moldea. (2018). 8.
29   Ibid. 8–9.

When questioned by Grant Cooper, Dr. DeVos explained that the MMPI validity scales, as he interpreted them, were a good measure to Sirhan's overall honesty; or whether he was malingering, faking, or attempting to distort the psychological picture he wanted to project. Cooper referred to these scales as the lying scales and accepted Dr. DeVos' in-depth conclusion that Sirhan did not attempt to distort these scales when he checked Drs. Richardson's and Schorr's testing protocols. Cooper then directed his attention to Sirhan's Rorschach results for signs of faking or malingering.

Dr. DeVos stated, "I have never seen it [malingering] done successfully," adding "that my impression is that this was a valid testing experience that was obtained by the two psychologists."

Based on Sirhan's reported spotty memory tracking he attributed to periodic recall deficits and to his chronic blackouts, two possibilities appear to explain these situational amnesic episodes. The first is psychologically connected to Sirhan's conscious attempt to provide false psychiatric information to enhance the probability that the diminished capacity defense would be more plausible to the jury. The results of Sirhan's testing results presented by Dr. Richardson and Schorr as reviewed by Dr. DeVos strongly support the position that Sirhan was not lying when he denied knowledge of the actual shooting of RFK at the Ambassador Hotel.

A second viewpoint concerning Sirhan's problematic memory history not previously addressed centers on his legitimate claims that he experienced isolated blocks of time during which he couldn't recall his activities. In my view, this possibility of a legitimate amnesic syndrome is only a part of his complicated personality psychodynamics that is tied into his diagnosis of disassociation as advanced by Dr. Diamond. Was Sirhan truly unable to remember critical events (like the shooting of RFK) that were blocked from his conscious awareness? Understandably Sirhan became frustrated, confused, and angry when repeatedly asked to recall certain information and was repeatedly unable to. Quite naturally, the prosecution took advantage of this, claiming that Sirhan was a liar.

To adequately explain his memory issues and other shrouded events in his life, it is necessary to consider Sirhan's psychiatric re-diagnoses. I proffer that his dissociated personality condition disallowed Sirhan from even knowing the real facts in his own case. For Sirhan, a considerable reservoir of information was recorded and stored that remains unavailable to him in a non-altered conscious state. This view is consistent with Dr. Diamond's perspective that Sirhan was experiencing a type of dissociated state when he murdered RFK, and his memory of the actual murder was at best fragmentary.

Furthering Dr. Diamond's psychodiagnostic position, I also suggest that Sirhan was experiencing a dissociative personality disorder characterized by the emergence of as second personality – the revenge-driven, criminal Sirhan. Along with other evidence that he had drifted in and out of this dissociated state for years, this clinical hypothesis suggests that neither of Sirhan's personalities (as defined by Dr. Diamond): the first, the usual unaltered Sirhan; and second, the altered Sirhan, had mutual access to each other; therefore they operated separately, one on a conscious level, and the other on a purely unconscious level.

I contend that when Sirhan murdered RFK, he was in an altered second personality. It is also my viewpoint that Sirhan's fractured personality began long before he became psychologically obsessed with RFK, in his childhood while he still lived in war-torn Palestine.

It must have been mentally anguishing for Sirhan to be continually questioned in his conscious state about facts and events that actually occurred while he was in an altered state of awareness. He had no answers.

CHAPTER 11

REASSESSING SIRHAN'S PSYCHIATRIC DIAGNOSES

PHASE II OF SIRHAN'S IDENTITY TRANSFORMATION

D r. Diamond's diagnostic assumptions lend support to my opinion that Sirhan was in a dissociated state when he murdered RFK, however we differ about Sirhan's definitive diagnoses.

So what were Sirhan's "real" diagnoses?

Describing and explaining each of the newly identified psychological conditions that were Sirhan's underlying mental destabilizers will help to clarify his rapid, pathological descent into a dark and confusing world that he didn't comprehend or consciously desire.

To completely recast Sirhan's story involves complicated and disturbing new issues tied to his societal deprivation, personal alienation, traumatic life events, buried rage, jealousy, rejection, and especially the vicarious "love/hate" relationship Sirhan had with his chosen victim, RFK. That troubling affinity for RFK formed a persistent psychological undercurrent throughout the trial, but was never considered to be a core part of Sirhan's motivational patterning that influenced his unprovoked anger and the homicidal rage fully expressed on June 5, 1968.

The criminological classification of erotomania-motivated murder is an insidious disorder (as previously described) involving an offender's delusional fixation. This deadly condition constituted Sirhan's Phase I of an identity transformation. Another of Sirhan's core psychological conditions was his "fractured or dissociative personality" structure, which affected him profoundly from childhood. This and three other key psychological conditions provide proof of Sirhan's identity transformation.

TWO SIRHANS

U sing psychological DNA to explain Sirhan's motives in killing RFK required a different research system from the traditional concept used in perpetrator identification patterning. This research-guided assessment approach has yielded significant results with hundreds of offenders when compared with other investigative methods, especially within the context of their potential to reoffend.

As noted, psychological DNA investigation is based on a search for key psychological components of criminals' lives that moved them from a law-abiding existence to pro-law violation. This process shares research components with behavioral or criminal sequencing. The unique aspect of psychological DNA is the attention given particularly to uncovering unconscious criminal motivators negatively influencing the criminal offender, which remain hidden until these buried factors are brought into the offender's awareness. Many offenders, including Sirhan, truly had no understanding of why they deviated and couldn't answer, "Why did you do it?"

Uncovering psychological DNA involves an in-depth, five-phase process of investigation into the offender's life.

1) Beyond a review of criminal records and any history of treatment, the goal is to identify a criminal's conscious negative factors impacting their pre-crime thought structure ("I've danced around the edge of crime all my life"), including early childhood components as suggested by R. Theodor Reik. This stage of psychological DNA involves gathering collateral, background information from family members, friends, associates, coworkers, and employers.

2) Quantification of these factors involves the use of psychological assessment tools to inform whether to rule in or rule out psychopathic deviation, lying/faking, or factual distortion, avoidance of personal responsibility, offender superficiality, and other related criminal destabilizers. The use of projective psychological tests to tap hidden thought streams is helpful. In this effort, the TAT and Rorschach are the tests of choice – the same ones used to test Sirhan.

3) Direct assessment of the impact of identified critical criminological factors is done, weighting these to measure their impact.

4) In the process of collecting offender information, a determination of the criminal's undermining, criminally oriented life factors are assessed as either static (immutable, fixed, or unchangeable – height, hair color, IQ, etc.), or dynamic and fluid (capable of change via lifestyle changes, or modification of habits: "I stopped shoplifting," "I've stopped drinking," or "I'm not doing drugs now," etc.), to identify pervasive self-defeating, personal life descriptors: "I'm no good, and I'll probably be like this the rest of my life!"

5) Search for and isolate unconscious, negative, criminological drivers in support of deviant patterning, and determine in each case the most appropriate psychiatric or criminological diagnosis.

When looking more closely at the use of projective, psychological tests like the Rorschach and TAT, forensic psychologists use these instruments customarily to tap into a patient's unconscious mind in ways that are not usually achievable using other non-projective tools. The results of these tests can open a vast reservoir of new content. For example, Dr. George Estabrooks, a Canadian psychologist and expert in the use of hypnosis, strongly urged the use of projective instruments that help explain obscured, covert, or unconscious personality factors that facilitate the formation of deviant behaviors.

In his book, *The Future of the Human Mind*, Dr. George Estabrooks suggests using a variety of psychological tests to better understand buried states. "...The use of one or more of a series of standardized tests known as projective tests ... all are based on the same general principle: that the way a person responds to material which in itself has no specific meaning is an indication how that person's mind works, on both the conscious and the unconscious levels, and, as an indication of his way of seeing things, is also an indication of the structure of his personality."[1]

Looking at Sirhan's pre-crime behaviors, using the psychological DNA research-guided method, it was immediately evident that his rational (non-criminal) reasoning that existed at some earlier point in his life was supplanted with an irrational thought system marked by negative thoughts or criminal ideations, a system later identified as dissociative identity disorder (DID). The identification of these types of unconscious criminal forces, including a dissociated state, can be traced back to the early writings of Reik.

In Reik's analysis of the criminal mind, he noted that the source of criminal thought emanates deep in the offender's mind. Reik also connected criminal behavior to earlier childhood trauma. He wrote, "Criminal psychologists should see the challenge in the investigation of the extent to which this unconscious connection can be proved also in the criminal, of whether here, too, there exists an underground connection between the primal crimes of childhood and the deed of the adult criminal ... the development of the person who later becomes a criminal."[2]

---

1   Estabrooks, G.H. and N.E. Gross. (2017). *The Future of the Human Mind: A Study of the Potential Powers of the Brain*. New Saucerian LLC Press, Edition. 65.
2   Reik, T. (1959) *The Compulsion to Confess: On The Psychoanalysis of Crime and Punishment*. Farrar, Straus and Company. New York, 285.

In my view, the unconscious, criminal drivers supporting Sirhan's homicidal thoughts and ultimate assassination of RFK must be approached from the psychological framework of his two distinct personalities – his "splitting," which can be discovered using psychological DNA to reach into his divided personality system.

SO WHO AM I TALKING TO?

For Dr. Diamond and many professionals who interviewed Sirhan prior to and after the trial, the same question came up: Which Sirhan was actually being interviewed? The issue persisted because of Sirhan's often amnesic responses to inquiries into the assassination, as well as his split, dissociative personality, making it difficult to determine which of his two personalities showed up during questioning.

This confusion in identity no doubt was also experienced during an interview with Sirhan arranged by Robert F. Kennedy, Jr., when he visited his father's convicted murderer at the Richard J. Donovan Correctional Center in San Diego on December 19, 2017. RFK Jr.'s contention was that, in addition to Sirhan emptying his eight-shot revolver, another gunman (the second shooter theory) fired additional rounds that killed his father.

Eyewitness confirmations that Sirhan's second personality surfaced spontaneously are unknown. Responding to questioning by defense attorney Berman concerning Sirhan's hypnotically induced sessions and his amnesia, Dr. Diamond stated, "It isn't the before or after that determines whether we call something a dissociated state. It's whether or not the individual has full consciousness, because the essential of a dissociated state is some degree of restriction of consciousness over the mind. ... The thing that is characteristic about a dissociated state is that the individual is now conscious only for a segment of their mind, and this can vary."[3]

Using hypnotic sessions, Dr. Diamond was able to elicit or manifest Sirhan's other personality, which came into full view in his words, gestures, and actions that substantially differed from his core or primary personality. During those sessions, Sirhan synthetically produced a very different-sounding and acting person. As Dr. Diamond stated during his testimony, he was only able to have Sirhan manifest his other personality as secondary to a preplanned posthypnotic suggestion. In this sense, Sirhan's evolvement into his alter was not spontaneously represented as a switching process, but rather one induced by Dr. Diamond.

---

3   Trial, March 21–26, 1969.

This created hypnotic state (personality 2) was able to produce an alternate Sirhan who shared some psychological characteristics with the primary Sirhan (personality 1). Personality 2 reflected many of Sirhan's mystical, occult-driven trance states (which he was able to self-induce), he manifested his dissociative personality, temporarily supplanting the primary Sirhan.

Dr. Diamond commented further concerning Sirhan's personality split, "It is my opinion that through chance, circumstances, and a succession of unrelated events, Sirhan found himself in the physical situation in which the assassination occurred. I am satisfied that he had not consciously planned to be in that situation ... I am satisfied that if he had been fully conscious and in his usual [non-dissociative] mental state, he would have been quite harmless, despite his paranoid hatred and despite his loaded gun."

Adding more, Diamond explained, "He was back in his trances, his violent convulsive rages, the automatic writing, the pouring out of incoherent hatred, violence, and assassination."[4] This unchecked violent, homicidal rage was a product of Sirhan's emergent, secret personality who carried out the plot to kill RFK.

Manifestation of Sirhan's dissociated personality was the counterpart to Dr. Diamond's "second Sirhan." Dr. Daniel Brown was also able to elicit Sirhan's switched alter personality as manifesting spontaneously, interpreted as his dissociative state.

Dr. Brown described Sirhan's altered state,

> In subsequent direct interviews with Mr. Sirhan, I directly observed Mr. Sirhan a number of times switch into at least one distinctively different alter personality state, a personality-state that responds in a robot-like fashion upon cue .... This altered personality state only occurs while Mr. Sirhan is in a hypnotic or self-hypnotic state, and only in response to certain cues. This state never spontaneously manifests. While in this altered personality state, Mr. Sirhan shows both a loss of executive control and complete amnesia.

During his interviews with Sirhan, Dr. Brown elicited flashback, fantasy, and dreamlike episodes as Sirhan described his partially dissociated memory of the shooting scene involving a girl in a polka dot dress. He told Dr. Brown: "I think she had her hand on me ... I am not sure if it was her hand or somebody else's ... then I was at the target range ... a flashback to the shooting range ... I didn't know I had a gun ... there was this target like a flashback to the target range ... I could be fantasizing or dreaming

---

4   Ibid.

that I was at the gun range ... I thought that I was at the range more than I was actually shooting at any person, let alone Bobby Kennedy...."

"What Mr. Sirhan eventually described as 'range mode' – wherein Mr. Sirhan takes his firing stance and experiences a 'flashback' that he is firing at circle target at a firing range, in a way that has been well practiced. While interviewing Mr. Sirhan, I, along with attorney Dusek [Sirhan's appeal attorney at the time], directly observed Mr. Sirhan spontaneously switch into range mode on several occasions."[5] Dr. Brown was clearly able to identify at least one additional personality state, as he and Sirhan's attorney observed this personality switching process.

All this established more support for Dr. Diamond's psychiatric theory that, when Sirhan pulled the trigger on June 5, 1968, he was in an altered mental state consistent with a diagnosis of DID. Moreover, that Sirhan was in a dissociated, self-induced state that mimicked a hypnotic trance, and therefore could only recall those events while in a simulated, alternative state, as provided under the altered consciousness trance produced by hypnotic aberration.

Dr. Diamond's belief that Sirhan was already in an induced trance state influenced by his past experiences with the Rosicrucian experiments and triggered by the physical circumstances at the Ambassador Hotel (flashing lights, external sounds, general confusion, and reflections in mirrors) when he killed RFK seemed to gain credibility.

According to Kaiser, who attended several of Dr. Diamond's hypnoanalytical sessions with Sirhan, "I believed him [Sirhan] ... I had sat in on most of the hypnotic sessions Sirhan had with Dr. Diamond. Although those sessions produced far less information than Dr. Diamond had hoped they would, they convinced me that – although Sirhan didn't tell the whole truth while hypnotized – he was not faking when he said he couldn't remember the specific details of the assassination. But why couldn't he? If he had programmed himself to kill Kennedy, he should have had some recollection, if not of the killing, at least of the programming. He didn't remember either. During Dr. Diamond's probe, he'd [Sirhan] learned it all from a book called *Cyclomancy*."

Under hypnosis, Dr. Diamond probed Sirhan about the notebook (diary) "RFK Must Die,"asking whether he drafted it alone "or did someone else participate?" And more importantly, "Were you hypnotized when you wrote the notebook?"

5   Declaration of Daniel P. Brown, 2/10/2016, United States District Court for the Central District of California.

Sirhan responded that, "Yes," he was hypnotized when he wrote sections of the notebook, stating "mirror mirror, my mirr [sic] my mirror."

Dr. Diamond was intrigued by Sirhan's strange response that he was hypnotized or believed he was in a trance when he wrote at least parts of the notebook, but what constituted the vague trance state that Sirhan alluded to? The alternate possibility suggested that he was in a trance, but was this evidence of Sirhan's alter personality who wrote at least large parts of the notebook (as Sirhan was in a confused state of consciousness)?

Quite possibly, the adjusted Sirhan had very little or no knowledge of the incriminating writings in the notebook written by the altered Sirhan. Because of this confusion in authorship, Sirhan merely supplied Dr. Diamond with what seemed to be a logical and convenient answer to an illogical situation he couldn't answer.

During many past interviews, Sirhan denied writing certain passages in the notebook. To an extent, he was able to provide Dr. Diamond with answers that made some sense, but still left Sirhan grasping for his own understanding of who really wrote some of the passages in the notebook. It seemed convenient for Sirhan to claim hypnotic status when faced with explaining the most controversial writings in the notebook.

Dr. Diamond went on the record, believing that Sirhan fulfilled his many fantasies while in a dissociated state, but all he could prove to the jury was that Sirhan had (for some unknown reason) the ability to shift into an unconscious, altered state of awareness.

When questioned by defense attorney Berman about Sirhan's not recollecting the controversial writings in his diary, Dr. Diamond provided new information. "I would prefer to say he had no recollection of those notebooks as being his … and he couldn't tell me when he did it, he couldn't tell me, when thinking of it, he couldn't tell me whether he agreed with them or whether he disagreed with them, and this is the way it occurred to me, and this applied not only to the Kennedy material but to all of the material in the notebook."[6]

Dr. Diamond had not yet solved this psychiatric conundrum of somehow tapping into Sirhan's lost memory, and still wondered if it could be solved. Sirhan's truthfulness or lack of it was not lost on the prosecution who saw this as a fertile area, easily assailed by sharp questioning. When prosecutor Fitts had Dr. Diamond on the witness stand, he aggressively challenged Diamond's interpretation of Sirhan's honesty as reflected during this heated exchange between the two during cross-examination.

6   Trial, March 24, 1969.

The confrontation centered on Sirhan's controversial experience at the shooting range earlier in the day of the assassination.

Fitts asked Dr. Diamond, "Can you suppose for a moment, taking in mind your entire diagnosis, that he lied to you about leaving the range with that gun fully loaded?"

Dr. Diamond said, "I suppose it's possible, but I don't think he did … I have tried my very best to examine him and reconstruct what is necessarily a psychiatric theory of what happened. I certainly never proclaimed this to be the Gospel truth or to exclude all possibilities. I present this simply as my opinion of what is the most likely, the most probable explanation of this crime. It's not the Gospel truth and there are alternative explanations."

As the cross-examination progressed, the term "dissociate" recurred throughout Dr. Diamond's testimony. Fitts again pressed the point that perhaps what Sirhan could remember wasn't reality, but his creation of a set of fantasies he constructed as his personal reality. He seemed to be laying a trap, moving Dr. Diamond's statements concerning Sirhan's truthfulness into a quagmire where the truth could not be differentiated from fantasy, lying, and fiction.

Dr. Diamond said, "I was uncertain in my own mind as to the authenticity of his [Sirhan] not being able to remember the notebook or at least parts of it. I was aware at the time of sharp differences in only parts of this notebook. It was done in an amnesic state or a dissociate state, and other parts were obviously not, and I was assuming that Sirhan, if he would be cooperative enough, to be able to at least recall all of the rest of it, might within his experiences under hypnosis again, as he has convinced me, he has greater ability to alienate the dissociate material. I have come to respect his claims that he doesn't remember, and he has demonstrated to me over and over again to an extraordinary extent that he is unable to remember actually the kind of experiments which we put him through, so that I felt better."[7]

ROBERT F. KENNEDY JR. COMES TO THE DEFENSE

Four years prior to the Parole Board decision to finally release Sirhan, RFK Jr. was persuaded by long-time survivor of the RFK shooting scene, Paul Schrade (deceased November 10, 2022), to review the voluminous crime files he assembled over the years on the assassination, especially the detailed ballistics report that indicated more than eight

---

7   Ibid.

gunshots were fired at the crime scene, whereas Sirhan's .22 caliber gun cylinder only held eight.

Up to the time of his death, Schrade was convinced that there was another person firing at the same time as Sirhan. Considering this new information, RFK Jr. arranged to visit Sirhan in the CDCR Richard J. Donovan Correctional Center in San Diego, California on December 19, 2017, to make up his own mind concerning Sirhan's role in his father's death.

RFK Jr. was finally meeting the man who had so profoundly impacted his life, the lives of his family members – his mother, brothers and sisters, and literally millions of his father's loyal supporters in the US and abroad. It seemed that RFK Jr. was prepared to have a first-time and maybe a one-and-only conversation with the man out of his past who, by any reasonable measure, he was supposed to dislike, maybe even hate. He no doubt guessed that making that judgment would come later after the interview, if at all.

Presumably, during the interview, RFK Jr. had no set agenda other than perhaps a sharing of the ballistics report given to him by Paul Schrade and questioning Sirhan about the circumstantial facts connected to his father's death more than fifty-years before. As far as Sirhan's plan for the interview, he probably had no inkling of what he might expect during the questioning, or what the outcome might be. What he did know is that Sirhan had spent the last fifty-plus years in several California prisons convicted of killing the father of a man he would shortly shake hands with and warmly embrace.

In deference to RFK Jr. and Schrade's theory of the assassination, both assumed the existence of an active second gunman who actually inflicted the fatal shot to RFK. According to many eyewitnesses at the time of the rapid gun fire in the midst of chaos, Sirhan was physically positioned directly in front of RFK, making it physically almost impossible to effectuate an entry wound from the rear. So there were doubts in the inquiring minds of many people. Additional essential questions arose: Why was Sirhan even there? And more importantly, were co-conspirators involved in the assassination?

After his three-hour interview, combined with Mr. Schrade's dossier material, RFK Jr. said he arrived at the unforeseen conclusion that Sirhan did not murder his father! RFK Jr. told the *Washington Post* in 2018, "I went there because I was curious and disturbed by what I had seen in the evidence ... I was disturbed that the wrong person might have been convicted of killing my father."[8]

---

8   Jackman, T. (January 13, 2022). Calif. "Gov. Newsom Denies Parole for Sirhan Sirhan,

Subsequent to his face-to-face meeting with Sirhan, in a letter to the California Board of Parole Hearings, RFK Jr. stated he was "impressed by the genuineness of [Sirhan's] remorse for the indisputable part he played in my father's assassination. Sirhan wept, clenched my hand, and asked for forgiveness."

During his revealing interview with Sirhan, RFK Jr. altered his view of the convicted assassin, at least regarding Sirhan's role in firing the final shot. After RFK Jr. spent time with Sirhan, Lisa Pease shared what he said about Sirhan: "He's a sweet man. Bobby told me after his visit. Bobby took the time to learn the truth about this case. What he found moved him to action, and rightfully so."⁹

Quite possibly, victim number one, Schrade, who was reportedly shot first in the melee, had long been convinced that Sirhan did not act alone, nor did he fire the fatal shot ending RFK's life. It appears that RFK Jr. had positive truth-seeking intentions when he interviewed Sirhan and seemed to be on the right track (e.g., the second shooter notion), but what he couldn't have possibly known is that the man responding to his sympathetic questions in a prison interview room manifested two distinct personalities, as argued throughout this book. It is my belief, the Sirhan personality RFK Jr. interviewed constituted the non-dissociative Sirhan personality 1, the adjusted, charming, conforming, socially adjusted Sirhan represented himself as the supplicant, tearful person sitting in front of him.

The intensive interview with Sirhan must have resulted in an emotional catharsis for both men, affecting RFK Jr.'s surprising conclusion that Sirhan was only one of the assassins, and he didn't fire the deadly round that ended his father's life. Unfortunately for RFK Jr., he didn't know which of the two Sirhans participated in the assassination or in his prison conversation. And in a sense for RFK Jr. and additional interviewers (for instance, David Frost and Jack Perkins), the adjusted Sirhan did the talking. RFK Jr. was correct in his reasoning because it is disturbing to think after fifty-five years that the "wrong person might have been convicted of killing my father!"

Equally unfortunate is the fact that if both had become aware of Sirhan's five previously undiagnosed psychological conditions including the split personality (DID) that, in a strange way, RFK Jr. might have been able to realize that he wasn't actually having a conversation with the man (or his personality) who fired at his father.

Convicted of Robert F. Kennedy Assassination." *Washington Post.*
9   Pease. (2018). 500.

207

The killing of RFK generated innumerable conspiracy theories as to what really took place during the assassination. One theory became tightly focused on the second gunman possibility – presumably the logical interpretation arrived at by RFK Jr. after his intense meeting with Sirhan.

RFK Jr. was probably correct in his assumption that a second person or at least a second personality shot his father – but I am convinced that "second" person was not the man he interviewed, but rather Sirhan's dissociated personality pulled the trigger, shooting wildly at RFK. This view is a central focus in this cold case analysis.

This of course leads to the question, which Sirhan did RFK Jr. interview during his prison session? My guess is that he had an intense three-hour meeting with the adjusted Sirhan, who could provide little factual information about the assassination, because he didn't do it! RFK Jr., absent of any clinical data regarding the two Sirhans, had no way to authenticate which Sirhan was speaking with him.

RFK Jr.'s much-anticipated, prison conversation with Sirhan is strikingly similar to Dr. Harold T. Brown's interview with Billy Milligan, the man with twenty-four personalities. Because of his odd out-of-body behavior as a teenager, Billy was referred to a psychiatric clinic for assessment. On many occasions, Billy appeared to wander as if in a mental fog, indicative of a dissociated trance – a multiple personality.

Billy described this state: "Sometimes my body feels funny, like I'm light and airy. There are times I think I can fly. ... Hey, I'm the only kid who can take a trip without LSD."

According to one of Milligan's alter personalities, when Dr. Brown believed he was conducting a psychiatric interview with Billy, he was, in fact, talking to one of the alters. Of course, there was no way that either RFK, Jr. or Dr. Brown could have known at the time they were possibly talking to the wrong person![10]

The presence of a secondary gunman during RFK's assassination was supported by conspiracy theorists who argued that a part-time rent-a-cop providing security for the senator's entourage, Eugene Thane Cesar (Gene) was identified as the co-assassin, "hit man." This theory was advanced by some researchers and apparently endorsed by RFK Jr. An armed Cesar was in fact observed in close proximity to RFK, even guiding him by the arm as they entered the Ambassador Hotel's kitchen area. Cesar said he went directly behind RFK and took his right arm at the elbow

---

10   Keyes, D. (1982). *The Minds of Billy Milligan*. Bantom Books, A Division of Bantom Doubleday, New York, 177.

with his left hand, while the hotel's assistant maître d' was ahead, holding RFK's right hand. Cesar said, "I'm on the [right] side of him. And what I'm doing is taking my hand and pushing people back, because Kennedy was having a hard time walking forward."[11]

Based on my own findings, there has been no attempt to support or negate Cesar's complicity in the assassination, therefore his role as the second gunman cannot be ruled out. Several books devote great detail to the assassination, identifying Cesar as the second gunman. In one account, the author even claims that a witness to the assassination told an interviewer that Cesar had his gun drawn and pointing toward the floor where the senator had fallen: "Why was the gun pointing toward the fallen Kennedy and not at the suspect?"[12]

In his own words, Cesar said, "There were dozens of articles that have come out saying that I carried a second gun [a .22 caliber in addition to his service-issued .38 revolver] , and that I possibly could've been the person who shot Bobby Kennedy – because the bullet entered the back of his head. But I think that was more my problem than anything else – because of where I was standing."[13]

Shortly after doing his own research, RFK Jr. began informal negotiations with Cesar to interview him about what happened on June 5, 1968. However before RFK Jr. could do so, Cesar fled unexpectedly to the Philippines in 2018. In 2021, the *San Francisco Chronicle* reported that RFK Jr.'s communication with Cesar had somehow broken down. RFK Jr. stated, "I was in negotiations with him [Cesar] in 2018, before reports of his death in September 2019. After first agreeing to meet with me, he gradually escalated his price to $25,000 for the privilege of interviewing him."

RFK Jr. called for a new investigation into his father's assassination, saying, "I believe Cesar killed my father. He was in the exact position to fire the shots as described in the autopsy. Three witnesses saw him draw his gun, which he later admitted, and one said she saw him fire it ... I firmly believe the idea that Sirhan murdered my dad is a fiction that is impeding justice."

From an analysis of the physical positions of Cesar and RFK, Cesar was in an opportune shooting position to fire from behind, because witnesses placed him standing directly in back of RFK when the gun reports began. Unless Cesar left behind undiscovered notes, photos, a second gun, a confession, tape recordings, films, or other information preserved

11   Moldea. (2018). 153.
12   Pease. (2018), 216.
13   Moldea. (2018). 150.

for later scrutiny, whatever knowledge he had of the assassination, including his direct or indirect participation or whether he was part of a larger murder plot, unfortunately died with him.[14]

RFK, Jr.'s analysis of who really executed his father is supported by an earlier and credible source – the LA Country Coroner Office. The coroner who performed the autopsy on RFK, Dr. Thomas Noguchi became kind of a macabre celebrity, later becoming identified as the "coroner to the dead stars." In view of how the actual crime was committed, especially the delivery of the fatal shot done at close range from behind RFK's head, Dr. Noguchi based his contrarian opinion on a physical-geometric reconstruction of the how the physical shooting occurred. Dr. Noguchi stated, "...there was other evidence to challenge the belief that Sirhan acted alone."

For example, four bullets were fired at Kennedy: three of them struck him, and one passed harmlessly through his clothing. Five people behind Kennedy were also struck by bullets, which were recovered in their bodies. And three bullet holes were found in the ceiling. Thus, the tracks of twelve bullets were found at the scene, and Sirhan's gun contained only eight.

The controversy about how many shooters were in that crowded pantry, and which ones fired at RFK was addressed by Dr. Thomas Noguchi who conducted the autopsy on RFK. His forensic identification of unburned-powder grains, known as a tattoo pattern, on RFK's right ear provided an obvious clue for the coroner. During the autopsy he conducted, Dr. Noguchi noticed this gun residue tattoo pattern at the base of RFK's skull, suggesting that the fatal shot was fired at very close range. Sirhan was several feet away and directly in front of the senator.

Dr. Noguchi commented further, "I now knew the precise location of the murder weapon at the moment it was fired: one inch from the edge of his right ear, only three inches behind the head. But I also realized that this evidence seemed to exonerate Sirhan Sirhan."

Almost all the eyewitnesses offered their opinion that "Sirhan shot and fatally wounded Kennedy openly and brazenly from in front."

Moreover, from Dr. Noguchi's three-dimensional recreation of the crime scene, he stated that there could only be two possible scenarios to explain the assassination: "One, either Sirhan lunged toward Kennedy and fired, a move unseen by anyone, and then, as Kennedy spun, lunged

---

14   Robert F. Kennedy, Jr. (December 8, 2021)." Robert F. Kennedy, Jr.: Sirhan Sirhan Didn't Kill My Father. Gov. Newsom Should Set Him Free." *San Francisco Chronicle*, Opinion & Open Forum.

back to fire from farther away, a second move also invisible to all, or two, a second gunman triggered the first shots up close, ducked away, and then Sirhan fired the other bullets from three feet away as Kennedy turned."

In his final assessment of the second gun hypothesis, Dr. Noguchi waffled, saying, "My own professional instinct instructs me that Sirhan somehow killed Senator Kennedy alone" then added, "…none of the eyewitnesses saw what actually happened. But until more is positively known of what happened that night the existence of a second gunman remains a possibility. Thus I have never said that Sirhan Sirhan killed Robert Kennedy."[15]

Perhaps RFK Jr. was moved by the somewhat ambiguous position ultimately arrived at by Dr. Noguchi ("maybe he acted alone, or maybe there was a second shooter") or from the information given to him by Paul Schrade in making his decision to exonerate Sirhan from firing the deadly, back-of-the-head kill shot. Of extreme interest to me is to know what information not available to the public (perhaps classified records?) that RFK Jr. used to inform his decision, culminating in his partial exoneration of Sirhan.

In my view, the Sirhan who surely shot RFK Jr.'s father in 1968 was not the same man he interviewed in 2017.

The explanatory psychological information developed within this book remains available for recognition by those parties interested in the appeals process. The psychological opinions expressed herein concerning the two Sirhans can better enable RFK Jr. and other family members or interested parties to determine that, by following Sirhan's psychological footprints, we have a better pathway for learning who killed RFK, and why.

MORE PSYCHOLOGICAL CLUES TO SOLVING SIRHAN'S COLD CASE

Key to my interest in reopening Sirhan's complex case was my desire to look further into his psychiatric diagnoses or misdiagnoses, particularly after I watched his performances during several TV interviews (e.g., with British journalist David Frost, and with Jack Perkins of NBC-TV News, in the LA County Jail after Sirhan's conviction and death sentence decision) as well as several California Parole Hearing Board hearings. During these sometimes-intense interviews, Sirhan appeared perfectly lucid, clear-spoken, well-oriented, cognitively organized, and he reflected

---

15   Noguchi, T.T. and J. DiMona. (1983). *Coroner.* Simon and Schuster, New York, 103, 105, 108.

a fluid speaking style. Sirhan's verbal fluency was quite unlike psychiatric patients I have diagnosed as psychotic and treated in the half-dozen mental facilities I have worked in.

Sirhan adamantly continues to deny any recollection of the actual shooting of RFK. During one of his sixteen parole hearings, he said, "Every day of my life, I deeply regret that I participated in a deeply horrible event which took place in the pantry in the Ambassador Hotel where Senator Kennedy was assassinated. I don't remember that exact moment. The reality of all of it hit me when I was on death row."

Beyond Sirhan's denial of the precise facts at the assassination scene, he had no overt, symptomatic manifestations of the florid psychiatric indicators I was trained to clinically identify (profound hallucinations and disturbing delusions), usually evidenced by patients diagnosed with a serious psychiatric condition like schizophrenia. It seemed clear to me from the start that something was off the mark when diagnosing Sirhan with ill-defined psychotic conditions, but alternatively I wanted to know what appropriate diagnosis matched his traumatic history, presenting symptoms, and proven homicidal acting out?

When conducting this retrospective psychological research into Sirhan's personality, three clinical clues immediately came to my attention. The initial clue to Sirhan's confusing psychopathology was derived from Sirhan himself as he repeatedly claimed from the start that he had experienced large gaps in his autobiographical memory for critical events such as what really happened when he shot RFK.

Sirhan claimed that there were many, critical, experiential pieces of his life that over the years he just could not reconstruct – they just seemed to be wiped clean from his memory. One of these memory gaps concerned the various, extraordinary entries he made in the rambling diary or the notebooks he kept. A second clue derived from Sirhan's disturbed and traumatic childhood living in Palestine that can be fairly characterized by death and destruction related to the ongoing Arab-Israeli war.

Sirhan's troubled history reminded me of my work with traumatized veterans at the San Francisco Veterans Hospital. During my experience with ex-combat soldiers, I learned how traumatic events can often produce remarkable psychiatric conditions such as PTSD, and a variety of other dissociative disorders (e.g., DID). The third clue tied to the second one: recall interruption, focused on Sirhan's compromised memory tracking, a symptom of a dissociative disorder like DID (termed multiple personality disorder, MPD when Sirhan was diagnosed).

This third essential clue was based on the testimony presented by three diagnosing doctors who, after examining and testing Sirhan, believed he could be experiencing a nonpsychotic dissociative disorder. The *DSM-II*, used at the time, made a limited reference to a dissociative reaction as part of a hysterical neurosis, dissociative type (300.14): "In the dissociative type, alterations may occur in the patient's state of consciousness or his identity, to produce such symptoms as amnesia, somnambulism, fugue, and multiple personality." The *DSM-II* had no reference to a diagnostic category supporting a PTSD diagnosis.

Sirhan made many statements to defense and prosecution doctors about his personal sense of mental disorganization, and possible dissociative confusion concerning simple events in his life, especially the essential details on the night of RFK's murder, and the true authorship of his diary writings.

When asked about these simple life events, Sirhan evidenced blank stares and said, "I don't know," "I can't remember," "That's not him" [strange third person reference], and "It's not me!"

Referring to himself in the third person many times, Sirhan never provided direct answers to simple questions posed to him by doctors and attorneys.

After review of hundreds of hours of court testimony including Sirhan's, it occurred to me that Sirhan was experiencing a psychiatric disorder not previously diagnosed by the team of defense doctors, a condition that profoundly affected his behavior and memory, and negatively impacted his life, making it impossible for him to retrieve even simple facts that he was expected to have a fingertip command of. More specifically, Sirhan seemed to be experiencing a multiple personality disorder (MPD) condition, but not definitively diagnosed as such, yet in my opinion he had evolved into two separate personalities coexisting in one physical body.

To confirm this notion, I needed to provide empirical proof to substantiate Sirhan's MPD diagnosis. In 1969, MPD was a somewhat unique personality disorder, although if proved it could help explain many of Sirhan's odd (but not necessarily psychotic) symptoms such as his substantial memory lapses. For a considerable period of time, I suspected that it was possible that, based on severe psychological trauma endured as a child, Sirhan had retreated from ordinary reality and emerged into a split personality, similar in many aspects to the well-publicized case: *The Three Faces of Eve*, an important multiple personality case that came to the public's attention in 1957.

Even prior to my provisional diagnosis of MPD (now labeled DID), confirmation using three dissociative scales, I suspected that Sirhan had developed an independent second personality; a split, malevolent, alternative personality capable of doing bad things, including committing the cold-blooded murder of RFK. Based on the results of these three dissociative scales and the testimony of Dr. Schorr and Dr. Diamond, I identified Sirhan's two distinct personalities as: 1) the adjusted or core, overt, conforming Sirhan as personality 1; and 2) the covert, dissociative Sirhan as the malevolent personality 2. I used the descriptive terms (adjusted, overt, conforming, law-abiding, social, and passive) interchangeably to depict Sirhan's personality 1, "The good Sirhan." Likewise, the adjectival terms (dissociative, alter, hostile, malevolent, angry, and vindictive) are similarly used interchangeably to depict Sirhan's (alter) personality 2, "the bad Sirhan."

Equally as important, I presented psychological evidence to support Sirhan's second missing psychiatric diagnosis: complex post-traumatic stress disorder (C-PTSD). These two newly formulated diagnoses combined with erotomania-motivated murder formed Sirhan's core personality dynamics.

SIRHAN: A SPLIT PERSONALITY?

My clinical experience in diagnosing murderers strongly suggested that many offenders struggle continuously, at least on a conscious level, to ascertain the exact reasons for their criminality, or at best they offer simple far-reaching guesses (confabulations) for why they took the life of another person, which leads us back to the real reason Sirhan assassinated RFK.

Dr. Diamond's theory that Sirhan was in an undefined, altered state of consciousness when he pulled the trigger added support to Sirhan's not remembering certain facts. Dr. Diamond reported that only when Sirhan was in an altered state of hypnosis was he able to recall and simulate the reenactment of the complete murder act. My perspective here is that Sirhan initially began to experience feelings of "splitting off," ergo the emergence of the second Sirhan during his war-drenched childhood.

Dr. Chu, who has diagnosed and treated several hundred dissociative identity cases addressed this splitting process: "The child attempts to disown unwanted impulses and feelings by splitting them off and attributing them to another imagined being (e.g., "I didn't break Daddy's CDs. The bad girl did it!").... The disowned feelings, impulses, and behaviors, are eventually spontaneously integrated into the child's psyche and sense of self as the child begins to achieve control of them. If seen in adulthood, imaginary companionship would be considered pathological as a kind of dissociative identity disorder."[16]

During his testimony, Dr. Diamond alluded to his clinical impression that Sirhan was experiencing a divided awareness or two distinct states of consciousness: "the usual Sirhan" (having full conscious awareness and recall of life events), and "the dissociated Sirhan" (where many of his memory events were unavailable while he was in a non-altered state). Although the psychiatric symptomology of Sirhan being in two states of consciousness was clinically supportable, Dr. Diamond did not come right out and diagnose Sirhan with MPD. However, based on my reassessment of new psychological evidence brought to light concerning dissociative personality disorders, this helps to fill in many of the unresolved aspects in Sirhan's complicated split personality case.[17]

Dr. Diamond came so close to applying the MPD diagnosis to characterize Sirhan as capable of mentally operating within two separate states of reality, possibly mutually exclusive from each other. Because this revised psychiatric diagnosis of Sirhan is explanatory, this interpretation takes us a long way into explaining Sirhan's variable memory deficits when interrogated about specific events he alleged to not recall.

Sirhan was either unable to understand the meaning of simple questions, or maybe he failed to supply well-thought-out responses, because the answers required a complete, memory base unavailable to him at the time. This suggests that Sirhan possibly had no idea how to answer the inquiries because the information requested from him remained in a dissociated memory bank, and when asked to respond he was in a non-altered, conscious state of mind – the notion that was marginally approached by Dr. Diamond.

During direct examination by Grant Cooper, Sirhan was questioned about the events as he recalled them on June 4, 1968, until the early morning of June 5 when RFK was shot. Cooper queried Sirhan about his activities when he entered the Ambassador Hotel. Sirhan repeated his statement that he was intoxicated from the Tom Collins alcoholic drinks he consumed at the Max Rafferty celebration prior to finding the Kennedy victory party. Sirhan claimed all he wanted was strong coffee with cream and lots of sugar to sober up.

16   Chu, J.A. (2011). *Rebuilding Shattered Lives: Treating Complex PTSD and Dissociative Disorders*. John Wiley & Sons, Inc. Hoboken, NJ, 49.
17   DSM-5-TR. (2022).

Mr. Cooper: "Now, you heard the testimony in here of at least a dozen witnesses I suppose."

Sirhan: "Yes."

Mr. Cooper: "That you were standing in the pantry."

Sirhan: "That is what I later learned in this court, Sir–"

Mr. Cooper: "That you walked up to Senator Kennedy and put a gun toward his head, possibly within an inch or two, and you pulled the trigger, and he eventually died?"

Sirhan: "Yes. I was told this."

Mr. Cooper: "Now, you believe it is true?"

Sirhan: "Obviously, Sir."

When Cooper asked Sirhan, "Did you know in the early morning hours, that is after midnight of the 4th and early morning hours of the 5th of June, that you had shot Senator Kennedy?," Sirhan gave a puzzling answer, "No, Sir, I did not."[18]

If this is representative of Sirhan's faulty memory and does not establish a pattern of deception, there must be a reason he has alleged all these years that he cannot recall important information that could cast light on this important murder case. The theory advanced here rests on the psychological premise that Sirhan's memory, in particular his autobiographical recall, became divided or cleaved into two separate parts based on his personality split.

The two Sirhan personalities, as far as I can determine, were independent from one another; separate psychological, cognitive and emotional entities; each with their own domain of autobiographical experience and separate memory histories. Sometimes these two states operated completely independently and, at other times, some memories spilled over into and were mutually shared between the two personalities.

Even as extensive and in depth as eight hypnotic trance sessions were with Dr. Diamond, experts for the defense and prosecution teams were left wondering why Sirhan couldn't even answer simple questions that could have helped his case. His vagueness went to his credibility as a witness in his own behalf.

During his seminars at Berkeley, Dr. Diamond discussed the complicated psychiatric bases underlying the case of *The Faces of Eve*. He was aware that in certain criminal cases, an insanity motion predicated on a multi-

---

18   Trial Vol 18, 5213–5232, March 6, 1969.

ple personality diagnosis had been used unsuccessfully in other criminal cases. For example, F. Lee Bailey, recognized as one of the nation's top criminal lawyers, used this defense in the Boston Strangler case of Albert DeSalvo, two years before the LA trial of Sirhan. DeSalvo was accused of, but not convicted of, strangling thirteen women in eastern Massachusetts and a state psychiatrist diagnosed DeSalvo as a schizophrenic with a split personality. After Sirhan's arrest, during a brief conversation with police, it was apparent to Officer Frank Foster, who was assigned to surveil Sirhan after his arrest, that Sirhan had read about or had knowledge of the Boston Strangler case, because DeSalvo's name came up. DeSalvo's name is also referenced in Sirhan's diary.

Dr. Diamond described how altered states of awareness could coexist in one person psychologically operating simultaneously on two different conscious levels without mutual disclosure – one personality really didn't know what the other one was doing. Using an MPD defense to account for Sirhan's wild personality swings from being a "nice guy to an inexplicable assassin" sounded like a fit.

Dr. Diamond struggled during his testimony to convey that Sirhan couldn't remember certain facts because his memory did not first record them. Fitts asked Dr. Diamond, "Did Sirhan have true amnesia at the time he shot Kennedy?"

"Yes," Dr. Diamond responded, "I think this was a true amnesia at the time he shot Kennedy.... He does not remember, in his conscious state, the shooting of Kennedy. He does remember, in a hypnotic state, the shooting of Kennedy."

Even so, Dr. Diamond's opinion about Sirhan's amnesic episodes remained troubling to him. In trying to explain it, he concluded that Sirhan had been in a trance, and unknowingly programmed himself to murder RFK, and unknowingly programmed himself to forget his crime, "a feat regarded as next to impossible by leading experts in the field of hypnosis." Diamond's "entire testimony teetered on this precarious point."[19]

Fitts continued, "If Sirhan was truly forgetful of the incidents relative to the immediate killing of RFK, should he not have inquired of the police why he was in custody and what he had done?"

Dr. Diamond said, "That's not how dissociative states respond to police apprehension. I have some familiarity with dissociative states [from arrestees] as they are arrested and what happens to them, and they do not, like in Hollywood movies, look around with a blank expression on their

---

19   Klaber and Melanson. (1997), 224.

faces and say, 'Where am I?' From my study of Sirhan's behavior following his being taken to jail, I think it is characteristic of this type of slow emergence from a state of dissociation. ..."

Dr. Diamond further differentiated a dissociated state from a schizophrenic reaction, and whether these dissociated states were the product of a highly hysterical reaction or of schizophrenia, saying, "I was quite satisfied that the clinical condition was of a dissociated state, not hysterical. ..."[20]

Fitts then delved into the details of the conversations when the group of defense doctors and one prosecution expert, Dr. Pollack, shared their respective, but divergent diagnostic opinions as to "what made Sirhan tick" at the February 2, 1969, case conference (or "roundtable" as it was called). Mr. Fitts read Dr. Diamond's summary comments to the court, pertaining to his diagnosis of Sirhan, favoring a primary diagnosis of a dissociated state, rather than a pure psychosis or schizophrenia. Then directing a question to Dr. Diamond, Fitts began, "Now, in my book this all adds up to hysteria."

Dr. Diamond said, "At the same time I am quite aware of the relationship between hysteria to psychosis, the theories that you know they have found, hysterical dissociation states with psychotic or schizophrenic trends. But all my clinical material points largely to this dissociative-hysterical, rather than a psychotic picture. I picked up a lot of paranoid stuff. To me the paranoid material is not terribly out of proportion to the sociocultural background, the environmental circumstances, the childhood trauma."

Fitts pressed, "I'll ask you again, Doctor; you had the benefit of all this material [from the conference] you have summarized for us, you had your clinical impressions based on the number of hours with the defendant, isn't that true?"

Dr. Diamond answered, "That it was not true."[21]

Apparently, after creating some controversy during his testimony and probably in concert with the defense attorneys, Dr. Diamond hastily drafted a rebuttal to his own testimony that he was about to present during redirect by defense attorney Berman.

Berman realized that part of Dr. Diamond's prior testimony needed clarification of some defense statements and the questionable inclusion of a prosecution doctor (Pollack) in the roundtable. Mr. Berman entered into a long discussion of that testimony as he spelled out Dr. Diamond's words verbatim for the jury.

---

20   Trial Vol 25, 7186–7198, March 27, 1969.
21   Ibid.

He read, "I agree that this is an absurd and preposterous story [Sirhan's], unlikely and incredible. I doubt that Sirhan himself agrees with me as to how everything happened. Sirhan prefers to deny his mental illness, his psychological disintegration, his trances, his automatic writing and his automatic shooting. He does this successfully through his loss of memory. I doubt that he believes to this day that I ever succeeded in putting him into a hypnotic trance. I doubt that he believes that it was truly his writing in the notebook threatening the assassination of Robert Kennedy."

Berman asked, "Now in that context, that is what you really referred to when you were on the witness stand?"

Dr. Diamond attempted to clarify, "I have stated that this is an absurd, preposterous story, unlikely and incredible, which is extraordinary and possibly, in a unique case such as Sirhan's, does raise the gravest probe of clinical proof and credibility … I was not, however, prepared for what I discovered, those stirring instances of correspondence courses, hypnosis, dissociated trances, and mystical occultism of the Rosicrucian mind power and black magic, and this type of psychological thinking could have resulted in the death of Senator Kennedy."

Despite an interjection by lead defense attorney Cooper, and then in agreement by prosecuting attorney Howard and Judge Walker, Dr. Diamond was allowed to continue, "In my opinion, this is the ultimate preposterous absurdity of it, and it is too illogical even for the theater of the absurd. I have investigated Sirhan's mind in every psychiatric means within my power, and I have related my findings; and upon them I base my opinion that Sirhan Bishara Sirhan's mental capacity as required by the legal definition of the crime of murder, I have little expectation of the belief, but I think it would be important that there exist this full record of how this assassination of Robert Kennedy came about…"

Howard interrupted, asking, "Did you just read something?"

Dr. Diamond said, "Part of it, yes."

Berman then asked, "When did you write it?"

Dr. Diamond answered, "Last night about midnight."

Whatever Dr. Diamond had in mind around midnight the night before, his final court appearance to explain his more-or-less trivialized characterization of Sirhan's psychiatric status as "absurd and preposterous" missed the credibility target. As guided by Berman, who seemingly could not formulate a cogent question to help clarify what Dr. Diamond's real intent was, Dr. Diamond quite possibly worsened an already bad impression. Berman had choked during his redirect examination of his own expert who appeared dumbfounded and confused by the questions posed to him.

He tried a third time to make sense of Dr. Diamond's portrayal of the assassination as essentially "absurd and preposterous." For the final time, Dr. Diamond struggled to provide an answer that would be convincing to the jury. Again he tried to explain what exactly he meant. "It's unlikely nature, Mr. Berman," Dr. Diamond replied coolly, clearly not pleased by this latest gaffe. "To me this is a script which would never be acceptable in a class-B motion picture; and yet these are the realities of the psychiatric findings."

Dr. Diamond descended from the witness stand clearly shaken from this maladroit performance. "He had been brought back to make a final impression on the jury, but whatever enlightenment the doctor was to impart was overshadowed by defense attorney Berman's inept performance. This was not a good ending, particularly for someone who had been the defendant's most important witness."[22]

Dr. Diamond's controversial wrapping up of Sirhan's psychiatric case was one more unforced error by the defense team, resting firmly on the shoulders of Berman, who should have known better.

Grant Cooper was also not pleased with this outcome, preferring that the defense delve more into Dr. Diamond's, or another defense doctor's, conception of Sirhan's dissociated states. The defense was losing critical points with the jury.

Oddly enough, Dr. Martin Schorr's testimony supported and, to a degree, vindicated Dr. Diamond's dissociated state hypothesis. Turner and Christian recapped Dr. Diamond's assessment: "So Sirhan, in Diamond's opinion, was a kind of automatic assassin, dissociated, a dual personality acting on both the conscious and subconscious levels, the subconscious being in control when he fired [at RFK]."[23]

Sirhan's so-termed dual personality structure was continuously debated throughout the trial, with defense Drs. Diamond and Schorr, in agreement with the psychiatric concept; and prosecution doctors, Marcus and Pollack, dissenting. During two later interviews in 1993 with William Klaber at California's Corcoran State Prison, Sirhan's duality was addressed. Describing his feelings toward RFK, Sirhan told Klaber, "I saw him as a caring, genteel person who stood up for the downtrodden, the blacks, the Latinos. ..."

---

22   Klaber and Melanson. (1997). 226.
23   Turner, W. and J. Christian. (1993). *The Assassination of Robert Kennedy: The Conspiracy & Coverup.* Carroll & Graf Publishers: An Imprint of Avalon Publishing Group, Inc., New York, 199.

When asked about the assassination, Sirhan continued, "Clearly I was there, but still it's a mystery, because I really don't have it in me to kill anyone – drunk or not. That's what I don't understand."

"In the space of twenty minutes, Sirhan has just demonstrated the strange duality of mind that he has consistently maintained.... On the one hand, he doesn't remember planning to kill Robert Kennedy and can't imagine performing the act, on the other, he believes that he murdered Robert Kennedy because he was a threat to the Palestinians. Which is the real Sirhan?"[24]

Sirhan reported his presence at the Ambassador Hotel as if he were wandering in a drunken fog, a trance state, or in a dissociative state taken over by his malevolent personality 2.

I don't believe Sirhan was a victim of self-induced or occult-influenced, altered states of consciousness, but rather a personality schism leading to the dissociative identity disorder diagnosis that could have been made, but wasn't. At points, several doctors, including Dr. Diamond, came close to making the same provisional dissociative diagnosis (MPD), reaching the same conclusion that Sirhan's personality was divided or simply split, manifesting into two segmented parts.

Sirhan's DID condition reflects what Farrell terms "the alter-in-control system," signifying that the "alter" dominating personality was in charge during the commission of a criminal offense. Farrell cited the DID case of a serial rapist, Billy Milligan, who was found not guilty by reason of insanity in Ohio ten years after Sirhan's trial and conviction. The court ruled that Milligan "was insane due to lack of one integrated personality, and therefore not culpable of the crimes he committed."[25]

Specifically, the court stated, "That by reason, respondent having been diagnosed as a multiple personality, his treatment should be consistent with such diagnosis ... and that respondent, due to mental illness, is dangerous to himself and to others, and therefore requires hospitalization in a maximum security facility."[26]

"TWO HEADS" ARE BETTER THAN ONE?
THE CONFUSING DIAGNOSIS OF MPD

At that time Sirhan was diagnosed, the 1968 *DSM-II* was comprised of only 134 pages, as compared with 1,050 pages in the 2022 *DSM-*

---

24   Klaber and Melanson. (1997). 331.
25   Farrell, H.M. "Dissociative identity disorder: No excuse for criminal activity." *Current Psychiatry*, 2011 June: 10 (6) : 33–40. https://www.mdedge.com/psychiatry/article/64330/personality-disorders/dissociative-identity-identity-disorder-no-excuse-criminal?reg=1
26   Keyes. (1982). 407.

5-TR edition. In 1968, the *DSM-II,* the diagnostic manual used to classify Sirhan's disorders, covered a relatively limited classification of mental disorders, excluding a direct reference to MPD. As mentioned, the only *DSM-II* reference to a dissociative condition classified it under the category of hysterical neurosis (300.1) "characterized by an involuntary loss or disorder of function. Symptoms characteristically begin and end suddenly in emotionally charged situations and are symbolic of the underlying conflicts. Often they can be modified by suggestion alone." This was a new diagnosis that encompassed the *DSM-I* diagnoses of conversion reaction and dissociative reaction.

The *DSM-II* referenced hysterical neurosis as a dissociative type 300.14: "In the dissociative type, alterations may occur in the patient's state of consciousness or his identity, to produce such symptoms as amnesia, somnambulism, fugue, and multiple personality." The 2022 *DSM-5-TR,* devotes a compete chapter to dissociative disorders, subclassifying DID (formerly MPD).

Table 1. Defining Symptoms in the DID Diagnosis
Defining symptoms in the DID diagnosis include:
A) Identity disruption characterized by two or more distinct personality states.
B) Recurrent gaps in recalling everyday events, important information, and/or traumatic events (inconsistent with ordinary forgetting).
C) Symptoms cause clinically significant distress or impairment in important areas of functioning.
D) The disturbance is not a normal part of a typical cultural or religious practice.
E) Symptoms are not attributable to the physiological effects of a substance (i.e., alcohol) or medical condition (i.e., seizures).

Although capable of diagnosing the more obvious forms of DID, the 2022 edition fell short in providing definitive diagnostic criteria necessary to make a truly accurate diagnosis of the disorder.

Dr. Daniel Brown, another diagnosing forensic psychologist who spent almost ten years assessing Sirhan intermittently, felt that he could not make a full DID diagnosis given the cookbook limitations imposed by the DSM.

Over the years, additional diagnosticians in psychology and psychiatry have taken issue with DSM's listed diagnostic criteria necessary for a DID diagnosis. For example, Dr. Ralph Allison, a forensic psychiatrist and expert on dissociative states, told me, "This academic criteria in the DSM to diagnose multiple personality syndrome has really never caught up with what we clinicians have found with our patients in the real world, and this applies to when and how many personalities emerge and the extent of their emergence as distinct entities emerging either spontaneously or when induced."

Although this diagnostic controversy concerning the labeling of a DID patient continues, i.e., exactly how many emergent, alter personalities are required to make a professional judgment, Dr. James Chu, a researcher into dissociative states and the author of *Rebuilding Shattered Lives,* agrees with Dr. Allison's opinion that when a second personality is evident, separate from the host personality, a DID exists.[27]

Dr. Allison added, "The DSM criteria has always been a problem because it was drafted by a group of academic researchers at the American Psychiatric Association, who had never even seen or treated a multiple as I have and I suspect you have. I have written extensive letters to APA study group who put together the dissociative identity disorder diagnosis and questioned the necessity of two additional personalities because that would make three – kind of like the three faces of Eve. Their criteria makes little sense to me."[28]

Dr. Allison also pointed out that even though the *DSM-5-TR* DID diagnosis does provide some latitude to clinicians making the decision to diagnose a patient with a dissociative disorder, the manual does not adequately spell out defining criteria necessary to separate a real dissociative patient from a feigned or false positive patient.

Based on the confusing language, Sirhan apparently would not meet the full *DSM-5-TR* criterion of "Disruption of identity characterized by two or more distinct personality states."

Based on the methodological proof presented here, using three dissociative rating scales and information gathered from a wide variety of primary sources, Sirhan clearly demonstrated at least one separate and distinct alter personality that occasionally manifested itself, although there may have been additional personalities yet to be uncovered; but whether they exist is not known at this time.

As an example, when we look back at Thigpen and Cleckley's (*The 3 Faces of Eve*) definitive investigation into Eve White's splitting into an independent second alter personality (Eve Black), tracing of the emergence

---

27   Personal communication from Dr. James Chu, February 2, 2023.

28   Personal communication from Dr. Ralph Allison, Sept 27, 2022.

of her alter personalities did not appear simultaneously. In fact, only after more than a year of psychiatric treatment did Eve Black suddenly come out. Thigpen and Cleckley described how Eve Black evolved when Eve White showed up for a therapy session seeming different, not herself, seductive, flamboyant, and displaying an impish smile, and she declared, "I know you real well, Doc ... lots better than she knows you ... and I kind of like you."

The doctor inquired further: "Well, who are you?"

"Why I'm Eve Black," she answered. "I'm me, and she's herself," she added. "I like to live, and she don't!"

Sometime later, another alter personality, Jane, came out, and finally Mrs. Evelyn Lancaster, emerged as a final and unanticipated personality.[29]

As Eve White's treatment progressed, Eve Black revealed herself more to the doctors. Thigpen and Cleckley did not hesitate to make a MPD diagnosis soon after Eve White's (host) personality split into the second, Eve Black. The third personality, Jane, emerged later, then surprisingly came a fourth, Evelyn. When considering the existence of what I conceive of as "two Sirhans," the adjusted Sirhan (personality 1) versus the altered Sirhan (personality 2) should be consistent with and reflect the *DSM-5-TR* diagnosis of DID.

Cautionary guidelines in the *DSM-5-TR* are set up to resolve this issue about a "magic number" of personalities necessary to make a differential diagnosis. "[The] DSM can serve clinicians as a guide to identify the most prominent symptoms that should be assessed when diagnosing a disorder. Although some mental disorders may have well-defined boundaries around symptom clusters, scientific evidence now places many, if not most, disorders on a spectrum with closely related disorders that have shared symptoms. ..."

It seems the identification of a true DID can be interpreted on a linear symptom spectrum, dependent on perhaps the number of emergent symptoms or isolated personalities reflected in the patient.

Sirhan's strange dual personalities, over an extended period of time, first emerged during the military turmoil he witnessed in childhood between Israeli and Arab forces just prior to the Six-Day War. At that point in his dissociative-riddled life, Sirhan unconsciously created an alternate existence or personality to simply cope, hoping that his new formulated self would provide more strength to mediate the traumas until they passed.

---

29   Thigpen and Cleckley. (1957). 25.

Sadly, just the opposite occurred: His alter personality began to incorporate and absorb the negative and even violent characteristics associated with the persecutors who had caused him indelible pain. During the next years of his life, Sirhan's newly formulated criminogenic self-identity sought prominence. The safety from what he perceived as a continuously dangerous world never developed.

This psychiatric evidence to support Sirhan's dissociative disorder is based on the doctors' clinical observations and diagnoses of Sirhan, on the results of the intensive psychological testing results, as well as direct interview information derived from his family members, associates, and friends. Dr. Martin Schorr, who used psychometric assessment tools to evaluate Sirhan, was in a favorable position to support my assumptions concerning Sirhan's dissociative symptomology. This differential diagnosis is also based on the three rating scales I applied to Sirhan's well-documented biographical information of multiple exposures to traumatic, life-changing events.

Unlike Dr. Allison, I am not the psychologist to try to unravel the confusing DSM dissociative identity disorder diagnosis. Dr. Brown spent multiple contact hours with Sirhan in three separate California penal settings, subjecting Sirhan to a series of psychological assessment tools to confirm or disconfirm whether Sirhan had, in fact, experienced a dissociative condition. When analyzing his results, he definitively concluded that Sirhan did not meet the diagnostic criteria for a dissociative disorder, although Dr. Brown believed that this altered state of consciousness could be hypnotically or synthetically induced and was resistant to spontaneous or non-hypnotic switching does not negate the possibility of Sirhan's second personality spontaneously switching.

Dr. Brown stated, "In subsequent direct interviews with Mr. Sirhan, I directly observed Mr. Sirhan a number of times switch into at least one distinctively different alter personality state, a personality state that responds in a robot-like fashion upon cue. ... This altered personality state only occurs while Mr. Sirhan is in a hypnotic or self-hypnotic state, and only in response to certain cues. This state never spontaneously manifests. While in this altered personality state, Mr. Sirhan shows both a loss of executive control and complete amnesia."

Additional psychologists enjoined the DID controversy. For example, according to Konovitz, et al.: "Every person with DID has a unique and complex internal system. The variety of personalities and the way they interact characterize each person's system. Every system is composed of one host, who is in control most of the time, and at least one [alter] alternate personality.… The initial separation of personalities (splitting) is induced by a traumatic event.… Each alternative personality performs a defined set of psychological tasks. The alters created and the tasks they are assigned are unique to each personality system."[30]

The conditional diagnosis I made of Sirhan's DID appears consistent with these researchers to the extent that the emergence of one additional personality within the total personality system is requisite to make the DID diagnosis according to Konovitz.

Dr. Brown and I appear to be in agreement that, regardless of the hypnotic spontaneity connected to the switching process, Sirhan had developed at least one additional, second, distinct alter early in his life. Nevertheless my clinical position remains unchanged, validating my premise that there were in fact two Sirhans.

Moreover, my professional position is more closely aligned to the interpretation of a linear or serial progression of emergent or switched personalities (e.g., one after another) proposed by Konovitz, et al. Another researcher, Dell, provides the tortured historical analysis of the deliberations and debates within the American Psychiatric Association subcommittee that formulated the diagnostic criteria for inclusion of MPD in *DSM-III, DSM-III-R* and *DSM-IV.* He argued that these successive sets of diagnostic criteria for MPD (DID, *DSM-5-TR*) have consistently presented only a vague structural criterion for its diagnosis, rather than a more typical set of shared clinical signs and symptoms. He believes the DSM continues to use a primitive set of unworkable diagnostic criteria probably of little value to clinicians or dissociative patients.

Based on my research into the Sirhan case, I acknowledge that the DSM criteria are user-unfriendly, unnecessarily controversial, and ensure the under-diagnosis of DID conditions, producing an artificially low base rate. Dell's research also shows that a DID condition can be efficiently diagnosed solely on the basis of its characteristic pattern of historic dissociative symptoms without the need for a clinician to independently determine the presence of two or more distinct identities or personality states.[31]

Dr. Numan Gharaibeh, a psychiatrist who works with dissociative patients, put it this way, "What is it about dissociative identity disorder (DISSOCIATIVE) that makes it a polarizing diagnosis? Why does it split

30   Konovitz, J.R., B.S. Konovitz, and P.P. Block. (1998) "Witnesses With Multiple Personality Disorder." In Sabra Owens, Diagnostic Evidence Admissibility and Multiple Personality Defense, I J. *Health Care Law & Policy.* 236. http://digitalcommeons.law.umaryland.edu/jhelp.vol

31   Dell, P.F. (2009). *The Long Struggle to Diagnose Multiple Personality Disorder* (MPD): MPD. In Dell, P.F. and J.A. O'Neil (Eds.), *Dissociation and the Dissociative Disorders: DSM-V and Beyond* (338–402). Rutledge/Taylor & Francis Group.

professionals into believers and nonbelievers, stirring up heated debates, high emotions, and fervor similar to what we see in religion? ... Proponents and opponents claim to have the upper hand in arguments about the validity of the dissociative diagnosis and benefits vs. harm of treatment."[32]

REACHING OUT TO THE OTHER SIDE

The application of and confidence in forensic hypnosis grew in the 1960s as memory retrieval systems became better refined. Dr. Diamond's probing of Sirhan's memory became a cornerstone in the case, because that was how he attempted to pull together the critical pieces of Sirhan's pre-crime mindset. He used Sirhan's autobiographical memory as an important aspect in the case, leaning toward the memory construct, and interpreting it as a tape recording that perfectly preserved past recollections, and capable of replay, similar to a tape recorder.

Notwithstanding the debate surrounding the use of forensic hypnosis in the courtroom, Judge Walker allowed Dr. Diamond to present copious testimony concerning Sirhan's responses recorded during his hypnotic sessions. The results of those sessions helped form many of Dr. Diamond's diagnostic conclusions as to Sirhan's mental status, including why there were so many obvious gaps in Sirhan's memory.

Dr. Diamond's testimony about what Sirhan told him under hypnosis was never challenged by the prosecution's attorneys using the applicable standards for the admissibility of evidence in a superior court, i.e., the Rules of Evidence. At the time of Sirhan's trial, the California Supreme Court was still being guided by the 1923 Frye Standard. This evidentiary test was the first ruling used to evaluate a witness's admissibility of scientific evidence, presumably including psychiatric results admitted in a California trial.

In California, the Frye decision quickly became known as the general acceptance test. "The use of a new or unique scientific technique, methodology, or system was inadmissible until the advocate clearly established that the scientific technique, methodology, or system had achieved reliability within the scientific community." The District of Columbia Circuit Court, "held that the expert testimony must be based on scientific methods that are sufficiently established and accepted."[33]

---

32   Gharaibeh, N. (2009). "Dissociative Identity Disorder: Time to Remove it From the DSM-V?" *Current Psychiatry*, September, 30–36.
33   Frye V. United States, 293 F, 1013, DC Cir., 1923.

From the outset of Sirhan's turbulent trial, all parties involved knew he had some buried secrets and even darker motives – but what were they and how can they be diagnosed? The problem was that they could not agree on the nature of those hidden, malevolent factors lying deep within the immature twenty-four-year-old's mind. Something was psychologically, terribly wrong with Sirhan, and no one seemed to be able to agree what psychiatric diagnosis or diagnoses best explained his behavior and a dark turn necessitating the use of violence.

Dr. Diamond guided Sirhan into multiple hypnotic states where isolated thoughts perhaps too painful were unavailable in Sirhan's conscious awareness. Dr. Diamond also realized that traditional forms of simple "talk therapy" as an informational gathering technique was simply not the method of choice, not designed to plumb the deepest reaches of a patient's functioning, where Dr. Diamond wanted to go.

Naturally, explaining a criminal's behavior is always problematic and challenging, often focusing on the most apparent causal reasons, and not searching for the real or hidden causes. Sirhan's case is a good example of the reductionist perspective where everyone (the prosecution and defense) seemingly agreed on a single cause: Sirhan acted because of his hatred for Israel and RFK's threat to send fifty bombers to Israel to be used against his people, the Arabs. This non-psychological political theory of causality provided a commonality that may be more grounded in misguided information than in psychological fact.

Dr. Diamond testified, "Through self-hypnosis, Sirhan B. Sirhan programmed himself 'like computer' to assassinate Senator Robert F. Kennedy.... The combination of events which led to the assassination of Robert F. Kennedy by Sirhan, I think, started with Sirhan's exposure to violence and death in Jerusalem in 1948, and it continued with his immigration to the United States, the development of his mental illness in which his whole personality altered and he became preoccupied with revolution, violence, destruction, paranoid fantasies of glory, power, and becoming the savior of his people. As his delusional fantasies grew bolder, his fanatical hatred and fear of the Jews increased with each radio and television broadcast concerning the tension in the Middle East, while in real life, Sirhan was withdrawing into a ruminative, brooding, isolated sense of failure and insignificance."[34]

---

34   News Release, Office of the District Attorney, The Hall of Justice, Los Angeles, CA, Wednesday, April 2, 1969.

Dr. Diamond continued to demonstrate the validity of the hypnotic trances. He gave Sirhan a posthypnotic suggestion, a form of programming that, when in a waking state, if the doctor reached for his pocket handkerchief, Sirhan immediately began to climb the bars in his jail cell like a monkey. After a demonstration of this, when asked what or why he was doing this, Sirhan claimed that he just needed the exercise. Dr. Diamond considered these as moments of insight for Sirhan, who was finally convinced that this hypnotic experience was for real. Mission accomplished for the moment.

Dr. Diamond tested Sirhan's hypnotizability in other ways. For instance, he instructed Sirhan to respond to the posthypnotic suggestion that when he arose from the trance that his arms would appear paralyzed and he could feel nothing. At first, Sirhan did not realize that he was responding to this command that his arm was paralyzed until he reached for his cigarette or match and, much to his surprise, he had no feeling in his hand and could not complete his task.

Under hypnosis, Sirhan provided Dr. Diamond with a loose chronology of events according to his best recall. He had to judge the veracity of what Sirhan said to see how it squared with other sources of information he had consulted. Dr. Diamond wanted to determine if Sirhan's amnesia was genuine or a product of his blocked memory recall.

To clear and unblock Sirhan's informational blockage, Dr. Diamond turned to a technique he used during World War II to treat US combat victims. He referred to this technique as aberration, the attempt to retrieve information by hypnotically taking the patient or combat veteran back in time to confront the trauma-causing current memory distortion or memory ablation. He explained to the jury how using the aberration technique could be equally effective in treating alcoholics and schizophrenic patients by bringing repressed memories back into full conscious awareness.[35]

As time passed, the technique of aberration became more commonly known as hypnotic age regression and memory retrieval or enhancement, was so controversial and under attack from the professional psychiatric community that Dr. Diamond took a professional risk, just as he did by venturing into the controversial area of dissociative states.

Dr. Diamond explained the importance of the true recovered memory process: "So, again I only want to emphasize that in producing this, you can't just hypnotize the person, but you have got to feed him, you have

---

35   Trial Vol 24, 6935, March 24, 1969.

to urge him." "You are right here, you are there, Sirhan, in the kitchen [in the Ambassador Hotel], look around you;" "You have to sort of play into the individual's unconscious and make him believe you are suggesting it happened right now, and not just recover as a memory, and then you evaluate the experience as to whether you, in your opinion, feel that it is a true story and what would happen. So on January 26, I took Sirhan step by step through all the events at the Ambassador on the night of June 4 and 5. Consciously we had taken him through (you will recall there was a missing part) again when he went back to the car and decided he was too drunk to drive, too tired, and he thought he went back to the hotel, and then he thought he had some coffee, and the next thing they were chocking him."[36]

Only under hypnosis was Sirhan able to recreate the chaotic scene at the Ambassador Hotel as RFK approached him when he drew his gun and fired. During this hypnotic reenactment scene, Sirhan acted like he pulled an imaginary gun out of his belt (proof that he had secreted it), and simulated repeatedly shooting the senator, over and over again, shouting, "You son of a bitch!"

Dr. Diamond indicated that this was the first indication from any source that confirmed what actually occurred at the time of the assassination. At the termination of the hypnotic session, Sirhan maintained that he had no recollection of this pivotal reenactment episode, only alluding to his suspicion that, as Dr. Diamond said, "we were bugging him, that we were playing tricks on him; and Sirhan knew nothing about the reenactment of the experience."

THE THREE FACES OF EVE VERSUS THE TWO SIRHANS

When Dr. Diamond described Sirhan's dissociated states, he seemed to connect them proximately to around the time of the assassination – April-June 1968. Whereas his conception of Sirhan's episodes of dissociation were framed more within a restricted time period, on the other hand, Dr. Schorr believed (as I do) that Sirhan's dissociated states had deep historical roots in his troubled background.

Dr. Schorr introduced the diagnostic context of MPD, referencing the book, *The 3 Faces of Eve*. Dr. Schorr accurately portrayed that the two original Eves (Eve White and Eve Black) unfolded serially, not at the same time, which supported my provisional DID diagnosis. During Thigpen and Cleckley's portrayal of *The 3 Faces of Eve*, Eve's two personalities were

36   Ibid.

diametrically different from each other, a connection that supports the validity of Sirhan's two split personalities.

Responding to prosecutor Howard's question, "The dissociated state occurs before the shooting of Kennedy?," Dr. Schorr said, "Yes, many times.... Well, this is a problem with the dissociative reaction potential. Given the conditions of stress that have been outlined in this case, this man has a facile capacity to dissociate."

When interviewed by Berman, Dr. Schorr clarified what he psychologically conceived of as Sirhan's dissociative states, likening them to a Dr. Jekyll/Mr. Hyde. "He doesn't really split off, but he does what we call in the trade 'dissociation.'"

Dr. Schorr continued, "It's sort of like what you would expect to find in a kind of a Jekyll/Hyde personality – one person doesn't know that the other exists, and vice versa." He then referred to the study Thigpen and Cleckley did in the 1950s on a personality that showed dissociative states, and he referred to the book and subsequent movie, *The 3 Faces of Eve.*

Dr. Schorr explained how one personality, Eve White, was distinctly different from Eve Black – two distinct personalities coexisting in one woman: "But under conditions of hypnosis or auto-suggestion and so forth, one personality submerged and the other personality emerged. The two personalities were sharply different. One was ... a portrait of a good girl [Eve White] and the other one was a kind of honky-tonk, free-wheeling antisocial sort of person. This is what I mean by the dissociation type of reaction ... as in a Jekyll/Hyde or—"

Continuing his inquiry, Howard pursued the Jekyll/Hyde analogy further with Dr. Schorr.

> **Mr. Howard:** "Let's stay with that for a minute. You're dealing with two ends of it. You're saying that Dr. Jekyll was in the police station [referring to Sirhan after his arrest]. The good Mr. Sirhan?"
>
> **Dr. Schorr:** "The many facets of Mr. Sirhan are with him, always, wherever he is."
>
> **Mr. Howard:** "At the same time he is Jekyll and Hyde, is that what you are saying?"
>
> **Dr. Schorr:** "I never said he was either Jekyll and Hyde except under dissociative states. I said he's got two personalities in one, so to speak. One is not aware of the other, because the conscious Sirhan conceives of himself as a nice guy."

Mr. Howard: "What I'm trying to get at, Doctor – let's perhaps illustrate it this way. He doesn't have two personalities at once. One is predominant?'

Dr. Schorr: "He is a classic picture of ambivalence, and the more ambivalent he feels, the more dichotomous is the nature of his personality structure, so that one could almost conceive of two personalities in one, just as one can conceive of three personalities in the concept of Eve, in *The 3 Faces of Eve*. In the dissociative state, as I indicated earlier, the personality that emerges responds to things in the environment in what appears to be a normal manner, just as in *The 3 Faces of Eve*, or in the Jekyll/Hyde personality."

When Howard asked, "Now, are you telling us the Hyde and Jekyll Sirhan are the same?" Dr. Schorr confirmed that they are "the same person, the same personality structure."[37]

Dr. Schorr appeared to comport himself well during his trip down the slippery slope into Sirhan's history of dissociated states, memory gaps, geographic disorientation, and the most important area: the lengthy discussion he made of *The 3 Faces of Eve*.

Dr. Diamond's reluctance to go all the way and make the MPD diagnosis appeared to be at odds with Sirhan's psychological symptomology when compared with Dr. Schorr's dissociated personality state diagnosis. If there were two Sirhans separated because of a dissociated mental state of consciousness, Dr. Diamond, as the defense's star witness, knew this controversial diagnosis would be difficult to sell to the jury.

Dr. Diamond described Sirhan's brother Munir's reaction to an altercation after returning home, after nine months, in September 1967, and was shocked and alarmed to find Sirhan had changed dramatically. Munir was confused to find that Sirhan, his otherwise close brother and "sweet personality" was "an angry, explosive kind of person, very suspicious and very distrustful...."[38]

Was this radical personality switch witnessed by his brother a phase of Sirhan's continuing dissociated MPD state, merging into his splitting into two Sirhans? Although all the clinical evidence was there to support an MPD diagnosis, Dr. Diamond seemed reluctant to actually diagnose Sirhan as an MPD. He kept trying to match or fit the symptoms of Sirhan's dissociated state into the diagnostic features that mirrored paranoid schizophrenia. As it turns out, it wasn't a good fit.

---

37   Trial Vol 20, 5731–5800, 5801–5850, March 11, 1969.
38   Trial Vol 24, 6891, 6892, 6896, March 24, 1969.

Dr. Diamond's hesitation to make the MPD diagnosis also troubled other diagnosticians as suggested by Dr. P. F. Dell, who conjectured that a diagnosis of DID was based on both the anxiety and confusion evoked by the MPD's bizarre, unsettling clinical presentation. Many of the clinicians who diagnosed MPD in their patients (78%) experienced professional criticism, even harassment, concerning the vague MPD diagnosis.[39]

Another reason for hesitation surrounded the professional dispute (as mentioned) over the exact number of distinct personalities necessary to make the diagnosis. The general notion was also that MPD was, at the time, somewhat rare, and some defendants may fake the disorder, raising the concern over the appearance that a criminal will "get off" without being punished by a "gullible" jury system.

Often during his testimony, Dr. Diamond referred to Sirhan's induced hypnotic state as a type of dissociated state, yet continuing to not diagnose Sirhan as a multiple personality as affirmatively deduced from Dr. Schorr's lengthy adventure into *The 3 Faces of Eve*.

Dr. Diamond realized that Sirhan was acting on two separate levels of consciousness as "... a kind of automatic assassin, dissociated, a dual personality acting on both the conscious and subconscious levels, the subconscious being in control when he fired [shot RFK]." In his summary to the jury, Diamond said it was "an astonishing instance of mail-order hypnosis, dissociated trances, and the mystical occultism of Rosicrucian mind power and black magic."[40]

Dr. Diamond's analysis of Sirhan's two dissociated states comes close to verification of two Sirhans made here. Clear to me was that the adjusted, nonviolent Sirhan personality 1 was not aware of the presence or the existence of his malevolent counterpart, personality 2 – the violent dissociated Sirhan, who carefully planned and fulfilled his intention to eliminate RFK, and who the alter Sirhan saw as a clear and present danger to the Palestinian people, his people. Because of this split in his foundation personality, the adjusted Sirhan (personality 1) took no responsibility for the actions of the emergent personality who murdered RFK.

Subsequent to the jury's imposition of the death penalty, when Sirhan was delivered to San Quentin's death row to wait his turn in the gas chamber, the prison warden ordered an additional psychological assessment. The job fell to Dr. Eduard Simson-Kallas, the chief of the prison's psycho-

39   Dell, P.F. "Professional Skepticism about Multiple Personality." *Journal of Nervous and Mental Disease.* 1998; 176: 528–531.

40   Turner, W. and Christian, J. (1993). *The Assassination of Robert Kennedy: The Conspiracy & Coverup.* Carroll & Graf Publishers: An Imprint of Avalon Publishing Group, Inc., New York, NY, 199.

logical assessment team, who became immediately aware that Sirhan did not present as a usual convicted murderer exhibiting violent tendencies (like, for example, Charles Manson, whose violent psychopathy was hard to conceal from Dr. Simson-Kallas).

Sirhan confided to him that he was convinced that he shot RFK although he seemed to be reading from a script and lacked conviction in his words. According to Turner and Christian, "As he grew to trust Simson, Sirhan confided, 'I don't really know what happened. I know I was there. They tell me I killed Kennedy. I don't remember exactly what I did, but I know I wasn't myself.'"

Dr. Simson-Kallas believed that Sirhan had been misdiagnosed by the defense doctors. He summarized, "Nowhere in Sirhan's test responses was I able to find evidence that he is a 'paranoid schizophrenic' or 'psychotic' as testified to by the doctors at the trial." He ended his discussion stating, "Whatever the full truth of the Robert Kennedy assassination, it still remains locked in Sirhan's other, still anonymous mind!" He also told Dr. Simson-Kallas, "Sometimes I go in a very deep trance so I can't even speak … I do not remember what I do under hypnosis. I had to be in a trance when I shot Kennedy, as I don't remember having shot him. I had to be hypnotized. Christ!"[41]

What Dr. Simson-Kallas calls "Sirhan's other still anonymous mind" is the key point here. If Sirhan was in a dissociated or altered state of consciousness, or manifesting MPD, he wasn't just blocking or faking; he simply could not retrieve information recorded in one state of consciousness and recall it in another.

Dr. Diamond's formulation of Sirhan's state of mind during the murder scene rested on a diagnosis of paranoid schizophrenia and, to a lesser degree, on a dissociated state, just as Dr. Schorr's had, but ruling out the larger and more complex MPD diagnosis (seeing Sirhan's personality as being truly split). Dr. Simson-Kallas (who spent more than thirty-five hours assessing and counseling Sirhan) only referenced Sirhan's other "still anonymous mind" as a possible form of DID.

Dr. Simson-Kallas needed more time to travel deeper into Sirhan's anonymous mind, but he was not afforded that opportunity. Associate Warden James W.L. Park intervened, saying that Dr. Simson-Kallas "appears to be making a career out of Sirhan," and curtailed his visits to conform with "the services offered other condemned prisoners."

---

41   Turner and Christian. (2006). 200–202.

The doctor's professional inquiry was simply cut abruptly off. Dr. Simson-Kallas tendered his resignation and never looked back at San Quentin's ominous barbed wire and medieval walls ... [42]

Sirhan commented on his relationship with the sympathetic prison psychologist, "He might have been right. I was on death row at the time. But he gave a good analysis of the work of the Jewish psychological team – which was supposedly part of my defense. They dismissed me as a paranoid schizophrenic. ... He might have been getting too close to what really happened."

The concept of MPD, or the presence of coexisting personalities within the same person has teased the imagination of the public for more than a century. Simply stated, the idea that the right hand literally doesn't know what the left hand is doing was at once fascinating and disturbing to psychologists who were committed to investigating the strange world of Dr. Jekyll and Mr. Hyde; the perplexing notion that a person could have two co-tenants residing within one body.

During the first decade of the twentieth-century, Dr. Morton Prince, a Boston-based neurologist and psychiatrist, and founding editor of the *Journal of Abnormal Psychology*, reported the case of Ms. Christine "Sally" Beauchamp who he diagnosed as MPD. He was preceded into the provocative world of dissociated mental states by the French doctor, Pierre Janet, who connected the multiple personality to clinical hysteria. At about the same time, controversial Viennese hypnotist Franz Anton Mesmer promoted the use of multiple trance states as a method of choice to investigate MPD.

After 1840, another French doctor, C.H.A. Despine, influenced by Janet's work, published a research paper describing what he termed the "dual personality." American physician, Dr. Benjamin Rush, a signatory to the Declaration of Independence described a psychiatric case, around 1800, of a patient being possessed with "two minds."

Also affected by Janet's work with hypnosis, Dr. Morton Prince modified the dissociated concept and began to use the term co-consciousness to describe the apparent situation where a patient was operating on what seemed to be two separate mental states simultaneously. He described this mental state or states as occurring outside ordinary personal awareness which nonetheless has, "conscious equivalents. Co-consciousness

---

42   Ibid.

characterizes both the fixed ideas underlying hysteria and the alter personalities of a multiple."[43]

Between 1898-1907, Dr. Prince treated a multiple personality case that would synonymize his name with the emergent MPD psychiatric condition: a twenty-three-year-old student, Ms. Beauchamp (a pseudonym for Clara Norton Fowler), whose presenting psychiatric symptoms included acute anxiety, fatigability, mental fogginess, and general nervousness. As a devotee to the field of hypnotic-induced trances, he put Ms. Beauchamp into a series of hypnotic inductions.

As the sessions continued, Dr. Prince noticed that she suddenly began to undergo a dramatic personality transformation that changed her from her ordinary unaltered self as passive, family oriented, caring person into an aggressive, almost childlike and irresponsible woman. In his further sessions with Ms. Beauchamp, Dr. Prince located two additional emergent personalities, and a third named Sally who told him that she was not a derivative or alter ego of Ms. Beauchamp, although she could remember her as a small child just learning to walk. This led Dr. Prince to trace Sally's transformation and switch into Ms. Beauchamp's far back in her life.

Thigpen and Cleckley's seminal work became the most well-known exploration into the murky waters of multiple personality investigation. An analysis of hypnotic work certainly could provide fertile psychiatric background that could cast some light on the Sirhan case and help frame it within the diagnostic arena of MPD. An intriguing aspect of their attempt to unlock the buried secrets of their initial patient, Mrs. Eve White, were the results of their psychological testing.

In 1957, the same year Thigpen and Cleckley published *The 3 Faces of Eve* book, Hollywood rushed a film version of the story to the big screen. The book and the film adaptation were both professional and commercial successes, garnering the best actress award for Joanne Woodard and a big hit for Twentieth Century Fox.

During the 1960s, just before the Sirhan case came to trial, Sutcliffe and Jones, who reviewed the psychological literature on MPD cases, reported only sixty-five cases, dating back to 1815. These researchers examined various conceptions of the multiple personality category, i.e., as a product of shaping; as simulation; and as a product of hypnotic suggestion. They discerned a peak flow of cases toward the end of the nineteenth century, supporting a diagnostic trend of fashion.

---

43   "Multiple Personality: A Mirror of a New model of Mind." *Institute of Noetic Sciences*, Vol 1, No .3.4, 1985.

Many DID cases remain where patients with presenting symptoms such as fugue state, somnambulism, and amnesia may in fact be examples of multiples, but are under-diagnosed. Sirhan's not being diagnosed with MPD clearly falls into the undiagnosed category specified by Sutcliffe and Jones.[44]

Just as Sirhan was exposed to a battery of psychological tests administered by Drs. Richardson and Schorr, Eve White was also psychometrically assessed. Thigpen and Cleckley wanted to determine if Eve's personality was indeed fractured or cleaved into three different parts or distinct components, then determine if each one was accessed whether the test results showed a difference. If these personalities were divergent from each other, could psychological assessment tease out those differences? To confirm or disconfirm this clinical hypothesis, combined with their observations of Eve's manifestations as Eve White, Eve Black, or Jane, the third personality, each personality was given the Osgood Semantic Differential method.[45]

The Osgood Semantic Differential rating system uses a seven-point Likert scale to access fifteen concepts such as: tense, important, weak, strong, and valuable as they affect a person's life. Because of my experience using this descriptive tool to assess various deviant populations, quite naturally it would be optimal to use this unobtrusive attitude measure with Sirhan.[46]

Thigpen and Cleckley's semantic differential results for the three Eves demonstrated distinct semantic structures. For Eve White: "The most general characterization would be that Eve White perceives 'the world' in an essentially normal fashion, is well socialized, but has an unsatisfactory attitude toward herself ... Eve Black has achieved a violent [acting out] kind of adjustment ... Jane displays the most healthy meaning pattern."[47]

In July 1952, to complete the diagnostic picture of the three Eves, Eve White was referred to Dr. Leopold Winter, a clinical psychologist and assessment expert at the VA Hospital in Atlanta, Georgia, for a psychological assessment (similar to Sirhan's assessment protocol conducted by Drs. Richardson and Schorr). Eve White was administered the Rorschach and the Wechsler-Bellevue Intelligence Scale, IQ scale. The results: "While

44   Sutcliffe, J.P. and J. Jones. (1962). "Personal identity, multiple personality, and hypnosis." *International Journal of Clinical and Experimental Hypnosis*, 1962, 10:4, 231–269.

45   Osgood, C.E. "The Nature and Measurement of Meaning." *Psychological Bulletin*, 1952, 49, 192–237.

46   Brady, J.C. (1990). *Drug Addicts: Are They Out of Control?:New Insights into the American Drug Dilemma*. Western Book Journal Press, San Mateo, California.

47   Thigpen and Cleckley. (1957), 247–249.

Mrs. White is able to achieve an IQ of 110 on the Wechsler-Bellevue Intelligence Scale, Miss Black attains an IQ of 104."

This differential intelligence scoring between alter personalities was also evidenced in the multiple personality case, the minds of Billy Milligan. Six of Billy Milligan's twenty-four personalities were given the Weschler Adult Intelligence Test (WAIS), the same IQ test given to Sirhan by Dr. Martin Schorr. The measurement of Milligan's six personalities IQs conducted established a wide range of intelligence ranging from a high of 120 (superior) for Allen to a low of 71 (borderline) for Danny. Dr. Schorr reported Sirhan's IQ as 97, which falls into the midrange of average intelligence.[48]

Psychologists and handwriting experts have also reported distinct differences in the handwriting exemplars between multiple personality alters. To see whether the Eves' handwriting was noticeably different, Thigpen and Cleckley hired a handwriting consultant who was a document examiner from the US Army, Document Section. The results showed a "consistent and significant difference between the two productions," but the examiner thought that "those with adequate professional training could establish sufficient evidence to show both were done by the same human hand." The expert concluded, "It readily appears the handwriting of each personality is of a different person.... However, extensive investigation of these handwriting materials establishes beyond any doubt that they have been written by one and the same individual."[49]

In addition to physical-stylistic variations (loops, lines, spacing, size, crossing t's), the writings of MPD patients in clinical settings often contain "information specific to a particular alter (alternative identity or personality state) who may express emotions repressed by other alters or provide information for which other alters are amnesic."[50]

An alter personality often produces a different range of affect or emotionally charged material when compared to normal handwriting samples taken from the general population, which convey a broad range of emotions and information compared to handwriting samples taken from an MPD patient's alter, which often reflect specific memories and emotions to which an alter may have exclusive access.[51]

---

48   Keyes, D. (1982). *The Minds of Billy Milligan*. Bantom Books, A Division of Bantom Doubleday, New York, 69.

49   Thigpen and Cleckley. (1957) 142–146.

50   Yank, J.R. (1991). Handwriting variations in individuals with MPD. Dissociation, Vol IV, No.1, March 1991.

51   Putnam, F.W. (1989).). *Diagnosis and Treatment of Multiple Personality Disorder*. The Guilford Press, New York.

Because of Sirhan's long, often rambling handwritten diary in the entries generally referred to as the "RFK Must Die" document, the topic of a dissociated patient's handwriting analysis takes on special importance. Whereas Thigpen and Cleckley encouraged their patients to submit a separate sample of their handwriting for forensic analysis by a professional document examiner, Sirhan's voluminous outpouring in his diary provided more than enough handwriting evidence to analyze.

The goal of such an assessment would be to determine what passages in the diary (if any) were written by Sirhan's alter vs. what parts he wrote when in a non-altered state of consciousness. The treasure trove of his supposedly private writings (sometimes expressed as random scribbles and disconnected streams of consciousness expressing his thoughts, emotions, and characterizations of his life) provided fertile information to support the task of determining which parts were done when he was in an altered state of awareness and which were not.

Based on a series of psychological tests, Thigpen and Cleckley were able to identify certain behavioral characteristics that differentiated Eve White from Eve Black, thereby establishing several points of psychological contrast. In a psychological analysis of Sirhan's personality, I outlined the principal behavioral differences between the adjusted Sirhan (personality 1, passive) and the dissociated Sirhan (personality 2, aggressive). An exhaustive listing of points of psychological contrast probably couldn't capture all the differences between the two Sirhans.

These composite categories were derived from Sirhan's accumulated biographical memories, the many interviews during the past fifty years, and from personal descriptions about Sirhan from his family members and friends. Moreover, a review of his psychological testing, especially the disturbing narratives he created on the TAT, proved helpful in constructing Sirhan's contrasting, psychological characteristics.

TABLE II: THE ADJUSTED SIRHAN (PERSONALITY 1) VERSUS THE DISSOCIATED SIRHAN (PERSONALITY 2)

THE ADJUSTED SIRHAN	THE DISSOCIATED SIRHAN
Pleasant, easy to get along with, likable	Irritable, unstable, unreliable
Balanced sense of humor, outgoing, seemingly happy	Droll, serious, not funny, stays to himself

People who knew him trusted Sirhan to "do the right thing." Altruistic. Helped care for his dying sister	Appears cold, distant, disconnected, alone, uncaring
Helpful to others, reaches out, provides assistance	Indifferent to others
Giving, sharing attitude	Devil-may-care attitude
Moves toward people including family members, loving feelings	Keeps distant, avoids most interactions with people
Displays a passive demeanor	Dominate, forceful, controlling. Questions motives of people around him, suspicious, paranoid
Nonjudgmental, "C'est la vie"	Distrusts why people do things – maybe they're out to hurt him. Signs of "identification with the aggressor"
Gregarious, fun loving, upbeat mindset	Isolated, cut off from human interactions, brooding attitude
Responsible and helpful, reaches out to others	Irresponsible, indication that he holds pro-law violation philosophy believes "ends justify the means"
Socialized, has circle of social and work associates and friends.	Misanthropic world view, dislikes his fellow mankind – Loner, cut off and alien
Forgiving philosophy	Distrusts the government, has an "enemies list"
Stable mood levels over time	Volatile, mood swings
Politically neutral or conservative	Radical, antiestablishment sentiments with anarchist views as expressed in his diary and readings. Leftist, communist beliefs

Many of those interviewed by the FBI and LAPD were not inclined to provide negative information about Sirhan's history. Quite to the contrary, the adjusted Sirhan was apparently viewed as stable and helpful to those who knew him. He was surprisingly different from his brooding, angry dissociative personality. For example, Jack Davies, Sirhan's former employer at a gas station, told FBI agents that Sirhan was responsible, worked hard at his job, was helpful with customers, presented no problems, always acted politely, and did not show any obvious, odd behavioral traits.

"Sidney McDaniel, who worked with Sirhan under Davies, also said "it was hard for him to believe that Sirhan could do this. Another employee at this station, Chester Yashuk, noted that when a security guard who collected money at night was overly profane, Sirhan asked him to tone it down. The guard tried to pick a fight with Sirhan, but Sirhan 'became very meek and would not fight this guard.'"

These positive evaluations of Sirhan's personality were followed up by other people who had worked closely with Sirhan at different places of employment, such as when he worked at a health food store and when Sirhan worked as a part-time gardener. According to Pease, "You can cherry-pick a few examples of people who saw Sirhan in an angry state. The one topic that definitely animated Sirhan was discussing the Palestinian-Israeli conflict...."[52]

Many of Sirhan's personality 2 psychological characteristics reflected his personality split as evidenced by a number of negative factors attributed to him. Sirhan's malevolent personality 2, the bad Sirhan (the one who killed RFK) filled with anger and rage is not uncharacteristic among persons who commit crimes including homicide while in a dissociated state. A study that tracked 21 reported DID cases "found that 47% of men and 35% of women reported engaging in criminal activity, including 19% of men and 7% of women who committed homicide."[53]

Dr. George Estabrooks researched patients with MPD, finding that the alter personality is often comprised of defined antisocial features. This analysis supports the view that Sirhan's alter personality 2 was suffused with anger, an accumulating violent tendency and, in the end, homicidal rage. According to Estabrooks, "Most cases of multiple personality follow this pattern: usually the unwanted intruder represents the less socialized and sensible aspects of human behavior, and secondary personalities are generally irresponsible at best."[54]

When looking at Sirhan's split personality, the development of his alter personality accurately fits into Estabrooks's description of the unwanted intruder. Remember that Sirhan did not plan to create a secondary identity, and have it turn out to be the "bad Sirhan" evolving into an assassin. His alter began as his personal defense against the emotional trauma he experienced as a child, and became over time a secret repository for evil dimensions he acquired along the way.

Howell explains, "In many remarkable ways, the dissociative mind bears witness to a multitude of human contexts and relationships.... [W]hen

52   Pease. (2018). 126–127.
53   Farrell, H.M. Dissociative identity disorder: No excuse for criminal activity. *Current Psychiatry*, 2011. June:10 (6) : 33–40. https://www.mdedge.com/psychiatry/article/64330/personality-disorders/dissociative-identity-identity-disorder-no-excuse-criminal?reg=1
54   Estabrooks, G.H. and N.E. Gross. (2017). 26.

evil overwhelms us, it may become part of us – until or unless we learn enough about it and our relationships to it. When we face this dilemma, we encounter a completely new realm of moral reality."[55]

In my view and the views of the quoted experts consulted here, the psychological roots of DID generally extend back into a person's negative, early life experiences when noticeable traumatic events have occurred. In a clinical sense, even though a dissociative disorder can be a life-changing experience for a person, more importantly, it can serve as a defensive or coping mechanism used to protect the person from further psychological disintegration.

Ultimate escape into an altered state of consciousness as Sirhan did is often sought as mental refuge from the pain associated with childhood adverse experiences, and this escape patterning mechanism becomes the goal to help insulate oneself. The conditions of safety become embodied in the confusing dissociative solution, seeking to protect the person from further psychological damage leading to the conditions for actual insanity. Dissociative states cannot be easily triggered by pulling a simple on-and-off mental switch voluntarily; the process is driven and occurs on a much deeper unconscious level, meaning it is not a volitional act or, as in Sirhan's case, a series of triggered events quite beyond his control.

Whether Sirhan was in an altered state of consciousness as personality 2 when he killed RFK continued to plague Sirhan's experts from the onset, probably because it was never resolved. A second question was whether Sirhan's "trance" was a voluntary alteration of his consciousness, or was his change in personality done without the knowledge of the adjusted Sirhan?

Dr. Diamond's theory that because of Sirhan's immersion into the Rosicrucian's hypnotic rituals, using intense lights, staring into candles, and self-hypnosis, he encountered a similar set of Rosicrucian-like almost psychedelic-like circumstances in the Ambassador Hotel on the night of the assassination, inadvertently propelling him into a dissociated state. Dr. Diamond had it almost right in his conclusion that the confusion in the pantry did affect Sirhan – it affected his alter personality who was already projected into the "killing mode." The excitement in the pantry only enhanced the dissociative Sirhan to carry out his plan to eliminate RFK, as he often stated in his diary. The dissociated Sirhan suddenly manifested itself fulfilling his intention to take out the current object of his vengeance,

---

55   Howell, E.F. (2005). *The Dissociative Mind.* Hillsdale, New Jersey: Analytic Press, 10. In Chu, J.A. (2011). Rebuilding Shattered Lives: Treating Complex PTSD and Dissociative Disorders. John Wiley & Sons, Inc. Hoboken, NJ, 46.

doing what he did, perhaps as an unwitting terrorist, but nevertheless still a terrorist. Chapter 12 explores Sirhan's complete personality conversion into the bad Sirhan from the good Sirhan.

CHAPTER 12

COMPLEX - POST-TRAUMATIC STRESS DISORDER (C-PTSD) AND THE CONVERSION OF SIRHAN
Phase III, Sirhan's Identity Transformations

A FRIGHTENING MENU OF TRAUMATIC EVENTS

A retrospective analysis of Sirhan's critical childhood existence reveals a horrific series of documented events that brought serious and life-long adverse psychological consequences for him. His dark journey into the oblique world of personality dissociation began around 1947 when he and his five siblings became refugees forced to relocate from their modest home into a cramped one-room apartment in the troubled Old Walled City of Jerusalem. Each Palestinian family was issued a United Nations ration card to help buy groceries. Sirhan's long chain of traumatic events began sadly when his oldest brother, Munir, died when run over by a careless driver of a military truck. Dr. Diamond was interested in searching into Sirhan's unsettling past principally aimed at finding out what past disturbing events in Sirhan's life could help account for his dissociative states, and if these could be tied to killing RFK.

Dr. Diamond found out that prior to Sirhan's relocation to Pasadena, California, he had experienced innumerable traumatic life events. After learning the details of these adverse experiences, Dr. Diamond tried to fit together all the disparate psychological pieces of Sirhan's life. Dr. Diamond's psychosocial history on Sirhan figured predominately in his diagnosis, seeing clearly that Sirhan did not emerge from childhood unscathed.

During his testimony, Dr. Diamond provided some examples:

> As you know they emigrated to the United States, leaving Jerusalem and arriving here in January of 1957. The whole family came, or the survivors of the family – originally there were thirteen children in this family but a number had died in infancy. The father was with them when they settled here in Pasadena. In the summer of 1957

an incident with the father occurred which I think is of considerable psychological significance, in that Sirhan's father and older brother Adel and Munir were digging a kind of irrigation ditch around a tree in their back yard, and Sirhan was sort of running around and not being very helpful, and was tramping in the mud, and then would trample on the cement of the driveway; and the father repeatedly warned Sirhan not to do that, and Sirhan kept it up, and the father finally got extremely angry and attempted to beat Sirhan. Now, the usual method of discipline in this family was to beat the children.

This time however, Adel interfered and protested and stepped between the father and Sirhan and did not allow the father to strike Sirhan, and the father was very angry and went in and demanded of Mrs. Sirhan that she choose between him, the father, and the children … and either he maintained the discipline or not. And Mary Sirhan [Sirhan's mother] said that she loved her children, and the father then told her he was going back to Palestine, what is now Jordan. He took the family savings and their bank account, bought an airplane ticket and returned to what was then Jordan, and I understand no one in the family has heard from him since. But I think that this episode had a considerable psychological effect not only on Sirhan but on the whole sort of relationship of all the members of the family."[1]

Somehow Sirhan tended to absorb the blame for the nasty, family confrontation with his father over a minor incident, thereby leading to feelings of abandonment and detachment that he could not escape from. Sirhan's school friends attested to the fact that Sirhan suffered multiple severe beating at the hands of his cruel father that they witnessed.

When still in Jerusalem, Sirhan's recollection of his childhood was anything but emotionally stabilizing, mentally congruent, and happy. His family and people were constantly under attack from the Israeli army that annexed more and more of the territory that was once the province of Palestinians. Sirhan felt the pressure of the sometimes-daily bombings and attacks that forced the Arab children to seek safety, going into makeshift shelters usually in poorly dugout basements and cellars. Sirhan witnessed the death of several Arabs blown to pieces as they waited at a bus stop. Sirhan recounted one emotional scene when he came upon the dead body of a dismembered soldier split into pieces. He saw the man's severed leg still wearing an army boot.

One of the most traumatic events in Sirhan's young life was the death of his older brother, Munir (Sirhan also has a younger surviving brother born in 1947 who the family also named Munir in honor of his deceased

---

1   Trial Vol 24, 6894, March 24, 1969.

brother). Munir was struck and killed in Jerusalem by an out-of-control British Army truck. Sirhan recalls the depressing moment when he was commanded to circle around Munir's body in the casket. His brother's death ushered in a series of psychologically damaging events, resulting in his many stress-related reactions.

Sirhan described another sobering emotional event that occurred at a communal well used by the inhabitants in Old Jerusalem: "It must have been Saturday because we cleaned our home on Saturday and we used to get water from the well for cleaning purposes. We never drank the water … we would lower the pail with the rope into the well and just draw up the water. That is when I brought up this piece of flesh, the hand. It was this part of the hand [pointing]. It sickened me."[2]

Sirhan's discovery of the human hand in the common well was verified by Ziad Hashimeh, a childhood friend of Sirhan's in the Old City of Jerusalem. Like Sirhan's family, Hashimeh's family was forced from their home into a communal living situation with nine other displaced families. He often visited Sirhan's family in their one-room surroundings. Ziad was questioned by Grant Cooper, who was interested in Sirhan's relationship with his father.

> **Mr. Cooper:** "Did you ever see him [Sirhan's father] strike Sirhan?"
>
> **Ziad:** "Oh, yes, quite a few times."
>
> **Mr. Cooper:** "I take it because he was a bad boy, or something?"
>
> **Ziad:** "Well, no. The husband, the man, was too emotional, you know.… Quite a bit of times he beat him."
>
> **Mr. Cooper:** "Did he strike him with his hands?"
>
> **Ziad:** "He used all sorts of sticks and hands."

Ziad recalled another time when he saw Sirhan crying: "I was in the room, and I hear him shouting, 'Mother, Mother.' The whole apartment, they goes out, and he was shaking, you know, like that, moving his body, and he was crying. 'Hand, hand,' so we all had to go to the well."

> **Mr. Cooper:** "What did you see?"
>
> **Ziad:** "We saw [a] hand in—"
>
> **Mr. Cooper:** "You mean a human hand?"
>
> **Ziad:** "A human hand."
>
> **Mr. Cooper:** "That was in the bucket?"

2   Trial Vol 17, 4834–35, March 3, 1969.

Ziad: "In the bucket, yes."[3]

Sirhan attended a Lutheran World Federation school in Old Jerusalem beginning in kindergarten. He regularly attended church and Sunday school at the Lutheran church. From the mid-1940s through 1956, innumerable off-and-on bombings occurred during the eight years he lived there. Sirhan described the bombing incidents: "The schools would close. They would close down on instructions and we would stay at home.... The fear of the bombings was always constant, throughout the whole population. We always had to go down into the basement of that building that we were in; the house we moved into in the Old City and my mother would stuff our ears with cotton, we knew there were bombings going on."

Sirhan was with his mother when he witnessed an open army truck pass on their street, carrying several young girls who were bleeding, their breasts ripped open by a group of sadistic soldiers. Such an incident is almost beyond the scope of what a trauma-dissociative scale can measure.

The graphic scene was reported by his mother during her trial testimony when questioned by prosecutor Russell Parsons.

> **Mr. Parsons:** "What was visible, what did you and he see?"
>
> **Mrs. Sirhan:** "Well, we saw an open truck with many young girls in the truck that were naked, and there was blood running from their breasts, and a big lot of the army that was going in, and I don't know what kind of soldiers they were, clapping hands, saying, 'Look what we can do,' and that is what Sirhan and I saw."
>
> **Mr. Parsons:** "What was the reaction of Sirhan to that?"
>
> **Mrs. Sirhan:** "Well, he looked at them and said, 'Mama, Mama, look at the blood,' and he began to shake again."

Prior to the family's departure from Old Jerusalem, Sirhan recalled more troubling events. Because of critical food shortages, he saw some people who appeared to be starving, some dying on the street of starvation. He said, "Well, we were really the more lucky people in the Old City of Jerusalem, because we had these ration cards. Some people did not have them, and those were the more miserable ones than us in the Old City. That's why we always tried to share what little we had with these people. And having to take care of ourselves first, we actually could not give too much to these poorer ones, and eventually these people would die of hunger."[4]

---

3   Klaber, W. and P. Melanson. (1997). 173–174.
4   Trial Vol 17, 4815–4825, March 3, 1969.

Sirhan recaptured still another traumatic episode involving a grocer the family did business with for six years. The man's store was bombed, and Sirhan saw his segmented body lying on the floor. "I didn't witness the actual bombing, to see the bombs come in the area of the store, this little shop where this man was, although I remember seeing his remains exploding or exploded, a part of the flesh around the shop and in the street."[5]

Even more serious as a victim of a bomb blast, Sirhan saw a man's body with the entrails exposed as he lay dying.

Dr. Diamond considered Sirhan's troubled background as a key contributing factor leading to his disturbed personality. The compounded series of traumatic occurrences that manifested in Sirhan's negative responses resulted in symptoms that included: a weak sense of self-identity, distorted fantasies, detached emotions, a persistent dread of his own death, a distorted sense that he was living his life as if he was in a horror movie, feelings of alienation from his thoughts, emotional numbness, amnestic episodes, and paranoid ideations. These primary symptoms were accompanied with repressed feelings of anger and deep-seated aggression. Sirhan's diverse cultural background could not be ruled out as a factor specifically tied to his repressed confrontational problem-solving style. Sirhan was certainly having difficulty with his problem-solving capacity.

Phase III: Sirhan's Identity Transformation – Cooccurring Complex Post-traumatic Stress Syndrome (C-PTSD)

When I factored Sirhan's multiple psychiatric symptoms against the diagnostic criteria in the *DSM-5-TR*, many mirrored those psychological symptoms usually associated with uncomplicated PTSD and, more importantly, they reflected the criteria associated with a new PTSD conceptualization: complex post-traumatic stress disorder (C-PTSD). When I compared the differential diagnostic components of Sirhan's dissociative disorder to C-PTSD symptoms, many appeared qualitatively the same, strongly suggesting that he shared common symptoms between his dissociated identity disorder and C-PTSD. The bottom line regarding Sirhan's definitive diagnosis is that his psychological condition is marked by a cluster of similar psychiatric symptoms that could easily be common to both a dissociative disorder and to C-PTSD.

---

5   Ibid. 4837.

But what is C-PTSD, and how does this diagnosis differ from its better-known disorder uncomplicated PTSD? C-PTSD is a rather recently introduced psychiatric diagnosis identified and classified – International Classification of Diseases (ICD-11) of the World Health Organization (WHO). WHO now classifies two variants of this condition: PTSD and C-PTSD, with diagnostic similarities and certain differences between these two related subclassifications.

The *DSM-5-TR* listed the symptoms necessary to make the PTSD diagnosis: intrusive memory of traumatic event(s), recurrent distressing dreams related to the traumatic event(s), dissociative reactions – flashbacks, intense or prolonged distress that symbolizes the original traumatic event(s), marked physiological reactions, persistent avoidance associated with the traumatic event(s), avoidance of efforts to avoid distressing memories of the traumatic event(s), inability to remember an important aspect of the traumatic event(s), irritable behavior, reckless or self-destructive behavior, hyper-vigilance, exaggerated startle response, and concentration deficit.[6]

The most differentiating symptom between PTSD and C-PTSD is that, while uncomplicated, PTSD is usually caused by a single traumatic event (e.g.; natural disaster, terrorist attack like the 9/11 event, traumatic combat, or accident); whereas C-PTSD results from a series of enduring, multiple traumatic experiences.

Whereas uncomplicated PTSD can result from adverse experiences anytime during a person's life, C-PTSD is typically the result of continuous childhood-induced trauma. The total psychological impact of the multiple traumas (associated with C-PTSD) result in more psychopathology than uncomplicated PTSD. Dissociative states are sometimes related to a diagnosis of C-PTSD, therefore this condition can share the symptomology of DID.

According to Boysan, dissociative states and trauma-induced PTSD are related in that, "These two symptomologies co-occur on account of not only shared vulnerabilities predating trauma but also are interconnected pathogenic mechanisms set in motion by trauma exposure."

Boysan calls complex PTSD a "prevailing conceptualization referring to somatization, dissociation, and interpersonal difficulties. Trauma-in-

6   American Psychiatric Association: *Diagnostic and Statistical Manual of Mental Disorders*, Fifth Edition, Text Revision. Washington, DC, American Psychiatric Association, 2022. Reed, G.M., M.B. First, M. Elena Medina-Mora, O. Gureje, K.M. Pike, S. Saxena. (2016). Draft Diagnostic Guidelines for ICD-11 Mental and Behavioral Disorders Available for Review and Comment. World Psychiatry. Official Journal of the World Psychiatric Association (WPA) 2016; 15:112–113.

duced dissociative states have long been recognized to be linked to chronicity in post-trauma psychopathology ... that dissociative tendency during and after the aversive traumatic experiences may serve as an adaptation mechanism...."[7]

Sirhan's extensive history of childhood traumas contributed to early onset of his PTSD symptoms, so in my clinical view, he meets the ICD-11 diagnostic criteria for C-PTSD. Some of the salient psychological symptoms ascribed to C-PTSD include emotional dysregulation; the presence of hostile, angry feelings; depression; persistent feelings of emptiness and self-estrangement; hopelessness, trust issues, alienation, and personal defeat patterning. The number and severity of impact on Sirhan's cumulative, early life traumas underscore his two, new major psychiatric diagnoses: DID and C-PTSD. His multiple C-PTSD symptoms, in some ways, are like his learned helplessness descriptors, Sirhan's fifth identity transformational factor.

The psychological impact of C-PTSD as a co-occurring psychiatric condition with DID share a similar set of causal factors as well as symptoms. In my clinical assessment, many of Sirhan's C-PTSD symptoms were internalized by his emergent alter, hostile personality when he was a child. Specifically, these C-PTSD symptoms listed in the ICD-11 coding are: 1. Deficit in managing a person's affective behavior resulting in emotional outbursts, and angry responses. Asked if he might kill the President and the Vice President of the US Sirhan angrily said. "I would have blasted anybody!," 2. Persistent feelings of hopelessness not accounted for by learned helplessness descriptors – "I can see the cards are stacked against me;" and 3, seeing the world as a dangerous place – "The Zionists are out to get all of us" [the Palestinians]; and faulty memory retrieval – "I didn't write that stuff in the notebook."

After examining the defining, diagnostic criteria for both DID and C-PTSD, establishing this connection prompts two clinical questions: Why did certain psychiatric diagnoses at the time Sirhan was originally diagnosed like a MPD and uncomplicated PTSD seem to be eschewed by the distinguished panel of doctors? Perhaps in their zeal to establish that Sirhan had a more profound and easily defined psychotic condition like paranoid schizophrenia, the defense doctors searched for a diagnosis they believed would further Dr. Diamond's diminished capacity defense.

The psychological evidence I was seeking to validate both Sirhan's DID and C-PTSD conditions was clear from an examination of his long

7   Boysan, M. "Association between dissociation and Post-Traumatic Stress Response." In: Martin, C, V. Preedy, and V. Patel (eds). *Comprehensive Guide to Post-Traumatic Stress Disorders*. Springer, Cham. 835, 845. https://doi.org/10.1007/978-3-319-08359-9_13

history of his extremely troubled and traumatized childhood experiences included situational amnesia, memory gaps, his odd behaviors, extreme mood fluctuations, periods of extreme nervousness and psychomotor agitation (reported by his mother), his retreat from social interactions, identity confusion ("Who am I?"), feelings of rejections, and periods of despair and social isolation ("It's better to be alone.").

Dissociative reactions are prevalently co-occurring psychological entities, sharing some causal factors with PTSD symptoms that were marked by the presence of one or more traumatic events. The causal factors increasing the probability of co-occurring PTSD and a dissociative disorder are also quite similar. The presence of traumatic events such as childhood sexual abuse, war, domestic violence, torture, and physical accidents can potentiate both disorders. Multiple categories of trauma can trigger both conditions.

A study conducted by Alisic, et al., found that 36 percent of children exposed to a traumatic event developed PTSD symptoms in their childhood. "Research conducted with the best available assessment instruments show that a significant minority of children and adolescents develop PTSD after trauma exposure, with those exposed to interpersonal trauma...."[8]

Research suggests that Sirhan wasn't alone in his childhood traumatic reactions to the events in war-torn Palestine. The majority of victims in the historic Middle East conflict were civilians. While the Sirhan family lived there, the Israeli forces continuously shelled the area, negatively affecting the lives of hundreds of innocent Arab residents, and destroying countless family residences. More than 4,000 homes had been destroyed in the Gaza Strip and the West Bank as recently as 2000. The October 7, 2023, attack on innocent Israeli civilians by Hamas-based terrorists from Gaza, resulting in the slaughter of twelve hundred, sparked still another Arab-Israeli war with similar atrocities to what Sirhan experienced as a child.

Homes constitute the cultural center of the Arab family and represent security, holding fond memories of life during better times. The psychological effects of bombing large areas of the Arab-occupied Middle East in the Jerusalem region, where the Sirhan family lived peacefully, has not gone unnoticed by psychologists. A study of PTSD reactions among Arab children is germane to the present analysis.

8   Alisic, E., A.K. Zalta, F. Wesel, S.E. Larsen, G. Hafstad, K. Hassanpour, and G. Smid. "Rates of posttraumatic stress disorder in trauma-exposed children and adolescents: meta analysis." *British Journal of Psychiatry*, 2014, 204:335–40. DOI:10.1192/bjp.bp.113.131227.

Qouta, et al. conducted research into children's responses to danger-ous and life-threatening experiences resulting from the devastating Middle East wars.[9]

Using a twelve-item checklist (like Sirhan's traumatic dissociative life factors) of military violence, these researchers sampled 121 Palestinian children and their mothers for stress-eliciting factors. Like Sirhan, the ma-jority were refugees from the 1948 war. Some of the violence areas Qouta and his team looked into included: witnessed direct shooting, fighting or explosions, saw a stranger being injured or killed, saw a friend or neighbor being injured or killed, and attended funerals.

Qouta states, "In addition to having their homes shelled, a substan-tial number of children had been tear-gassed (94.9%), and had witnessed shootings (97%) and seen funerals (86%). Half of the children had wit-nessed strangers being injured or killed (51.7%).... More than half (54%) of the children were suffering from a severe level of PTSD symptoms, and a third from a moderate level." Qouta also reported less than 2% (1.7%) scored no or doubtful severe PTSD symptoms.

These war-related experiences are quite similar to those reported by Sirhan, his family members, and people who knew him in Palestine prior to his move to California when he was twelve years old.

Outside the academic confines of graduate school, my exposure to pa-tients with PTSD came a few years after graduation with a doctorate in criminology from UC, Berkeley. These cases of diagnosed PTSD were the result of overwhelming combat stress incurred during the Vietnam War. I soon encountered many Vietnam vets who carried the PTSD diagnoses after graduation, as a psychology intern at the San Francisco VA Hospital, Psychology Division. To be licensed as a psychologist (forensic or other specialty) in the state of California it was (and still is) required to do a two-year, psychology internship.

The winding down of hostilities in Vietnam meant that thousands of returning young, military personnel found it necessary to face the chal-lenge to reintegrate back into civilian society. Sadly, for many, the damage caused by their psychological wounds exceeded their obvious physical in-juries. Obviously, some vets experienced physical and mental symptoms. I was confronted with a similar traumatized patient population that prob-ably confronted Dr. Diamond twenty-five years earlier with returning World War II vets he treated.

9   Qouta, S., R.L. Punamaki., and E. El Sarraj. (2003). "Prevalence and Determinants of PTSD Among Palestinian Children Exposed to Military Violence." *European Child & Adolescent Psychiatry*. 12:265-272 (2003). DOI 10.1007/s00787-003-0328-0

At the top of the list were battle-tormented patients telling their incredulous tales of war-associated trauma, experiencing varying degrees of PTSD, with certain dissociative reactions not far behind. My assigned responsibilities as an intern centered on conducting initial intake interviews and engaging the new patient in some nonthreatening brief psychological testing – usually a military background questionnaire that included a chronology of either physical or psychological events, the TAT and MMPI.

Because each new veteran entering the VA is presumably under considerable stress, the obvious goal during an initial intake assessment is to establish rapport. After all, they voluntarily contacted the VA psych unit and made an appointment for some reason, so whatever happened during that first session can drastically affect how they reacted to treatment. It was pointed out to me by my supervisor that 99 percent of these outpatient admissions were experiencing severe emotional trauma, and our job (my specific job) was to ease their pain – the pain connected to scenes they should never have witnessed, and maybe their own acts of brutality which they now deeply regret and attempt to repress from their consciousness.

The stories they told me were shocking and sad at the same time – seeing scorched dead bodies of their fellow soldiers cut down in the absolute prime of their lives, innocent civilians accidently immolated with the US's Agent Orange, and children wounded and alone and thrust into a world at war that they didn't create.

Their chronic exposure to dioxin, for example (the toxic chemical used in Agent Orange), toxic agents like napalm, polluting the air they breathed and making safe drinking water almost impossible to find. Ripped from the safety of their Stateside homes, families, children and friends, these were not happy draftees into the U.S. Army by any means, yet they had been pressed into involuntary service to fight a war about halfway around the globe that they knew almost nothing about. And if I asked them directly, they could have cared less about the outcome – the just wanted to go home.

After a few months of interviewing and conducting intake evaluations of many of these traumatized ex-soldiers, I realized that dissociative conditions like PTSD and other dissociative reactions were real, very real, and in some cases, when left untreated, ruined ex-soldier's lives including innumerable suicides. That VA experience helped inform my increasing data bank of what constituted these puzzling, dissociative experiences. As I reflected on the symptoms these soldiers presented, I began to reformulate my viewpoint concerning Sirhan's specific symptomology being impacted by the never-ending series of horrible events in his early life, which mirrored the ex-soldiers sitting in front of me filling out government forms and taking the MMPI and later administered the TAT.

These were the same psychodiagnostic tools used to assess Sirhan as he languished in his jail cell awaiting his fate placed in the hands of the jury – life or death. The psychological similarity between my VA patients' combat experiences and Sirhan's long list of traumatic events was striking, appearing as two disturbed, psychological bookends. This prompted me to pose the question: Did Sirhan actually begin his drift into a longstanding dissociative syndrome based on his firsthand traumatic experiences as a child as a certain victim of the Palestinian-Israeli conflict?

Clinically I have found that whenever a diagnosis of DID is made and is derived solely from a patient's self-report data, these memories may easily be fabrications, distortions, and enhanced beliefs or even some events that never occurred or were imagined. An experienced clinician needs to corroborate the materials or narratives generated by potential dissociative patients, especially related to the reportage of one's own traumatic life experiences.

How this diagnostic process can go awry is exemplified by the well-publicized case of Sybil that served to bring into light how an alleged case of MPD can be manufactured by three colluding women promoting their own self-interests, and not Sybil's welfare. The 1973 book *Sybil*, unraveling a supposed MPD case, became an overnight best seller.[10] Unfortunately, this case as presented to the public was almost a complete fraud right from the start, but was still made into an NBC miniseries in 1976, seen by forty million people, and won four Emmys. The treating doctor, Cornelia Wilbur, was played by Joanne Woodward who two decades earlier played the MPD patient in *The 3 Faces of Eve*. Sally Field gave an impassioned and award-winning performance as Sybil in the miniseries.

Although the Sybil fraud represents a step back for the entire professional concept of MPD, and left those who believed the *Sybil* story stunned when the facts emerged that the three women who perpetrated this hoax had incorporated Sybil into a money-making machine, "and the contract they signed designated a three-way split of all profits and spin-offs from their book, including *Sybil* movies, *Sybil* board games, *Sybil* tee shirts, *Sybil* dolls, and a *Sybil* musical."

10   Schreiber, F. R. *Sybil*. (1973). Grand Central Publishing, Hachette Book Group, (2009) New York, Boston.

During an interview conducted in her later years, Dr. Wilbur described her contribution to the field of psychiatry, demurely characterizing herself as a "maverick psychiatrist[11] – obviously she was that and much more.

Dr. Wilbur's involvement in controversial MPD cases did not end with Sybil. A few years later, Dr. Wilbur became involved in another famous MPD case, published as *The Minds of Billy Milligan* by Daniel Keyes. Apparently, Dr. Wilbur's reputation for both her insights and criticisms preceded her, derived from her highly publicized experience on the Sybil case. The chief psychiatrist in the Milligan case told defense attorney, Gary Schweickart: "Well, I must tell you, Mr. Schweickart, I have great grave reservations about the syndrome known as multiple personality. Although Dr. Cornelia Wilbur did give a lecture at Harding Hospital about Sybil in the summer of 1975, I'm not sure I really believe it.… Well, in a case like this, it's too obviously possible for the patient to feign amnesia."[12]

Notwithstanding the psychiatrist's criticism, Milligan's MPD defense proceeded, and in the end proved successful. Milligan was found NGRI for the first time in US courts wherein the MPD defense was upheld in a criminal trial. This proved to be a marginal victory for Dr. Wilbur. During Milligan's psychological assessment by a psychologist, it was discovered that his multiples (alters) tested with differing IQs.

The release of the Sybil transcripts convincingly showed that her story was a phony, enhanced and distorted by a doctor who desired more than anything to have her name in the newspapers and be famous. The Sirhan case as unfolded here demonstrates that he met the diagnostic criteria to make a real dissociative diagnosis; Sirhan is the real deal, not a figment of a Hollywood director's imagination.

To make a valid dissociative diagnosis, a clinician must apply some specific, objective measures or scaling process to determine if a person like Sirhan reflects those supporting psychological symptoms of a dissociative disorder. At the time Sirhan was first examined, no accurate scales existed to access DID. More currently, several appropriate scales can assess the symptomology of dissociation. Each of the three rating scales used here are based on Sirhan's history, thereby they derive their content validity from an analysis of those identifiable factors associated with dissociative conditions. As noted, in some ways similar to making a PTSD assessment, the main set of factors indicating when to make the dissociative diagnosis

---

11 Nathan, D. (2011). *Sybil Exposed: The Extraordinary Story Behind the Famous Multiple Personality Case*. Free Press: A Division of Simon & Schuster, Inc. New York.

12 Keyes, D. (1982). *The Minds of Billy Milligan*. Bantom Books, A Division of Bantom Doubleday, New York, NY, 47.

rests on a person's history of traumatic events and not exclusively on patients' direct recounting of their traumas.

In addition to Sirhan's recorded, firsthand account of the life experiences that negatively impacted him, this analysis is based on select collateral sources of information. This diagnostic patterning, relying on collateral, biographical rewiew and secondary sources, has been used in other applications to assess personality factors such as psychopathy, or psychopathic deviance (PD). The psychopathic deviance "gold standard" measure, the *Hare Psychopathy Checklist–Revised: 2nd Edition* (PCL-R) (2003) allows the use of a collateral or file review process (a "blind analysis") in certain cases to diagnose psychopathic deviation.

The author of the PCL-R, Dr. Robert D. Hare, comments on the use of a file, chart, biographical, or collateral review to assess a condition like psychopathy, "In some situations (e.g., research using archival information, clinical assessments of active psychotic patients), it may prove impossible to conduct a useful interview. A considerable amount of research … indicates that reliable and valid PCL-R ratings can be made solely on the basis of collateral information if it is of sufficiently high quality."[13]

Reviews of clinical records or charts and historical patient data have been effectively used, especially with inpatient psychiatric patients and a variety of prison populations where barriers to one-on-one interviews exist, such as the COVID-19 epidemic, which posed a deterrent to the direct interviewing process. Researchers suggest that a clinical records review usually focuses on specific areas of inquiry.

According to Sarkar and Seshadri (2014), "Clinical records review is a process aimed at obtaining retrospective data to answer specific clinical queries. A clinical records review, as used by forensic psychologists, called a "retrospective data analysis, clinical chart review, chart review, and so on.… The effective utilization of record reviews for seeking answers to specific clinical questions requires adequate planning and use of appropriate data sources."[14]

In Sirhan's situation, the issues addressed centered on the validity of his prior psychiatric diagnoses. The insight into Sirhan's personality dynamics was not based on a single police report or a doctor's clinical assessment, but on a wider universe of retrievable biographical data I accessed

---

13   Hare, Robert. D. (2003). *Hare PCL-R, Technical Manual, 2nd Edition*. Multi-Health Systems, Inc. North Tonawanda, New York.

14   Sarkar, S. and D. Seshadri. (2014). "Conducting Records Reviews in Clinical Practice." J. Clin Diagn Res, 2014, Sep: 8(9): JG04. 10.7860/JCDR/2014/8301.4806 http://www.ncbi.nih.gov/pmc/articles/PMC4225918/

over the years since first becoming involved in the case as a graduate student during Sirhan's trial.

The enhanced window into Sirhan's personality presented here is based on hundreds of hours of researched statements he made over many years and during many interviews, including retrospective professional assessments (i.e., by Dr. Dan Brown and Dr. Simson-Kallas), combined with the probing by investigative journalists such as Dan Moldea and my own extensive time spent with Dr. Diamond. Dr. Diamond's select audio-taped conversations with Sirhan added to the in-depth context provided here. Based on a factor analysis of potential questions to present to Sirhan to assess his psychological conditions, the sampling of areas of inquiry in a review of his clinical case file review supports the psychological opinions extended herein. In my view, the structure of this retrospective survey exceeds the general clinical guidelines necessary to conduct an in-depth case, historic, or file review as established by prior researchers (e.g., Hare, and Sarkar and Seshadri).

Not a surprise to me, the product of this psychological DNA inquiry into Sirhan's personality dynamics yielded five previously unidentified psychological conditions that have substantially changed Sirhan's personality, unalterably shifting his mindset to the "bad" Sirhan (personality2) from the "good" Sirhan (personality 1).

To confirm or disconfirm Sirhan's DID status and other newly diagnosed psychological conditions, I took a step further beyond the ordinary case review suggestions proffered by Hare and Sarkar and Seshadri. To achieve this, I analyzed many passages of "Sirhan in his own words" from trial transcripts as well as an inordinate number of complementary sources of information derived from innumerable interviews to verify Sirhan's history of traumatic events.

The following list of some high-impact trauma factors of Sirhan's known life events is not chronicled in any particular order.

Table III Sirhan's traumatic dissociative life factors
• Death of his older brother, Munir
• Physically forced to circle his brother's casket at the funeral
• Forced relocation of family to war-torn East Jerusalem
• Being thrust into cramped and impoverished living conditions
• Experiencing physical and psychological brutality and infliction of physical punishment by his father (Bishara)

• Witnessing constant bombing raids near Sirhan's home
• Seeing disturbing dismemberment of soldier's foot still in his boot
• Discovering a human hand in the water well, affecting Sirhan's sleep behavior
• Death of his beloved sister, Aida
• Sighting of a deceased man's entrails
• Seeing partial remains of local storekeeper and family friend
• At age seven, witnessing a nine-year-old child hit by shrapnel, with blood streaming down her leg
• Sirhan's horse riding accident and head injury
• Witnessing several young girls who were maimed by military personnel who bragged about their actions
• Witnessing the disembowelment of a man struck by a bomb
• Seeing a group of Arab civilians blown apart at a bus stop

Sirhan's being made to parade around the casket of his deceased older brother, who was struck and killed by a military truck in Jerusalem was reminiscent of a similar scene occurring in the story of *The 3 Faces of Eve*. At age six, Eve White's mother forced her to kiss the face of her dead grandmother as she laid in a casket, ignoring Eve's vehement protests, "Mother, please don't make me … I can't do it!," and hysterical screams of "NO, NO, NO!"

In her case, this symbolic "the kiss of death" provided the psychological impetus for Eve's strange descent into a state of dissociation. Engaging in such a morbid act obviously had an emotional impact that was devastating to a six-year-old. And in a similar way, Sirhan was forced into an emotional conundrum when forced to view his older brother's dead body after witnessing him being hit and killed by a military truck. He was told to circle around his dead brother's casket – an image he later referenced when responding to a Rorschach card. He alluded to his brother's tragic death on Rorschach card IV when he describes what he calls "very dark-serpents and, in another response on the same card, as he grimaced and said, "…it looks like a casket to me. It represents death!" It makes sense that this oblique Rorschach content response was triggered by the image of Munir's casket left imprinted in Sirhan's mental data bank.

According to Dr. Meloy, "The witnessing of extreme violence outside his home and physical abuse by [Sirhan's] father in his home would disrupt the safety necessary for autonomous striving…. [15]

The identification of these known negative, dissociative factors in Sirhan's life can be assessed using one or more of these three current dissociative scales used to diagnose dissociative disorders. Each evaluative scale has been extensively used to assess potential patients with presenting dissociative symptoms. These are not the only dissociative scales in current professional use to help make a differential diagnosis of this complicated disorder, but they remain at the top of my list.

THE WES VERSUS LEE CASE

Several years after the conclusion of the Sirhan trial, during my second psychology internship this time at Oakland General Hospital, Psychiatric Unit, in Oakland, California, many new admissions presented with long histories of substance abuse and/or chronic psychiatric diagnoses. Some patients who, subsequent to an arrest evidenced signs of mental illness, were sent by the sheriff's or Oakland Police Department.

Because Highland served 1.3 million residents of Alameda County, it was a busy place. The Highland psych unit (D-1 only had fifty beds available to treat acute, psychiatric patients, and the demand greatly exceeded the supply). At the time Wes Nelson was hospitalized, California was struggling to deal with massive changes in mental health care policies including the closure of major mental health facilities throughout the state. Rapidly apparent to most mental health workers was that closing psychiatric hospitals was a colossal political and social blunder.

Thousands of mentally disturbed and addicted patients suddenly became dispossessed as societal "throwaways," and turned to the streets out of desperation for refuge. With nowhere for acutely disturbed mental patients, substance abusers, and other patients to go, the overwhelming crisis of homelessness began as we can still see on the streets throughout the once "golden" state.

Initially, I was assigned to do assessments of new patients, "intakes" on newly referred patients regardless of who made the referral and for what clinical reason. I served as a kind of triage doctor, hoping to assign the patients to the most appropriate section of the psych unit. Month after month as my one-year internship progressed, I saw at least one hundred troubled souls come in for acute psychiatric treatment and then be discharged to their families, to community halfway houses, or to whomever in their lives was willing to care for them. Some of the discharged patients remained homeless and, in many instances, I saw them again as their coping skills again became overly challenged.

Often a male patient (new or repeat referral) was referred by his wife because he apparently was out of control and exhibited aggressive behaviors and seemed to meet the criteria under the California Welfare and Institutions Code, 5150, as a danger to themselves or to others, or gravely disabled. Almost immediately I sensed that something was a little different about Wes Nelson, beginning with his loud protestations: "I don't need to be here again. I didn't do anything wrong this time, and now I'll be locked up like some sort of a criminal. I haven't done a crime or anything!"

As Wes made his statement, his wife of twenty-years, Carole, patiently tried to calm him down. She encouraged him saying, "It'll be okay, honey, you've been here before, I know, and the doctors are here to help you. Maybe medications will help you. They worked before."

I introduced myself and explained that my job was to do whatever I could to assess their situation, provide treatment, and get this troubled man back home as soon as possible. I said, "Mr. Nelson, you're here for a routine psych evaluation so, as Carole said, we can help you. I see you've been here before, so that should make this easier."

I extended my hand to Wes to shake his, and he obliged, finally shaking mine, and we were off. I paused my conversation with Wes and asked, If he would like a drink: soda, coffee or whatever." He said, "Yes, coffee, cream and sugar would be great."

I motioned Carole to accompany me, and I told Wes, "We'll be right back. Please sit there and try to relax."

This coffee break provided the perfect opportunity to talk to Carole alone and gather new information about Wes's situation including his previous history of psychiatric admissions. She told me that she referred Wes because "almost for no reason, he just started acting crazy-like. Throwing things around our apartment and saying nonsense stuff. This has been going on for about two weeks now. For some reason, he's having these terrible nightmares over and over again about his mother's death. He wakes up in a cold sweat and says that he just can't forget what happened to her. I know the story – maybe not all the details – but from what I do know, it's very tragic, her killing herself and all. And right in front of him when he was little."

From the conversation, it was evident that Wes would need Carole's continued support to help him navigate the strange psychological journey he was about to take, or I should say, all three of us were about to embark on. We returned to the interview room with the coffee, and Wes was admitted to Ward D-1 and assigned to a bed. Ward D-I housed about ten other male patients, many who, like Wes, could only be treated for up to fourteen days (the county could not legally hold him without his consent longer under California Welfare and Institutions Code 5150).

With two days on medication, Wes was stabilized. Wes's initial confusion and resistance to be hospitalized greatly diminished. Once he was in a composed state, Wes seemed gentle, his mannerisms polite. He was respectful of the other patients and appeared to be just a quiet guy. During treatment sessions, he spoke softly, choosing his words carefully as he assumed an almost passive demeanor, easy to get along with and certainly not aggressive or violent. I learned about his violent temper and proclivity to act out later as described in several Oakland Police Department's police reports.

During subsequent sessions, Wes kept conversation on the light side, making me wonder if he was talking just to talk, and not addressing important areas that were only unwrapped later. Because this was his third or fourth admission, I contacted central records in the main hospital to retrieve his complete psychiatric file. The file was almost three inches thick, containing the psychiatrists' varied diagnoses and nursing notes, doctor's notes, and progress notes from his prior admissions. Wes's conflicting psychiatric diagnoses were made by a variety of doctors who had seen him during the past five years. In the middle of the large file, I found several police reports from Oakland PD.

When I thumbed through them, I saw that Wes had been arrested numerous times on a variety of criminal charges ranging from assault to assault with a deadly weapon and attempted murder. These seemed uncharacteristic of the polite man I talked to daily. Several more serious charges (assault with a deadly weapon: a knife) were plea bargained down to simple assaults for which he was placed on probation and two sixty-day county jail terms. Still this was not consistent with the passive man I continued to interview. He was also accused of first-degree robbery of several liquor stores in East Oakland.

Because my knowledge of these arrests for his violent offenses could have sabotaged my interaction as well as with Wes's treatment goals, I decided to momentarily put aside Wes's fairly extensive "rap sheet," considering it a possible confrontational issue. After all, this psychiatric admission wasn't based on any pending criminal charges; so during the next few days, I entered my own comments on Wes's condition in the progress notes section of his hospital file.

Unexpectedly Wes was the one who raised the issue of his police reports as we sat in an interview room, with his ever-growing psychiatric file sitting on the desk between us. His revelatory and candid comments provided the key to answering, *Who really is Wes Nelson?* Wes revealed an important diagnostic issue that was not discussed with previous doctors who, as I noticed, entered various psychiatric diagnoses in the doctors' notes section in his psychiatric file, none of which mentioned Wes's true underlying condition.

The varied diagnoses ranged from paranoid schizophrenia, personality disorder, to psychopathic personality disorder, with a few additional psychotic disorders thrown into the mix. After reading these, I wondered why his core condition still remained shrouded after all these hospitalizations. That is similar to Sirhan's case, where too many doctors couldn't arrive at the bottom-line, agreed-upon diagnosis!

Throughout *Psych DNA*, I have emphasized that Sirhan's defense doctors completely missed his most important psychiatric diagnoses – multiple personality disorder (MPD) or dissociative identity disorder (DID), and complex post-traumatic stress disorder (C-PTSD), and three additional, destabilizing conditions. Much to my astonishment, Wes Nelson, the man sitting in front to me, confined to a locked psychiatric ward, was about to reveal something he had not acknowledged to any previous doctors. During a particular session when we discussed his symptomatic history, Wes informed me that he suspected for a long time that he was actually two people – Wes and Lee Nelson coexisting in one person, a man with two distinct personalities became infinitively more complicated than I originally assumed. *So much for clinical assumptions,* I thought.

For a long period, Wes sat in his chair and fixated on his file on the desk between us. As his eyes narrowed, he appeared deep in thought when he asked, "Dr. Brady, when were you going to bring up those police reports on the desk there?"

This was a cathartic moment for both of us. I answered: "When I thought that information could best help you. You know, somehow fit into your treatment plan."

Wes responded with another unanticipated statement. "How would you like to know that I didn't do any of that stuff you can see in those police reports. I'm telling you, it was always Lee, not me, who did that stuff. Sure, he wanted to blame all that bad stuff on me, but that was just a joke. He was always trying to blame me! I guess that's his way."

I asked, "And what exactly do you mean, 'I didn't do any of that stuff?'" This session paved the long road of investigation into the intriguing Wes vs. Lee case. I was finally able to confirm the underlying psychiatric diagnosis for Wes, the confused, fifty-three-year-old male psychiatric patient whose strange behaviors were later diagnosed as MPD.

As Carole mentioned, the key repressed, traumatic event in Wes's life was witnessing his mother's gruesome suicide when he was eight years old. Painfully, Wes recounted how she impaled herself in the stomach area with a large butcher knife and bled profusely from her abdominal area until she finally died. A frightening scene for the young boy, and one Wes just couldn't eradicate from his mind, thus explaining his recurrent nightmares, repeating this tragic incident again and again. For him, this emotionally charged experience was more than his ordinary state of consciousness could filter out, thus he relegated it into a separate compartmentalized zone that was later confirmed as an alter personality, Lee Nelson. Lee emerged as more or less Wes's evil twin, a Dr. Jekyll/Mr. Hyde situation not unlike the two Sirhans.

Almost immediately after his mother's suicide, Wes began his rapid personality split, and a second (alter) personality, Lee, the nefarious one, emerged, who seemed better equipped psychologically to mediate his perceived guilt about his mother's death. During the course of hypnotherapy two additional personalities were introduced, joining Wes and Lee.

Later while serving a second-year internship at the San Francisco VA Hospital, I was exposed to returning Vietnam veterans, several of whom, because of the horrors of war, had dissociated, and formed a second identity in order to escape the pain they experienced seeing their comrades cut down by the Viet Cong Army. The dramatic emergence of their coexisting personalities reminded me of how Lee had developed alter personalities, Lee, as the stronger, more aggressive personality who was somehow able to deal with the childhood trauma of seeing his mother stabbing herself, and his own futile attempt to save her.

Based on prior research into diagnosing multiple personalities, I knew that some psychological assessment was required to substantiate Wes's multiple personality condition. Similar to the assessment of Sirhan conducted by Drs. Richardson and Schorr, I used the tools available to psychologists focusing on the MMPI to assess Wes's hysterical characteristics in a same way Sirhan was assessed. Wes's MMPI profile pointed out the hysterical features in his personality, a feature consistent with MPD. At the time, about 1969, hysteria as a primary psychiatric diagnosis was closely tied to the emergence of an MPD condition. An analysis of Wes's MMPI scales showed a distinct elevation on the hysteria and the paranoid scales.

In many ways, Wes's MMPI profile was similar to Sirhan's, perhaps helping to explain the identification of his paranoid thoughts, believing that the world was "out to get him." However, when considering the information used against Sirhan during his trial, perhaps he had good reason to appear suspicious.[16]

Research into MPD, or what is now identified DID, convincingly establishes that DID in females greatly exceeds males. As diagnostic measures to access DID became more focused during the 1980s, the occurrence of male-related DID increased. The male frequency began to rise for this once thought to be rare psychiatric condition in men.

On several occasions under hypnosis, Wes was induced to manifest or switch into the malevolent Lee Nelson, the constant troublemaker no doubt responsible for the commission of crimes unfairly attributed to Wes as he protested.

Under hypnosis as Lee, he told me, "I knew he [Wes] wasn't strong enough to deal with the suicide situation [his mother's]. Somebody had to stand up and be strong. And I guess it was me. I guess that all my life I wanted to, you know, just get even for what happened to Helen [his mother]. Sure, I robbed a liquor store or two and got into street fights. One of us had to stand up and fight, and Wes was just a weakling not able to deal with it. He just didn't have the guts to do what I did. He's never been with it, if you know what I mean."

Referring back to the Sirhan case, my viewpoint, based on the accumulated psychiatric evidence at the time of the trial, is that Sirhan met the criteria for a dissociative disorder, and could have been diagnosed with DID. To confirm this definitive diagnosis, I needed to find considerable psychological proof to substantiate my clinical impression. When considering Sirhan's tumultuous history, it was easy to piece together all the necessary elements consistent with a DID diagnosis.

At an early point in Wes's life, he (like Sirhan) split his personality, dividing into two independent, opposing states; the first (personality 1) was the adjusted personality perfectly capable of remaining honest, socially outgoing, and law-abiding and happily married, and then a second (personality 2), the dissociative Lee, characterized as an argumentative, malevolent, plotting, alternative personality, quite capable of doing bad things, stopping short of murder. Sirhan's personality 2 included the motivation to commit the cold-blooded murder of RFK.

---

16   Brady, J.C. (1976). "Wes and Lee: One Person or a Divided Self?" Unpublished paper, Clinical-Criminal Psychology Services Center, Oakland, CA.

All the subsequent elements necessary to develop the composite mental picture of Wes and Sirhan presented here flow from this primary MPD diagnosis. During treatment, Wes continued to struggle with the sometime spontaneous switching (changing personalities) at those times when Lee became prominent – "I wish he [Lee] would never come back. I'd really like to kill that bastard. He's already caused me lots of problems including being here."

Over time, Wes's splitting episodes into the antisocial Lee, though still problematic, decreased in frequency. After Wes's fourteen-day involuntary psychiatric hold in the hospital, Carole was able to take him home.

Agreeing to a limited number of follow-up outpatient sessions, Wes kept most of his future scheduled appointments. With the assistance of medication, using the antipsychotic drug Stelazine, Wes's impulse controls appeared to be in check, and his former acting-out episodes, according to Carole, appreciably decreased. Most importantly, Wes's unwanted intruder, Lee, became somewhat of a stranger rather than a meddlesome companion.

Unfortunately, because of the limited resources available through the county, I was only able to see Wes on a limited basis several times with Carole, who had provided strong emotional support and a caring attitude. Moving forward, Carole verified the fact that Wes's night terrors, triggered by the thoughts of his mother's grizzly suicide, had decreased in frequency. Of course, a more in-depth treatment approach would have been preferential, but I had to work within the county's guidelines. A more prolonged therapeutic approach might have centered around the possible elimination of Lee's occasional disruption as the hostile alter personality.

Of import to Wes's case, during one of his seminars presented at the San Francisco VA hospital, Dr. John Watkins explained the process he used to decondition what he termed the malevolent alters, MALS. Though Watkins's MALS intervention seemed to be a good fit to finally banish Lee's intruder personality from Wes's life, I was not afforded the chance to use it.

DR. ALLISON'S MARK VERSUS CARL MULTIPLE PERSONALITY CASE

During my research on Sirhan's case, Dr. Ralph Allison's work with MPD cases came to my attention. For many years working as a forensic psychiatrist, he devoted himself to unwinding the mysteries of these complex cases, specializing in MPD research. During an interview with him, I discovered that he, like myself, wondered about the frequency of male multiples. He commented, "There was a time when I might have concluded that male multiple personality patients were unlikely to exist, because so few men suffer the same kinds of trauma endured by my female patients: rape or extreme sexual abuse. However, as first one and then another male sought my treatment, each showing signs of multiplicity, I realized there were no certainties in this field, especially regarding the sex of a MPD or the exact diagnosis."[17]

In agreement with Dr. Allison's perspective, I also learned that there was no set primer guiding the inquiry into the multiple personality patient. Now understandably, along with Dr. Allison, I was on a road less traveled. In his book, *Minds in Many Pieces*, Dr. Allison described one of his first cases of male MPD, the Mark vs. Carl saga; a multiple personality case involving trauma and ultimately a conviction for first-degree murder. Dr. Allison's first, clinical tip-off to Mark's host personality's multiplicity centered on his memory deficit. "Mark's lack of memory was the first clue to his illness, although I did not initially think of multiple personality in connection with his case. At the time I only knew he had tremendous emotional problems stemming from the death of his mother in an auto accident for which he felt responsible."

Dr. Allison noticed the spontaneous emergence of Mark's first alter, Carl, during an emotional treatment session: "All of a sudden an enraged monster emerged.... When I called him 'Mark' he cursed me loudly and made it quite clear that his name was Carl." In many ways, Mark's trauma connected to his mother's death was similar to the description of Wes's initial personality demarcation that led to the emergence of the maladapted, law-violating Lee, in my case.

Dr. Allison discovered that Mark's initial or precipitating trauma also involved a more serious event around the death of his mother. He relived the scene of his mother's tragic fatal auto accident, "...the sight of his mother's head separating from her body as she was killed instantly ... a nightmare that may have replayed itself endlessly inside his head, although he never shared his feelings with anyone else."

Mark's alter personality in the form of Carl – the vengeful, violent alter, was responsible for murder but not tried, and his presence was never revealed. Mark was tried and convicted of first-degree murder in a Califor-

17   Allison, R. with T. Schwarz. (1980). *Minds in Many Pieces: The Making of a Very Special Doctor.* Rawson, Wade Publishers, Inc., New York, 159.

nia court and, like Sirhan, sentenced to death. Again like Sirhan's, his prison sentence was commuted to life in prison with the possibility of parole.

Just as, throughout his trial, Sirhan firmly resisted the introduction of the diminished capacity defense (the psychiatric reasoning explaining his felonious killing of RFK) because he insisted he was "not crazy," Mark's greatest fear (as Dr. Allison recounted) was that he did not want to be labeled as a "psych head case."

Mark and Sirhan shared the same illogical belief that there was no convincing reason that their dark secrets should be exposed to a jury or to the public even if it could spare their lives. Dr. Allison preserved Mark's dark secrets, including his MPD diagnosis. He did not testify as a defense witness at his trial, and Mark willingly walked into death row unembarrassed.

DR. EDUARD SIMSON-KALLAS CAME THE CLOSEST

The psychologist who probably learned the most about Sirhan's mental status, Dr. Eduard Simson-Kallas, who analyzed Sirhan post-conviction as Sirhan also sat on death row, entered the diagnostic wars too late to provide information in Sirhan's behalf, nevertheless his professional viewpoint was essential in furthering our understanding of Sirhan's complete psychodynamics.

Though Dr. Simson-Kallas came closest to comprehending Sirhan's personality structure, he was overshadowed by the experts who assessed Sirhan before and during his trial in early 1969. Dr. Simson-Kallas had developed important, new insights into Sirhan far beyond what the assessing doctors could have possibly garnered from an analysis of Sirhan's Rorschach and TAT tests. A portion of his analysis was exposed to a Monterey, California radio audience during a recorded interview by Brussell in 1977.

Simson-Kallas interviewed Sirhan on San Quentin's death row more than twenty times for more than thirty-five hours, and he commented from a transcript that, from the start of the trial, he did not trust the defense team of doctors and attorneys comprised mostly of Jewish men. Sirhan told Dr. Simson-Kallas that he wanted to be represented by Arab attorneys, because he "just didn't trust Jews!"

A year before Simson-Kallas's radio interview, he was questioned by CBS reporter Dan Rather. Simson-Kallas told Rather that he suspected that Sirhan was covertly set up to take the fall for the RFK killing, just like Lee Harvey Oswald was set up as a "patsy" to take responsibility for the assassination of JFK in 1963. He told Rather, "My hypothesis is there had to be other people involved; someone else who set him up as the lone gunman. He [Sirhan] is the ideal person because he is a follower. Essentially he follows orders and is willing to die. He doesn't even ask many questions."[18] Simson-Kallas suggested that Sirhan was possibly hypnotically programmed, assuming the role as a distractor, as a "Manchurian Candidate," as the real killer fired the fatal shot that killed RFK.

However, Sirhan's complaint about only being represented by Jewish attorneys wasn't altogether representative of what actually occurred during the trial. Sirhan was also represented by a young Arab attorney, Abdeen Jabara, a Detroit-based attorney appointed by defense attorney Russell Parsons to serve as a defense legal consultant.

The trial judge, Judge Walker, also welcomed in a second Arab attorney, Mr. Issa Nakhleh, the director of the Palestinian-Arab Delegation to the UN, a member in good standing of the English Bar, and a well-recognized Palestinian lawyer. Defense counsel, Mr. Cooper quickly moved, "to admit Mr. Nakhleh's brief appearance into the case simply as an advisor to Sirhan for approximately one week."

Judge Walker granted Cooper's motion, so Sirhan had his requested Arab legal representation as the trial moved forward.

Even with Jabara at his side at the defense table, Sirhan continued to voice a lack of trust and confidence in what he believed to be "a weak Jewish-dominated defense team. Maybe coming too late, Sirhan renewed his trust, placing it in prison psychologist Dr. Simson-Kallas.[19]

Shortly after Sirhan arrived on San Quentin's death row, Dr. Simson-Kallas recognized that Sirhan was free of florid psychotic symptoms and that included paranoid schizophrenia, and he suggested that Sirhan was psychologically operating in an alter or dissociative state of awareness.

THE HILLSIDE STRANGLER CASE

The Hillside Strangler Case demonstrates how a validly diagnosed MPD or DID can be differentiated from a pseudo-diagnosis. Dr. Ralph Allison told me that in 1979 he became involved in probably his most well-known murder case involving a man who ostensibly manifested a MPD diagnosis. Kenneth Bianchi was one of the two convicted murderers in the Hillside Strangler case. During the two-state (California and Washington) murder rampage, two male cousins, Kenneth Bianchi and

---

18   Dan Rather, *CBS News*, American Assassins. 1976.
19   Brussell, M. Interview with Dr. Eduard Simson-Kallas. June 13, 1977. Dialogue Conspiracy Show, Radio Station KLRB, Carmel, CA.

Angelo Buono were ultimately implicated and arrested for the murders of up to ten women who they sometimes raped and then discarded their lifeless bodies on the hillsides adjacent to freeways.

Dr. Allison's well-publicized analysis of half of the infamous duo, Kenneth Bianchi, provides valuable insights into Bianchi's claim of being a multiple personality and has direct implications to the present discussion of the two Sirhans. Dr. Allison had persistent professional problems with the diagnostic criteria developed by the American Psychiatric Association formulation of what clinically constituted a dissociative identity disorder. He was particularly troubled because he had to diagnose then present the Bianchi case in court as a man experiencing MPD, but he wasn't sure.

When I began to research the confusing MPD diagnosis, and its application to Sirhan, I quickly learned that even the pioneers in the field of dissociative disorders, such as Dr. Morton Prince (the Chambeau case) and Dr. Thigpen and Dr. Cleckley (*The 3 Faces of Eve* case) also had to overcome diagnostic barriers of their own. As I read more about these doctors' travels into the murky area of dissociative states, I shared their feeling as if they were alone wandering in a fog the more I dug into my Sirhan analysis.

Dr. Allison also told me that during the course of his decades of experience, he too struggled to match the more than forty-eight multiple personality cases he treated using the varied criteria for MPD as loosely defined by the American Psychiatric Association. He said that all patients with MPD have been in such different situations, changing motives, and show such variations in behaviors, mood, and thought patterns that, in reality, "there is no typical MPD patient."

I thought that Sirhan could easily fit within Dr. Allison's framework of MPD. Dr. Allison mentioned that he offered diagnostic suggestions to the DSM's Review Group for Dissociative Disorders to modify the restricted, diagnostic criteria for DID. He argued as I do that the diagnostic criteria to make the diagnosis is confusing and limiting to the practitioner. Dr. Daniel Brown, who also identified Sirhan's second personality, felt that he was prevented from making a DID diagnosis because of the DSM's restrictive language: "Disruption of identity characterized by two or more distinct personality states...." Dr. Brown instead classified Sirhan with dissociative disorder not otherwise specified (DDNOS).

Between October and early November in 1977, the Hillside Strangler case made front-page headlines in the *Los Angeles Times,* sparking the public's fear throughout southern California that perhaps another

Charles Manson serial killer was once again slaughtering unsuspecting females. The murders began again in December and February when two more women were found strangled to death, this time in Bellingham, Washington.

The LA sheriff's Strangler Task Force initially was left baffled in their search for the killer or killers until the stranglers struck two more times, this time in Washington State, when Bianchi was finally arrested and linked by the Task Force to the LA cases. Bianchi's cousin, Angelo Buono, was implicated, indicted, and then tried and convicted for first-degree murder in a separate California courtroom. Bianchi's trial was held in Bellingham, Washington, for his raping and murdering two young women: a twenty-two-year-old and a twenty-seven-year-old in a vacant house in Bellingham, Washington, in 1979.

Dr. Allison was faced with another psychiatric conundrum when he was called upon as an expert witness on dissociative MPD disorders to assess and diagnosis Bianchi, a codefendant who claimed that he didn't really kill the two women, because he was a multiple personality, thus his alter Steve Walker did it!

Dr. Allison was a good choice to check out Bianchi's alleged MPD claim and was joined by five additional doctors all charged with determining if Bianchi was sane at the time of the murders, and if he suffered from MPD.

The issue of the differential diagnosis of MPD in Sirhan's case and in the Bianchi case still remained problematic for me, for Dr. Allison, and apparently for Dr. Brown. Dr. Allison discussed how difficult it is to make the MPD diagnosis: "The diagnosis of the multiple personality condition is difficult enough in the case of clinical patients, with their extensive us of denial, repression, and dissociation. The difficulty is greatly compounded when the individual under consideration is charged with first degree murder and is facing the death penalty."[20]

Initially, Dr. Allison diagnosed Bianchi as experiencing a true MPD as he wrote to the trial judge, The Honorable Jack S. Kurtz, on April 22, 1979: "Mr. Bianchi suffers from what is currently classified as a hysterical neurosis, dissociative type (multiple personality). He is a dual personality and has been so since the age of nine. At that time, he created an alter personality which took the name 'Steve Walker' ... Ken Bianchi is able to understand what he is charged with, but his amnesia for the actual in-

20   Allison, R. (1984). "Difficulties Diagnosing the Multiple Personality Syndrome." *Inter. Journal of Clinical and Experimental Hypnosis*, Vol 32, No.2, 102–117.

stances [murders] during which his body was under the control of Steve Walker. ...Whenever the Steve Walker personality takes over, there is no awareness of wrongfulness of any conduct he wants to do, his impulse control is nonexistent. ..."

Dr. Allison forewarned the judge that these diagnostic conclusions are only "first glance" professional views subject to him receiving additional corroborating data from other sources, including reports from the additional doctors who also assesses Bianchi.[21]

After Dr. Allison gathered more important background data on Bianchi sometime later, he changed his professional diagnosis of Bianchi, thereby rejecting his previous MPD diagnosis as he explained, "This was not a usual situation for me in working clinically with multiple personality syndrome patients, as many times bits of data emerged which could not, at the time, be understood in the total context. ... The facts which I now looked at with more attention, however, fitted a dissociative disorder, but not what I knew to be the multiple personality syndrome. In court, I testified that I had come to a new conclusion regarding Bianchi's psychiatric diagnosis."[22]

After Dr. Allison changed his MPD diagnosis, he added a footnote to the Bianchi story. He told me that because he was in the minority of the doctors who had verified Bianchi's MPD, Dr. Allison was subtly pressured to change the diagnosis back. Three of the six doctors believed that Bianchi was legally insane experiencing MPD at the time of the crimes, and three rejected this claim.

Dr. Allison continued to resist the pressure, and ultimately he was proven right because Bianchi turned out to be diagnostically nothing more than a psychopathic serial killer. Based on the three-three split decision, Bianchi's attorney, Dean Brett, agreed to a plea bargain in which Bianchi would plead guilty to two counts of first degree murder in Washington and five counts of first degree murder in California in exchange for his testimony against Angelo Buono.[23]

Dr. John Watkins was one of the psychologists who strongly believed Bianchi's MPD story. As a full professor of psychology at the University of Montana, he specialized in the use of hypnosis to treat a variety of dissociative conditions. His seminal book, *Hypnotherapy of War Neuroses: A Clinical Psychologist's Casebook,* first published in 1947, is still a standard

---

21   Allison, R. (April 22, 1979). Bianchi Report #1 to The Honorable Jack S. Kurtz, Judge of the Superior Court, Whatcom County Courthouse, Bellingham, WA.
22   Allison. (1984). 102–117.
23   Personal Communication with Dr. Ralph Allison, September 27, 2022.

reference on the subject. I listened to his many lectures presented at the San Francisco Veterans Hospital where I was a psychology intern. Many of his presentations explored his use of clinical hypnosis and deep-trance work he employed with MPD patients.

He always brought with him an intriguing selection of audiotape recordings made with a variety of MPD cases he had diagnosed and treated. I looked forward to his dynamic presentations, and he never failed to deliver. These seminars during my second-year internship were always informative, instructional, and at times very dramatic, demonstrating how he used hypnosis to bring out or switch one or more personalities from a MPD patient. One of his unique tapes concerned the integration of two distinct personalities in one patient as the host personality was about to eliminate the alter.

Dr. Watkins' extensive background with multiple personality cases paralleled Dr. Allison's. Dr. Watkins' recorded sessions with Bianchi were considerably less dramatic nevertheless convincing enough to him to believe that Bianchi was the real deal – as it turned out Bianchi wasn't. He was a psychopathic serial killer, a liar, and a fairly good actor.

Despite the fact that, in the end, Dr. Watkins' view of Bianchi's MPD proved faulty, he consistently put forth the valid notion that oftentimes with multiple personalities there is no direct communication between the alter states. This is the same belief I had developed with Sirhan whose two distinct personalities never reached a point of mutual awareness, therefore they remained separate from each other. Watkins and Allison both argued that there is no single identified pattern of shared awareness or coconscious states between MPD personalities.[24]

Dr. Allison presented two necessary psychological factors he used to ultimately reject his original MPD diagnosis of Bianchi: "Before I list the factors in this particular case which caused me to change my original diagnosis, I must emphasize that there is no typical patient with multiple personality syndrome against which to match any future patient.... Diagnosis from any list of necessary findings, as implied by the *DSM-III*, leads one into the pigeonhole myth."[25]

Referring to these two important factors Dr. Allison ultimately felt he could establish that Bianchi wasn't a true MPD case. Conversely, these same factors confirmed for me that Sirhan was a multiple. His first factor – no witnesses to personality changes – is essential. Dr. Allison could not

24   Schwarz, T. (1988). *The Hillside Strangler: A Murderer's Mind.* Peabody Books, c/o Vivisphere Publishing, Poughkeepsie, NY, 252.
25   Personal communication with Dr. Ralph Allison, September 27, 2022.

locate anyone, especially family members, to corroborate the presence of any noticeable changes in Bianchi's moods, interaction patterns, general demeanor, or the existence of what might be considered a different personality, and clearly not a multiple personality.

When we examine similar life factors in Sirhan's case that could evidence a separate personality (personality 2), a different picture emerges. Ample firsthand accounts of Sirhan's sudden shifts in personality style, mostly based on his early childhood personality changes, were witnessed by his mother and others after he was exposed to innumerable traumatic scenes related to the Arab-Israeli war that tore apart his physical world and emotional anchor. Sirhan's mother Mary documented many observable changes in Sirhan's personality and behavior and how she tried to provide comfort and aid to him during the street bombings in Jerusalem.

Periods of social withdrawal and confusion persisted in Sirhan's life reconfirmed by his brother, Adel, who witnessed Sirhan's progressive personality alterations. Adel wanted to reach into Sirhan's "dark world," rescue him, and provide security for his struggling brother.

Dr. Allison's second psychological factor – aggression toward victim(s) – is an element he has seen in almost all his MPD patients who committed murder (e.g., a read hatred toward the selected target). In the Bianchi situation, leading up to the double murders of the two women in Washington State, Dr. Allison wrote, "None of the victims had any emotional tie to Bianchi. They were not threats to him in any way. ... Defendants with multiple personality syndrome, whom I have met since the Bianchi case, each killed a spouse or a parent figure when their anger toward that individual overwhelmed their repressive abilities."[26]

In Sirhan's case, his personality 2 (the aggressive Sirhan) was filled with anger and hatred toward RFK who he saw as a real threat to himself and his Arab people (his paradoxical love-then-hate relationship with RFK, characterized as an erotomania-motivated murder syndrome). From Sirhan's court testimony and his interviews with the diagnosing doctors, he held nothing back, revealing his hatred of all things RFK: "If he was standing here now in front of me, I'd blast him!"

In an interview with Robert Kaiser, about Sirhan's deep-seated hatred and anger toward everything Israel, Sirhan told Kaiser, "I was all tied up.; The Arab Israeli [conflict] ... " sounding quite confused, and in a manner quite unlike a political terrorist. Referring to this hate pattern he had developed, Sirhan said, "This is what puzzles me ... I have hatred, but

---

26   Allison. (1984). 102–117.

not that much. Hatred was very foreign to me. That bothers me. I can't understand it."

For Sirhan's personality 1 (adjusted and conforming), this hatred represented a negative emotion somewhat foreign to him, yet a serious, psychologically contaminating factor when he switched from the law-abiding, adjusted Sirhan into the retaliatory, vindictive dissociative Sirhan. Sirhan's adjusted personality 1 was not infected with any of the homicidal thoughts of his personality 2 counterpart.

Dr. Allison's focused, acute anger patterning directed at victims absent in the Bianchi case was continuously present in Sirhan's dissociated, rage-filled alter. Sirhan's anger was directed toward a single goal leading up to the RFK assassination: destroy a powerful force before it destroyed him.

Although Dr. Allison's revised diagnosis of Bianchi did not include MPD, he said, "I do not believe Bianchi was deliberately and consciously faking the multiple personality syndrome clinical picture – the clinical elements just weren't there."

Because of Dr. Allison's treatment-centered approach with Bianchi, he was able to elicit what was assumed to be Bianchi's alter self in the form of "Steve Walker," bringing him out.

If Dr. Diamond had followed through with his initial "clinical hunch" that Sirhan had a dissociated alter personality that occupied a considerable space lodged somewhere in his hidden mind, the two Sirhans might have been equally exposed, leading to filling in many informational gaps the adjusted Sirhan simply did not have access to. To expose Sirhan to the reality of being a multiple personality, in Dr. Diamond's view, seemed remote, in that Sirhan already felt over-psychologized and was tired of the constant psychiatric probing process.

Dr. Watkins puts forth another unique concern about uncovering or exposing a patient, or making them aware of their status as a multiple, or that they may have two or more distinct personalities, because the multiple status may be a defense against becoming overtly psychotic. In other words, in his view, the multiple status insulates the patient from a deeper plunge into a world of psychosis. He applied this reasoning in the Bianchi case. "He was being forced to face aspects of himself he hated, and his denial mechanism has always done this by letting a different personality take control.... If this was the case, then the personality writing to me might very well be innocent. This personality did not commit the crimes. It was some other personality."[27]

27   Schwarz. (2001). 250.

Dr. Diamond also addressed the issue of Sirhan's hiding, or masking his psychiatric disorder by faking or simulating sanity to avoid the negative stigma ascribed to the mentally ill. This was a particularly touchy cultural issue Sirhan faced because, in Arab culture, the acceptance of a psychiatric diagnosis portends moral weakness. Dr. Diamond was constantly fighting this battle with Sirhan, even though Sirhan knew that even a partial psychiatric defense like diminished capacity was in his best self-interest to spare his life.

As Dr. Diamond stated, "It has been my experience that the willful concealment of mental illness, that is sanity, is very frequent, even in persons accused of serious crimes where mental illness would be an adequate defense.... Since biblical times, people have feared that criminals would escape punishment by feigning insanity. Yet in actual fact, feigned insanity is very uncommon."[28]

As it turned out, Steve Walker, Bianchi's alleged alter personality according to Dr. Allison, was an artifact, simply a mental creation that Bianchi held onto and could be used in an MPD defense; but in actuality, the character Steve Walker was what Dr. Allison termed an "immature, imaginary companion" not a multiple personality.

Although Dr. Watkins disagreed with Dr. Allison's reasoning for decades, he cultivated an interest in the diagnosis and treatment of MPD. He was qualified in several states as an expert witness to testify in various dissociative criminal cases. It was Dr. Watkins's professional opinion that Bianchi definitely was the real deal – a multiple personality. The doctor's opinion was contrasted with a second doctor's assessment of Bianchi's mental status.

Dr. Allison initially believed he misdiagnosed Bianchi as experiencing MPD, although as more disconfirming evidence came to his attention, he changed his diagnosis. He stated, "The facts which I now looked at with more attention, however, fitted a dissociative disorder, but not what I knew to be the multiple personality syndrome. In court, I testified that I had come to a new conclusion regarding Bianchi's psychiatric diagnosis."[29]

In Dr. Schorr's clinical assessment, when asked whether Sirhan was aware of his second personality, he said, "I don't believe that he is at all aware that the personality of the killer, the personality of the assaulter, the preying guy on society, is his personality at all. He is not consciously aware of it.... One is not aware of the other...."

28   Diamond, B.L. (1956). "The Simulation of Sanity." *J. Soc. Ther.*, 2:158–165.
29   Allison. (1984). 102–117. Personal Communication with Dr. Ralph Allison, September 27, 2022.

About the same time as Sirhan was on trial, Dr. George Estabrooks raised an interesting question, "What if a multiple personality could be created using a variety of hypnotic techniques?"

On the other hand, Dr. Estabrooks wrote, "The potential dangers of hypnosis are as real as its potential benefits. But both the benefits and dangers derive from the human condition. Hypnosis will not determine the future of the human mind. But the future of the human mind will determine the future of hypnosis. If we choose to emphasize the least desirable qualities in ourselves, hypnosis will reflect that choice."

Dr. Estabrooks' notion of the least desirable qualities might be manifested in a synthetically and hypnotically produced multiple personality, like the hypno-programmed killer in the 1959 novel by Richard Condon, *The Manchurian Candidate.* The book's premise is constructed on a Soviet cold-war communist vision of turning a former military officer into a sleeper agent to carry out a planned assassinations – by using hypnosis as a brainwashing technique, thereby creating what can be construed as an alter or multiple personality to do the dirty work.

Dr. Estabrooks, who chronicled hypno-analytical research dating from biblical times, addressed the real-life possibility of using a hypnotic state to create a multiple personality. "The job would take time, but it would be entirely possible to carry out. Because hypnosis is such a powerful tool, and dissociation such a common psychological mechanism – after all, all the material in the unconscious that has been pushed there by repression is dissociated from the conscious personality, and some such dissociated material can be found in even the healthiest of us – an able hypnotist, working with a good hypnotic subject could, if he went about it in the proper way, split the subject's personality into two completely dissociated parts."

Dr. Estabrooks went on to caution how the bond between the hypnotist and subject could affect the outcome: "For in no case of hypnotic behavior can we be really sure which member of the partnership, hypnotist or subject, is being hypnotized: the unconscious mind has such extraordinary sensitivity and acuity that the subject often knows the hypnotist's expectations and wishes better than the hypnotist does himself."[30]

Forensic psychiatrist, Dr. Colin Ross, told me during an interview that, in his view, Sirhan could have been a self-created Manchurian candidate. He went on to say that he wasn't persuaded by the conspiracy theories that Sirhan was set up as an externally programmed killer, yet he agreed with

---

30   Estabrooks, G.H. and Gross, N.E. (2017). 219–222.

the notion that Sirhan was probably in a self-induced trance state when he shot RFK. He wrote, "The major trance technique Sirhan used was staring at candles and mirrors for long periods of time. This is an important detail because there were lights and mirrors in the area of the Ambassador Hotel where Sirhan stood immediately before shooting Robert Kennedy. In combination with four Tom Collins drinks, the lights and mirrors probably helped trigger Sirhan into his dissociated assassin state."[31]

Moreover, Dr. Ross contends that Dr. Diamond and the other defense-team doctors believed that: "... Sirhan's thought processes were always organized and coherent outside the dissociated trance state. In the 1960s, the term "schizophrenia" was overused and loosely by American psychiatrists. There is no reason to think that Sirhan Sirhan would receive a diagnosis of schizophrenia if interviewed with the more reliable diagnostic procedures of the early twenty-first century."

He continued, stating that there are generally four pathways to the development of MPD: 1) childhood abuse; 2) childhood neglect; 3) factitious (self-generated); and 4) iatrogenic or created (sometimes even inadvertently) by a mental health therapist. The third causal system contributing to MPD, the factitious category, Dr. Ross psychologically connected to Sirhan's dissociated state. "Sirhan Sirhan corresponds to the auto-hypnotic sub-pathway of the factitious pathway to dissociative identity disorder. He was a self-created assassin, but not consciously so."

Dr. Ross confirmed his belief in the authenticity of a "Manchurian candidate," noting the goal in his book, "My focus in *The CIA Doctors: Human Rights Violations by American Psychiatrists* is on psychiatry and the dissociative disorders. My intent is to prove that the Manchurian Candidate is real, and to set the Manchurian Candidate programs in a historical and clinical context."[32]

I concur with Drs. Diamond and Ross's assessment of Sirhan as being in a dissociative state when he fired eight shots at RFK. Dr. Diamond also suggested that Sirhan's history of Rosicrucian hypnotic experiences, and the large mirrors and flashing lights in the confined pantry, supported his view that Sirhan was in a hypnagogic state – a hazy area somewhere between wakefulness and sleep; and due to Sirhan's ingestion of at least four Tom Collins alcohol drinks this may have also helped move him into a partial state of alcohol-induced hypnagogia.

---

31   Personal communication, Dr. Ross; US Journal Training. Ross, Colin A. (2006). The C.I.A. Doctors: Human Rights Violations By American Psychiatrists, Manitou Communications, Inc. Richardson, TX. 219, 220, 232.
32   Ibid, 12.

When Sirhan shot RFK, he was certainly in a dissociative state, and his appropriate diagnosis is dissociative identity disorder (DID). To confirm this finding, I present results of his three dissociative rating scales.

AN ANALYSIS OF SIRHAN'S THREE DISSOCIATIVE RATING SCALES

Since the early part of the twentieth century when Dr. Morton Prince discovered the seminal Beauchamp multiple personality case, psychologists and psychiatrists have searched to unlock the psychological-emotional factors underlying MPD, and find reliable psychological measures to substantiate the MPD diagnosis. This was not an easy task, taking many years for researchers to develop a valid assessment tool or a series of tests.

The first objective and comprehensive attempt to measure and define MPD using psychological testing was conducted by Thigpen and Cleckley in their case, *The 3 Faces of Eve,* to determine whether Eve's initial two personalities were truly differentiated from each other. They were the first investigators to use psychological tests to delineate distinct personalities (as time passed, four different ones emerged), perhaps proving that psychological assessment is necessary to isolate individual MPD alters.

Thigpen and Cleckley used the variety of psychological assessment tools available to them during the 1960s: intelligence testing, personality assessment using the Osgood Semantic Differential and Rorschach, handwriting analysis, and even electroencephalographic (EEG) measures. Their clinical findings verified that Eve White was functioning as one woman, yet she was wrapped up in a constellation of multiple personalities.

In the fields of criminology, psychology and psychiatry, methodologies and times have changed quite a lot since then, especially with the evolution of new and more sophisticated psychological tests and methods for identifying specific symptoms associated with different dissociative categories.

As of 2024, several different and more sensitive tests can better help define a dissociative condition. To assess Sirhan for signs and clinical symptoms of a dissociative disorder (not a diagnosis) or a different dissociated state of consciousness, I used three validated scales, two of which were unavailable at the time of Sirhan's assessment: the Holmes and Rahe Social Readjustment Rating Scale (SRRS), the Dissociative Experiences Scale II, DED-II, and the Clinician-Administered Dissociative States Scale (CADSS).

The clinical data necessary to provide ratings for these scales principally derives from Sirhan's personal historical information as related
to his past stress/trauma-related experiences and not on a face-to-face
interview process. Sirhan's projected rating scores based on the present research were assessed to confirm or disconfirm his probability of
manifesting symptoms consistent with a dissociative identity disorder.
These results are not aimed at making a definitive DID diagnosis, but
are interpreted as highly probable.[33]

Sirhan's scoring on these three scales is derived from his verified autobiographical information collected from a wide variety of background
sources, which is consistent with Dr. Hare's clinical approach to scoring
of a structured interview inventory he used to assess patients' psychopathic behaviors, although indirectly and not in person.

The three dissociative assessment scales I am most familiar with have
some similarity in their application and some differences among them.
This new generation of specialized assessment techniques were not available in 1969.

A review of the studies conducted to assess dissociative conditions
indicates that two critical psychological areas are necessary to substantiate the presence of a dissociative disorder. The first area is the
assessment of the psychological amplitude of the actual precipitating
traumatic event(s) – death of loved one, physical abuse (sexual and/or
nonsexual); and the second is to measure the subjective psychological
impact that the precipitating stressful event has on a person – amnesia, feeling outside of oneself, finding oneself in a strange place and not
knowing how you got there, and partial or complete amnesia. In order
to support these two areas, we must use one or more evidenced-based
psychological rating scales.

Dr. Daniel Brown achieved this scaling process by accessing Sirhan
for a dissociative condition using the Structured Clinical Interview for
the Diagnosis of Dissociative Disorders (SCID-D). He spent seven-
ty-plus hours interviewing and assessing Sirhan in jail, summarized his
findings, and submitted his results in his Declaration to the court on
November 19, 2011, to support Sirhan's appeal.

Dr. Brown also addressed the unavailability of adequate assessment
tools when Sirhan was initially assessed by defense and prosecution
psychologists/psychiatrists prior to trial:

33   Hare, R.D. (2003). *Hare Psychopathic Checklist (PCL-R): Technical Manual, 2nd Edition*. Multi-
Health Systems, Inc. North Tonawanda, New York, 19.

> In developing guidelines for such forensic psychological assessment, Brown and others have recommended the use of a combination of generally accepted, empirically derived standardized structured interviews, normative self-report and actuarial tests, independently compared to accumulative evidence from medical records as the best approach to achieve incremental validity (reliability in the legal sense). None of these contemporary psychological assessment instruments were available at the time of the petitioner's [Sirhan's] trial ... the opinions reached by the defense and prosecution experts regarding the petitioner's mental status are likely unreliable and inaccurate.[34]

Now with my work to reconstitute the TAT results, presented for the first time in more than fifty-years, employing a unified method of interpretation, this information could have been useful to Dr. Brown in his appraisal of Sirhan's dissociative symptoms. Sirhan's SCID-D structured interview results established that he suffered from a major dissociative disorder.

In his Declaration, Dr. Brown commented on the paucity of rating scales available to the psychologists who examined Sirhan: "Had these scientifically based assessment tools been available to the defense and prosecution experts at the time of the trial, they would have drawn a similar conclusion that the petitioner had both a dissociative coping style (a stable trait over years) and a major dissociative disorder.... Respondent states that the prosecution expert at the time of the trial found no evidence of a dissociative state at the time of the shooting. Dr. Pollack [prosecution psychiatrist hired to assess Sirhan] could not have found evidence of dissociation because no scientifically based instruments were available in that time period to detect dissociation accurately and reliably."

I devised a retrospective research design, using a projected response model combined with a collateral review to assess Sirhan's dissociative symptoms. This was accomplished using three evidenced-based, rating scales that are dependent on an individual's history of cumulative traumatic events. The results of these three scales constitute the projected direction Sirhan may have taken, if he had filled these scales out in person. As such, these results are only suggestive as to Sirhan's actual psychiatric diagnosis, DID. These scales and Sirhan's projected results are presented here.

---

34   Exhibit H. to Petitioner's Reply Brief – Declaration of Daniel Brown, November 19, 2011, 1.

The Three Dissociative Scales Used

1. The Dissociative Experience Scale-II (DES-II)

The initial dissociative measure I used to do a retrospective factor analysis of Sirhan's dissociative symptoms based on his historical trauma issues is the DES-II. Differing somewhat from the SCID-D used by Dr. Dan Brown, the DES-II is construct-founded, based on the identification of discreet traumatic dissociative events in a person's life, separating these from normal or quasi-dissociative experiences – daydreaming ("winning the lottery") or fantasy thoughts ("They say I look like a movie star").

The DES-II measures both a person's normal and their pathological dissociations. The manifest impact of these twenty-eight disturbing, trauma events usually tax or exceeds a person's ability to cope. Each traumatic area on the twenty-eight-question DES-II is rated on a 0 to 10-point scale (scored from zero to ten). A summary score of 48 is the cutoff point to identify DID.[35]

The DES-I and, more currently, the DES-II have been used as diagnostic tools and in research applications. For example, Barlow and Chu directly administered the DES-II with a sample of eleven women diagnosed with DID to verify their symptoms and check on communications patterns between their alter personalities, the switching process. These psychologists reported that the participants had a mean DES score of 56.16, which is consistent with a DID population, and well above the normal range.

These scores compare favorably with Sirhan's DES-II score equal to 55, obtained in the present investigation using a projected, file review (a "blind analysis") methodology as suggested by Hare. A score greater than 48, according to the DES-II authors, suggests the presence of a DID condition. When a person scores in the elevated range (>30.00), the DES questions can be used as a more definitive measure of DID using a structured clinical interview, similar to the SCID-D used by Dr. Brown to diagnose Sirhan's dissociative condition.[36]

The following eight select questions taken from the DES-II represent select content areas affecting Sirhan's emotional reactions to his defined traumatic life experiences. These substantiated, biographical experiences are taken directly from Sirhan's Traumatic Dissociative Disorder Life Fac-

---

35   Carlson, E.B. and F.W. Putman. (1993). An update on the Dissociative Experience Scale. *Dissociation* 6 (1), 16–27. http://traumadissociation.com/des
36   Barlow, M.R. and J.A. Chu. (2014). "Measuring fragmentation in dissociative identity disorder: The integration measure and relationship to switching and time in therapy." *European Journal of Psychotraumatology*, 2014: 5: doi10.3402/ejpt.v5.22250.

tors. Similar to the scoring on the Modified Holmes and Rahe Social Readjustment Rating Scale (SRRS), these items are retrospectively scored based on the many comments made by Sirhan himself, or by credible collateral sources about Sirhan's emotional reactions to the cumulative traumatic events that occurred in his life and direct comments and statements he made as a witness during his trial.

DES-II Select Questions
#3: Some people have the experience of finding themselves in a place and have no idea how they got there.
#9: Some people find that they have no memory for some important events in their lives (for example, a wedding or graduation).
#10: Some people have the experience of being accused of lying when they do not think they have lied.
#15: Some people have the experience of not being sure whether things that they remember happening were real or whether they just dreamed them.
#18: Some people find that they become so involved in a fantasy or daydream that it feels as though it were really happening to them.
#25: Some people find evidence that they have done things that they do not remember doing.
#26: Some people sometimes find writings, drawings, or notes among their belongings that they have done but cannot remember doing.
28: Some people sometimes feel as if they are looking at the world through a fog, so that people and objects appear far away or unclear.

SIRHAN'S PROJECTED RATINGS ON THE DES-II

Sirhan's projected rating score on the DES-II, as derived from his verified autobiographical information collected from a representative variety of background sources, overall score at 55.00, is suggestive of those symptoms usually associated with a dissociative condition.

2. The Modified Holmes and Rahe Social Readjustment Rating Scale (SRRS)

The second dissociative scale examined and rating Sirhan's projected responses is the SRRS. I applied SRRS criteria against Sirhan's many cumulative stress responses and statements he made in court testimony before, during, and after his trial to determine his trauma-stress impact level, a critical component necessary to make the dissociative diagnosis.

This assessment area, the stress associated with an identified stressor or series of stressor events, as in Sirhan's situation, lends itself to measurement using a more traditional stress rating scale like the SRRS or similar assessment tool. Because of Sirhan's documented multiple, cumulative traumatic life events, I believe that examining each impactful area separately as to their psychological effect on Sirhan's mental status is essential. The SRRS measures the subjective impact of forty-three possible life events that a person responds to either "yes" or "no" to affirm or negate the presence of the identified stress category.

This SRRS has been in continuous professional use since I was in graduate school, providing important feedback in facilitating the diagnosis of PTSD as well as dissociative disorders. The original scale used here has been modified to embrace some traumatic-related events that help explain Sirhan's cumulative stress events. The scoring on the SRRS ranges from a low traumatic stress score equal to 11 to a maximum of 600. The connection between excessive stress and elevations in trauma levels and dissociative states of consciousness is well founded. Examining these areas is necessary to engage in any appraisal to find the underlying factors causing a dissociative state.

TABLE IV. SIRHAN'S RATING ON THE MODIFIED HOLMES AND RAHE SOCIAL READJUSTMENT RATING SCALE (SRRS)

PRECIPITATING FACTORS

(Sirhan's dissociative impact factor)	(SRRS factor weights)	
Death of older brother	Death of close family member	63
Circling the dead body of his older brother	Death of close family member	63
Move to poor area	Forced change of residence	25
Family uprooted	Forced change in residence	20
Father's physical brutality	Physical Injury	53
Bombing raids	Social life disruption	19
Dead soldier	Death of person	36
Human hand in well	Nightmares	36
Death of sister	Death of family member	63
Deceased man's entrails	Nightmares	63
Death of friend (local storekeeper)	Death of close family friend	63
Serious injury to nine-year-old girl hit with shrapnel	Witness/experience physical/ psychological suffering	23
Injured young girls' bloody chests/ laughing soldiers	Witness/experience physical/ psychological suffering	63

The results of Sirhan's retro-analysis of his SRRS stress level measuring the impact his 11 identified dissociative impact factors suggests the following. Sirhan's total Score=590 on the SRRS represents a significant trauma-stress level that can be considered consistent with a dissociative symptomology, supporting a dissociative condition, and ranking his score significantly in excess of the cutoff SRRS threshold point.

3. The Clinician-Administered Dissociative States Scale(CADSS).

The CADSS is a twenty-seven-item scale with nineteen subject-rated items and eight items scored by the observer.[37]

The observer items are representative of patients' behaviors consistent with the presence of a dissociative state. The subjective component the patient completes or here represent Sirhan's projected responses supported by his recorded life esperiences to the nineteen completed items, which are administered by the clinician were of most interest here. These items were rated based on a judgment on each about the degree of fit in Sirhan's life experiences – potential trauma events that precipitate a dissociative reaction.

The CADSS has been used as a companion scaling technique with the DES-II and other validated dissociative tests. Each item is endorsed using a possible range of responses: 0=not at all, 1=slightly, 2 =moderately, 3 =considerably, 4=extremely. The total scoring is a summation of all items rated.

CADSS Select Questions
#2: Do things seem to be unreal to you, as if you are in a dream?
#3: Do you have some experience that separates you from what is happening; for instance, do you feel as if you are in a movie or a play, or as if you are a robot?
#5: Do you feel as if you are watching the situation as an observer or spectator?
#14: Do things happen that you later cannot account for?
#18: Does it seem as if you are looking at the world through a fog, so that people and objects appear far away or unclear?

SIRHAN'S PROJECTED SCORING ON THE CADSS

Sirhan's projected scoring on the CADSS exceeds (>19.3) the cutoff point for the identification of suspected dissociative symptomology. Each of his projected ratings was compared against his known life trauma factors outlined above. There is convincing evidence that for many years

37   Bremmer, J.D., J.H. Krystal, F.W. Putnam, S.M. Southwick, C. Marmar, D.S. Charney, and C.M. Mazure. (1998). "Measurement of Dissociative States with the Clinician-Administered Dissociative States Scale (CADSS)." *Journal of Traumatic Stress*, 11: 1. 125–136. https://doi.org/10.1023A:1024465317902

Sirhan had experienced many inexplicable trancelike departures from ordinary reality curiously marked by memory lapses not based on head trauma or drug ingestion– LSD, or other hallucinogenic drugs agents.

During an interview with Dr. Chu he told me that the use of the DES-II is an adequate measure of dissociative conditions if the goal is to identify these types of states. He has conducted many studies to assess dissociative states including the one referenced in this book.

Dr. Chu provided no opinion whether the DES-II could be administered on a projected "cold case, file review basis," as used here, but did not reject this possibility in the Sirhan case when incarceration is involved. He cautioned against using somatic scales such as the Somatoform Dissociation Questionnaire (SDQ-20) that is targeted to assess those physical items related to a dissociative state.[38]

The results of Sirhan's three dissociative scales (SRRS, DES-II, and CADSS), combined with his revised TAT and MMPI interpretations, strongly indicated that Sirhan had experienced many symptoms that verify a dissociative condition. For example, his projected responses on these four CADSS items:

1. Do things seem to be unreal to you, as if you are in a dream?

2. Do you have some experience that separates you from what is happening; for instance, do you feel as if you are in a movie or a play, or as if you are a robot?

3. Do you feel as if you are watching the situation as an observer or spectator?

4. Do things happen that you later cannot account for?

Of course, Sirhan still alleges he can't recall killing RFK, and that he no doubt was in some type of undefined trance state during times in his life, beginning prior to his relocation from Palestine to Pasadena, California.

An individual like Sirhan with a dissociative condition, a second personality begins to emerge then dominate and, unbeknownst to him, splitting into two or more independent personalities occurs because the person is struggling to escape from their traumatic memories and trying to preserve their sanity from further decomposition. This psychological picture reflects the personal psychodynamics of Sirhan's obviously fractured mental state. All the consulting doctors who examined Sirhan had no doubt that Sirhan was suffering from some type of an unspecified mental disorder, but no one could precisely label this condition.

---

38   Chu, J.A. (2014). Personal communication with Dr. James Chu, February 2, 2023.

This mentally imprinted trail of adverse, childhood experiences that haunted Sirhan (and probably still does) constitutes a nonerasable chapter in his life that he could never escape from. The interpretation of his early life experiences helps to bring us forward to the night that Sirhan's deadly impulses sought full expression in an act of vengeful and unstoppable rage. But for Sirhan's traumatic-laced history and the unrestrained emergence of the altered Sirhan, the killing of RFK would not have become an American tragedy. His dissociative rage, expressed through his personality 2, persisted at such an intense level that, if RFK wasn't the target, then perhaps, as Sirhan said, Ambassador Goldberg or even President Johnson might have been put squarely in his sights.

The results of Sirhan's projected dissociative state scales (DES-II, SRRS, and CADSS) demonstrate scores that exceed the suggested cutoff threshold to make a clinical judgment consistent with a dissociative disorder. The psychological elements comprising a dissociative condition do not suggest that it is activated or triggered by a volitional act. The predecessor cases referenced here (e.g., the Dr. Prince case of Christine Chambeau, and Thigpen and Cleckley's *The 3 Faces of Eve*) both indicate that the altered states experienced by these patients were not under their direct control in order to switch. Sirhan's movement into and out of one alternative state, I assert, was also a reactive event emerging spontaneously rather than planned.

Similar to the Gorshen case (Chapter 4), when Sirhan shot RFK he appeared to be acting robotically, striking out and disregarding the devastating consequences of his deadly act as well as the obvious inevitability of being apprehended. Sirhan had no possible path for escape. He was wrestled to the floor by a half-dozen people as he continued wildly firing his gun. Clear to me is that Sirhan's non-volitional and automatic act was committed as the altered Sirhan, which was captured by Dr. Schorr during his testimony. He noted that prior to the assassination, Sirhan entered into dissociated states triggered by his enormous stress levels. Dr. Schorr described Sirhan's dissociated state as "a kind of Jekyll-Hyde" situation. This divided personality – one person with two alternative and disparate personalities – where one is unaware of the other's existence and vice versa seems consistent with Sirhan's dissociative split, or as Dr. Schorr put it, "two personality structures residing in the same person."[39]

Dr. Schorr repeated his clinical view that for several hours prior to the assassination Sirhan was cycling between the real world and a dissocia-

---

39   Trial Vol 20, 5732, March 10, 1969.

tive world. He also believed that Sirhan was unaware he was drifting from one state of consciousness to another, and while he may have wanted to murder RFK, he was, and probably still is, genuinely unaware that he is dissociative.[40]

As mentioned previously, Dr. Diamond remarked on the Gorshen case, noting that Gorshen, like Sirhan, was particularly prone to entering into dissociated or trancelike states that he unconsciously used to protect himself from others discovering he that was mentally disturbed. Sirhan perceived that something was wrong with him, yet he adamantly denied that he was "a crazy person." In this sense, as Dr. Diamond alleged, Sirhan's trance states or dissociative episodes served on one level as a defense mechanism to insulate him from further and perhaps more observable symptoms of a mental illness, and on another level as a method of escaping from his cumulative trauma.

When further analyzing the Wells case (Chapter 4), Dr. Diamond reminded us that Wells's psychiatric issues while in prison were attributable to his cumulative stress resulting in "a dysfunctional state of psychological tension." According to Dr. Diamond, Sirhan's well-documented and long history of traumatic episodes contributed to his mounting levels of stress, resulting in a split from ordinary reality much like Wells did. Wells dissociated into "an aggressive bad identity possibly begetting the 'Bad Wells's.'"

Certainly, Sirhan's reconstitution into his alter Sirhan, differentiated from the adjusted Sirhan, represents a psychological move from the good Sirhan to the bad Sirhan. As Dr. Diamond carefully laid out the complicated psychodynamics in the Wells case, some of these psychological factors he identified are reminiscent of Sirhan's own psychiatric features. The "Bad Wells" had over time accumulated layers of negative, destructive, and dark forces that lay dormant until he exploded in a fury of deadly violence. The altered Sirhan, remained in an unconscious reservoir of equally contaminated thoughts and feelings diffused in nature and loosely connected similar to Wells's.

Based on my analysis of Sirhan's history, the domineering, aggressive, and homicidally altered Sirhan, shielded from the awareness of his non-altered state, was perfectly capable of developing a clear plan to assassinate RFK.

However, in my view, Dr. Diamond's analysis of Sirhan's darker side, the hidden second personality 2, is descriptive, but does not explain Sirhan's real second identity – the one suffused with anger, rage, and homi-

---

40   FBI FILES, LA 56–156, Vol 13, in the *LA Times*, March 10, 1969.

287

cidal vengeance. In the Gorshen case, Dr. Diamond specifically unfolded the elements of Gorshen's good versus the evil side that projected him into killing his boss, Red O'Leary. Correctly enough, Dr. Diamond also saw dissociative features in Gorshen's weakened hold on reality.

During his testimony, Dr. Diamond clearly described Sirhan's trance states still relying on a volitional entrance into and out of these states of altered consciousness. Assertively, he stated to defense attorney Berman his definition of dissociated states of consciousness:

> There are degrees of consciousness and unconsciousness, extending from very deep coma states in which there is apparently no activity whatsoever of the human mind, all the way to a state of full alertness. But the abnormal examples of dissociated states exist in various trancelike conditions or various states of twilight states or twilight consciousness. Hypnosis or hypnotic trance is an example of artificially induced dissociative or twilight state, and this can be accomplished in relatively normal persons.... Now the thing that characterizes the dissociated is not, as is popularly believed, the element of amnesia. It is true that following many dissociated states, the individual has no recollection of what actually took place and they may be amnesic.... The thing that is characteristic about a dissociated state is that the individual is now conscious only for a segment of their mind, and this can vary. One of the most common types of things, or at least common that you read about in newspapers and see in motion pictures, would be the multiple personality type thing, where somebody thinks that they are two different people....[41]

Again Dr. Diamond accurately noted how Sirhan's troubled childhood had adversely affected his chances of achieving positive or a normal psychological development. Dr. Diamond also knew how these negative events impacted by a sequence of adverse, childhood experiences began to form the foundational elements of Sirhan's dissociative personality. My view is that these cumulative traumatic episodes in Sirhan's life became intolerable to his ordinary state of mind thus, in order to survive, a competing personality emerged able to defend itself against the infliction of more aggression. At that time, Sirhan's secondary personality formed around a core of aggressiveness that he needed to strike back at his perceived enemies: his father, the Jews, the British occupying forces, Israeli soldiers, all the people who fought against him, and his current nemesis, RFK.

---

41   Trial Vol 24, 6888–6892, March 24, 1969.

Sirhan's altered personality emerged as a powerful warrior for his cause (save Arab people), a countervailing force, capable of doing what the adjusted, weak Sirhan (personality 1) was unable to do, strike back and retaliate against a cruel society that traumatized his childhood and cut off his viable options to finally "be somebody."

THE SIMULATION OF SANITY

One of the most opaque, psychological areas in my analysis of the Sirhan case was whether he was distorting, lying (we know he told a few), faking, or malingering when he was interviewed by a "parade of shrinks." His memory erosion of what happened when he shot RFK is relevant, as is his selective forgetting pattern (perhaps Sirhan's not knowing what was written in his "RFK Must Die" diary). In criminal cases, this faking or malingering is usually related to the concept of "faking bad," that is, claiming they are experiencing some type of mental disorder that will benefit their case.

In my experience, some defendants will fake a psychiatric disorder to lessen responsibility for a criminal act; I have seen this intentional malingering many times with defendants that I was court-ordered to assess. It is also evident from these cases that some engaged in "faking-good," that is – "I'll prove to the doctor that there is nothing wrong with me. I think there is something there, but that's my business not the shrink's."

In conducting forensic assessments, it is essential to know if the person sitting in front of me (criminal defendant or civil plaintiff) is telling the truth, a modified version of the truth, or is lying or distorting the facts to somehow influence my diagnostic opinion. Malingering or faking is an important psychological variable that must be controlled for to believe everything I am told by a defendant.

Many defendants, to avoid responsibility for a particular crime, or a series of crimes, create the most implausible, crazy stories to circumvent their guilt and, in the process, engage in malingering behavior. This issue, which goes to the core of truthfulness, is especially important when assessing a defendant like Sirhan, who was literally fighting for his life being criminally charged with first-degree murder.

In forensic psychology, the issue of psychological malingering dates back almost 100 years. To rule in or rule out this conscious, deceptive ploy, the first area that ought to be addressed by a psychologist or psychiatrist during the assessment/testing phase of a valid psychodiagnostic assessment of a defendant. In Sirhan's case, ample evidence already exists that he lied at certain times (i.e., concerning his presence at the shooting range earlier on the day of the assassination) to ostensibly shield himself from what might be considered damaging evidence.

The measurement of malingering has been widely expanded over the years, compared to its less accurate measurement when Sirhan was evaluated. The possibility of Sirhan's malingering or denial capacity falls generally into three psychological areas of concern: 1) his denial of recall of the shooting itself in the Ambassador Hotel's pantry; 2) his steadfast and repeated denial of having mental issues – "I'm not insane!" Obviously, an appropriate psychiatric diagnosis could be beneficial to Sirhan's effort to not end up on death row, however he strenuously resisted being labeled as a "mental case;" and 3) his confusion and denial of writing certain entries in the "RFK Must Die" document.

Conversely, this irrational reluctance flew directly in the face of Sirhan's diminished capacity defense, clearly a psychiatric defense that fell short of necessitating a diagnosis of a psychosis. In a strange way, Sirhan almost preferred the gas chamber over being characterized with a permanent stigma as a psychologically deranged murderer. His cultural background was deeply woven into his avoidance of the stigma attached to mental illness.

Sirhan's brother Adel told Klaber and Melanson that: "In Arabic culture, there is a great stigma attached to mental illness. Not only is the person involved outcast, but also his family. Here [The United States] it is a somewhat romanticized notion, but in the Middle East it is better to be a thief than to be thought of as crazy ... Sirhan's choices were two: either he was crazy, or he murdered Robert Kennedy to defend his people. A third possibility, that he had been an involuntary dupe, was not seriously considered."[42]

Certainly, a part of Sirhan's reluctance to accept a mental illness label lay in the fact that his doctors continually put pressure on him to admit to an illness he did not believe applied to him.

In the *DSM-IV* (1994), malingering is defined as "the intentional production of false or grossly exaggerated physical or psychological symptoms, motivated by external incentives," or "Intentional reporting of symptoms for personal gain." The manual directs clinicians to "strongly suspect" the presence of malingering when a diagnosis of antisocial personality disorder is made.

Psychological research suggests that up to 40 percent of criminal defendants and 20 percent of civil litigants engage in some form of faking,

---

42   Klaber and Melanson. (1997). 170–171.

lying, deception, distortion, selective memory retrieval, and psychological confabulation (making of facts to fit a narrative favorable to his/her defense position). Researchers contend that "no single test score or combination of test scores alone can determine the presence of malingering."[43]

For Sirhan, the possibility of his faking behavior was evidenced by his repeated claims of being amnesiac to the assassination scene where he was obviously a participant, and his persistent denial that he was experiencing psychiatric problems. Furthermore, at first glance, his chronic denials of writing some passages in his diary could be construed as malingering.

Dr. Diamond was fully aware of the importance of faking or malingering when he interviewed then diagnosed Sirhan. During several of his graduate seminars at U.C. Berkeley he often discussed psychogenic amnesia as a form of malingering. He also stressed how essential it is to gather the truth from a defendant and not be swayed by carefully crafted false and misleading statements. To reach a modicum of truth, Dr. Diamond said he sometimes relied on hypnotic sessions with Sirhan, hoping that, when in a hypnotic trance, Sirhan would recall and reveal the true facts of his involvement in the assassination.

According to Dr. Diamond: "It also was clear to me where he tells lies. He tells lies when it comes to revealing anything that shows an indicator of mental illness."

Dr. Diamond stated that consistently throughout the trial, Sirhan attempted to deny that he had any mental issues, or that he was "a head case." He certainly did not desire to offer any assistance with his psychiatric defense because, in his way of thinking, being labeled as mentally ill was worse than being labeled a cold-blooded killer, who might be issued a one-way ticket to San Quentin's gas chamber. But was he malingering regarding the recurrent issue that he claimed he couldn't recall, the actual shooting of RFK?

Evidence mounted that on several occasions, Sirhan stalked RFK and made what seemed careful plans to show up at the Ambassador Hotel at precisely the right time and complete his crime in full view of many witnesses. Again, Sirhan's biggest fear might have been that he was in fact going insane and had little control over certain dark forces that began to infiltrate deep into his unconsciousness.

Dr. Diamond felt that hypnosis could provide the only valid window to the facts basic to "Sirhan's whole story." He discounted the position that

---

43   Widows, M.R. and G.P. Smith. *SIMS, Structured Inventory of Malingered Symptomology.* (2005). Psychological Assessment Resources, Inc. Lutz, FL, 3.

Sirhan was faking mental illness in the expected direction ("appearing to be a crazy person to fool him").

Maybe Sirhan was trying to fool Dr. Diamond, but not necessarily in a way one might expect. Dr. Diamond explained to his students that paranoid patients (and it can be conceded that Sirhan demonstrated lots of paranoid ideations) actual intention was paradoxical – they wanted to "fake sanity" not the expected direction, to appear insane.

Dr. Diamond continued to confirm that Sirhan's behavior fell into this classification of "faking good." To support his reasoning, Dr. Diamond reached back to 1957 when he wrote a penetrating article stating his position of why a person might fake sanity rather than faking insanity. He said that a small number of patients, often criminal defendants, attempt to protect themselves and preserve their egos by masking their psychiatric symptoms and thereby faking sanity.

In Sirhan's case, Dr. Diamond surely recognized that the simulation of sanity was antithetical to his defense of his case, i.e., insanity, at least a diagnostic description of insanity, was at the core of the defense team's efforts to spare his life. Throughout the trial Sirhan feared that his mental disorder would be exposed by the day-after-day psychiatric diagnoses casually tossed out by the team of psychologists and psychiatrists and defense attorneys. [44]

For instance, during one memorable court session defense attorney Berman proclaimed to the jury that, "Sirhan was an immature, emotionally disturbed, and mentally ill youth."

When issues concerning his mental state were voiced, this prompted Sirhan to rise from his chair at the defense table interrupting the attorney and loudly state: "No, no!"

Pease recounts one emotional moment: "He desperately did not want to be painted as mentally ill, despite the fact that was the defense's strategy for saving him from the death penalty. Sirhan felt that if he had to go down for a crime he didn't remember committing, it should at least stand for something, and he had settled on the Palestinian-Israeli conflict as his motive."[45]

Characterizing Sirhan's many outbursts in court, defense attorney Parsons made the obtuse comment to the press that, "Like most mentally ill people, Sirhan doesn't like to be told he is mentally ill. He doesn't like it when I tell him."

---

44   Diamond, B.L. (1957). "With malice aforethought." *Arch. crim. psychodynam*, 2:1–45. In Quen, J.M. (1994). *The psychiatrist in the courtroom*. (Ed.) The Analytic Press. Hillsdale, NJ and London.
45   Pease. (2018), 141–142.

How odd that because of Sirhan's Middle Eastern cultural patterning, he feared public exposure as a mental case far more than a date on death row. Sirhan was kind of trapped between the ill-advised comments made by Parsons and his Arab-oriented cultural beliefs inculcated in him concerning the inherent moral weakness associated with the admission of mental illness.

Sirhan tried vigorously to influence the doctors working on his defense that he did not suffer from any mental disorders – which was exactly contrary to the foundation of his diminished capacity defense.

When a psychological issue like an insanity plea enters into the fray of the courtroom, a fair amount of skepticism is commonly aroused. Usually the primary focus is related to the validity of the psychiatric defense, i.e., Is the defendant claiming insanity or a variant of insanity just trying to minimize his/her mental element necessary to commit a crime, especially first-degree murder?

To rule in or rule out these conditions, several valid and reliable measures are used to assess a defendant's truthfulness. The Structured Inventory of Malingered Symptomology (SIMS) is one of these tests. The authors of the SIMS describe three types of instruments used in the detection of malingering: (a) structured interviews, (b) general psychological or cognitive instruments, and (c) tests specifically designed for the detection of malingering.

Unlike the assessment of conscious malingering or faking, no psychological assessment tools to date are specifically developed to measure the simulation of sanity. Therefore, psychological opinions as to whether a defendant engages in the process of simulating sanity is a professional judgment call.

As Dr. Diamond stated, "There is a considerable literature on the subject of malingering, particularly the simulation of mental disease. Yet very little has been written about the simulation of sanity, even though the pretense of mental health seems to be a much more frequent and more important problem than is malingering.... It has also been my experience that the willful concealment of existing mental illness, that is, the simulation of sanity, is very frequent, even in persons accused of serious crimes where mental illness would be an adequate defense.... To conceal his delusions he will confabulate logical reasons for his crime and resist all attempts of the psychiatrist to discover his psychopathology."[46]

---

46   Ibid, Diamond, (1957)..

Referring to a pejorative newspaper story about him in the *West Los Angeles Times Sunday Magazine,* Sirhan said, "Well, I'm too psychotic. That article they wrote about me in *West* says I was psychotic, that I envied the Kennedys." Sirhan shook his head side to side vigorously, saying again, "I'm not psychotic."

When, in another interview with defense investigator Kaiser, he tried to define psychosis for Sirhan in laymen's terms, "A true psychotic would not have the ability, the strength, the power, the cunning to be able to do the necessary things to pull off something like that [referring to the RFK assassination]." Sirhan retorted, I'm not psychotic ... I don't think I am. Except when it comes to the Jews."

"If he told me once, he told me a hundred times that he doesn't want to be considered as mentally ill," Dr. Diamond commented.

Throughout his psychiatric interviews, Sirhan engaged in the simulation of sanity head game. For instance, his initial interview with Dr. Marcus (a supposedly neutral, court-appointed psychiatrist) Sirhan displayed indifference and denial in the diagnostic process. "So you're the doc who's supposed to see whether or not I'm crazy." Then he asked, "Are you Jewish?" Sirhan clearly did his best to convince anyone who would listen him to that, "he simply wasn't a crazy person."

In his article, "The Simulation of Sanity," Dr. Diamond highlighted several clinical cases where patients choose to hide their mental conditions, even risking jail time to cover up a condition they considered too embarrassing to disclose. In a San Francisco kidnapping case, kidnapper Betty Jean Benedicto unlawfully carried away a two-day old infant from Mount Zion Hospital, claiming to her husband that it was hers, and actually went to jail, never disclosing the delusions she had about her "mystery pregnancy."

Clearly mentally ill, she chose to conceal her delusions from Dr. Diamond and Dr. Agron who each evaluated her mental status. In Dr. Diamond's words, "She described how she had wanted to have a baby and some six months prior to the kidnapping she had been delighted to learn she was pregnant. Her abdomen enlarged, and she had all the signs of pregnancy, yet her immaculate conception was a delusion obscured by her simulation or feigning sanity."[47]

In many ways, Sirhan's denials mirror Dr. Diamond's experience with other psychiatric patients who he noticed either simulated or disguised their psychiatric symptoms trying to look normal. "The motive for the con-

---

47   Ibid.

cealment of mental illness seems clear in these cases.… To admit that one's actions were motivated by delusions, rather than reality, and that one was and is mentally deranged is a public humiliation destructive to one's self."[48]

Dr. Diamond described the simulation of sanity process in Sirhan's case. Sirhan's list of dissimulations never stopped before, during, or after his case was adjudicated. In Dr. Diamond's recap of Sirhan's case, he said, "I was able to elicit a good deal of psychopathology through the use of hypnosis during which Sirhan recalled the shooting. In the waking state, Sirhan admitted none of this and claimed amnesia for the shooting. After listening to the tape recording of the hypnotic interviews, he claimed that his attorney and I faked the tapes and had hired an actor to impersonate him."

Amazingly, when Sirhan testified in his own defense, he also claimed that he was never hypnotized at all, and that he faked being induced into several hypnotic trances as a kind of conformity exercise. Sirhan's simulation, the obsessive denial of his critical symptoms worked against a well-conceived and explanatory psychiatric defense predicated on his profound dissociated disorder that resulted in the emergence of two Sirhans.

Dan Moldea's Key Interview

Though not a psychologist or psychiatrist, Dan Moldea was faced with many of the same factual issues that confronted Dr. Diamond: When was Sirhan telling the truth, or when was he lying, claiming he couldn't remember the actual killing of RFK?

During a lengthy interview with Sirhan at California's Corcoran State Prison on June 5, 1994, Moldea got his answer. He was accompanied by Adel Sirhan, Sirhan's loyal brother, who made the necessary arrangement to interview his brother with the California Department of Corrections and Rehabilitation.

Moldea took Sirhan all the way back in time to June 4, 1968. Sirhan began with his recollection of leaving the gun range, restlessly wandering through Pasadena, searching for a party in downtown LA, arriving at the Ambassador Hotel, drinking several Tom Collins, returning to his car, and again going back to the hotel to find coffee. This initial part of his recollection is substantially the same as the timeline he provided Dr. Diamond.

"At that point," Sirhan told Moldea, "I blacked out."

Moldea asked, "You don't remember anything about the shooting?"

Sirhan said, "No nothing in my mind. I just remember being choked."

---

48   Diamond, B.L. (1986). "Newsletter of the American Academy of Psychiatry and the Law," Dec 11:27–18.

Moldea followed up, "You have no recollection about the shooting at all?"

"I don't remember aiming the gun and saying to myself," Sirhan said, "that I'm going to kill Robert Kennedy. I don't remember any adrenalin rush."

Concerning his role or culpability for the assassination, Sirhan told Moldea: "I would not want to take the blame for this crime as long as there is exculpatory evidence that I didn't do the crime. The jury was never given the opportunity to pass judgment on the evidence discovered since the trial, as well as the inconsistencies of the firearms evidence at the trial. In view of this, no, I didn't get a fair trial."[49]

Moldea plunged deeper into a serious inquiry into the possibility of Sirhan being set up as a fall guy for a more sinister, conspiracy plot. "Let me ask you this, what do you think about the theories that you were programmed to kill and programmed to forget? Do you think that you were the victim of mind control by a person or persons unknown as has been suggested by Dr. Edward Simpson at San Quentin, among others? What did you think of him?"

In a very revealing answer, Sirhan stated, "He might have been right. I was on death row at the time. But he gave a good analysis of the work of the Jewish psychological team, which was supposedly part of my defense. They dismissed me as paranoid schizophrenic."

"Why do you think Dr. Simpson was dismissed from his job at San Quentin?" pressed Moldea.

Sirhan said, "He may have been getting too close to what really happened."

"Do you really think it's possible that you were under mind control, that you had been programmed?" asked Moldea.

Sirhan smiled politely and replied, "It's probably too diabolical to suggest that I was controlled by someone else – but I don't know. I only know that I don't remember anything about the shooting. And I only remember being choked."

Although Moldea's interview with Sirhan did not produce many new psychiatric revelations that differed significantly from what Sirhan told Dr. Diamond, even after a quarter century, Sirhan continued to claim that he was amnesic to the actual shooting of Kennedy.

Sirhan had nothing to gain from continuing to lie about what he did or did not remember about the shooting scene. In a deliberate way, Sirhan may have seen a benefit from continuing the deception especially for future parole board hearings.

---

49   Moldea. (2018).

Although Moldea was not aiming at revealing the existence of Sirhan's alternate personality structure during his in-depth interview, he almost inadvertently provided very compelling evidence that Sirhan could be psychiatrically diagnosed with MPD.

Moldea asked Sirhan, "Were you a participant in a conspiracy?"

Sirhan answered, "Do you think I would conceal anything about someone else's involvement and face the gas chamber in the most literal sense? I have no knowledge of a conspiracy ... I wish there had been a conspiracy. It would have unraveled before now."

"Then why do you even talk about the possibility of being mind-controlled?" asked Moldea.

Sirhan's answer surprised Moldea. Sirhan had said, "My defense attorneys developed the idea of "The Manchurian Candidate" theory."

Again, Moldea asked him why he doesn't just accept responsibility for this crime. Sirhan's answer to this question helps us frame his state of awareness or altered, dissociated state: "If I were to accept responsibility for this crime, it would be a hell of a burden to live with – having taken a human life without knowing it."

"Why did you take credit for the murder at your trial?"

Again, Sirhan's response suggests that only a vague part of him could recall what really happened, because the real homicidal actor was his dissociated Sirhan, when he says, "Grant Cooper conned me to say that I killed Robert Kennedy. I went along with him because he had my life in his hands. I was duped into believing that he had my best interests in mind. It was a futile defense. Cooper sold me out. Charles Manson [with whom Sirhan had spent some time] once told me that the defense attorneys treat their clients like kings before their trials. After he trial begin they treat their clients like shit."

Moldea pressed Sirhan, "You were willing to go to the gas chamber for a crime you didn't remember committing?"

"I did a lot of self-exploration while I was on death row. It changed my whole vision of the world. I was trying to justify that I was going to the gas chamber. I wanted to search myself to find the truth, but I could never figure it out. I had nothing to lose. ..."

Moldea confronted Sirhan directly, "Sirhan: did you commit this crime?"

Sirhan fired back, "I would not want to take the blame for this crime as long as there is exculpatory evidence that I didn't do the crime."

For Sirhan, the intense interview with Moldea raised more doubts about his present state of consciousness, and which personality was responsible for pulling the trigger the night RFK was shot. Clearly, Sirhan steadfastly denies remembering the incident. During many interviews, the adjusted (non-dissociative) Sirhan certainly acknowledged that he was physically present on the evening of June 4, 1968, in the Ambassador Hotel's crowded pantry. Yet cognitively since he can't recall the murder act, he expunges the incident from his memory.

The position here is that he simply doesn't know that his alter (personality 2) committed the crime. Not possessing the information that his alter personality, of which he has no reciprocal communication, has always put Sirhan into an impossible psychological conundrum; simply stated, he can't possibly remember what was occurring in his altered state that was never recorded in the first place. Nor for that matter has the diagnosis of MPD or DID been the focus of any of Sirhan's select team of psychologists and psychiatrist, Dr. Diamond, which could help to explain why the adjusted Sirhan (personality 1) cannot remember the actions engaged in by the altered Sirhan (personality 2).

Dr. Diamond continuously struggled to accurately explain Sirhan's amnestic episodes as either a way to reduce his responsibility for the murder or because his non-dissociated, alter personality had no access to the memory. Sirhan was operating within two distinct personality states that shared no information with each other.

The memory-amnesia factor also extended to parts of Sirhan's diary that he cannot recall writing, or even if he did write them. Dr. Diamond admitted that many writings in the diary were wandering thoughts. Some of the content was so confusing that authorship was impossible to absolutely establish.

Dr. Diamond concluded that major portions of the diary were written when Sirhan was in an amnestic or dissociated state of consciousness, and still isolated sections were apparently done when Sirhan was not in an altered state.

In Sirhan's case, there was no need for an outside mind-controlling agent or a team of influencers who programmed him to kill as a kind of Manchurian Candidate, because, in concert with Dr. Diamond's viewpoint, at the time of the shooting, Sirhan was not in a conscious state conducive to total recall.

CHAPTER 13

SIRHAN'S ADDITIONAL IDENTITY TRANSFORMATIONS
Phases IV–V

PHASE IV: TRAUMA-INDUCED PARADOX, AKA STOCKHOLM SYNDROME

A few years after Sirhan's trial ended, we were introduced to what psychologists believed at the time was a new, psychological phenomenon, the trauma-induced paradox" that came to be popularly labeled Stockholm syndrome. This condition has been compared with the psychological concept of "identification with the aggressor." The term was first used by the media to cover the events surrounding a bank robbery gone awry in Stockholm, Sweden, that quickly devolved into a dangerous hostage dilemma for four Kreditbanken employees.

The six-day hostage saga began on an ordinary business day as two men with extensive criminal records suddenly burst into the bank, carrying automatic weapons, and opened fire, not specifically aiming at bank employees, but creating extreme fright and signaling that they meant business.

The would-be bank robbers held three female and one male employee at gunpoint during the well-publicized standoff. When police finally rescued the hostages, they had an unexpected reaction to their traumatic experience. As described by writer Kathryn Wescott, "It became evident that the victims had formed some kind of a positive relationship with their captors."

Disturbed by the police's apparent inability to end the stalemate, Sweden's prime minister had put in a call to the kidnappers, demanding the immediate release of the hostages. One unhappy female employee picked up the telephone kind of indignantly, saying that she was, "Very disappointed with him … I think you are sitting there playing checkers with our lives. I fully trust Clark [one of the captors] and the robbers. I am not desperate. They haven't done a thing to us. On the contrary, they have been very nice ... what I'm scared of is that the police will attack and cause us to die."[1]

During post-release interviews with the hostages, all four described a similar kind of identification or psychological bond with their alleged captors and felt they had been protected by the criminals from adverse police action. Such upside-down reasoning applied to a potentially life-and-death situation was difficult to sort out.

The lone male hostage perceived the kidnappers in a strange sense as "kind of God-like figures." The question in the mind of the public and puzzled psychologists remained: What could possibly explain this odd reaction from the victims as they attest to openly, emotionally connecting to their oppressors to the extent that they began to identify with them?

Sometime later, criminologist Nils Bejerot, while facilitating a US Task Force on Terrorism and Societal Disorder during hostage situations, attempted to explain the bank saga. Sharing his analysis of the psychological elements constituting this newly identified psychological concept with the FBI and Scotland Yard, he coined the term "Stockholm syndrome."

Bejerot described the identity reversal process, "First people would experience something terrifying that just comes at them out of the blue. They are certain they are going to die, then they experience a type of in-fantilizing where, like a child, they are unable to eat, speak, or go to the bathroom without permission. The hostages experience a powerful, prim-itive positive feeling toward their captor. They are in denial that this is the person who put them in that situation. In their mind, they think this is the person who is going to let them live."[2]

The now well-documented, trauma-induced paradox, aka Stockholm syndrome, found its way into popular psychology and has been applied in hundreds of similar perpetrator/victim situations. The syndrome has been used by psychologists to explain maladaptive behaviors in many abusive contexts such as: abused and molested children, abusive interper-sonal relationships, incest victims, and even WWII concentration camp victims.

Only a year after the Stockholm bank standoff, a wealthy heiress, Patty Hearst, was abducted from her Berkeley apartment close to the Univer-sity of California campus where she was a sophomore, by a violent, an-archist group named the Symbionese Liberation Army (SLA). Patricia

---

1   Westcott, K. "What is the Stockholm Syndrome?" BBC, August 22, 2013, 4.
2   Ibid, 3.

Hearst was the daughter of Randolf A. Hearst, Jr., a San Francisco-based publishing magnate who owned the *San Francisco Examiner* and other newspapers.

In the nineteen months that followed her kidnapping, Hearst seemingly and voluntarily joined the anti-American cult, and even participated in several bank robberies with them, wearing the SLA military camo-fatigues and combat boots. Her transformation into a gun-wielding SLA member included adopting the name Tania, honoring East German Marxist revolutionary and constant companion to Che Guevara, Haydee Tamara Bunke Bider.

Similar to the Stockholm hostages, Patty Hearst later, after her arrest, claimed during an interview that her decision to join forces with the SLA was done on her own accord. This flawed admission reflected her own headfirst plunge into the murky waters of the Stockholm syndrome.

To try to make sense of what happened to this naïve nineteen-year-old college student, media accounts of her out-of-character behavior put forth the theory that Patty Hearst had been systematically brainwashed, resulting from being locked in a darkened closet for days at a time. Psychologically, this seemed a far too simple answer for such a highly complex case. Something just did not make sense. To contend that she made a conscious decision to hook up with a violent, revolution cult left the public wondering whether she was lying, and maybe she had other motives yet to be determined.

The history of her case fit hand-in-glove with the psychological conditions set forth in the Stockholm syndrome. Since the basis of the syndrome involves an unconscious element, Hearst was probably clueless on a conscious level to any ex-post facto determination about what happened to her.

Because the Stockholm syndrome can effectively operate as a strong, vicarious force operating below personal awareness, Sirhan also unwittingly adopted the negative characteristics of his persecutors and then incorporated the negative actions of his enemies: the Jews, the Zionists, the Israeli forces and anyone else he believed was "holding him back," thereby making him more like his enemies than different from them. Much the same as Patty Hearst, Sirhan slowly began to psychologically identify with his believed enemies.

The origin of the psychological concept of identification with the aggressor is tied to the trauma-induced paradox, which dates back to the work of Hungarian analyst, Dr. Sandor Ferenczi, during the first decade of the twentieth century. The concept of identification with the aggressor was later advanced by Dr. Sigmund's Freud's youngest daughter, Anna Freud, who also became a psychoanalyst and visited the US many times, delivering lectures on various aspects of psychoanalysis, including the origin and maintenance of psychological defense mechanisms. Freud described her analysis of various defense mechanisms including the identification with the aggressor in *The Ego and the Mechanisms of Defense.*[3]

Anna Freud focused particularly on the psychology of the identification process as taking over an abused child's awareness, which she observed in many traumatized children who appeared to take on or mimic the negative aspects of their oppressors and became unduly influenced by status figures who exerted unrestrained power over them. Instead of rejecting the oppressors, Freud noticed that some children subsequently adopted the same antagonistic and negative aspects of the abusers.

She often found that these traumatized child victims used this maladaptation process to insulate from further victimization, but then counterproductively began to display the same negativity of their oppressors that was earlier directly at them. Freud's conceptualization of the identification with the aggressor was that this defense mechanism served as the disenfranchised child's incorporation of the adverse actions directed at them as if this negativity had irreversibly invaded their existence. At the time of this assimilation, the victim simultaneously fears the abusers and strangely identifies with them, amounting to a similar process as in Stockholm syndrome.

The identification with the aggressor can occur as a real, yet vicarious psychological circumstance based on their victims' cumulative traumatic status as collected or filed away in their unconscious state, to erupt at some later time. Children progressively victimized by gun violence early in their lives may one day themselves turn to gun violence against later victims. Research has demonstrated that victims of childhood sexual abuse often themselves become sexual predators.

Dr. Ferenczi was affiliated with the European faction of psychoanalysis and worked closely with Anna Freud's father, Dr. Sigmund Freud, founder of the psychoanalytic movement. Dr. Ferenczi accompanied Freud during his only visit to America in 1909 when Freud delivered a series of lectures at Clark University in Worcester, Massachusetts.

The identification with the aggressor construct is directly connected to the psychological defense mechanism "introjection," which was first

3   Freud, A. (1956). *The Ego and the Mechanisms of Defense.* C. Baines (Trans.) Hogarth Press, London, England.

introduced into the psychiatric lexicon by Dr. Ferenczi. He most likely helped Dr. Freud more precisely define introjection as an ego defense mechanism. Introjection is defined as an unconscious process wherein an individual psychologically attributes from the identity of another person such as emotions, feelings, attitudes, values, and even spirituality. These internalized components can be either positive (compassion, empathy) in nature or negative (anger, hostility, vindictiveness). In this way, the incorporation process is like either a positive (exercising) or a negative (drug-alcohol abuse) addiction process.

Introjection is the opposite of psychological projection, where an individual rejects their negative characteristics, instead attributing them to another person. Introjection forms the psychological core of identification with the aggressor. Ferenczi's work with introjection easily blended into his concept of identification with the aggressor. This represents an important step to our understanding of how good people can sometimes engage in bad behaviors, and can help us piece together the fragments of what went terribly wrong in the Stockholm, Hearst, and Sirhan cases.

The psychological communality in these cases that is fueling their foundations is the paradoxical identification with the aggressor. Some psychologists have termed this connection as "the terrifying or traumatic bond." After the traumatized person begins to assimilate the unsavory attributes of the oppressor as in the Stockholm bank situation, they become even more vulnerable to additional traumatizing behaviors, leading to increased victimization. This strategy aims at the survival of the victim, hoping that their fractured self can be reunified.

Because the traumatized individual perceives that they live in a constant state of existential danger submersed in a perilous world, they may elect to become armed, purchase a weapon (perhaps a gun) and train to use it, to reduce more trauma and protect themselves. If and when they perceive an imminent life-threatening danger, they can legitimately strike back at the enemy. At the unconscious level, their retaliatory actions become neutralized, because they have now become the proxy extension of the aggressor.

Perhaps the most profound impact of the identification with the aggressor concept is taken from tragic, personal accounts of survivors provided to researchers from the Nazi concentration camps that spread throughout Europe before and during WWII. The central focal concern of the professionals who studied the prisoners from these death camps was: how could severely damaged and depersonalized Jewish captives come to identity with their brutal Nazi SS overlords? It seems almost impossible to imagine that some Jews, already traumatized by their confinement status and tortured by sadistic German guards, could look to them as idealized persons to identify with. Yet that took place.

These Jewish prisoners slowly began to progressively incorporate the heinous aspects of the German sentinels. According to Dutch physician Elie Aron Cohen, a survivor of Mauthausen concentration camp during the war, there were benefits to be derived from the identification with the aggressor and many prisoners began to at least partially identify with their Nazi controllers: "... Similarly, I am certain, the partial identification of the greater number of the prisoners with the SS must be explained: it is not the moral standards of the SS, which he despises, that the prisoner identifies himself, but he cannot escape identification with the aggressive manifestations of the SS...."

Dr. Cohen witnessed this negative identification with the aggressor by some Jewish prisoners with their Nazi SS captors firsthand. "I am aware that my statement, to the effect that only a small number of the prisoners, perhaps not even one, was able to escape a certain measure of identification with the SS, will cause some surprise."[4]

Curiously, during his identity surrender, his dissociative personality became more like his real or perceived enemies than different from them. Sirhan's inexplicable conversion into the negative alter personality couldn't be understood, reconciled, and integrated into his adjusted personality 1, because his alter personality evolved as a separate entity – a different personality, a malevolent Sirhan who was perfectly capable of striking back with ferocious intensity against his targeted enemy, RFK.

Dr. Cohen extended his reasoning on what caused these concentration prisoners to slide into the dark world of identification with the enemy, attributing this to two main psychological factors. First, they saw in the SS reminiscent signs of a father image and, through regression, they (childlike) wanted to form some type of human bond; even if this bonding process was flawed, they just couldn't stop themselves.

Dr. Viktor Frankl, like Dr. Cohen, a physician and prisoner of the SS and held in several WWII concentration camps, explained his conception of the identification with the aggressor process with the SS. He contended that the creation of the "capo status" (also kapo) for some prisoners amounted to a type of trustee standing, and accorded this higher status, they quickly developed a special affiliation with the SS. "These kapos,

---

4   Cohen, E.A. (1953). *Human Behavior in the Concentration Camp*. The Universal Library, Grosset & Dunlap, NY, 178–179.

of course, were chosen only from those prisoners whose characteristics promised to make them suitable for such procedures, and if they did not comply with what was expected of them, they were immediately demoted. They soon became much like the SS men and the camp wardens.... But apart from the selection of kapos, which was undertaken by the SS, there was a sort of self-selecting process going on the whole time among all the prisoners."[5] As these pseudo-guards became more comfortable in their ignominious roles, they began to imitate and act like the real SS guards.

During an interview with Stanford University Professor Emeritus, Dr. Phillip Zimbardo, he was questioned why, in some cases, persecuted people, such as concentration camp prisoners, so closely identified with their captors and why they even took steps to fashion their uniforms like Nazi SS guards. Dr. Zimbardo referred to an observation made years before by psychologist, Bruno Bettelheim,

> He was in a Nazi concentration camp for an actually short time at the beginning of the Holocaust and wrote some books about it. A lot of prisoners, he said, would identify with these terrible Nazi guards. He even has a button or something [that] came off a Nazi guard's uniform, they would pick it up and put it on – like carry it in their pocket to have a piece of the power. And instead of hating the guards, what he's saying is, some prisoners identified with the aggressor. Anna Freud said earlier that this is like the anti-Semitic Jew. People who know that others despise them, but then come to accept that; and by identifying with the aggressor, you try to minimize the gap between you and this powerful aggressor.[6]

Frankl's concept of the identification with the aggressor contends that the traumatized individual often displays an accompanying splitting or breaking apart of their personality. He noted, "... As the shocks increase during a child's development, so do the splits, and soon it becomes extremely difficult to maintain contact without confusion with all the [personality] fragments each of which behaves [as] a separate personality yet does not know of even the existence of others .... It is clear that he is describing writing of various functions of splitting-off of self-states."[7]

5   Frankl, V.E. (2006). *Man's Search for Meaning.* Beacon Press, Boston, 4–5 .
6   Wanis, P. (2013). "Holocaust Jews, Informing, Identification With the Aggressor: A Love for Power." https://www.patrickwanis.com/holocaust-jews-informing-identification-aggressor-love-power/
7   Howell, E. F. (2014). Ferenczi's Concept of Identification With the Aggressor: Understanding Dissociative Structures With Interacting Victim and Abuser Self-States. The American Journal of Psychoanalysis, 0002-9548/14, 55. www.palgrave-journals.com/ajp/

Dr. Ferenczi further conceptualized this splitting process as a turning away from reality, forming a type of psychological break in the individual's personality under the influence of shock. The dissociated part, however, seems to live on, hidden; and tries ceaselessly to make itself known.

Howell put the notion of personality splitting within the diagnostic context of a dissociative condition:

> With respect to splitting, it might be more specific and experience-near to formulate the inherent alterations in terms of aggressor and the victim self-states. Splitting in this sense seems to involve this organization of alternating dissociated submissive/victim and rageful/aggressor self-states of which I have been speaking, that reflect the impact of relational trauma.... Thus the victimized child learns both roles – victim and abuser.... This is evident in the aggressor state, and may help explain the isolated rage, contempt, and omnipotence often termed 'identification with the aggressor.

Dr. Ferenczi's conceptualization of the identification with the aggressor blending with dissociative features may help us cast new light into Sirhan's operating as a dissociative personality when he killed RFK. Ferenczi's connecting the identification with the aggressor to a dissociative state is critiqued by Howell: "The dissociative structure involves identification with the aggressor which involves the person being emotionally attached to inner persecutors, just as he or she was to the earlier outside aggressor."[8]

Dr. Frankl discusses his third concept, states of dissociation "that Ferenczi focused on as a response to trauma. Ferenczi's understanding of dissociation is similar to that of other writers; he saw it as a splitting off from immediate perception of experience that is intolerable. At this point, I leave the explication of Ferenczi's ideas to propose my own understanding of how dissociation, identification, and introjection often function as a unit during trauma. How does this work? During an overwhelming and inescapable attack, the victim surrenders himself to the attacker. He gives up his own sense of self, and his personal feelings and reactions – that is, he dissociates large chunks of his own experience – both because it is unbearable and because it is actually dangerous. ..."[9]

As pointed out by Ferenczi and others familiar with a dissociated patient like Sirhan, and as admitted by Dr. Diamond, the splitting or fracturing of one unified personality into two or more separate entities occurs

---

8   Howell. (2014), 54.
9   Frankel, V. (2002) "Exploring Ferenczi's Concept of Identification with the Aggressor: It's Role in Trauma, Everyday Life, and the Therapeutic Relationship." *Psychoanalytic Dialogues,* 12, 101–139.

306

because the individual is struggling to save his sanity, thereby protecting himself. Dr. Diamond agreed that this radical personality fracture results from an overwhelming chain of traumatic conditions beyond a person's control. In the Gorshen case (Chapter 4), Dr. Diamond clearly affirms the proposition that trauma-induced factors or cumulative trauma, such as that experienced by Sirhan stemming from his many childhood adverse events, can effect a drastic personality alteration that resulted in Sirhan's dissociative disorder.

Sirhan's highly charged trauma history, like Gorshen's own traumatic history, resulted in his personality split. Both men were similar victims to their circumstances and seeking refuge when they created an alternate identity to protect themselves and, seemingly in both cases, an evil twin was born, allowing them to seek a measure of personal revenge just to even the score with their perceived enemies.

Sirhan did not stroll into a bank armed with an AR-15 rifle and demand cash (as Patty Hearst did more than once). Sirhan's crime was far worse – he murdered the possible next President of the United States. Hearst's identification with her aggressor, two gun-wielding criminals, resulted in her temporary personality transformation. Sirhan's transformation into the aggressor was more complete and longstanding, precipitating the emergence of the morally challenged, altered Sirhan. This altered, violent, and vengeful Sirhan had moved into a criminal killing zone.

Over the years, Sirhan experienced so many serious traumatic experiences, more than enough to cause his personality to fracture, divide, and split, that he had moved away from his passive non-altered state of consciousness, where he was unable to defend himself against further traumatizing, into a deviant state where he could defend himself against the aggressors he had connected with vicariously for so long. Sirhan progressively became more similar to rather than dissimilar from the behaviors demonstrated by the aggressors. RFK represented the last man standing, so to speak, as just another potential aggressor filling Sirhan's growing reservoir of enemies committed to taking down the Arab cause.

Somewhat delusional, Sirhan saw his homicidal act as a way to achieve martyrdom by engaging in a violent, narcissistic act, unleashing the rage incorporated via years of his uncontrolled identification with his perceived aggressors. In a psychologically convoluted way, stemming from his identifying RFK as an oppressor, his killing of RFK represented (to Sirhan) the substituting of an obvious bad act, transforming it into a noble one supported by his cause to save the Palestinians from further destruction. I see Sirhan's wanton act of homicide rage as clearly tied into the criminological concept of erotomania-motivated murder.

Sirhan's complex motives in carrying through with his violent act, committed during an alter state of dissociation into his retributive personality 2, blocked from the awareness of his core personality 1, the passive or adjusted Sirhan; his repeated denials of recall of those critical moments just prior to and during the assassination of RFK that continuously evaded recollection by the adjusted Sirhan.

Although Dr. Diamond testified that, under deep hypnosis, Sirhan was able to recall some of the missing elements of the murder scene, it is possible that what he told Dr. Diamond was merely a reiteration of what Sirhan had learned about his actions from multiple media sources and what he was told from the beginning by police and others.

Sirhan's description of the assassination, as told to Dr. Diamond under hypnosis, could have been reconstructed based on the facts Sirhan learned from outside sources. He was pleased to pass on this information to Dr. Diamond and the prosecution's psychiatrist, Dr. Pollack. Sirhan, in one interpretation, may have been giving a convincing performance to conform to the demands of Dr. Diamond. Sirhan could have certainly viewed Dr. Diamond as another powerful authority figure. Because Dr. Diamond, like Dr. Pollack, was Jewish, Sirhan had his own personal and political reasons to distrust them; and he told them what they wanted to hear.

During his testimony regarding hypnotizing Sirhan, accompanied by Dr. Pollack, Dr. Diamond said this was the only time Sirhan described the assassination scene. When this particular hypnotic session ended, Sirhan told the two psychiatrists that he had no recollection of this pivotal reenactment episode, and he alluded to his suspicion that, "we were bugging him, that we were playing tricks on him; and Sirhan knew nothing about the reenactment of the experience."

Dr. Diamond noted that Sirhan's inability to recall the facts surrounding the murder scene was additional proof that, when Sirhan murdered RFK, he was in a dissociated state of consciousness. But the state of awareness he was immersed into was not a place where even under hypnosis he could have a conscious window into. After Dr. Diamond visited Sirhan's mother, he told defense attorneys Cooper and Berman, "Sirhan is sick, and this is a sick murder. I feel Sirhan killed Kennedy while he was in a dissociated state. I really don't think he knew what he was doing."

Dr. Diamond hypothesized what actually triggered Sirhan's homicidal act: "Sirhan consumed three or four Tom Collins drinks at the Ambassador, went back to his car to go home, discovered he was too drunk to drive, picked up his gun off the back seat of his car because he thought someone [the Jews] might steal it, and returned to the Ambassador to get some coffee. Then at some point, surrounded by mirrors and a great many lights, he became confused, probably went into a dissociated state, perhaps a kind of trance – then after the shooting – suddenly found himself being choked and beaten.… When he dissociated he was under a very special combination of circumstances. He fulfilled his fantasy in a dissociated state.…"[10]

I believe that Sirhan began to psychologically dissociate quite early in his life as verified from his mother's critical statements to Dr. Diamond during his visit with her. Sirhan displayed many of the symptoms consistent with a patient experiencing a dissociative disorder, as listed by, for instance, by Thigpen and Cleckley's study of Eve White reported in their book, *The 3 Faces of Eve:* trancelike states of consciousness, blackouts, headaches, time loss, odd handwriting, and gruesome nightmares. Eve's most disturbing nightmares centered on murdering her mother: "The fear and horror in the dream also reveal guilt and dread of retaliation for her wishes as a child to kill and do away with her mother."[11]

Mrs. Sirhan told Dr. Diamond that her son's reaction to the bombings and physical mayhem enveloping their home in Palestine left Sirhan frightened and pale, leading to his isolation from others for long periods of time. At times he acted as if he was frozen in place and did not or could not shift from one position for extended periods of time making him seem like a statue. Then at other times Sirhan seemed hyper-agitated. She continued describing Sirhan's other symptoms of sequestering himself in his room for days, lacking communication with other family members; then there were the blackouts when he seemed to be totally disconnected from his surroundings, what she called "his fainting" episodes. In my diagnostic experience, these symptoms are characteristic of an early onset dissociative condition.

Long after the childhood occurrences, Sirhan reported a continuing history of keeping to himself, closed off in his bedroom in the Pasadena home, as he engaged in occult Rosicrucian exercises such as intense mirror gazing and staring into candle flames, producing what appeared to be trancelike states. I contend that during these semi-hypnotic episodes, Sirhan became dissociated into his altered state as personality 2 from his adjusted Sirhan as personality 1.

---

10   Kaiser. (1970). 307, 309.

11   Thigpen and Cleckley. (1957). 214.

During these transient episodes, core psychological components of the bad Sirhan formed around his identification with the many aggressors who he saw either directly or vicariously as tormenting him, and to some degree were ruining his life. Most strikingly (like Eve White), he developed a retaliatory impulse to eliminate his tormentors, culminating in taking out his most recent threat, RFK.

Counterintuitively, Sirhan's killing of RFK was, in his distorted reasoning, substituting what his alternate personality considered justified, retaliatory behavior for obvious criminal behavior, deeming the murder act as a positive rather than negative event. Sirhan's wanton act of murder was triggered by his perverse attachment to his victim, RFK, thereby he was eliminating a person he once held in high esteem; then when he perceived that RFK turned against him and his Palestinian comrades, Sirhan decided to retaliate by killing him.

His vicarious love-hate relationship with RFK fits into the identification with the aggressor syndrome as well as fulfilling the diagnostic criteria of the erotomania-motivated murder condition.

At the same time that Sirhan moved into the stage of pathological fusion, his core personality 1 radically shifted into his altered personality 2, at that point becoming the bad Sirhan capable of eliminating what he perceived as RFK's direct threat to him and his Palestinian people. By splitting into this secondary personality, Sirhan immediately became powerful, potent, and capable of projecting who he really was.

Early in his life, Sirhan began to search for "who" he was, employing whatever tools he could to fill an existential void that continued to elude him – that different self he knew was there – all he had to do was find it. Over time, Sirhan's perception of the world became imbued with what he perceived as his failures; it seemed that whatever he did was met with defeat. This is an operational definition of learned helplessness.

PHASE V: LEARNED HELPLESSNESS

Adding to the psychological concepts (the trauma-induced paradox, Stockholm syndrome, and the identification with the aggressor) that help account for Sirhan's alter personality, turning him to the dark side of his world, a third psychological factor that negatively affected Sirhan's adjustment patterning is learned helplessness.

Sirhan's history of learned helplessness, extending back into his childhood, was marked by his reaction to extreme traumatic events he experienced in war-torn East Jerusalem. My interpretation of how the psychological principles of learned helplessness directly affected Sirhan centers on how these factors began to accumulate over time in his dissociative and irrational personality.

The psychological concept of learned helplessness is most associated with the research conducted by Peterson, Maier, and Seligman, who defined the terms "learned helplessness" and "learned optimism" in the 1970s. For purposes here, learned helplessness is defined as "a noxious mental state of frustration created when an event or series of traumatic events beyond one's control, with escape options few or none, contribute to feelings of losing control, and helplessness."[12]

Many of Sirhan's most serious traumas happened when he was still living in Palestine, prior to his move to California in 1956. Most of these adverse experiences were directly tied to the brutal horrors attendant to the war between the Palestinians and the Israelis and the abuse from his father as described previously.

At an early age, Sirhan realized that physical escape from these frightening events occurring in his homeland was beyond his control, therefore to insulate himself from further psychological degradation he did what persons with acquired learned helpless sometimes do – he created a safe place in his mind to protect himself from additional mental trauma. His psychological move toward a safe mental milieu is indicative of the second learned helplessness descriptor: the mental awareness that, no matter what he does, it won't change the adverse outcomes facing him. The dynamics of learned helplessness do not serve as a method to abdicate one's responsibility for a serious crime like murder, but provides us with new information to explain how, for instance, Sirhan became a murderer.

Peterson, Maier, and Seligman's work promulgate three criteria necessary to characterize a learned helplessness condition: "First the person (or group) would act in an inappropriately passive way ... second, the person would have a history of uncontrollable events ... and third, if someone's self-defeating actions are to be well described as learned helplessness, then her passivity would be mediated by her beliefs in helplessness."

These psychologists add, "The best way to demonstrate the applicability of learned helplessness is longitudinally, because helpless theory – in both its original and reformulated versions – is a theory of process."[13]

Generally, at least seven psychological, learned helplessness descriptors are derived from the three criteria used to account for this condition.

12   Peterson, C., S.F. Maier, and M.E.P. Seligman. (1995). *Learned helplessness: A Theory for the Age of Personal Control.* Oxford University Press, New York.
13   Peterson, Maier, and Seligman. (1995). 229–230.

These reformulated descriptors are particularly germane, as I interpret how Sirhan's learned helplessness helped mold his thought process and produce the mind of a killer.

Table V. Sirhan's Learned Helplessness Descriptors
1. Abdication of personal control over one's life.
2. Feelings that no matter what they do, it won't change the behavioral outcome.
3. A compromised ability to resolve everyday problems fosters personal resentment and envy.
4. A perception that their lives are controlled by external agency.
5. The impression that "I'm doomed to fail."
6. The strong belief that there's no one to trust, "It looks like I can't trust anybody, so betrayal is always out there."
7. A feeling that there is no clear pathway to escape, "Regardless of what I try, nothing has worked out for me, and "I'm trapped."

Beginning in his early childhood, Sirhan's belief system concerning his perception of the world fit into the framework of a learned helplessness model. In his diary, Sirhan described a guiding philosophy he read about that was similar to his: "Life is ambivalence, life is a struggle, life is wicked," and then he wrote, "If life is any way otherwise, I have honestly never seen it. I always seem to be on the losing, l-o-s-i-n-g, always the one exploited to the fullest."

Asked by defense attorney Cooper about this specific diary entry, Sirhan responded, "I must have been manic at the time. I don't remember what was on my mind."[14]

This statement reflects Sirhan's learned descriptor number 1: "I can't change the outcome of my life, so why try?"

Again referring back to his diary, Sirhan seemed at times to be preoccupied with money, getting it and hopefully becoming wealthy, then fluctuating between his opposition to and the attraction and envy of the American capitalistic system. In his diary, he expressed the learned helplessness descriptor number 2: "No matter what I do, I can't get what I want." (wealth and status). He wrote, "Whatever can be said in praise of poverty, the fact remains that it is not possible to live a really complete life unless one is rich."

This expression of his personal frustration at being poor indicates that he believed he was unable to change his life circumstances, thus he re-

---

14   Trial Vol 17, 4998, March 4, 1969.

mained frozen in his opportunity as reflected in the learned helplessness descriptors: I don't know where to turn or what to do next.

As time went on, Sirhan's learned helplessness drifted ever so closely into a fantasy world marked by frustration, and perhaps even into a delusional space as he again expressed his rejection of the principles of the unfair capitalist system. This time his frustration focused on his desire to own a new Ford Mustang, a popular and desirable vehicle in the mid-1960s, yet well beyond the financial reach of most people in their early twenties. Nevertheless, he still wanted one. Again, he wrote in his diary, "I must plan to come home in a new car today, I must plan to go home ... in a new Mustang in a new Mustang ... tonight, tonight, tonight, I must buy a new Mustang tonight, tonight, tonight, tonight...."

Sirhan's persistent fantasy about driving a flashy Mustang around Pasadena, as expressed in his diary, is in concert with learned helplessness descriptor number 3 – a compromised ability to resolve everyday problems, fostering personal resentment and envy.

As already noted, Sirhan's learned helplessness extended far back into his history to the time he lived with his family in East Jerusalem when the decision was made by his father to move to America, a decision Sirhan rejected, but again a choice he had no control over. This absence of control over his life is suggestive of learned helplessness descriptor 4: a perception that one's life is controlled by an external agency. Sirhan made it clear that he desired to stay in Jerusalem and not relocate to a foreign land that was not "an Arab place." He ran away from his parents the night before they were supposed to depart for the US. Sirhan said, "I was very hesitant, Sir. I didn't want to leave ... I wanted to stay in my own country, Sir, with my own people ... I went to a neighboring town of Ramallah – it's about 15 miles away...."[15] At age twelve, Sirhan lacked the ability to change his father's mind about relocation. He had to move first briefly to New York then on to Pasadena, California, where he lived until his arrest for killing RFK.

Because of Sirhan's interest in horses, the sport of horse racing, and especially due to his unique small physical stature (approximately five feet four and between 110–115 pounds), he had fantasized about training as a jockey, and he had his chance. Sirhan had worked at Hollywood Park, Del Mar, Granja Vista Del Rio Stable, and Santa Anita racetracks doing various menial jobs, including as a "hot walker," which required a license so that he could cool off race horses after a vigorous workout.

---

15   Ibid. 4856–4857.

In 1966, when Sirhan finally got the opportunity to physically ride, he was involved in the two riding accidents that led to the end of his dream fantasy of being a jockey, and psychologically represented another blow to his ability to control his life.

Sirhan recalled the accident at the Granja Vista, responding to defense attorney Mr. Cooper's questioning. "And on this morning when you had the accident, did you ride this horse on the track alone, or were there any other horses on the track?"

Sirhan responded: "Yes, Sir, I was the only one on the track."

"And the horse you were on?"

"It was a quarter horse filly, Sir, called Hy-Vera."

"Obviously you got on the horse and you started? Were you supposed to ride the horse fast?"

"I was supposed to work it, Sir. Three hundred yards.... After fifty yards, Sir, I don't remember. Something happened."

"Do you remember where you – were knocked unconscious?"

"I fell from that horse, Sir, and I was knocked unconscious."[16]

Once again, one of Sirhan's dreams turned into a frustrating nightmare. It seemed that whatever he tried was met with overwhelming defeat, reflecting learned helplessness descriptor number 5: "I'm doomed to fail."

Even at age twenty-two, Sirhan saw his opportunities rapidly slipping away and began to conceive of himself as a failure, maybe asking himself, *Will I be able to grasp that brass ring, ever?*

During an exclusive one-on-one interview with Robert Kaiser, Sirhan discussed his interest in becoming a foreign diplomat, his experiences at Pasadena City College (PCC), and his frustration with trying to get ahead in life.

Sirhan said, "The way they did things at PCC helped detach me from society, or at least campus society. But for me, that was society. I majored in political science, foreign languages. Diplomacy was my main interest. But soon I gave up on the idea of being a diplomat. When I figured the score, I saw that the odds were stacked against me. You gotta be rich to be a diplomat. You have to give big parties. After that, I realized that being an Arab is worse than being a Negro."[17]

The sixth learned helplessness descriptor, the perception that there's no one to trust and, because of betrayal, is directly related to number 5 – and is probably the most definitive factor in Sirhan's case. Sirhan had be-

---

16   Ibid, 4887.

17   Kaiser. (1970). 199.

come vicariously attached to RFK, many times expressing his admiration for him, then he suddenly turned against RFK, exploding in a fuselage of hate, firing eight shots at his one-time hero. This drastic change in Sirhan to a hate-driven motivation from love-oriented position for RFK was explained previously as the concept of erotomania-motivated murder.

As time passed, Sirhan developed an almost mythical worship and false connection to RFK as he had to his brother, President John F. Kennedy. Sirhan initially praised RFK as a kind of savior. The applicability of the erotomania diagnosis, in Sirhan's case, the initially positive identification with RFK, was converted into a homicidal rage based on his perception that the object of affection had somehow turned against him, automatically almost forcing him to act out, culminating a devastating, homicidal climax.

Sirhan's distorted thinking may have gone something like: *How could you do this to me? I've been deceived and betrayed. Now you deserve to be punished!*

This symbolic betrayal, terribly distorted by Sirhan, supports the learned helplessness descriptor 6 – the perceived and real loss of trust in a valued person.

Sirhan's feelings of betrayal are reminiscent of Patrizia Gucci's story of the murder of her husband. Initially, Patrizia worshiped the ground Maurizio walked on, and then the love turned sour, then fatal.

Many times Sirhan alluded to his admiration for RFK, and then Kennedy became a dark obsession as he described to the prosecution psychiatrist, Dr. Pollack: "I liked him, Sir, I think that is the crux of it, Sir. He was a hero, an idol. I really went for him, Sir, but he failed me, Sir. He betrayed me, Sir."

Not believing this, Dr. Pollack said, "Betrayed you. Well, that idea – that is twisted thinking. That is twisted thinking. ... I think that what failed you, what betrayed you, were your own unrealistic expectations, your own ideals. You wanted more than the world was going to give you. ... It was normal enough to have dashed hopes. It was not normal to murder a real person who symbolized those hopes. Many people share your feelings, so I don't see you as crazy. And that doesn't help you."[18]

To help clarify the odd fixation that had long troubled Sirhan, Dr. Pollack also tried his hand at hypnotizing Sirhan. Dr. Pollack's hypnotic induction procedure differed a little from Dr. Diamond's, and the result was not equally effective. But Sirhan froze up and failed to communicate with

---

18   Kaiser. (1970). 361 –362.

Dr. Pollack, giving him no usable psychiatric information that could confirm or disconfirm his clinical diagnosis. Dr. Pollack continued to probe Sirhan, urging him to speak to him about the murder scene, still Sirhan only gave guttural sounds and nothing more.

Exploring the betrayal aspect of Sirhan's learned helplessness, Dr. Diamond asked, "Did you feel Robert Kennedy had betrayed you?"

Sirhan answered, "Yes, his solid promise. Saying he would give fifty jet bombers to Israel."

Dr. Diamond continued, "When did you decide to do something?"

"I don't think I ever decided," Sirhan said, "I'm mad, and it's good as long as it lasted for the duration of the aggravation."

Dr. Diamond asked, "So you don't think you carefully planned this, then?"

"Oh, hell, I never planned it," Sirhan responded.

Because of the split into two Sirhans, while in his adjusted state, he sincerely believed that he never planned to assassinate RFK; yet the altered Sirhan, possessing the requisite, retaliatory criminal intent planned and carried through the murder plot.

The descriptor, that there is no pathway for escape, is tied to Sirhan's paranoid, political thoughts that the Zionists, the Jews, and Israelis were dedicated to the destruction of himself and the Palestinians. During his testimony, Sirhan made many statements that the "Jewish State will never stop trying to destroy my people."

These intrusive thoughts marked by violent overtones even pervaded his dream states. Recall the terrifying dream-turned-nightmare that Sirhan reported as he viewed the TAT card 16 (a blank card) presented to him by Dr. Schorr. Sirhan's retaliatory feelings, saying, if given the opportunity, he would murder Moshe Dayan [Israeli Defense minister during the critical Six-Day War] looking down at people. Sirhan put it this graphic way: "There's a bullet that's crashing through his brain at the height of his glory. Sirhan was not part of the scene. He was the scene. Sirhan paused and said, 'I'm the one killing him!'"

Sirhan felt trapped and persecuted by the unstoppable Jewish forces he saw all around him as he explained during his testimony about another one of his diary entries: "Sir, the whole thing was in this volume [about] the Zionists and it involved the State of Israel, Sir, and it invoked in me something that I can't describe, and the Zionists to me is just like the communists to you."

Sirhan could not seem to escape his continuing obsession with his perception of the Jewish State as the enemy, therefore verifying the learned helplessness descriptor number 7 that he had "no clear pathway of escape" from the Jewish peril. Throughout his twenty-four years, Sirhan was unable to defeat the Zionist's forces he perceived were clearly out to get him and his Palestinian people, leaving him trapped in a paranoid belief system from which there was no escaping; and in this sense, he was saw himself as a failure.[19]

Listening to a radio interview, Sirhan learned that RFK was going to make a campaign fundraising speech at a Jewish gathering in Beverly Hills, California, his dissociative self, personality 2, became agitated and then enraged. He painfully recalled that RFK's image was almost diabolically haunting him as he practiced his Rosicrucian "mirror-gazing exercises." He recounted that his personal facial image strangely transformed and was replaced with RFK's.

He told defense attorney Grant Cooper, "I just thought right then, Sir, he [RFK] bugged me to the point, Sir, where I was concentrating in the mirror instead of seeing my own face, that [sic there] was Robert Kennedy's face in front of me in the mirror. ... Again, Sir, this is an illusion. I can't prove it but I saw it in the mirror. His face ... I actually saw his face, Sir, I was that burned up about him."[20]

Apparently, RFK's fantasized image, real or not, had so penetrated Sirhan's alter personality that, in line with learned helplessness descriptor number 7, Sirhan felt he was held captive psychologically and could not escape from the plan he was constructing to eliminate the man who betrayed and now haunted him. At that moment, the altered Sirhan personality 2 knew exactly what course of deadly action was to follow.

Further characterizing learned helplessness, Peterson, Maier, and Seligman wrote, "As it is currently formulated, helplessness theory may only explain who falls victim to misfortunes for which they are predisposed by other factors.... Perhaps the helplessness reformulation should be considered less a model of one or a few human difficulties and more a mechanism involved in all manner of problems."[21]

When examining these seven learned helplessness descriptors, they clearly mirror many of the life experiences negatively impacting Sirhan's early childhood. These traumatic life events contributed to his mounting levels of stress, resulting in a break from ordinary reality, paving the way for his learned helplessness condition, helping to account for the emergence of the altered Sirhan, the personality who was inclined toward eve-

---

19   Trial Vol 17, 4972, March 5, 1969.
20   Trial Vol 17, 4978, March 4, 1969.
21   Peterson, Maier, and Seligman. (1995). 181.

ning the score with all those he perceived made him helpless in the first place; and first on his "hit list" was RFK.

SIRHAN'S MOVE INTO THE WORLD OF SELF-HELP

To aid with his self-discovery process, Sirhan availed himself of as many self-help reading materials as he could locate. Many of these books, pamphlets, and printed articles veered into the opaque world of mysticism, spiritualism, and occult studies. I contend that Sirhan thought moving into areas of mysticism could facilitate his personal trip into self-awareness as a seeker of truth, and finally discover the identity that had consistently eluded him.

My contention is also that Sirhan, on a surface level, perceived he was psychologically damaged goods. After arrest, when he was jailed, a search of his house (without the benefit of a legal search warrant), Sirhan's brother Adel gave investigators a sampling of Sirhan's books, including some oriented toward occult studies and a substantial amount of information concerning Rosicrucians.

Dr. Diamond testified that Sirhan had to do something about "his condition," so he developed this very intense interest in the occult, the mystic, and he started reading all kinds of books on mind control, yoga, thought control, etc., in which the human mind supposedly transcends or overcomes the limitations of the physical reality. A Rosicrucian Society, the head of which is centered in San Jose, had a standardized advertisement in many magazines, especially appealing to seekers like Sirhan, who are failing, who aren't making it in life, and offering them instructions on how to control one's mind, how to gain the ancient mysteries of the power of thought so that one can become a master of one's own destiny: "They [Rosicrucians] are not religious, but like the Masons ... they speak of themselves as AMORC, the Ancient Mystical Order of the Rosae Crucis."[22]

Dr. Diamond was correct in his analysis of Sirhan's moving toward the weird attraction of the AMORC philosophy and practices because he was seeking enlightenment and identity resolution. Sirhan's immersion into the world of the Rosicrucians presented positive facets as Dr. Diamond stated, "He was particularly interested in an article entitled, 'Put it in writing' of the *Rosicrucian Digest*. This is a quite innocuous, harmless article in which basically what it says is, 'If you really want to succeed in life, put it in writing, write it over and over again; pick a date; believe it, and it will start to come true; start acting as if you will achieve your goal and most of

---

22   Trial Vol 24, 6989-6990, March 24, 1969.

all to put everything in writing' – it ends in the quotation: 'I dare you to write it down.'"[23]

Sirhan heeded the Rosicrucian's suggestion and "dared to write it down," and parts of his diary are evidence that he did commit his thoughts to writing, accounting for certain entries in his diary done either by Sirhan's personality 1 or 2. Other less-constructive passages Sirhan does not recall, written by the altered Sirhan, reflected his emergent vengeful and homicidal impulses.

During the late 1960s and well into the early 1970s, millions of disenfranchised youth like Sirhan looking for "the right path" in their lives were magnetically drawn to alternate, New Age solutions. This led to the use of LSD and other supposedly mind-expanding chemical agents promulgated by drug gurus such as Dr. Timothy Leary and his associate Ram Dass (Dr. Richard Alpert) at Harvard University, whose magical, instant nirvana slogan to the youth of America was to "Turn on, tune in, and drop out."

The Hare Krishna movement swept up new loyal followers who hung around bus stations and airports, chanting ancient Hindu scriptures. Beatle George Harrison, a spiritual advocate of Eastern religious thought, chanted "Hare Krishna, Hare Rama" lyrics in the song he wrote, "My Sweet Lord," after he became a loyal follower in the late 1960s, and remained a devotee until his death in 2001.

These supposed words of wisdom barked out at a youthful population led a generation of mind-numbed, pill-popping, weed-smoking kids who had to finally face the music that age twenty only lasts for twelve months; then it was time, as their parents urged them, "to grow up and get a job."

The New Age therapy was quite unlike Sirhan's concerted bibliotherapeutic journey to locate the missing elements from his consciousness. That takes time, and the gurus of self-discovery promised it in a heartbeat.

Added to the invasive drug solution, the self-help and countercultural movements were suddenly ushered in, widely promoting such unique experiences as Werner Erhard Training sessions (EST), rage reduction, rebirthing, *Dianetics* and Scientology (both developed by science fiction writer L. Ron Hubbard), Gestalt therapy, sensitivity training seminars, and the father of all the New Age fulfillment quests, primal therapy, founded by Dr. Arthur Janov, a southern California psychologist with big expectations for fame and fortune. Dr. Janov boldly claimed one's center or finding your true self was merely a scream or two away from reality. Almost immediately, primal therapy spread from meager beginnings in LA to around the globe.

---

23   Ibid.

John Lennon and Yoko Ono, convinced that primal therapy was just the ticket for them, flew Dr. Janov to England where they screamed away their anxieties in a multimillion-dollar mansion, and produced their record album, *John Lennon/Plastic Ono Band*. Seemingly, a renewed, spiritual awakening was out there for anyone, and it was as easy as replying to widely promoted magazine and TV ads and "for a small fee," as promised in Scientology, you too could "be clear."

Set against this psychological backdrop, Sirhan's turning to the mystical side of self-enlightenment doesn't seem so out of place for a confused, traumatized, and suspicious person who believed he had psychological problems, but never realized that the real psychological conundrum feeding his troubled existence was his undiagnosed dissociative identity disorder. The condition continued to resurface even though he had no conscious knowledge of why this was happening to him, or when his adjusted personality would be invaded and replaced by the alternative Sirhan.

Sirhan had no clue why, for most of his life, he had split off into odd, inexplicable, and frightening trances comprised of deeply troubling thoughts involving violent and dark retaliatory actions centered on striking back at the people he perceived had harmed him. For the adjusted Sirhan, these thoughts were not only disturbing, but unlike him. Dr. Diamond was correct again, implying that Sirhan was like a child who became lost in his search for his true identity that could only be solved with the identification and reconciliation of the two Sirhans.

Sirhan wasn't a societal loser as much as he was simply losing the struggle to identify, and then acknowledge his alternate personality – the one suffused with anger and rage, that was suddenly unleashed on a warm June night in 1968. One clue to why could be related to his accumulated collection of reading materials.

SIRHAN'S BOOKS: "IN SEARCH OF SELF"

When Sirhan's home was searched, probably illegally, in addition to his diary, his brother Adel mistakenly gave defense investigator Michael McCowan many of Sirhan's books, some of which reflected his interest in the occult and the writings of the Rosicrucians as well as more evidence of his automatic writing. During Sirhan's questioning by lead defense attorney, Cooper, he reviewed several of these books, some that Sirhan recalled and some he did not. Cooper asked Sirhan if he could remember reading *The Laws of Mentalism* by A. Victor Segno. Sirhan said that he had read the book, but could not recall specifics. Oddly, Sirhan had inscribed his name serially over and over in his books.

Cooper inquired. "I notice you have your name, Sirhan Sirhan."

"Yes, Sir," said Sirhan.

"Sirhan Sirhan Library, Sirhan, Sirhan, is that right?" asked Cooper.

"Yes, Sir," Sirhan said.

"And whose is that writing?" asked Cooper.

Sirhan answered, "I doubt if that is mine!"

Cooper then asked, "And the writing 'good one, not copy yet' that is not your handwriting?"

Sirhan said, "No."

Cooper followed up, "Sirhan, Sirhan, Sirhan, Sirhan Library, Sirhan; you wrote your name four times?"

"Yes, Sir," Sirhan stated.

"Do you know why you wrote your name four times?" Cooper asked.

"No, I really don't," said Sirhan.

Sirhan's repeating of his name was done like so many other examples, indicating that the alter Sirhan penned this writing in his various books while in a mechanical, dissociated state; thus when asked by Cooper in a non-altered state, he came up blank.

Cooper continued inquiries into the underlining of certain additional passages in the books removed from Sirhan's collection, and Sirhan continued denying that he placed the underlined markings on many of the pages.[24]

Sirhan's convoluted route into self-defeating, learned helplessness led him to unresolved existential issues concerning what his life was all about. He probably thought that by reading selected books, he could find the happy destination he sought. Sirhan's reading choices seemed eclectic and random to the investigators who examined his books and other occult-oriented materials; yet my view is that Sirhan's reading choices were focused toward one goal – to figure out why he maintained these strange, alternative feelings he could not identify. Like the New Age truth seekers, Sirhan was unknowingly engaged in a psychological process known as bibliotherapy and, in each book he read, he hoped he could find the answers to his psychological confusion.

Maybe Sirhan believed there was a magical answer, or perhaps many of them that would help explain his confusing state of consciousness; i.e., why was he engaged in such odd behaviors he could not recall (e.g., the

---

24   Trial Vol 17, 4944-4946 March 4, 1969.

assassination and his wandering diary entries, for example), and why were large slices of his conscious life mysteriously shrouded from his conscious awareness? Sirhan's own explanations for his obscured behaviors seemed to have hit a wall, resulting in him turning to the occult and black magic to find the answers he desperately sought. He wasn't himself, and he knew it; he felt alien and somehow outside of himself, almost like a stranger in his own body.

The issue of Sirhan's reading materials was addressed by prosecutor Compton as part of cross-examination of Sirhan is characterized by the following exchange:

> **Compton:** "Now, let me talk to you a minute about these studies of your books about how to improve your mind. When you read these things, you really didn't expect to acquire some supernatural power, did you?"
>
> **Sirhan:** "Sir, that is what they claimed, Sir, that you would...."
>
> **Compton:** "I know what they claim, but you didn't really expect to do that, did you?"
>
> **Sirhan:** "You're wrong, Sir. I did."
>
> **Compton:** "Then what did you mean by your answer the other day when your counsel asked you if you read these books to become a better-developed person mentally? He asked you the question: 'A superior development?' and you said, 'I don't know about superior, but better development.'"
>
> **Sirhan:** "Well, superior and better, Sir, are better than normal, no?" Sirhan responded.
>
> **Compton:** "So you were really trying to improve your mind?"
>
> **Sirhan:** "Improve my ability, Sir, yes ... yes, from normal to superior – If I better myself, I would actually be superior, no?"
>
> **Compton:** "But that's all you really wanted? You didn't want to gain some supernatural power over other people, did you?"
>
> **Sirhan:** "If I could, Sir, why not? That's what they claimed you could do in those books."
>
> **Compton:** "Did you really believe it?"
>
> **Sirhan:** "Sir, the Bible says if you have as much faith as a drop of mustard, you can move mountains, Sir. I believe that, Sir. It has been proven to me, Sir."[25]

---

25   Trial Vol 18, 5255-5256, March 6, 1969.

Sirhan's incessant reading of enlightenment books was fueled by the promise to facilitate his "seeing the light," yet during the process he continued to live in a frightening and delusional world of psychological confusion, darkness, and dissociative experiences.

It follows that Sirhan used his books as a psychological stepping stone to bring clarity into his confused existence, attempting to answer the existential question, "Who am I?" Some of his readings were certainly a form of bibliotherapy or self-discovery. The term bibliotherapy suggests combining psychotherapy with reading to ameliorate a psychological issue. Bibliotherapy has been used in a wide variety of clinical, psychiatric, and nonclinical settings, often with favorable outcomes. I have seen bibliotherapy used in hospital settings for patients to better understand their individual issues: clinical depression, PTSD, anxiety, as well as general self-esteem deficits – reading along with the printed text, and then engaging in "guided self-talk."

Because several of the books in Sirhan's collection seemed to promote revolutionary themes vs. self-discovery analysis, they became targets of inquiry for the prosecution's attorneys, and even a defense investigator. Fidel Castro's book, *History Will Absolve Me*, was singled out by defense investigator McCowan, who said, "This guy is a fuckin' communist." (Maybe Mr. McCowan missed another book in Sirhan's collection on the life and times of the peaceful advocate of social revolution, *Gandhi*.)

Sirhan's Connection to the Occult

In addition to his "searching for self" books, prior to the tragic events on June 4-5, 1968, Sirhan was preoccupied by a fascination with occult-related matters. Pursuant to a search of his bedroom, investigators located lots of occult-related reading materials, including his personal diary that came to be known as the "RFK Must Die" document that was thoroughly scrutinized during the Sirhan trial.

The product of this search provided valuable insight that helped shape Sirhan's thought process. Theoretically, a look into the content of Sirhan's vast reading materials may offer some insight into his frame of mind just prior to killing RFK. When Sirhan took the witness stand to give testimony in his own defense, he showed no reluctance, explaining his penchant for acquiring then reading these magazines and books, and then plunging into occult practices. The defense and prosecution both wondered if the unraveling of this fascination with occult studies could help explain his vicarious love-hate relationship with RFK.

It seemed worthwhile to investigate whether Sirhan's interest in the occult altered his personal life view, or conversely if his pursuit was driven by an undiagnosed, pre-existing mental condition? This included his preoccupation devoted to themes, such as understanding the difference between black magic and white magic, or using his mind to modify the physical environment, thereby defying the laws of physics as, for example, willing the flame of a candle to change colors – apparently, a practice Sirhan learned from the teachings of the Rosicrucian Order.

Rosicrucian Order (AMORC) literature describes a primary goal as to help followers awaken their spiritual faculties and wisdom in harmony with natural laws. The order's origins can be traced to ancient Egypt. By the seventeenth century, they associated its principles of a brotherhood of alchemists and sages whose quest to turn base metals into precious gold was a metaphor for the desire to seek higher truths by transforming human mental states into greater spiritual awareness. The Brotherhood claims Sir Francis Bacon, Sir Isaac Newton, and Albert Einstein as followers.

The Rosicrucians, "traditionally secretive, have entered a period of glasnost and even runs a correspondence course for members through Rose-Croix University International. This particular sect of the Rosicrucians was started by a New York advertising executive in 1909, and moved to San Jose, California, in 1927."[26]

Rosicrucian advocates suggest that telepathic communications are possible, providing a bridge into a new dimension in one's life, yielding inner peace and universal truth, providing a transcendent path. The organization promoted Sirhan's mental immersion into telekinesis, the movement of physical objects using a person's mind, or simply willing them by mental command. With practice, Sirhan convinced himself that he could move objects and practiced this ritual many times with mirrors, candle flames, and a pendulum strung from the ceiling, moving back and forth supposedly at his command if he willed it to move. The organizing principle in all Sirhan's occult exercises seemed to be to gain control over his behavior, as if he sensed that at times at least part of him was uncontrolled.

On more than one occasion when Sirhan began to gaze in the candlelit mirror, he suddenly and unexpectedly saw RFK's clear image, which aroused his anger at a man he once claimed to respect, if not love.

When questioned by defense attorney Cooper about his initial interest in the Rosicrucians by filing an application, Sirhan explained the process

---

26   Shapiro, Stephanie. "Once secretive Rosicrucians beginning to open up." *Seattle Times.* Oct 3, 1990. http://archive.seattletimes.com/archive/?date=19901003&slug=1096412

as the attorney showed him a copy of his original Rosicrucian application. After a court recess, Cooper shifted his area of inquiry to examine a book titled *Cyclomancy*. By engaging in multiple mind expansion and behavioral control exercises, Sirhan's search for meaning was viewed as an attempt to preserve his sanity.

About *Cyclomancy*, Sirhan mentioned that the author described the benefit of practicing white magic: "The basis of what he says is you can do anything with your mind if you know how. ... He gave exactly how the mind operates and how you can [put] a thought in your mind and how you can have it work and become a reality if you want it to."[27]

Obvious to Dr. Diamond, Sirhan was searching his own personality to not only improve himself using perhaps the principle of spiritual alchemy and additional techniques, but also to survey his own mental state – that he was not "going crazy," his constant fear.

Sirhan's extensive readings into occult and mystic studies, combined with his affiliation with the Rosicrucians were methods he chose to self-diagnose and deter those troubling thought intrusions in search for self-mastery that Dr. Diamond diagnosed as being consistent with paranoid schizophrenic symptoms that formed part of Sirhan's psychosis. Progressively, Sirhan began to involve himself in ritualistic behaviors he believed would infuse clarity into his alienated life.

Defense attorney Cooper asked Sirhan to describe the exercises he used as prescribed in Rosicrucian literature.

Sirhan said, "One of them was, Sir, to put your hand in a very hot pail of water and think cool. I know this sounds queer but, Sir, the boiling water on my hand was cool when I put it in. I thought it was cool, and I felt that it was cool. And I did it the other way around with ice cold water, and I thought it was hot; and believe me, Sir, it was hot."

Focusing on the candlelight exercises again, Sirhan said, "After repeated exercises and attempts, I managed to do it, and I cannot prove this, but goddamn it, it worked!"

When Cooper asked Sirhan about other Rosicrucian or occult or metaphysical exercises he performed such as thought transference, Sirhan said, "I played with that a little bit, yes."

Another of Sirhan's most unique claims was represented as human thought transference from one person to another. During a session with Dr. Diamond, Sirhan recounted what I'd diagnose as a visual hallucination or delusional depersonalization. As Sirhan continued his mirror-gaz-

---

27   Trial Vol 17, 4905, March 3, 1969.

ing rituals using two flickering candles placed on each side of the mirror, he experienced a frightening, perhaps prescient episode.

Cooper asked, "And would you be convinced in your own mind that you were able to project these thoughts?"

Sirhan said, "If I knew enough about it, it will happen. It will work."

When Cooper asked Sirhan where he felt such experiences would lead him, Sirhan said he had high hopes he could become a better person, regain control over his life. He reiterated this later when cross-examined by prosecuting attorney Compton.

Under cross-examination from Mr. Compton, Sirhan explained his peculiar connection with the Rosicrucians and again described being able to change the colors of a candle flame with his mind.

Compton asked, "As far as you were concerned, the experiment was a success?"

Sirhan said, "Yes, Sir … I didn't have any trouble believing, Sir, that this stuff works … I was impressed that it happened, that what they said, Sir, become true."[28]

The evidence of Sirhan's dissociative trance states is reported by Sirhan himself and verified by his family members. He had a history of isolating himself, sequestering in his bedroom in his mother's Pasadena home and in the Pasadena City College library for hours at a time. He would meditate, light candles, stare into mirrors, and chant to himself. It is my opinion that during those sequestered times, the altered personality 2 took executive control, and also wrote many of the inculpatory statements in his diary.

When Sirhan took the stand to testify, he was in a non-altered, ordinary state of consciousness as personality 1 when he disowned authorship of many of the statements in his diary. Citing one such entry, Cooper quoted Sirhan, "My determination to eliminate RFK is becoming more, the more unshakable obsession. …"

Quoting a different diary entry, he pointed out that "RFK must be assassinated" was repeated five times. He asked Sirhan, "Do you remember writing that?"

Sirhan answered that he did not remember writing that or any of the other similar passages Cooper read to him. In one case, Sirhan agreed that "It looks like my handwriting, Sir," but I still didn't remember writing it. "That's the problem, Sir. I can't explain this."[29]

---

28   Trial Vol 18, 5261–5262, March 3, 1969.
29   Trial Vol 17, 4721–5026, March 4, 1969.

During the exchange, all the basic inquiries about these diary entries appeared totally foreign to the adjusted Sirhan (personality 1). And for good reason, he could not possibly fill in the blanks as requested. Quite simply, it would be impossible for the adjusted Sirhan's personality 1 to retrieve some of the diary contents, because they were written as he admitted in his own hand; however, done when he was in his alter personality 2.

Sirhan's responses, quite naturally, attracted the attention of the jury who were also puzzled by Sirhan's plausible deniability, and the prosecution's claim that Sirhan was just flat-out lying to protect himself. But from what?

Sirhan's self-imposed isolation became more apparent after he joined the Rosicrucians, yet these moments of retreat began much earlier, when he was a child suffering from a series of senseless violent scenes he experienced in Palestine.

Sirhan only became affiliated with the Rosicrucians in 1966, two years prior to the assassination. While working at the Santa Anita Race Track, Sirhan met Thomas Rathke, an older horse groom, who exposed Sirhan to study of theosophy – the teachings about God based on Buddhist and Brahmanism theories stressing reincarnation. He had also provided Sirhan with brochures explaining the Rosicrucian's smooth path to enlightenment.

Besides offering the road to enlightenment, Sirhan's extensive trips into the Rosicrucian sect did a lot more for him. It gave him a mental roadmap to enhance his penchant for differing meditative techniques merging with his dissociative states created by Sirhan personality 2. On one level, these techniques, combined with his already automatic, dissociate identity trances, allowed him to reach an even higher plateau as an alternative, yet potentially malevolent second personality.

According to Pease,

> But there is something odd about the role of the Rosicrucians in Sirhan's life. It was almost as if someone used his association with the Rosicrucians as cover to hide Sirhan's trancelike states ... Mrs. Francis Holland, the "Southern California Grand Counsellor of the Rosicrucian Order" told the FBI on June 12, 1968, that Sirhan had attended the Pasadena chapter meeting on June 4,1968 [one day prior to RFK's murder], the night of the California primary. Holland said she had confirmed this with the supervisor of the Pasadena Chapter, Sherman Livingston. Holland noted in the same

interview that Livingston and the Master of the chapter, Theodore Stevens, were concerned about negative publicity stemming from Sirhan's association with the Rosicrucians. So it should surprise no one that when the FBI talked to Livingston, he said he reviewed his notes and found Sirhan appeared at their chapter on May 28, not June 4. This may be the truth, but this may also be a lie to distance the organization from any hint of involvement.[30]

The cliff-hanger ending to that story is that no one knows with specificity when Sirhan last visited the Pasadena Chapter of the Rosicrucians. What we do know, via Sirhan's own testimony, is that his affiliation with the group influenced his belief system and facilitated his rapid drift into trancelike states. My interest here is to focus on the psychological impact this had on Sirhan's personality decomposition and how this connection contributed to his disenfranchisement from his family members.

During his court testimony on March 3, 1969, Sirhan's older brother, Adel, took the witness stand. He discussed Sirhan's isolating behaviors, using a time frame at about the same time as Sirhan's riding accident. This critical time period corresponds with Sirhan's peaked interest in theosophy and the Rosicrucians. He was observed by his brother, gazing into mirrors, watching flashing lights, deeply concentrating on lighted candles arranged on the desk he used to study on, and quietly chanting and mumbling to himself. As part of the Rosicrucian methods, Sirhan began chanting and talking to himself. Adel described Sirhan's social withdrawal, isolation, and more odd behaviors affected by his Rosicrucian rituals. Adel also mentioned how Sirhan's riding accident affected him in a negative way.

Under direct examination by Mr. Cooper, Adel described the difference in Sirhan's personality before and after his fall from a horse. "He was getting a little more nervous as time went by…. He was more ambitious than he was after. Like he used to go out and look for work; work when he found work. He was in school. So far as I know, he was doing well in school, except for the period that my sister was sick, and he was staying at home for a while, while she was sick.…" He described his attitude before as "friendly," but after, "It seemed like he wanted to stay at home most of the time, read, stay in his room."

Sirhan became cut off from his ordinary social and familial relationships subsequent to his journey into the occult Rosicrucian world. This was noticeable and somewhat troubling to his family, especially because he was at the same time recovering from physical injuries incurred in his

---

30   Pease. (2018). 437-438.

riding accident that had a deeper psychological effect on Sirhan. In large measure, this accident represented the end of the road for his fantasized career as a future jockey, earning a big salary and commanding respect, thus another setback for a man who felt the world was against him. This negative event provided another reason for Sirhan to become sidetracked, evidencing an entirely new but darker side to him.

When Fitts followed up Cooper's direct questioning Adel, he generally explored the same areas touched on by Cooper – Sirhan's day-by-day retreat into an entirely separate psychological reality. Fitts probed Sirhan's background, highlighting his studies into the occult, specifically the Rosicrucians. Adel noted that Sirhan had an inquisitive mind, using it to control his surroundings and himself. Adel confirmed that he had frequent conversations with Sirhan about how "if you think something, it would happen, you don't actually do it, and things of that nature."[31]

This discussion of Sirhan's mental state, as outlined here and verified using the three separate dissociative rating scales, convinced me that he was a genuine dissociative personality. Unquestionably he shared many psychological dynamics as the first reported American case of the twentieth century, Dr. Morton Prince's case of Christine "Sally" Beauchamp, and the 1957 (three faces of Eve) case uncovered by Thigpen and Cleckley. Though this diagnosis was not directly made by Sirhan's defense doctors, they nevertheless came close with innumerable references to Sirhan's dissociative states.

Several citizen investigators who explored the RFK assassination have claimed that, at the time of the crime, Sirhan was in a hypnotic or altered state of consciousness perhaps effectuated by a handler when he killed RFK. According to Pease in her exhaustive study of Sirhan's case,

> Most researchers on this case who get this far believe that Sirhan was in a hypnotic state or acting out a posthypnotic command at the time of the firing. But why would any conspirator go to the trouble to program an assassin when so many were readily available for hire? Wouldn't a man in a hypnotic state pose a risk? What if someone inadvertently said something that brought him back out of hypnosis? It's a risky variable.[32]

Consistent with other writers' viewpoints, Pease characterized Sirhan's mental state accurately as reflective of a trance-induced episode. Dr. Diamond, who assessed Sirhan at the time of his trial, failed to consider that

31   Trial Vol 17: 4748–4785, March 3, 1969.
32   Pease. (2018). 376.

he was in an altered state of consciousness the night he shot RFK. Pease conjectures that Sirhan was unwittingly set up in a preprogrammed mental state when he killed RFK. I suspect that she was partially accurate to assume that Sirhan was experiencing a kind of synthetic awareness, an alternative reality, in an unconscious mental state when he shot RFK, which I label here as a dissociative condition attributable to Sirhan's personality 2.

In 2011, Dr. Brown used his clinical experience with hypnosis and the Structured Clinical Interview for the Diagnosis of Dissociative Disorders (SCID-D) process to detect and diagnose Sirhan's major dissociative disorder. The SCID-D instrument was not yet developed when Sirhan was first assessed, therefore in Brown's view, if the doctors had used an evidenced-based assessment tool like SCID-D, they probably would have reached a similar diagnostic conclusion.

I find support for Dr. Brown's professional opinion based on the present investigation's assessment results where Sirhan's trauma-based experiences were measured prospectively against the reliable rating criteria on three dissociative scales: the Dissociative Experience Scale – II (DES-II), the modified Holmes and Rahe Social Readjustment Rating Scale (SRRS), and the Clinically-Administered Dissociative States Scale (CADSS). The results presented here demonstrate that Sirhan was experiencing a dissociative disorder at the time of the murder of RFK.

The "RFK Must Die" document provided some essential psychological clues to the crime.

CHAPTER 14

SIRHAN'S MYSTERY DIARY

Sirhan probably knew deep down that there was something psychologically wrong with himself, perhaps an undiagnosed condition or two going back in time, or just a feeling that he was becoming different – estranged from society, and from himself. It probably puzzled him. Some factor or cluster of psychological factors somewhere in his mind pushed him to pick up a gun and shoot RFK without any obvious, conscious provocation; he simply failed to put his finger on what it was, or what the troubling mental elements below his level of awareness were that drove him to the dark side.

In my view, seeking resolution to this nagging enigma led Sirhan on a perpetual self-discovery journey he hoped would quell his uneasiness and return him to "normalcy." But that did not happen. No matter how hard he tried or what techniques he employed, he still came up empty, still no doubt wondering, *Why do I have these thoughts? Who am I really? Where am I going?*

It is safe to say that, prior to the RFK assassination, Sirhan wandered in a cloud of confusion, remaining clueless to what was motivating him to commit a premeditated, political assassination.

Unfortunately for Sirhan, he was searching in all the wrong places for answers to his questions about his own identity and perhaps sanity. Desperately, he sought relief from his mental confusion by accessing a collection of unorthodox reading materials and becoming absorbed in murky, occult pursuits. But the road of self-discovery he traveled down only resulted in a dead end, yielding no new insights. The unresolved psychological issues he struggled with demanded a keen professional expertise far beyond his naïve and untrained acumen.

The interpretation of Sirhan's diary ("RFK Must Die") rests on five clinical assumptions that I propose. The first assumption is that the psychological drives and motivations evidenced by Sirhan when he wrote in the diary represent speculative hypotheses derived from my analysis of the many cryptic messages he left in this important document that were later used as evidence of his guilt as anticipated by the prosecution's legal team as well as by Sirhan's own defense attorneys – and unexpected outcome. For obvious reasons, the diary information was self-defeating and incriminating to say the least for Sirhan, necessitating further clarification as to why he even wrote it.

The second assumption is that the contents of Sirhan's diary can be best understood within the psychological framework of a dissociative "split personality" or multiple personality disorder (MPD), and that Sirhan developed two distinct and very different identities early in his life. Throughout *Psych DNA,* the discussion of Sirhan's two polarized personalities are interchangeably referred to simply as Sirhan's core, foundation, or host personality 1 – the conforming Sirhan, and Sirhan's dissociative personality 2, or alter – the malevolent Sirhan. I maintain that a great deal of the diary writings were written by his personality 2, separate and unknown from his personality 1.

A third assumption is that Sirhan's personality 2 left many of the incriminating messages intentionally, as an interpersonal technique to communicate with his personality 1. Further, Sirhan's personality 2, because of the internalized guilt associated with the prospective assassination of RFK, placed incriminating messages in the diary to try to covertly inform personality 1 of the plan to eliminate Kennedy before the crime occurred.

This communication technique between Sirhan's two personalities created "the assassination paradox," because, although personality 1 was now at least partially informed of the plan, it was powerless to prevent the anticipated murder from taking place. Sirhan's personality 2's guilt for the planned killing far outweighed the obvious consequences of being caught and/or being punished.

A fourth assumption is based on Sirhan's projected thoughts and free-floating ideas imputed to him in certain diary passages. These statements are set off in italics, indicating what Sirhan might have said in some hypothetically defined situations generating self-posed questions – *If I really did it, then why can't I remember it? I don't know, they told me I killed Kennedy!*

Additionally, the dissection of Sirhan's diary is based on my own informed, clinical judgment blended into fifty-plus years of working knowledge of Sirhan's case, first achieved as an informed graduate student working with Sirhan's lead psychiatrist, Dr. Diamond; and on my professional expertise as a forensic psychologist working with criminal defendants who have been diagnosed with a DID condition.

Early into Sirhan's defense case, his traumatically destructive history was referenced by Dr. Diamond as the primary basis for a diagnosis of a dissociative condition. As pointed out here, Sirhan's dissociative diagnosis was also suggested by other doctors (Drs. Schorr, Simson-Kallas and Marcus) when they evaluated Sirhan prior to and after his conviction. Drs. Diamond and Schorr both agreed that Sirhan's personality was fractured and segmented into two distinct, not necessarily equal, separate parts during his childhood.

Throughout Sirhan's diary, innumerable, hidden messages are woven into the document that have not been previously decoded. His diary provided a wealth of speculative, evidentiary support that helped seal his criminal fate, leading to a conviction of first-degree murder.

During intense court testimony conducted on February 25, 1969, the prosecution argued to the court to introduce Sirhan's diary as *prima facie* evidence of his guilt in the assassination of RFK. After all, Sirhan wrote that "RFK Must Die" over and over again; so it seemed clear, at least to the prosecution, that Sirhan had carefully planned the assassination, and then carried out that plan. But what if parts of Sirhan's diary were written by the hand of his personality 2, and shielded mostly from awareness of his personality 1?

Because of the confusing nature of the diary itself, with long rambling political passages, including a kind of political manifesto, interwoven with very clear death threats to RFK, and carelessly scribbled statements as well as what appear to be random, nonsense writings, it is at times difficult to discern which entries were written by Sirhan's personality 1, versus those by personality 2.

Although important psychological implications directly affecting Sirhan's case arose from the diary content, these factors have eluded prior researchers. After a careful examination of the diary's multiple meanings, a more complete psychological dissection and commentary has been long overdue. As Dr. Diamond opined, the diary entries can be characterized by three specific types of writings. It is difficult to determine exactly which passages were done when Sirhan was in a distinct dissociated state, apart from those written when he was not in an altered state of consciousness. But which were which?

Dr. Diamond offered some clarity: "Because of the uncertainty as to the precise times and circumstances in which all the various entries in the notebook were made, there is necessarily an element of uncertainty in my opinion, but my best clinical judgment is that there were three types of entries. One had no apparent relevancy to politics or to the assassination of RFK, and revealed no evidence of mental disease. The second type was in the nature of a political manifesto about America facing an abysmal downfall. The third type was specifically about RFK's assassination."

Dr. Diamond felt that the third type of writings were written "in a self-induced hypnotic-trance, a dissociate state similar to that in which I believe he committed this killing itself, and that these entries here, this third type, shows more evidence not only of paranoid schizophrenic psychosis, but additional evidence of a dissociated state."

Sirhan's opening statement as a witness in his own defense, concerning the introduction of the diary into evidence, detonated a veritable bombshell admission in the courtroom, unleashing his full measure of anger and hostility that the diary could and would be used as evidence by the prosecution against him. Sirhan began his courtroom diatribe with a startling admission to the court and to Judge Walker: "Your honor, if these notebooks are allowed in evidence, I will change my plea to guilty as charged. I will do so, Sir, not so much that I want to be railroaded into the gas chamber, Sir, but to deny you the pleasure, Sir, of after convicting me turning around and telling the world: 'Well, I put that fellow in the gas chamber, but I first gave him a fair trial,' when you in fact, Sir, will not have done so."

Indignantly, Sirhan added, "The evidence, Sir, that was taken from my home was illegally obtained, was stolen by the district attorney's people. They had no search warrant. I did not give them any permission, Sir, to do what they did to my home. My brother Adel had no permission to give them permission to enter my own room and take what they took from my home, from my own room!"[1]

Previously, Sirhan told Dr. Diamond that he knew all about the 4th Amendment to the US Constitution against self-incrimination and, if the diary was used against him and, if he was convicted, "it wouldn't hold up" in an appeal of his case. After Sirhan made his provocative statements, defense attorney Cooper quietly rose and began to address the court in Sirhan's defense, "I knew he was going to object to the use of the notebooks; but in the light of his statement, I would like to have a few minutes to talk to him."

Sirhan immediately responded, "No, Sir, I'm adamant on this point."

Mr. Cooper interjected, "Well, if Your Honor please, we would like to have an opportunity to talk to him."

---

1   Trial Vol 25, 7350–7351, March 26–28, 1969.

After a brief consultation with Sirhan, Cooper said, "We have him calmed down, temporarily at least, and we don't know when he might blow again and, if there is any indication, we would appreciate a quick recess."

When the brief recess ended, Judge Walker made his controversial ruling on the admissibility of Sirhan's diary, also making himself crystal clear, "Now Mr. Sirhan, let me tell you this. The Court has ruled on the admissibility of this evidence in court, and if there is an error, the upper court can reverse this case."

Sirhan said, "Yes, I understand."

Judge Walker added, "You have three counsel, and they are all very competent, and you appreciate that?"

Calmed down, Sirhan said, "I appreciate that."

Judge Walker ended his summation, stating, "They are running this lawsuit to your very best interest, and there is no question in the Court's mind about that. Now just remember this ... !"

"I understand, Sir," Sirhan conceded and that was that – the notebook was in, and Sirhan's emotional protests were out.[2]

A fifth assumption connected to Sirhan's diary, and perhaps the most devastating affecting the outcome of his trial, is the defense team's questionable decision to use or misuse the controversial diary information, introducing large parts of it into evidence, strangely enough, on Sirhan's behalf. The prosecution built an extensive part of its case against Sirhan based on revelations in the diary, never realizing of course that, in line with my assumption, it had been largely written by Sirhan's altered personality 2.

When the police came to Sirhan's house, officers without a court's search warrant had asked Sirhan's brother Adel if they could search the house. Adel said they could as far as he was concerned, however, it was his mother's house. When asked if he wanted the police to call her for permission, Adel said his mother did not know Sirhan had been charged with a crime yet, and Abel did not want to alarm her.

With Adel's permission, the police officers were admitted into their house, and directed to Sirhan's bedroom in the rear of the house where they opened a closed dresser drawer and found an envelope with these words, "RFK must be disposed of like his brother was."

They also spotted two notebooks that looked like student composition books, with notations "RFK must be assassinated" and "Ambassador

2   Ibid.

Goldberg must die" as well as a prediction of America's downfall, an attack of its leaders, and comments relating to doing away with US leaders.

Officer Young, who was assigned to secure the home's perimeter, keeping unauthorized people away, had secured the back yard of the house. As he discarded his paper coffee cup into the trash, he noticed an envelope in clear view with similar writing on it: "RFK Must Die," and "Robert Fitzgerald Kennedy must soon die die die…!"

During an evidentiary hearing with Judge Walker, prosecution attorneys persuasively argued for inclusion of only select portions amounting to only a few pages of the diary to be exposed to the jury. Curiously, the defense then made the disastrous call to offer to the court the majority of Sirhan's diary entries into evidence – a surprise to Sirhan.

Instead of making further objections to what certainly appeared to be incriminating statements made in the diary, the defense opted to use the most controversial material ostensibly as "proof of diminished capacity," because only a "crazy person" would commit these perverse criminal thoughts to writing.

I cannot determine what reasoning the joint legal and psychiatric defense teams used to encourage the unveiling of innumerable inculpatory statements beyond the more limited ones provided by the prosecution. From the outset, this strategy seemed to be a fool's errand.

Insofar as Sirhan's courtroom protestations and the subsequent 1972 California Supreme Court appeal process, an automatic appeal process based in part on the grounds of "Alleged Illegal Search and Seizure violation to the 4th Amendment" to the US Constitution, the California Supreme Court, in its appeal ruling, affirmed their denial, stating, "Under the circumstance we are satisfied that defendant by introducing the remaining pages of the notebooks did not waive his right to contend that the introduction of the evidence by the prosecution was error."

The California Supreme Court continued, "The defense may have been seeking to show that the pages introduced by the prosecution, when viewed in the context of the notebooks in their entirety, should be considered by the jury as containing merely declarations of a mentally unsound person."

The defense's desired effect backfired in a big way. Clearly, the impact of these many damaging statements did not provide support for a diminished capacity defense or any other defense as theorized, and instead served to reinforce the jury's belief in Sirhan's guilt beyond a reasonable doubt, thereby making their ruling in favor of the death penalty a less-burdensome task. This ill-conceived decision reigns as the major blunder made by Sirhan's defense team during the trial.

In retrospect, this decision could have constituted one of those rhetorical moments when Sirhan might have asked: *What were they thinking to allow this information into evidence, and all against me?*

The clear downside risk of exposing Sirhan's homicidal wishes (expressed by his dissociative personality 2 throughout his diary) to eliminate RFK without weighing the full, negative impact of these disclosures was shortsighted when compared to any anticipated benefit.

Sirhan's courtroom outburst and intense protest had a well-founded foundation to disallow the defense's (and not to mention the prosecution's) use of the notebook's contents coming into evidence. Clearly, this damaging information, openly exposed to the jury, should have signaled trouble; and Sirhan's appeal should have been directed toward his own attorneys for professional malpractice, and not just the faulty evidentiary ruling made by Judge Walker in the matter. Yet alternatively, Sirhan's attorneys who professed allegiance to their client, nevertheless still chose to pursue a risky path, allowing inculpatory, *prima facia* evidence supposedly in support of an already shaky psychiatric defense, a strategic move that was not in Sirhan's best legal interest, as the imposition of the death penalty by the jury proved.[3]

The fact remains that Sirhan's diary as analyzed here includes new interpretations that have not been addressed by previous psychologists. A complete understanding of this document (necessitating a complete do-over of its content) could potentially comprise several additional chapters or perhaps an entire book. Without a doubt, this multifaceted document is replete with latent psychological content, providing new clues in the hunt for Sirhan's motivation in killing RFK.

Maintaining a personal diary or journal (journaling) is not an uncommon method that a person with a dissociative disorder (or as referred to here Sirhan's "split or divided personality") uses to generally communicate with the external world. Specifically, an individual may also initiate communications between the core personality and its alters. In some cases, the hidden alter may attempt to channel the host personality using various written contacts like diary passages as a method to enhance messaging between the two personalities. This nonverbal communication patterning is often represented in the form of letters, incomplete notes,

---

3   Supreme Court of California, June 16, 1972, Crim. No. 14026, People v. Sirhan, 7 Cal. 3d 710, The PEOPLE, Plaintiff and Respondent, v. SIRHAN BISHARA SIRHAN, Defendant and Appellant.

brief memoranda, or even revealing artwork, as evident in the Billy Milligan multiple personality case.

More often, an alter personality can reach the host personality, reducing the separation between them and can lead to therapeutic integration and possible unification of both personalities in the dissociative system. Mental health professionals who treat dissociative identity patients maintain that journaling should remain a private endeavor protected from the prying eyes of the outside world: "The journal is meant to be a safe place. There must be some ground rules for yourself, and each alter to feel safe enough to write in the journals."

In addition to this communication function, journal entries can serve as an adjunct therapeutic aid, recording a history of intrusive events such as blackouts, flashbacks, recurring nightmares, or other psychologically conflicting experiences. "It will also be helpful for you to write about your experiences of switching [transitioning from one personality to another]. If you are going to therapy, journaling is an excellent way to reflect on your sessions." [4]

This is notably the case when competing personalities do not have mutual awareness of each other (known as non-co-consciousness or non-co-presence), one personality (i.e., the host) is unaware of its alters. Sirhan's dissociative system was, and perhaps still is, a closed system. In my view, Sirhan's personality 1, the host, was not co-conscious with his alter personality 2 until personality 1 began the emotional experience of digesting the troubling messages left in his diary by his alter.

Sirhan's alter left an extensive trail of cryptic notes sometimes hastily written, even leaving partially written ones on scraps of paper in addition to his more extensive journal efforts that, once discovered by the police, quite naturally, provided a rich reservoir of potential evidence for the prosecution's case against Sirhan.

Prosecutors Compton and Howard joined with Fitts to exploit the incriminating statements left in Sirhan's diary that would certainly facilitate his conviction for first-degree murder – the evidence was right in front of them in mostly black and white. Then the question presents itself: Were Sirhan's dramatic outbursts in court solely based on the revelation of the damaging messages he had supposedly authored and left in the personal diary? Or were there other less obvious, and perhaps even more important but not yet clear, psychological reasons that he desired to protect his confidential diary?

---

4   Alex Caroline Robboy, CAS, MSW, ACSW, LCSW. "Journaling with Dissociative Identity Disorder." Center for Growth. Phila., PA. https://www.thecenterforgrowth.com/tips/journaling-with-dissociative-identity-disorder

Sirhan's alleged, motivational factors underlying the assassination, expressed innumerable times in his diary, support the view that he had conscious presence of mind, the ability to premeditate, including malice aforethought, clear awareness, and criminal intent, knowing exactly what he was doing prior to the killing of RFK. I maintain that Sirhan's alter personality carefully followed a self-orchestrated plan and carried out the assassination scheme unbeknownst to his personality 1 (who didn't have foreknowledge of the contemplated assassination). Furthermore, I believe that Sirhan's core personality remained clueless as to the malevolent undercurrent of seething rage and homicidal impulse possessed by his alter, that culminated in a barrage of bullets unleashed on RFK.

My assumption is that Sirhan's loud reaction in court had a deeper psychological basis. Visibly upset, Sirhan screamed, "Those notebooks are PRIVATE [author capitals]! They're my property. The police had no right to take them. They had no search warrant!"

Once the journal became a centerpiece of the prosecution's case against him, its contents were continuously read and reread to the jury.

Because Robert Kaiser was hired as a defense investigator working for Sirhan's defense lawyers, he was provided with unfettered access to Sirhan with whom he met alone on many occasions, interviewing him almost at will. One of those meetings was conducted on New Year's Eve 1968 when Kaiser attempted to delve further into the nature of Sirhan's mystery diary, emphasizing the phrase, "Robert Kennedy must be assassinated, assassinated, assassinated," then suggesting that Sirhan may have been in a dissociative state of awareness when he made this and other entries in his diary. Kaiser asked Sirhan directly, "I pointed out that some of the notebook writing seemed to have been written in a trance. You wrote certain things over and over and over again. ... And when you wrote about killing Kennedy, you join to it the unexplainable phrase [a reference to money] I have never heard 'Please pay to the order of. ...'"

Sirhan had no recollection of what this reference meant and stated he could not recall ever writing it. This was another example of Sirhan's personality 1's unfamiliarity with many of the damaging entries that his alter made in his diary, as he insisted, "They're not mine! I'm not familiar with them."

Sirhan had been keeping a diary for some time prior to the assassination, yet time after time when confronted with the reason he left these incriminating statements in his diary, Sirhan was at a loss to explain these devastating disclosures that were definitely not in his best self-interest and not at all helpful in his defense.

When examining Sirhan's consistent denials of authorship, it appeared as if many of the most injurious diary entries were written by his personality 2, and he became confused and visibly upset when the damaging sections were pointed out to him. The defense and prosecution attorneys agreed that the disclosures in the diary were seemingly written by a disturbed person.

Was the vengeful and malevolent Sirhan's personality 2 responsible for leaving an unmistakable trail of disturbing messages in the diary? And did these harmful statements serve as covert psychological clues that Sirhan's alter was attempting to break through, to communicate with his core personality 1, as the latter remained in the dark concerning Sirhan's altar's intentions to commit a murder? One possible explanation for Sirhan's extensive writings by his alter was to reduce the divided personality fragmentation (the nondisclosure between two disparate personalities) between his two distinct identities.

In the furtherance of this task, Sirhan's alter was disclosing the plan to eliminate RFK in advance. Sirhan's personality 1 also appeared to be terribly confused. To leave behind self-incriminating information in writing that could easily seal Sirhan's fate seemed to be at cross purposes, if the goal was to spare his life. In so many words, Sirhan attempted to explain this conundrum to Robert Kaiser, telling him, "How could I have been so stupid?"

In a desperate attempt, Sirhan's alter was reaching out and leaving a chain of cryptic clues to inform his personality 1 of his alter's intent to murder RFK. In essence, Sirhan's alter was confessing to a planned assassination before the fact. Sirhan's alter was providing ample evidence of a unique pre-crime thought process accompanied with a large dose of malice aforethought.

Sirhan's alter's contemplation of committing a future crime is reminiscent of the plot in the sci-fi film, *The Minority Report,* where a criminal's pre-crime thought processes are detected before the criminal act. In the film, Tom Cruise plays a policeman and pre-crime task force leader (John Anderson) who's assignment is to follow telltale clues in order to arrest potential murderers, based on reading their inner cognitions before they can act. As it turns out, Anderson himself becomes wrongly profiled as a future murderer and is forced to go underground to avoid capture by corrupt government enforcers.

In Sirhan's situation, using the diary, his personality 2 also engages in a kind of pre-confession to his naïve personality 1 about what was going to happen, information that Sirhan's personality 1 simply could not know prior to this access. This disclosure was no doubt founded on Sirhan's alter's mounting guilt, and on the need to confess even before the murder of RFK.

This perspective also brings to mind the work of psychologist and criminologist Dr. Theodor Reik who years ago argued that many times murderers have an unconscious need to express their guilt even before they confess their crimes. This compulsion to disclose their crimes can neutralize their instinctive, conscious resistance to not confess. As Reik states,

> Why does a murderer talk in a thousand tongues? It is clear that in the criminal, two mental forces are fighting for supremacy. One tries to wipe out all traces of the crime, the other proclaims the deed and the doer to the whole world. It is impelled by the unconscious desire for punishment which expresses itself in faulty acts of this kind.... But in some cases, this unconscious need for punishment becomes so strong that it overwhelms the culprit and, from the very outset, seals his fate.

In keeping with Reik's analysis, the new information outlined here strongly suggests that Sirhan's personality 2 continuously sought to deal with the tormenting guilt connected to the anticipated crime, while at the same time welcoming the deserved punishment for it. Dr. Reik further asserts that the criminal's need to confess represents a primitive attempt to assuage troubling, internal guilt patterning: "We believe these confessions which serve the purpose of releasing the person from an oppressing feeling of guilt.... In these exceptional cases too, we are therefore left to seek the continuation of the confession into the unconscious and search for its motives....."[5]

Moreover, according to Reik, criminals often leave behind obvious clues in order to be intentionally apprehended somewhere down the road, and then be subjected to a measure of punishment for their criminal acts. Returning to Sirhan's pre-crime cognitive process, it became apparent to me that his personality 2 left behind a trail of extremely damaging statements in his diary, striving to both explain the future assassination and expiate his guilt associated with the planned demise of RFK. From this perspective, Sirhan's personality 2 certainly provided a veritable treasure trove of criminal evidence specifically outlining the planned assassination.

Surprisingly, when Sirhan's personality 1 began to peruse his diary, he began to discover these alien messages from an unknown source. At that

---

5   Reik, T. (1959). *The Compulsion to Confess: On The Psychoanalysis of Crime and Punishment.* Farrar, Straus and Company. New York

point, he probably had to address the same psychological puzzle facing his doctors and defense team, who continued to ask who wrote these strange messages anyway? And why? Dr. Diamond's opinion that Sirhan failed to recall many sections he journaled eluded the crucial point that Sirhan's personality 1 (undoubtedly the personality he interviewed) couldn't have been amnesic to the origin of the self-incriminating statements left in the diary by Sirhan's alter, because he didn't write them; however at later times, he painfully became aware of them, causing him to wonder, *Could I have written these? And if not me, then who did?*

Sirhan's personality 2 sought expiation for the guilt associated with his pre-crime desire to kill RFK, and apparently, using the psychological defense mechanism of projection, he cleverly attempted to displace these guilt feelings connected to the assassination onto Sirhan's core personality 1, who in turn would be punished for a crime it did not understand, or in large measure did not want, and, in this analysis, this is the chain of events that happened.

Sirhan's alter's underlying projected guilt necessitated a demand for punishment, a covert need to be apprehended, and that the punishment be meted out to Sirhan's terribly confused core personality 1 – who had been repeatedly told so many times and finally became generally convinced that he killed RFK. After finding these incriminating entries in his diary, Sirhan's personality 1 became even more confused as to the authorship of the unrecognized entries.

Sirhan's core personality may have wondered at this point, *Could this plan set out in the diary actually become a reality, and am I responsible for it? And if I'm not, then who is?*

Reading the fatalistic diary entries once the plan was put in motion, the assassination of RFK became inevitable, and at that point Sirhan's personality 1 was powerless to change the sequence of events already moving quickly forward. This would have led to Sirhan's thinking, *Them just telling me that I did this terrible crime doesn't mean I actually did it!*

Throughout the trial, Sirhan was presented with this no-win dilemma over and over as to whether he actually planned the assassination and pulled the trigger to shoot RFK point blank. He couldn't recall the murder scene, only what he heard, read in the newspapers, or was told by his attorneys and doctors, just as his prosecutors alleged. *Well, this is what they told me so I must have done it.*

Over time, the pervasive implanted persuasion that Sirhan shot RFK plunged his personality 1 deeper into an unresolvable state of cognitive dissonance, prompting the impossible reconciliation of two opposing fact sets. *They continue to tell me I did it, but I have no recall of the actual scene at the hotel, so how can this be?*

The legal outcome of this paradox, the jury's guilty verdict, sealed Sirhan's fate when he was sentenced to the gas chamber for a crime he may have only pondered. Once he became ingratiated to the notion that he may in fact be a cold-blooded murderer, or at least part of him was, Sirhan probably became tormented by his own mounting guilt associated with the acceptance of the fact that conceivably he may be a real, even psychopathic, killer.

Ultimately, the recognition that perhaps part of him, his personality 2, was the real assassin was also no doubt difficult for Sirhan to psychologically reconcile, a thought pattern inconsistent with his personality 1 self-image as maybe a troubled person, but nevertheless not a murderer. But at this late date, who would believe him? Finally, the explanation of Sirhan's diary, elucidating the implausible interaction between his two nonintersecting personalities operating at cross-purposes, may never become a reality for him. However, the opportunity still exists that this complex psychological conundrum can be put to the test with Sirhan if and only when the opportunity presents itself.

Dr. Diamond faced many of these same cognitively dissonant inconsistencies with regard to the interpretation of Sirhan's diary that I addressed here. At times during Dr. Diamond's interviews, Sirhan denied writing some of the most incriminating sections of the diary, and conversely at other times he acknowledged he was the author. So which is it? If Sirhan's personality 2 wrote the incriminating passages in the diary, then his personality 1, as he sat in court, would have almost no way of recognizing what had been written. However, there were some entries in the diary that Sirhan admitted to Dr. Diamond that he acknowledged.

Dr. Diamond was on target when he affirmed that Sirhan could not recall one particular entry: "He told me he didn't write it. I have no reason to disbelieve him.... Some of the notebook material is quite incoherent. There's one page that may be a full year out of sequence. I have no way of knowing for sure.... The most I can say is that some material to me obviously was written in a dissociated state; some material obviously was not written in that state; and there is some I can't tell."[6] Reflecting on Dr. Diamond's statement, I became convinced that the concept of the "two Sirhan's" was valid, perhaps somewhat abstractly, but nevertheless a representative assessment.

---

6   Trial Vol 25, 7147, 7151, 7158. March 26–28, 1969.

Referring to specific pages in Sirhan's diary, defense attorney Berman asked Dr. Diamond, "Do you have an opinion as to the mental state at the time he [Sirhan] made entries into these notebooks?"

Dr. Diamond described how, under hypnosis, Sirhan was able to recall writing some of the material in the diary, and concluded, "It was done in an amnesic state or dissociated state and other parts were obviously not, and I was assuming that Sirhan, if he would be cooperative enough to be able to at least recall all of the rest of it … as he has convinced me, he has greater ability to alienate the dissociate[d] material when he has decided it was not possible for him to do it. I have come to respect his claim he doesn't remember...."[7]

This raises the contentious issue surrounding Sirhan's memory or lack of it and his continual denial of remembering the actual shooting on the night of the assassination, which has never been resolved, and affects the present discussion of Sirhan's psychologically provocative diary: Were some passages simply ablated from Sirhan's working memory? Or more likely, were certain entries done while he was in a dissociated state of consciousness, supporting Dr. Diamond's viewpoint?

During Sirhan's pre-conviction interviews, Dr. Diamond and prosecution psychiatrist Dr. Pollock both tried to determine whether Sirhan displayed any signs of remorse or guilt for the alleged assassination of RFK. My hypothesis is that before being found guilty of first-degree murder, Sirhan's personality 2's alienation and rejection supported his projected guilt associated with killing RFK.

Sirhan's troubled personality 2 desired to expiate his guilt for the planned crime, and his various diary entries demonstrate a desire to share this potential crime with personality 1 as well as to project away a measure of guilt for what was to happen. His personality 2, similar to Reik's belief, was troubled by a guilty mind in anticipation of what was to come, and found that personality 1 was a convenient target to put the blame on.

Sirhan's pre-crime expiation of guilt expressed in his diary is reminiscent of the guilt patterning demonstrated by the main character in Fydor Dostoevsky's novel, *Crime and Punishment*. Dostoevsky presents a timeless psychological portrait of the workings of a murderer's inner sanctum, attempting to justify his contemplated homicidal act. The main character, Rodion Raskolnikov, becomes guilt ridden, anticipating the murder of a ruthless pawnbroker, the aged Alyona Ivanovna, onto whom he projects his life's misfortunes and failures. Raskolnikov, as a poverty stricken stu-

---

7   Ibid, 7174.

dent, mentally struggles to justify why he should kill the old woman, and then steal her cash box containing valuable jewelry and money ill-gotten, in his view, from other poor, disadvantaged people like himself.

Raskolnikov tries to convince himself that Ivanova's existence is solely based on the exploitation of society's marginalized citizens, like himself; therefore, in his rationalized thinking, he would be doing society a favor by murdering and then robbing the exploitative predator. Seeing the pawnbroker as a parasite on Russian society, Raskolnikov further reasons that his negative behavior is both justified and morally correct, as though appealing to some self-directed higher purpose.

At the crime scene, things do not go as Raskolnikov planned. First he is interrupted by Ivanova's sister who is in the wrong place at the wrong time. In a fit of rage, Raskolnikov also murders her, apparently without such moral justification. Panicky after the double murder, he cannot find the coveted cash box and expensive jewelry. He escapes with a variety of cheap trinkets rather than lots of valuable jewelry and the anticipated cash. Conveniently, Raskolnikov juxtaposes ordinary societal moral values and laws, instead substituting his relativistic Machiavellian sense of right versus wrong in concert with his view that the ends truly justify the means. His attempt at rationalizing his crimes by invoking a higher moral principle supports his role in society as he perceives it – to impose his will to create a more equal society by the elimination of the evil pawnbroker. In essence, Raskolnikov sees his actions as the furtherance of his own values and legal system.

From this point on, Dostoevsky paints Raskolnikov's progressive mental deterioration fueled by his pangs of overwhelming guilt and remorse, facilitating his rapid psychological breakdown. Prior to his arrest he reluctantly confesses to his confidant and prostitute friend, Sonya Marmeladova, who urges him to inform the police of what he has done. Although initially it appeared that Raskolnikov would not be arrested, the magistrate in charge of investigating the murders, Porfiry Petrovich, from the start, suspects Raskolnikov of the brutal, double murder and robbery. Raskolnikov's mounting guilt and remorse after the crime begins to torment him, first leading to his confessing to Sonya, and then ultimately to Petrovich.

In a parallel view, Sirhan's personality 2 was also deeply affected by a number of moral choices he had to make, having a belief that RFK was determined to encourage a military strike against his Arab brethren by Israeli forces, he concluded that RFK, like Raskolnikov's victimized pawn broker, must be eliminated. From a moral viewpoint, also like Raskolnikov, Sirhan seems to desperately strive to convince himself that society and specifically Arabs would be better off without RFK, who vowed support for his enemies.

Again there seems a comparison between Raskolnikov's psychological justification for committing a murder, and Sirhan's. Sirhan's alter's pronouncements of guilt and remorse (like Raskolnikov's) forced him to struggle to accept his guilt. Sirhan may have been misguided and deeply influenced by his faulty moral judgment that he was acting in a way consistent with a virtuous code predicated on the belief that the protection of his people outweighed the taking of the life of a man who represented a threat – the ends justify the means.

Whereas Raskolnikov had good reasons to confess his crimes to Magistrate Petrovich; Sirhan's personality 1, who was shielded from disclosure that his alter committed a murder, surely had no similar motivation. It remains my opinion that, as extraordinary as this analysis of the two Sirhan's is, there is little doubt that these conclusions drawn from this assessment may still continue to be incomprehensible to Sirhan.

Dr. Diamond had invited Dr. Pollack to witness a light-hypnoanalytic session with Sirhan. Hopefully, Dr. Diamond could elicit new information from Sirhan to tap into various aspects of his personality specifically into the hidden parts unknown to both doctors. The conversation with Sirhan challenged their belief systems as they struggled to make sense of Sirhan's responses. It was as if they were interviewing an entirely different person; and in a very real, psychological sense, they were. Dr. Diamond slowly guided Sirhan through a series of questions comprising a mental status examination, or psychological orientation, identifying the date, time, place, day, and additional self-anchoring inquiries.

To elicit new information pertinent to achieving a better understanding of his diary, Sirhan was presented with a yellow legal pad and pencil and instructed to write his responses to a series of questions. Dr. Diamond wanted to compare these responses to the various writings in Sirhan's diary. He believed that certain entries in the diary were done during a process of automatic writing, when Sirhan was in a trance or dissociative state of consciousness.

During the hypnotic induction, Sirhan answered questions about his diary with the goal to better comprehend his impressions of the now deceased RFK. Incredibly, at one point Sirhan denied that RFK was even dead! How could his perception be so errant?

Dr. Diamond began by asking, "What about Kennedy, Sirhan?"

Sirhan scribbled the same language that appeared in his diary – "RFK Must Die" nine consecutive times.

"When must Kennedy die?" questioned Dr. Diamond.

Unexpectedly, using future tense, Sirhan wrote, "Robert Kennedy is going to die," repeating it twice.

Oddly, Sirhan's written answers repeatedly connoted that RFK was still alive.

A little taken aback, Dr. Diamond continued, frankly asking, "Is Kennedy dead?"

Sirhan wrote, "No, No, 'Now.'"

Dr. Diamond then asked, "When is the 'now?'"

Sirhan immediately wrote the day's date, "Friday 31, January, Friday."

Pursuing this unusual line of questioning, Dr. Diamond asked Sirhan, "Is Kennedy alive?"

"Yes, yes, yes," Sirhan wrote.

Based on these contrary responses, Dr. Diamond concluded that Sirhan had somehow emotionally and psychologically convinced himself that RFK was still alive.[8]

Looking at what Sirhan had written, Dr. Diamond and Dr. Pollack both reacted with the same first impression – total disbelief. How could Sirhan so nonchalantly doubt RFK's assassination as he sat in a LA County jail cell, facing a first-degree murder trial for the killing of RFK?

Another possibility was based on the notion that Sirhan was simply lying to deflect his actual role in killing RFK and then falsely claiming amnesia.

Sirhan's vacillating belief that RFK was not dead centers on the recurrent issue that Sirhan was amnesic to the fact that RFK was indeed dead and, more to the point, that he pulled the trigger. After all, Dr. Diamond testified that he thought that at the time of the assassination Sirhan was experiencing an amnesic condition and could not recall any of the events connected to the actual murder scene, but could that extend to his almost delusional belief that RFK wasn't really dead?

The explanation for Sirhan's negating that RFK was dead is consistent with my primary opinion that there are two Sirhans operating on two levels of awareness – one conscious and the other unconscious. Therefore, a possible resolution to this denial-recall issue is that Sirhan's core personality 1 was not cognizant that his personality 2 had already committed the

---

8   Kaiser. (1970).

assassination, thereby this alter contributed many entries into the diary prior to the murder to prove it. It was obvious that the doctors were not having the revelatory conversation with Sirhan's personality 2, who could with certainty confirm that RFK was deceased. Instead, they were interviewing Sirhan's personality 1, who was not part of the plan to assassinate RFK.

Psychologist Dr. Simson-Kallas, who extensively interviewed, tested, and diagnosed Sirhan on death row in San Quentin State Prison, believed that Sirhan's mental state at the time of the assassination was more in concert with my diagnosis of a dissociative condition. He concluded that Sirhan should have carried a dissociative diagnosis, not one symptomatic of a psychotic condition like paranoid schizophrenia as believed by Dr. Diamond. Dr. Simson-Kallas did not make a definitive split personality diagnosis, yet he came close, like Drs. Diamond and Schorr had. Research has demonstrated that, as a dissociative disorder develops, it can block away parts of memory traces shielded from the foundation personality, therefore it is feasible that Sirhan's denial (the death of RFK) is consistent with the nondisclosure between his two personalities.[9]

Objectively, when we look at Sirhan's case in terms of the emergence of more than one distinct personality, it is apparent that his dual personality structure differed from Eve White versus Eve Black's dissociative personality system, for instance. For a long period of time, Sirhan's personality 1 was aware that there was an ill-defined dark, anxiety-eliciting cloud hanging over him, creating recurrent mental instability that he was becoming increasingly unstable to an extent that he could become insane just as the doctors believed.

There is considerable evidence that Sirhan's recurrent thoughts of going insane created an identity crisis obstructing his own perception of who he was. At times, doubting his own sanity only confused Sirhan more, because he couldn't account for the inculpatory statements made or left by someone else in his diary. Inquisitively, he may have pondered: *Where did these statements come from? Did I actually write them, or did someone else plant them there?*

Yes, he admitted to Dr. Diamond that some passages were definitely written in his own handwriting, but what about the others? Did he write all of the entries? Some of them? Or none of them? The possibility arises that maybe his memory lapses were connected to the blackout periods he'd chronically experienced.

---

9   Ibid.

Kaiser characterizes Sirhan's cross-examination by Deputy DA Lynn Compton, who questioned Sirhan about any history of lapses in his consciousness or blackout periods. This is a direct reference that substantiates Sirhan's "zoning out" or blackout episodes, and is connected to his diary entries.

Compton began his questioning, saying, "[Sirhan] You look nervous?"

Sirhan admitted, "A little bit." His voice was very soft, and he gripped the counter tightly.

Compton asked him immediately whether he had ever blacked out in Jerusalem. Sirhan said he didn't remember this happening.

"The only occasion then was at Ambassador Hotel?" asked Compton.

"No," said Sirhan. "When I wrote in the notebooks and the fall from the horse...."[10]

During his extensive interviews with Dr. Diamond, Sirhan provided many subtle hints concerning the different types of writings in his diary. The nuanced statements were not particularly enlightening, but nevertheless were unguarded moments to peer into Sirhan's mind. When Dr. Diamond probed the memory lapses, Sirhan generated vague and nonspecific answers, at one point, leading to him blurting out, "Goddam it. That's not me, Doc."

A string of these references to the "not Sirhan," or "not me" aspect of his identity leads to the conclusion that Sirhan's personality 1 was only partially aware of inculpatory statements made in the diary by Sirhan's personality 2.

In the end, he simply couldn't remember what he couldn't remember, because personality 2 was the diary's major contributor and, most important, the killer!

Sirhan claimed that he was resting at home when he heard a radio newscast that RFK had given a pro-Israeli speech at a Jewish temple, making Dr. Diamond wonder if this contributed to his diary entry: "Kennedy must fall, Kennedy must fall." Together Sirhan and Dr. Diamond casually paged through the diary, looking at various entries related to the "Kennedy must fall" statement.

Sirhan said that some of the writings were related to his classroom work, and he didn't know a lot about the additional material though apparently done in his handwriting. Asked about similar entries, he claimed that his mind was a blank, and he only had a vague recollection of the content.[11]

---

10   Kaiser. (1970). 429.
11   Pease. (2018).

Sirhan's reference to this vague recollection, although not fully aware of some of the writings, is interpreted as his unconscious awareness by his personality 1 that something must be occurring, because these statements were right there in his own scrawled handwriting. During the trial, these writings were painfully brought up to Sirhan again and again, often within the framework of challenging his credibility, honesty, connoting that he was just a liar. Even so, as Dr. Diamond stated, "I believe him. He just can't remember."

The amnesic memory issue involving Sirhan's not recognizing important information he had written down looms as secondary to his puzzling unawareness that the journaling ever occurred in the first place. Dr. Diamond commented on Sirhan's amnesic conundrum during his own testimony under questioning by prosecutor Fitts, who wanted to know why Sirhan couldn't remember some of the critical facts concerning the assassination: Did Sirhan have true amnesia at the time he shot Kennedy, or was he merely lying?

Dr. Diamond responded, "Yes, I think this was a true amnesia at the time he shot Kennedy." He quickly added: "I'm sorry, I want to correct that. A true amnesia for the time he shot Kennedy. Now, obviously whether he was in a state of amnesia at the time he shot Kennedy, I think one has to give a very qualified answer to that and to define it precisely. You will notice that I did not use the term 'amnesia' and I don't use it, because it doesn't quite make clinical sense to me. Amnesia refers to loss of memory. Now loss of memory can occur after an act or it can occur before an act…. He [Sirhan] does not remember in his conscious state the shooting of Kennedy. He does remember in a hypnotic state the shooting of Kennedy."

Fitts tried to discredit what Sirhan could and could not recall under hypnosis as perhaps a repeating back only what he had read about his own case. Fitts asked Dr. Diamond, "Well, there again with respect to the hypnotic state, he read the newspapers, you gave him lots of suggestions, it's very questionable in your mind, but he was just acting out what you told him to do, isn't it?"

In disagreement, Dr. Diamond responded, "No, it's not questionable in my mind, but I cannot guarantee the authenticity, because I am more aware than you are, Mr. Fitts, that hypnosis produces the content, that gains access to one's mind."[12]

At this juncture, Dr. Diamond was struggling to explain Sirhan's troubling, amnesic episodes, particularly whether this was the reason Sirhan

---

12   Trial Vol 25, 7186–7187, March 27, 1969.

couldn't remember many of the passages in the diary. Based on Sirhan's innumerable probing into the question of who even wrote the diary I believe that there was no co-consciousness or equal access, nor a flow or shared information between the two Sirhans. Therefore, the behaviors engaged in by Sirhan's personality 2, such as the scribbling of homicidal messages in the diary was not accessible to Sirhan's personality 1 until later when he was shocked to read them.

At one point, Sirhan audaciously accused the prosecutors of distorting critical time lines, chronology, and specific dates in his diary to be used against him. He also accused the LA County Sheriff's Department of bugging his jail cell.

Sirhan's personality 1 was perfectly capable of determining that these entries were untoward and damaging to his case, but he struggled to determine their exact origin and true authorship. Sirhan was cognizant that he did not write lots of them, so who did? And when were they written?

More recently Dr. Daniel Brown, an associate professor at Harvard University Medical School at the time and expert in hypno-analysis, met with Sirhan for extended periods of time and conducted a number of hypnotic sessions with him. Dr. Brown has been critical of Dr. Diamond's hypnotic techniques during sessions he conducted with Sirhan. Dr. Brown's perspective is that Dr. Diamond may have implanted certain beliefs into Sirhan's memories, therefore Sirhan merely affirmed what Dr. Diamond had told him. Dr. Brown respectfully disagreed with Dr. Diamond's diagnosis of Sirhan: "Dr. Brown noted that Sirhan does not have schizophrenia and that the diagnosis at the trial was incorrect. Dr. Brown retested Sirhan and applied a 'modern, scientific approach' to the results to come to this conclusion."[13]

This was particularly relevant concerning the specific events during the assassination that Sirhan continuously claimed he could not recall the actual murder scene. In other words, perhaps the version of those events as he describes them to Dr. Diamond may have been artifactual or implanted, and Sirhan's real recollection of the facts remain buried, only available in the awareness of his "evil twin," personality 2.

Dr. Brown's general findings are consistent with my analysis that throughout the inquiries made by innumerable doctors with Sirhan, the critical facts concerning the evening of June 4 and early morning of June 5, 1968, were simply unavailable for recall.

In analyzing Sirhan's case, Dr. Diamond was faced with the same identity issue that confronted Dr. Thigpen and Dr. Cleckley ten years prior

---

13   Pease. (2018). 417.

with Eve White in *The 3 Faces of Eve* case. Understandably, and more dramatically, the initial information and identity-sharing process between Eve White as a multiple personality and Eve Black was unidirectional, not supporting a state of co-consciousness: It was evident that Eve Black knew about Eve White, but not vice versa.

When Eve Black suddenly emerged, becoming the dominant, altered personality, she dramatically informed her doctor od the news: "Now, Doc, that's one for you to answer! There's a lot about it I can't explain ... an awful lot I don't understand. But I do know I'm not her, and she's not me. I've been getting out a lot more recently, too.... Now Eve White would worry about all those questions you've been asking, but not me ... Eve White was completely unaware of Eve Black's existence.... And don't you go and tell her either. When I get out, she don't know a thing about it. I go where I please, and do like I please, and it's none of her damned business.... On the other hand, Eve White had no contact with Eve Black's consciousness, no suspicion of her existence.... Eve Black could not, she admitted, emerge at will to express herself freely in the body of the sober and retiring woman known as Eve White."[14]

Trying to add clarification to Sirhan's wandering and often incriminating entries scattered throughout his mystery diary, Dr. Diamond hypnotized him again and witnessed Sirhan engaging in a psychological process termed automatic writing. According to Koutstaal, "Automatic writing has been of interest to psychologists, clinicians, and theoreticians of the mind both as a phenomenon in its own right and as a technique for exploring aspects of dissociation and normal and pathological consciousness.... The conceptual and methodological challenges posed by automatic writing persist in such contemporary concerns as divided attention, implicit memory, and dissociation of awareness and intentionality."[15]

Psychological research into the concept of automatic writing extends back to the early work conducted by Dr. Morton Prince, a neurologist-psychiatrist, in the early part of the 1900s. Additionally, he was one of the first US doctors to chronicle a multiple personality disorder case. Examining the process of automatic, or spontaneous writing with an MPD client, Dr. Prince asserts that, during this process, the writing must be executed not simply as a motoric, reflex action, but as a concerted effort of the second personality to seek expression.

14   Thigpen and Cleckley. (1957). 27–28.
15   Koutstaal, W. (1992). "Skirting the Abyss: A History of Experimental Explorations of Automatic Writing in Psychology," *Journal of the History of the Behavioral Sciences*, 28(1), 5–27.

In the Beauchamp case, Dr. Prince stressed that one of Miss Beauchamp's personalities claimed to be co-conscious with another of her personalities, both in her normal state and when hypnotized. This disclosure, a one-way experiencing, is similar to Eve Black's knowledge of the presence of Eve White although not vice versa.

Dr. Diamond was initially questioned by defense attorney Mr. Berman, and then by prosecutor Fitts concerning Sirhan's rather odd diary entries, especially those derived from a type of automatic writing. His testimony was critical because he was dissatisfied with Sirhan's explanations that, in his opinion, there were really no explanations at all. It was true that Sirhan denied the authorship of many diary entries. It occurred to Dr. Diamond that at least parts of the diary's contents were highly influenced by Sirhan's self-induced hypnotic, Rosicrucian experiences, as Sirhan slid in and out of altered states of consciousness.

After asking a long series of questions, Dr. Diamond brought Sirhan out of the hypnotic state and showed him what he had just written, and Sirhan replied: "It's too scribbly to read ... they are not Sirhan."

Dr. Diamond pressed Sirhan on the various details of the ostensible automatic writing. Sirhan "observed that some of the r's were made in an unusual manner, and he answered, he wanted to know whether we had hired a handwriting expert to forge the papers, because they were not his."

Dr. Diamond described a session with Sirhan on February 8, 1969: "I questioned him again about the automatic writing notebook and again he had no recollection of it...."[16]

Dr. Diamond believed that not only were many of the statements in Sirhan's diary done in a dissociated state, they also seemed to be valid examples of the automatic writings process.

During cross examination by prosecutor Fitts, Dr. Diamond was sharply questioned about the entries in Sirhan's diary, as well as Sirhan's "alleged" automatic writing samples (done during an alleged altered state consciousness). As expected, Fitts expressed considerable doubt concerning the veracity of Sirhan's dissociative personality theory.

The prosecutor expressed his confusion over Dr. Diamond's inability to discern between Sirhan's conscious (usual personality 1) versus the nonconscious, dissociated, writings done by personality 2.

Mr. Fitts: "The thing I am trying to arrive at is the difference between the 'dissociated Sirhan' and the 'usual Sirhan.' You will agree with me that they harbor the same kind of ideas, 'Kennedy must fall,' is that right?"

Dr. Diamond: "There are three statements written on top and obviously different from the other. Now I do know that when he did the automatic writing [dissociated], or when he went into these Rosicrucian things, he would have his notebook here, and he would end up writing in between the spaces, on top of things, and out of sequence. The most I can say is that some material to me very obviously was written in a dissociated state; some material obviously was not written in that state, and there is some I can't tell."[17]

Was Sirhan in a dissociated state when he wrote the diary, or even part of it? Were the incriminating phrases – "RFK Must Die," and "Kennedy must fall" proof positive that Sirhan had the full capacity to premeditate with malice aforethought in the killing of RFK? Was Sirhan engaging in a form of dissociative, automatic writing when he wrote the diary, as believed by Dr. Diamond? These unanswered questions further compounded the diary's controversy.

Another insight into Sirhan's diary by Dr. Diamond rested on his evidence of Sirhan's automatic writing comparing it with the writing samples Sirhan did for him under hypnosis in his jail cell. A side-by-side comparison seemed to verify that at least some of the diary entries were done as Sirhan automatically wrote. However, Sirhan's many statements denying authorship of the diary ("That's not me," "I didn't write that!") persisted as problems for the defense attorneys who finally came to the conclusion that Sirhan's writings constituted the "diary from hell."

The diary's authenticity also presented special problems for Dr. Eduard Simson-Kallas. He had worked for the California Department of Corrections for six years, and when Sirhan was referred to him, he wanted to do whatever he could to make the death-sentenced man's confinement more tolerable. Based on his many interviews with Sirhan, Dr. Simson-Kallas established good rapport with him. Sirhan finally began to trust the concerned psychologist who he felt was working in his behalf.

Probably because of this rapport, Dr. Simson-Kallas was able to uncover a great deal of revealing new information not available during Sirhan's trial. For instance, he approached Sirhan's diary from a differing perspective. First, in Dr. Simson-Kallas's opinion there is evidence that the handwriting in the diary, even some of the scribbled entries, do not come close to matching up with Sirhan's handwriting samples he examined.

17   Trial Vol 25: 7158–7162, March 26–28, 1969.

His analysis of the diary differed substantially from Dr. Diamond's, particularly the authorship of certain parts. Surprisingly, Dr. Simson-Kallas's position concerning the diary's content rested on his bold assumption that many sections were not written by Sirhan at all. He believed that, even if Sirhan wrote selected sections in the diary, perhaps he was in an altered state at the time.

During his many prison sessions with Sirhan on death row, Sirhan asked him, "Who wrote this, it's not me! Who wrote it? I don't know it!"

Dr. Simson-Kallas said that Sirhan told him the diary, or some of its passages, were probably done by someone else, again saying, "But not by me."

Dr. Simson-Kallas said that when interviewing Sirhan, "It was like two people talking to me at once."

On the one hand, Sirhan told him, "Yes, I committed the crime," yet on the other hand, Sirhan remained puzzled and deeply concerned about the details of the assassination. Expressing his vagueness, Sirhan added, "I want to find out what really happened. I have no memory, no recollection; can you help me remember what took place? I do know that I just wasn't myself. I don't know what I did and didn't write, and I have no memory of the shooting. The last thing I can remember is having coffee with the girl, then I was choked. They broke my left finger, then I was in a courtroom with a lady judge who read some charges. 'It was dreamlike.' Then six months with doctors. Always a problem with my notebooks. Doesn't look like my writing. I can't remember ever writing it."[18]

The results of Dr. Simson-Kallas's direct interviews with Sirhan open up wide new vistas into Sirhan's personality, or two personalities, not previously addressed. Sirhan's statements to Dr. Simson-Kallas about the night of the assassination and the authenticity of the diary support my contention that Sirhan's host personality 1 played no active role in either the murder plot or the scrambled writings, whereas the altered Sirhan, personality 2, filled with years of seething rage, formulated and fulfilled his retaliatory wish to destroy his enemy before he was destroyed by a political figure who was once his hero, and then turned nemesis.

It follows that Sirhan was manifesting his personality 1, when speaking to Dr. Simson-Kallas. Sirhan wanted and solicited his help in putting the disparate pieces of what really happened on the night of the assassination back together again. Dr. Simson-Kallas, I believe, came closest to unraveling the tightly would ball of psychological string that still continues to

---

18   Brussell, M., Interview with Dr. Eduard Simson-Kallas. Dialogue Conspiracy Show, June 13, 1977. Radio Station KLRB, Carmel, California.

unravel, because Sirhan's diary is still an unsolved mystery. Similar to Sirhan's case, handwriting analysis was also an important issue in *The 3 Faces of Eve* multiple personality adventure.

Thigpen and Cleckley desired to find out if Eve White's handwriting was noticeably different from Eve Black's. To achieve this, they called upon a document examiner who concluded: "Though considerably impressed by consistent and significant differences between the two productions, it was his opinion that those with adequate professional training could establish sufficient evidence to show both were done by the same human hand." The expert concluded: "It readily appears the handwriting of each personality is of a different person.... However, extensive investigation of these handwriting materials establishes beyond any doubt that they have been written by one and the same individual."[19]

Throughout Sirhan's trial proceedings, Fitts maintained a no-nonsense, fact-driven DA approach – he wanted just the facts and not more of what he deemed "psychobabble." It was apparent that he was continually frustrated when he had to deal with quasi-scientific inferences such as: "During automatic writing, your hand just mechanically moves without your conscious awareness."

To cut through the maze of confusion surrounding the handwriting in Sirhan's diary, Fitts brought in the LA County DA Office's own forensic handwriting expert to analyze Sirhan's separate writing samples taken from the diary.

Laurence W. Sloan was sworn in as an expert witness having made more than 1,500 court appearances, qualifying as a calligrapher during his twenty-year career. Sloan seemed to be almost too eager to testify in such a high-profile case and wasn't a stranger to the press, maybe hoping that the Sirhan case would be a career builder for him. He testified that he carefully analyzed approximately eight pages from Sirhan's diary that were admitted into evidence by the prosecution (as noted against Sirhan's adamant protests).

Sloan's results indicated that there were measurable differences between the two writing exemplars he described as a qualitative breakdown in the automatic writing sample conducted by Dr. Diamond. In Sloan's opinion, the notebook entries he examined were not written by Sirhan when he was under hypnosis. His analysis does not address whether Sirhan was in an altered state of consciousness when he wrote various sections in the diary. Sloan's general findings were in agreement with *The 3*

---

19   Thigpen. and Cleckley. (1957). 142–143.

Faces of Eve examiner to the extent that, although there were some variations, the samples were no doubt executed by the same person.

Even so, it eluded me why a handwriting specialist could offer his expert opinion as to Sirhan's state of consciousness when he made various entries into his diary; Sloan testified that he knew zero about the psychodynamics of the automatic-writing process. His opinion that there were wide variations page to page in the diary was fairly obvious to anyone even at this late date who even casually perused the diary's contents.

Mr. Sloan's interpretation aside, it has been my position throughout my research into Sirhan's psychodynamics that certain passages in the diary were written by Sirhan's alter, personality 2, the personality who made the more violent threatening statements against RFK, Ambassador Goldberg, President Johnson, and others. This does not rule out the possibility that some of the entries may have subliminally been influenced by the process of automatic writing as suggested from the results of Dr. Diamond's experiments.

Under cross-examination by prosecutor Compton, Sirhan continued to express his doubts about the incriminating materials in the diary. When asked about the diary entries, Sirhan didn't give the answers Compton or the prosecution wanted to hear: "No, I don't remember.... If you show it to me and it's my handwriting and I recognize it as my handwriting I will say, that's mine, yes, but I don't remember doing it.... No I don't remember."

Compton followed up, "But you do have a general recollection that you used to write in these books from time to time, right? Do you remember doodling in the past, whether you wrote parts of words or something else?"

Sirhan still answered, "No, Sir, I don't remember."

Though Compton pressed further, he achieved the same result. Unless Sirhan had become a skilled liar, and even under the pressure of fighting for his life, it seemed as if his denials supported my belief that his dissociated personality 2 wrote many of the passages cited by Compton.

Quite similar to the Christine Beauchamp and *The 3 Faces of Eve* cases where secondary personalities emerged, Sirhan's transient, altered personality ascended to dominance unpredictably at various times throughout his life from the first time he began to dissociate, beginning his personality split when he was a traumatized Palestinian child.

Since that initial personality split, he attempted to escape from a world he perceived as populated with multiple oppressors and enemies out to do him harm. Unlikely as it might seem, like the bank employees in the Stockholm robbery and the Patty Hearst saga, Sirhan was unaware how profoundly he was affected by the identification with the aggressor and symptom facets of the trauma-induced paradox, AKA the Stockholm syndrome, that contributed to his becoming what seemed almost impossible – a violent, dissociated killer.

During his examination of Dr. Diamond, Mr. Berman moved into the critical area of whether Sirhan, being in alternating dissociated states, was fully able to premeditate to commit first-degree murder under existing California law?

Dr. Diamond addressed the issue, "It is my opinion that the defendant was unable because of mental disease to maturely and meaningfully reflect upon the gravity of his contemplated act and that he was unable, because of mental disease, to comprehend his duties to govern his actions in accordance with the duties imposed by law."[20]

Somehow during the defense doctors' confusing testimony, they mostly omitted the major principles forming the foundation of the diminished capacity defense as outlined by Dr. Diamond. This concerned the conceptualization that it was not that Sirhan was insane when he assassinated RFK, but rather if he was able to maturely and meaningfully capable of reflection upon the gravity of his alleged criminal act. Unfortunately, most of the doctors avoided this issue, being lead into the prosecution's trap of falsely connecting Sirhan's sense of responsibility to the issue of knowing right from wrong – the antiquated M'Naghten standard.

When considering the doctors' testimony concerning what diminished capacity is and is not, in addition to Dr. Diamond's trial statements, Dr. Richardson probably came closest to capturing the meaning of diminished capacity: "My general feeling is that at least for a year or two, Mr. Sirhan couldn't be characterized as capable of maturely premeditating or of comprehending his duty as most of us would understand it. As I said in my report, his comprehension of his duty has been that of a kind of soldier and a representative of his nation."

SIRHAN'S DIARY EXPOSED ON *NBC-TV* NEWS INTERVIEW

The mysteries surrounding Sirhan's diary did not go away when the trial ended. After he was sentenced on May 21, 1969, and before being transferred to San Quentin's death row, he gave an interview to NBC-TV's correspondent, Jack Perkins. The interview paid for by NBC offered about $1,000 per minute for fifteen minutes of exclusive access to the now-convicted Sirhan who would later that day be transferred to

20   Trial Vol 25: 7712A-7397, March 26–28, 1969.

San Quentin via helicopter from the LA County jail to Van Nuys Airport, then into a waiting twin-engine Beechcraft aircraft to Hamilton Air Force Base in northern California. There the entourage was met with a six-car caravan and, in the early morning, Sirhan was escorted to San Quentin.

NBC-TV provided two camera crews, a TV producer, and Jack Perkins, who conducted the interview that was broadcast live to a national audience of twenty million people on June 3, 1969. Many descriptions of this interview have been already reported by others, but my focus was directed at Sirhan's steadfast claims that he did not remember making incriminating journal entries in his diary.

Perkins was particularly interested in Sirhan's diary. According to Kaiser: "Sirhan was, as usual, less than cogent about them. They were still a mystery to him, part of his experimentation with the occult."

Sirhan stated, "There's something here, sir, that has something to do with it [the diary], and I don't know what it is."

Perkins responded, "They're the writings of Sirhan Sirhan."

Sirhan said, "Yes, Sir, but they're not the writings of me now, Sir."

> **Perkins:** "Well, in court you claimed you didn't – you don't even remember writing in the notebook?"
>
> **Sirhan:** "I don't, Sir."
>
> **Perkins:** "You don't remember any of those writings?"
>
> **Sirhan:** "I know, Sir, that they are my writings."
>
> **Perkins:** "...talking about 'Robert F. must be sacrificed' and so forth and so on?"
>
> **Sirhan:** "It's my handwriting – they are my thoughts, but I don't remember them, Sir." [This represents a critical point regarding Sirhan's amnesic dissociative state.]
>
> **Perkins:** "Well, did you only write them when you were, when you were in great fits of anger?"
>
> **Sirhan:** "I must have been, Sir, I must have been. Why they are the writings of a lunatic, Sir."

Perkins moved the interview into a rather odd exchange pertaining to his diary and the planning for the assassination: "You were planning to kill Senator Kennedy."

> **Sirhan:** "Only in my mind."
>
> **Perkins:** "Well, that is the only place you can plan it."

> **Sirhan:** "Not to do it physically. I NEVER THOUGHT OF DO-ING IT [author capitals]. I never, never, I don't see myself, Sir, as doing it. I don't have the guts to do anything like that."
>
> **Perkins:** "You don't have the guts?"
>
> **Sirhan:** "It's against my nature, Sir, to do that."
>
> **Perkins:** "Well, you did it!"
>
> **Sirhan:** "I DID IT, BUT I WAS UNAWARE OF IT, SIR" [author capitalization]."

After more than two hours of filming, the NBC-TV producer abruptly said, "Cut," the interview came to an end, leaving Perkins with more unanswered questions. The recurrent pattern in Sirhan's answers to Perkins' questions remained unchanged from those he had provided when testifying in court in his own defense. An analysis of Sirhan's responses began to take on the tone of a mystery novel at the center of the plot – what was he aware of, and what wasn't he aware of?

To illustrate Sirhan's awareness and recognition of certain of his diary's entries and denial of others left Perkins confused. He asked Sirhan if he thought he was mentally ill.

Sirhan responded, "I'm not mentally ill, Sir, but I'm not perfect either." This response followed the claim that, "No one in his right mind, he added, could have done such a thing!" Further confusing the issue, Sirhan added: "I did it, but I was unaware of it, Sir."

I contend that, during the interview with Perkins, Sirhan's personality 1 really had no idea what his violent counterpart was capable of doing as he explained to Perkins: "I don't have the guts to do anything like that! It's against my nature!" Of course, Sirhan's personality 1 may have from time to time entertained ill-will toward his perceived aggressors even singling out RFK, nonetheless he remained incapable of planning and carrying out the necessary steps in the assassination plot. Conversely, Sirhan's violent personality 2 was psychologically well equipped to get the job done.

The planning for and actual murder of RFK as expressed in Sirhan's diary entries remained the private repository of Sirhan's personality 2 plan to kill, with only occasional and minimal leakage into his personality 1. Sirhan's often-claimed statements (by his personality 1 to the effect that – *It was like someone else did the killing*) were in fact his actual representation of reality. His alter personality 2 assassinated the senator unbeknownst to his conforming personality 1.

For obvious reasons, developed through this account of the two Sirhans, none of this essential background information of Sirhan's split personality could have been available to Mr. Perkins or even to Sirhan's doctors and attorneys. In the end, the Perkins interview merely reinforced the existence of two Sirhans, and the questions Perkins and the public most wanted answered still remained unanswered.[21]

21   In Kaiser, R.B. (1970). Perkins, J. (5-22-1969). "First Tuesday: The mind of an assassin," NBC-TV broadcast, June 3, 1969. 522–526.

Epilogue

Throughout this cold case analysis, I have demonstrated that Sirhan Bishara Sirhan was not lying about having no memory of the specifics of the assassination of RFK, and he was instead experiencing multiple, undiagnosed psychological disorders that affected his memory of the event. As it turns out, the man who did this particular assassination had a kind of Dr. Jekyll/Mr. Hyde split personality, two sides of the same person – one side fairly benign and the other fairly deviant.

As noted from the start, I approached Sirhan's story as an unsolved cold-case psychological mystery, similar to how an FBI profiler might approach a cold-case file. But *Psych DNA* is not as much a straightforward "Who dunnit?" as a "Why he dunnit?"

Methodologically the psychological DNA framework I adopted differs from a search that focuses on the discovery of new, physical evidence inadvertently left by a perpetrator at the crime scene, or on DNA tracings. I concentrated instead strictly on pieces psychological evidence not previously explored.

Accordingly, my chief intent has been to uncover and identify the hidden and undiscovered factors that dramatically affected Sirhan's life, negatively impacted him, and helped to shape the homicidal path he was thrust into.

This fact-finding approach, anchoring psychological DNA, also identified as criminological research-guided assessment, involved a search for and identification of those salient criminological factors that dramatically changed the direction of Sirhan's life, and the lives of Senator Kennedy's family. The death of RFK has had the greatest impact on the American political landscape in the decades since his assassination.

The results of this search explain how Sirhan, a law-abiding, fully functioning person living an unremarkable life for the most part with his family in Pasadena, California, evolved into an unwitting assassin.

This newly constructed psychological DNA system helps to explain why ordinary noncriminal-oriented people begin to deviate from societal norms and laws and then turn to the "dark side." I have used the psychological research process to quantify the conscious and especially the essential unconscious criminal-psychological destabilizers that drove Sirhan's thoughts and subsequent homicidal actions.

My search for the first causes of Sirhan's criminal actions was built using a five step process:

1. Identify conscious deviant thought patterns in the pre-crime phase;

2. Quantify these factors using a cohesive criminological methodology;

3. Using factor analysis, weigh the impact of these identified-critical factors;

4. Assess whether these variables, including psychiatric diagnoses and related mental conditions, are fixed (static) and immutable, or if they are amenable to change (dynamic); and,

5. Search for critical, unconscious criminal drivers mostly unavailable in the offender's conscious state.

At the outset, I posed three seminal questions:

1. Why write another book devoted to a retrospective psychological analysis of RFK's assassin?

2. Why did Sirhan target RFK as the victim?

3. What difference can the results of this retrospective analysis now make in the ultimate outcome in Sirhan's life?

Hopefully, the results presented here resolve these three critical areas of concern. I am convinced that, if the newly revealed information I present, specifically the five newly formulated identity transformational processes (criminal-psychological conditions), had been made available to the jury at the time of Sirhan's trial, the result could have resulted in Sirhan being charged with (and surely convicted of) second-degree murder, rather than first-degree murder imposing the death penalty.

This would have likely shortened Sirhan's confinement (possibly by decades), which could have made a real difference for a man who probably continues, fifty-five years later, to wonder, *Will I ever get out of prison?*

My attention in this comprehensive review of Sirhan's overall mental status focused on realistically assessing Sirhan's defense team's characterization of the man they were defending, including the presentation of a confusing menu of questionable psychiatric diagnoses rendered by a team of defense doctors. I found that an essential factor that contributed to Sirhan's questionable diagnoses was based on the results of the psychological testing results offered principally by two psychologists, Drs. Richardson and Schorr.

These tests were administered at various times when Sirhan was housed in the LA County Jail. Consulting psychiatrists for the defense (Dr. Diamond) and for the prosecution (Dr. Pollack) relied heavily on those testing results to help inform their various psychiatric opinions, fueling the controversy I raise about Sirhan being misdiagnosed as a paranoid schizophrenic. This (essentially unsolved) diagnostic dilemma contributed to Sirhan's misdiagnoses; even though there was very little evidence that he ever showed psychiatric symptoms consistent with a psychotic diagnosis, he was nevertheless classified as a paranoid schizophrenic.

Using the results of these tests, the doctors working for the defense team arrived at rather standard psychiatric classifications popularized and overly used during the 1960s, concluding that Sirhan somehow met the criteria for a psychosis such as paranoid schizophrenia. Clearly, he didn't, and this did not help to explain the wide cluster of accumulated symptoms not connected to a psychosis, such as Sirhan's memory deficits, intermittent trancelike states, dissociative experiences, learned helplessness, identification with the aggressor, a pathological love-hate connection to RFK, and other psychological conditions not fitting with a diagnosis of schizophrenia.

After I reviewed the totality of Sirhan's psychological testing results, it was apparent that several of these results were misinterpreted, and one test (TAT) was not scored using any accepted (by forensic psychologists) scoring protocol. After engaging in this review and then reconstructing the results from certain tests, including the TAT, I found very little clinical support for diagnosing Sirhan with a psychotic disorder at all.

Equally as important, I concluded that at least five non-psychotic, psychological conditions that served as criminal destabilizers were completely missed by the examining doctors. Several of these conditions are not specifically categorized as psychiatric diagnoses, but can be interpreted as ancillary criminological-psychological conditions which negatively impacted and helped explain Sirhan's mental dysfunctioning.

Dr. Diamond, a strong proponent for the use of hypnosis, believed that using this method could facilitate unlocking hidden dimensions in Sirhan's mind that were unavailable using other approaches or traditional "talk interview techniques." He knew that other varieties of psychological inquiry were simply too time-consuming, and there was little time available before and during the trial. The goal was to find out who Sirhan was, and present a psychiatric diagnosis, or combination of diagnoses, in support of a diminished capacity defense, which Dr. Diamond brought to the attention of the jury when he testified.

From a diagnostic standpoint, Dr. Diamond never got there, leaving him with the unsupported paranoid schizophrenia diagnosis derived from the psychologists' assessments. Nevertheless, during his testimony, Dr. Diamond stated, "The defendant suffers from chronic paranoid schizophrenia. For years the defendant had trances during which he heard voices and experienced visions ... devils in disguise, committing abnormal sexual acts, sometimes on the defendant."

Dr. Diamond's testimony summed up his position that in some way, Sirhan ingratiated himself into a kind of mail-order hypnosis acquired during his plunge into the philosophy of the Rosicrucians, "programming himself like a computer" to kill RFK. Dr. Diamond's experience with Sirhan, using hypnotic inductions, further convinced him that Sirhan was in a dissociative state of consciousness at the time of the crime, and that he was amnesic to the shooting scene itself– he simply "blacked out."

Still for his own professional and maybe for personal reasons, Dr. Diamond did not come out and diagnose Sirhan's multiple personality or dissociative identity disorder, relying instead on the dissociative, trance-state condition combined with paranoid schizophrenia. The jury, bombarded with four months of confusing psychiatric testimony, didn't buy it and brought in a guilty verdict accompanied by a death penalty sentence.

Based on Sirhan's long history of multiple childhood traumas, I considered how profoundly these events had negatively impacted his early developmental history. In this effort, I was not the first doctor who believed that the key to solving Sirhan's complex case lay somewhere far back in his childhood. For instance, Drs. Schorr and Diamond, in agreement, confirmed that the psychological roots of Sirhan's homicidal ideations derived from his maladaptive and traumatic childhood experiences, even though they couldn't quite arrive at an explanatory psychiatric diagnosis aside from the loosely fitting paranoid schizophrenia concept, and to a lesser degree the more applicable dissociative reaction.

Unfortunately no definitive psychological analyses of Sirhan's divided personality were undertaken previously by either forensic psychologists or psychiatrists who took up the challenge to explain why he did it. Even

Dr. Diamond only discussed Sirhan's case on a limited basis with his graduate students at the Berkeley campus after the disappointing guilty verdict was brought in; and he choose not to write a book about his experience or his pivotal role as the lead defense psychiatrist in the case.

After the trial, Dr. Diamond did grant at least one interview to a reporter from *Psychology Today* where he acknowledged, "His [Sirhan's] mind is truly split, with part of his life on one side and part on the other."[1]

From the start of Sirhan's trial, his defense doctors were urged to use the unique diminished capacity defense as his primary strategy. Dr. Diamond tried to explain to the jury that this particular defense forms a unique method to weigh or assess a defendant's responsibility for the commission of a criminal act, using a linear, responsibility spectrum, not one based on the more popular either/or approach – the simplistic notion, i.e., either sane and totally responsible for the commission of a crime, murder for instance, therefore adjudicated sane, or not responsible for one's actions, therefore not guilty by reason of insanity. Alternatively, the diminished capacity defense aligns responsibility for one's behavior, forming the basis of entering a lessor plea such as manslaughter or second degree murder. In Sirhan's case, the defense was striving to plead him to second degree murder, and thereby eliminate the death penalty option.

However, the ongoing problem for the jury was that Dr. Diamond's mixing of psychiatry, arcane academic language, and complex legal concepts with complicated, philosophical doctrine (as he explained these) fell on deaf ears for the most part. The jury just didn't get it. Equally important as the diminished capacity defense was Sirhan's vehement resistance to being labeled as having any type of a mental disorder.

Sirhan steadfastly maintained that he was not a mental case, probably thinking, *I'm not crazy, I'm not crazy – They can't prove it! They're just bugging me, trying to prove I'm a crazy killer!*

Referring to a negative newspaper story written about him in *West Los Angeles Times Sunday Magazine*, Sirhan said, "That article they wrote about me in *West* says I was psychotic, that I envied the Kennedys." Sirhan shook his head side to side vigorously, saying, "I tell you, I'm not psychotic."

Sirhan's reluctance to be labeled with any psychiatric condition was counterproductive, and at variance with the diminished capacity defense, thereby further sabotaging his own defense strategy.

During the trial, Dr. Diamond had confrontational exchanges with Sirhan concerning his mental conditions, pointing out to him that a psychi-

---

1   Harris, T.G. (1969). "Sirhan B. Sirhan." *Psychology Today*, 3, 48–55.

atric diagnosis would best serve his defense interests, potentially saving him from a death sentence.

Dr. Diamond concluded that Sirhan was attempting to deceive himself and the doctors by attempting as best he could to convince them that he wasn't the insane person portrayed by his own doctors and in the media. On the other hand, Dr. Diamond surmised that Sirhan was "faking" sanity in order to protect his already damaged ego and repress his suspected belief that he was truly mentally disordered after all.

Dr. Diamond labeled this "faking" condition the "simulation of sanity," describing it as when a person attempts to cover up or mask their perceived, underlying mental illness by feigning or pretending to be perfectly sane. This strategy is also referred to as "attempting to fake good" a defendant's denial of their obvious psychiatric symptoms. Of course, the big payoff for Sirhan was his attempt to avoid being stigmatized by the public and, more important to him, by the Arab community at large as a "crazy person" as suggested in the *West Magazine* story.

The concept of mental illness was obviously a very sensitive area for Sirhan and for his family, especially when considering his strong ties to Arab cultural mores, believing that an admission of mental illness is directly equated with a moral failing or weakness. Sirhan's brother Adel brought this reasoning into focus: "In Arab culture, there's a great stigma attached to mental illness. Not only is the person involved outcast, but also his family ... it is better to be a thief than to be thought of as crazy!"

The corollary question: Is it better to be a convicted murderer facing the death penalty than admit mental illness?

A number of documentary productions, film treatments, true-crime magazine articles, newspaper articles, and other accounts of Sirhan's case have been previously produced. There is no shortage of books written by historians and conspiracy theorists alleging that either Sirhan was a hypno-programmed "Manchurian Candidate," a psychologically trained killer conditioned by one or more nefarious governmental agencies (e.g. CIA, FBI), robotically conditioned to kill RFK, and that he had accomplices to the crime, or that there was an unknown second shooter who actually fired the single fatal shot from behind where RFK was positioned. Of course, there is no direct proof, and scant evidence exists that can corroborate these conspiratorial perspectives.

To date, no books devoted to Sirhan's case have been written by forensic psychologists or psychiatrists, especially anyone who was there at the time of the trial (as I was). Although psychological descriptive information given by the two primary psychologists provided valuable insight into Sirhan's personality, the results of their tests are seen as seriously compromised.

The most devastating evidence used against Sirhan at trial was allowing the prosecution to introduce limited pages from Sirhan's diary, "RFK Must Die," into evidence against his vehement protestations that it was obtained illegally without his permission and absent any search warrant. This controversial document is one of the strangest evidentiary items I have ever seen admitted into any murder trial that I've worked on, and perhaps represents the master blunder committed by Sirhan's defense team. From my viewpoint, an important point to keep in mind is that a considerable amount of the incriminating evidence left in Sirhan's diary has not been previously explained as a direct product of his altered personality 2, the angry, homicidal Sirhan.

Looking back, it is apparent that the prosecution's use of the diary, even limited sections, should have never been exposed to the jury. Nevertheless, the prosecution was allowed to use selected pages from the diary as evidence against Sirhan, then the defense went a giant step further. Almost inexplicably, the defense team made the unwise decision to introduce even more incriminating evidence from the diary than what was requested by the prosecution!

The misguided theory leading to this counterproductive decision centered on the defenses' false belief that by exposing the jury to many of Sirhan's strange "crazy sounding" statements, not in his self-interest, would help advance the diminished capacity defense, establishing that he did suffer from a profound mental disorder. The strategy clearly backfired, and this had a dramatic impact on the jury, and no doubt contributed to a guilty verdict.

In my analysis of Sirhan's diary, I espouse that the preponderance of the incriminating entries were written when Sirhan was in a dissociative or altered state of awareness. Unfortunately during the trial, this interpretation of Sirhan's diary, as written by his alter personality, was not brought to the attention of the jury; and in large measure, this negatively influenced their decision to convict.

I have identified one of the most influential psychological drivers pushing Sirhan to kill RFK, a relatively new and intriguing, criminological condition identified as erotomania-motivated murder. For Sirhan, the symptoms of this condition were widely evidenced from the many conflicting statements he made about RFK. In particular, at one time, Sirhan claimed, "Senator Kennedy was my hero. I loved him. When I saw him it was as if there was a halo around him. He looked like a saint."

Then inexplicably, at other times, Sirhan characterized RFK very differently. For instance, he wrote in his diary over and over again, "RFK Must Die!" Additional negative statements attributed to Sirhan include: "Kennedy got what was coming to him," "That bastard isn't worth the bullets," and "That bastard isn't worth my life."

These negative statements were deeply grounded in his obsessive, erotomaniac attachment to RFK, a person he had never met; yet somehow Sirhan personalized it as if he had, forging a synthetic, emotional bond in his mind with him. This fatalistic identification with a potential victim supports this unique "love hate" homicidal attachment concept, as expressed in the diagnosis of erotomania-motivated murder.

But the question remains: Which Sirhan pulled the trigger? This fundamental issue is addressed throughout *Psych DNA*. In an earlier chapter, I made the statement that: "This is an intriguing story about a man with two personalities – one good one, and one not so good – kind of a Dr. Jekyll/Mr. Hyde" situation where the bad one (personality 2) commits a well-planned political assassination, however the good one, (personality 1) has no knowledge of it, denying any responsibility. That's exactly what I have tried to demonstrate, establishing that early in his childhood, Sirhan's personality cleaved into two, polar opposite personalities: the good, adjusted or host, personality (1), and the dissociative, bad Sirhan, the malevolent, alter personality (2) who gunned down RFK in cold blood. Consequently, the adjusted personality remained almost clueless to the homicidal expression by his alter personality.

The diagnosis of a multiple personality disorder, now termed dissociative identity disorder (DID), is the most salient psychological factor uncovered in this retrospective analysis of Sirhan's complex murder case, and this helps to explain why he (or even who) chose to assassinate RFK. This dissociative identity disorder is identified as phase II of Sirhan's identity transformation and personality conversion. Combined with his phase I, erotomania-motivated murder syndrome, phase II provides multiple clues into Sirhan's motivational reasoning, psychologically driving him to kill RFK.

Verification of the two Sirhans lends support to the opinion that, at the time of the assassination, Sirhan was in a dissociated state of consciousness that mimicked a self-induced hypnotic trance. In addition to Sirhan's personality split, I diagnosed Sirhan with co-occurring complex post-traumatic stress disorder (C-PTSD) – Sirhan's Phase III identity transformational factor. This condition shares many clinical symptoms with Sirhan's dissociative identity disorder.

Sirhan's multilevel dissociative symptoms that formed his dissociative identity disorder originally derived from his innumerable recorded traumas experienced while he and his family lived in East Jerusalem. This mentally imprinted trail of adverse, childhood experiences began to haunt Sirhan and probably still constitutes a non-erasable chapter in his life that he can never completely escape from whether in or out of penal custody.

The interpretation of Sirhan's past life experiences bring us forward to the deadly night of June 4-5, 1968, when Sirhan's homicidal personality (2) sought unrestrained expression in an act of vengeful and unstoppable rage. But for Sirhan's trauma-laced history, and the emergence of his altered dissociated personality (2), the killing of RFK would not have become an American tragedy.

After Sirhan's conviction, Sirhan's lead attorney, Grant Cooper, hastily drafted a legal brief listing thirteen tentative grounds in support of a motion for a new trial. On the face of it, Judge Herbert Walker would obviously reject such a motion because, in effect, he'd be ruling against himself.

Cooper's legal brief contained one claim that was of special interest to Sirhan, and thought to be constitutionally valid, charging Judge Walker with judicial error – a Fourth Amendment violation – admitting Sirhan's private diary into evidence (and used extensively against him throughout the trial). Absent a valid search warrant, the fact that the authorities entered Sirhan's home, searching it illegally, seemed sustainable on appeal, but it wasn't. Paradoxically, the presentation of Sirhan's more complete diary as proof that he was experiencing a mental disorder was an ill conceived defense decision, therefore Cooper would be appealing his own judicial error.

Judge Walker's pronouncement of the death penalty and the denial of the motion for a new trial did not end the controversy swirling around Sirhan's fifty-five-year old case. The 1972 automatic appeal of his death sentence to the California Supreme Court stated, "The judgment is modified to provide a punishment of life imprisonment instead of death for the murder and as so modified is affirmed." The same year, the California Supreme Court ruled the death penalty unconstitutional, allowing Sirhan and an additional 107 inmates on death row to be resentenced to life terms with the possibility of parole.

Another appeal filed by Sirhan's former legal team, William Pepper and Laurie Dusek, challenged the validity of Sirhan's diagnosis as a paranoid schizophrenic. Additionally, the door opened, asserting the theory that Sirhan was a preselected and mentally programmed "patsy," covering for the presence of a second shooter, a similar accusation leveled at Lee Harvey Oswald after he allegedly shot President John F. Kennedy five years before.

In a 2012 appeal ruling of Sirhan's conviction based on evidentiary issues related to ballistics reports presented at trial court, California Attorney General Kamala Harris stated, "All claims in the petition should be dismissed as both untimely and procedurally barred." Harris added in her legal brief that, at trial, there was enough evidence to uphold Sirhan's premeditated murder conviction. In a later ruling however, the California Parole Board dissented.

Sirhan's appearance before the California Board of Parole Hearings on August 27, 2021, provided the newsworthy story that a two-person Board panel voted in favor of Sirhan's request for release from confinement after more than fifty-plus years spent in captivity.

This news came as somewhat of a welcome surprise to myself, a disappointment to some, and still quite baffling to others. Even more unsettling is that Sirhan's quest for freedom extends as far back as 1984, when he was scheduled for release by the California Board of Prison Terms, "However Los Angeles district attorney John Van de Kamp persuaded the Board to rescind its decision."

In pleading for his release, Sirhan is now contrite for shooting RFK, saying, "I wish it had never happened, for the Kennedys' sake, and for my own."[2] However, he has always maintained that he does not remember the key events of June 5, 1968.

Related to a more current decision, the key element in the Board's decision is that, in agreement with the California Department of Corrections and Rehabilitation (CDCR), they found Sirhan no longer posed a societal threat. Interestingly enough, this was Sirhan's sixteenth parole hearing, apparently setting aside his life sentence originally imposed in 1969.

At the most recent California Board of Parole Hearings meeting in 2022, Sirhan's was recommended for release on parole, as Commissioner Robert Barton, directly addressing Sirhan, said, "We saw the improvement you've made, and all of the other mitigating factors, and we did not find your lack of taking full responsibility for the crime as proof of your not being dangerous to society."

2   Moldea. (2018). 342.

The decision by the limited panel would later be reviewed by the full board for 120 days prior to finalizing Sirhan's release from custody and, at that point, California's Governor Gavin Newsom had thirty days to uphold the full board's decision if in favor of Sirhan's petition for parole, reverse the board's decision, or send it back to the Board.

Because the Sirhan murder case was originally tried in the City and County of Los Angeles where he was convicted and sentenced, the LA District Attorney retains the authority to contest Sirhan's release and the Board's decision, however the current (2023) Los Angeles DA, George Gascon, elected not to challenge the Board's decision, stating, "I believe the prosecutor's role ends at sentencing, and they should not influence the decision to release prisoners."

Moreover, Gascon issued a broad sweeping directive stating that the LA prosecutors will no longer even be allowed to attend parole hearings, thus no one from the Los Angeles District Attorney's Office will be allowed to attend any of Sirhan's parole hearings in order to advocate for the victim in the case.

From his political vantage point, Governor Newsom saw things quite differently after he reviewed the board's decision to grant parole. On January 13, 2022 he denied Sirhan's parole, contending that Sirhan is an assassin who continues to pose a real threat to recidivate as well as remaining a safety risk to the public. Additionally, the governor claimed that Robert F. Kennedy was one of his political heroes: "The assassination was among the most notorious crimes in American history.... Mr. Sirhan killed Senator Kennedy during a dark season of political assassinations in the US, just nine weeks after Dr. Martin Luther King Jr.'s murder, and four-and-a-half years after the murder of the Senator's brother, President John F. Kennedy.... Sirhan still lacks insight, refuses to accept responsibility, and has failed to disclaim violence committed in his name. That adds to his current risk of inciting further political violence."[3]

Sirhan will have to wait and see whether Governor Newsom's successor will affirm the Board's decision and ultimately parole RFK's assassin.

Only a handful of politically motivated assassinations committed during the twentieth century continue to spark controversy and present puzzling outcomes, especially when posing the most important questions: *Who really did it?*, or *Did the defendant they convicted actually do it?*

In Sirhan's case, the answers to these questions have propagated endless investigations and generating seemingly nonstop controversies. The

3   *The San Jose Mercury News*, January 14, 2022.

controversy over the appeals process did not swiftly end when Governor Newsom denied Sirhan's parole –maybe the battle had just begun.

Apparently the governor had a different reaction to the July 11, 2023 release of seventy-three-year-old Leslie Van Houten from a California State women's prison. Van Houten, one of Charles Manson's deadly cult followers during the 1960s, was convicted in 1971 for the savage murders, at Manson's request, of supermarket executive Leno LaBianca and his wife Rosemary in their home in an upscale Los Angeles neighborhood on August 8, 1969.

Van Houten admitted to killing Mrs. LaBianca by stabbing her at least fourteen times in the back as an accomplice held the woman down as she struggled to survive. The night before this double homicide, an additional four Manson cult members slaughtered five more people in another fashionable LA neighborhood. Van Houten did not participate in that mass killing scene that took the life of a pregnant Sharon Tate, a rising Hollywood star married to film director, Roman Polanski.

Van Houten, like Sirhan, spent more than fifty years in prison after her 1971 conviction. The decisions made by the California Board of Parole Hearings to previously release her from custody were reversed by California governors Jerry Brown – twice – and Gavin Newsom – three times. However, California's Second Court of Appeals in Los Angeles reversed Newsom's opinion, leading the way for Van Houten's release. Governor Newsom could have elected to petition the California Attorney General's Office to file an appeal to the California Supreme Court in his behalf to continue to block Van Houten's freedom. Newsom chose to not file with the high court in this matter, resulting in her being placed on supervised parole.

Quite naturally, the speculation swirling around Sirhan's on-again off-again parole status has now shifted back to an earlier contention that reaffirms Sirhan's confinement as designated far beyond the point where he was professionally viewed as a societal danger to anyone, yet Governor Newsom extended this controversial belief that Sirhan continues to be a threat to public safety. The governor's position has so far found little or no support from the many forensic psychologists who have continuously assessed and monitored Sirhan for decades, reaching the consensus that he does not represent a danger to anyone.

In Sirhan's case, more recently, Ms. Angela Berry, Sirhan's current appeal attorney, told me that she filed a fifty-three-page writ of habeas corpus (a fundamental right guaranteed in the US Constitution that protects against unlawful and indefinite imprisonment), asking a LA County Superior Court judge to rule that Governor Newsom violated State law which holds that inmates can be paroled unless they pose a current unreasonable public safety risk. Seeking a reversal to Newsom's denial, Ms. Berry persuasively argued that there is no evidence that Sirhan remains a societal danger. She also argued that she is challenging the governor's reversal of Sirhan's parole as an abuse of discretion, negating his constitutional right to due process in violation of California law to finally resolve the issue of why Sirhan remains in prison.

During a conversation with Ms. Berry, I mentioned that the results of my intensive retrospective, criminological reassessment of Sirhan's historical, criminal risk factors, including his rescored and reinterpreted psychological tests, strongly indicating that his risk for engaging in a future criminal behaviors, especially crimes of violence, in my opinion, is reduced to almost zero.

I added that this retrospective analysis of Sirhan, could easily be blended into a more current face-to-face meeting in the San Diego prison seting or a video assessment with her client, and a comparison of his past criminal risk factors with more current ones could be helpful in securing Sirhan's ultimate release.

Because of my long history and knowledge of Sirhan's case (longer than any psychologist who assessed him), I offered to do this evaluation pro bono, which could provide important new data with regard to both Sirhan's next parole hearing, and be of material import, in his appeal filing, and perhaps most important for Sirhan's self-enlightenment.

Concerning the appeal, Ms. Berry stated, "The governor acted with personal bias, incorporated the wrong law, ignored mitigating evidence, and did not afford Sirhan the same rights as others eligible for parole." She added that it's her position that the governor has politicized the parole process.

Again I believe that, for Sirhan, being apprised of this revised psychological information, presented in *Psych DNA,* could help inform him about his critical split into two personalities. To be able to explain to Sirhan that his dissociated personality 2 is responsible for shooting RFK, without the awareness of his host personality 1, represents a psychological breakthrough that could help him better comprehend how this tragedy actually unfolded.

At this juncture, I pose the question: Wouldn't it be helpful for Sirhan to finally understand the complex psychodynamics of his fractured personality, helping him to clarify the oblique statement he made? – "No one in his right mind could have done such a thing [assassinated RFK]!"

It seems to me that, during these passing years since the crime, perhaps Sirhan has wandered in a perpetual, psychological fog of discontent, every day asking himself the same question, *If I did what they said I did, then why does it feel like someone else did it?*

Clear to me now, Sirhan's doubts have a solid psychological foundation not yet fully explored with him.

Referring again to the night of the assassination as recently as 2021, Sirhan told the California Board of Parole Hearings' members, "It pains me to experience the knowledge that I'm responsible for such a horrible deed, if I did in fact do that."

For fifty-five years, Sirhan has wondered how and why he became woven into RFK's death. Likewise, RFK's family members continue to struggle to put all the pieces of their historic and personal tragedy into some kind of sensible perspective.

The 2021 Board's decision to grant Sirhan release from the California Department of Corrections and Rehabilitation, resulted in a mixed reaction from RFK's family members, producing a split in the usually tight family ethos and locking the family into a battle involving Sirhan's release.

After all these years, the news of Sirhan's pending release from custody left Kennedy family members divided, with six of RFK's children, and surviving widow Ethel Kennedy, voicing strong opposition to any type parole for Sirhan; although two sons, including Robert F. Kennedy, Jr. (a 2024 candidate as an independent nomination for US President) and Douglas Kennedy, offering their support for Sirhan's release.

At the time of this writing, Sirhan remains housed in the Richard J. Donovan Correctional Facility in San Diego County. Although he was granted parole in 2021, he now faces an unprecedented seventeenth parole hearing and, must wait for the decision of his appeal's case filed in his behalf by his appellant attorney Ms. Berry.

On Wednesday, September 28, 2022, in her filing, Ms. Berry asked the court to overturn the governor's decision because she asserts that the governor broadly overstepped his judicial authority. Commenting on the pending appeals case, she added, "It's not unreasonable to assume that this may not be resolved by the next parole hearing, but we will just forge ahead on with the next parole hearing as well, and I don't expect the Parole Board to come to a different conclusion."

As I write this, Sirhan continues to sit, locked up, wondering whether all the right legal moves were made by his appeals attorneys to secure his freedom over the last five decades. I too ponder his fate, especially after closely following his case, first as an informed graduate student and later as a forensic psychologist, for the past five-and-a-half decades. I suppose for Sirhan, hope springs eternal!

I feel that Leslie Van Houten, confined for fifty years, assuredly had the same yearnings for liberty and freedom as Sirhan. Perhaps her attorney, Ms. Nancy Tetreault, framed it best, saying her client "has gone through courses to confront what she did – to take responsibility for what she did, along with forty years of psych evaluation to gain parole."

In a recorded message presented at a news conference, Sirhan was heard saying that he feels remorse every day for his actions, and he is now dedicated to nonviolence and wants to "go home to my brother and live the rest of our days in peace."

For Sirhan, tomorrow is certainly another day – maybe the day when he can walk as a free man and feel the warm southern California sun once again not filtered through rows of deflecting bars.

APPENDIX

Sirhan's Rorschach Coding
(Real-time scoring)

Below is the annotated record of Sirhan's Rorschach scoring results card by card. This includes the author's comments and Dr. Richardson's interpretive clarification of response items made during the inquiry phase of the test's administration as presented during his court testimony. The bracketed statements are taken directly from Dr. Richardson's testimony combined with the record of Sirhan's Rorschach responses, and preserved by Kaiser (1970).

Sirhan's direct responses (impressions of what he reports seeing appear in the left-hand column) with the inquiry responses (probing, asking questions about the initial impressions) appear in the right-hand column.

CARD I RESPONSES	
I've seen it before I still don't know. Looks like the back part of a chicken. That's the only thing I can...	It's the whole thing, this being the center. I've eaten some chicken. I never used to like that part, if I could avoid it. It's very bony. [Now Sirhan began by seeing a chicken on the whole blot, by that I mean a chicken carcass, a chicken you might fry (or cook), and he saw the whole thing, this being the center]
A butterfly in flight	The body is here and here are the wings. [The butterfly or the bat with a large natural whole response to the bat. On the center detail what is seen is a woman, a very common response. Now empirically and through clinical experience it has been found when an individual looks at this card in a way, which way is quite different than the way other individuals looks at it, then he is looking, in other words, in a different fashion.]
A frog	Looks like the internal dissection of it. From the little of what I remember, this looks like the cloaca. He is then looking at the frog in the center and then two birds or doves right here [pointing]
Two birds – doves	[Inquiry] How does it appear as though they have just landed?)

Coastline	From a top view like from an airplane. Looks like both a photo and an aerial view could be either. I can see islands. [The last response is a coastline, in the clouds, and cliffs, and, a scoring standpoint, and from a concept standpoint it represents a somewhat chronic response … looking far away, loneliness, isolation, this kind of thing. These responses then have in common (theme) a loneliness, an isolation, and a perspective of deep loneliness.]
Mountains	Looking down from a plane, the darker areas.
Clouds	Is very dark. Just about ready to start to rain. Dark clouds.
Cliffs	This reminds me of cliffs looking far away. The space is the water.
A bowl [scratched-out "bull"]	It looks like the top of a bowl ["bull" scratched out], like it's curved here.
CARD II	
A crown	It's in the space here, a crown for a queen or a king.
A diamond	It looks like a diamond or the top of a mosque. A minaret up here. It's the same space, the cut of it.
A satellite, you know, space	It's the same area, you know, just the shape of it.
A blood smear on a microscope thing	In here looks like blood smeared around. [red shading in the dark area, lower right] The response "blood" is an uncontrolled color response. It is interpreted as a breakdown in intellectual (and impulse) control … and Mr. Sirhan is having trouble managing his aggressiveness, terrific impulses; he is disturbed by his own hostile impulses.
A cross	It's at the top, a Rosicrucian cross is the way I think of it.
6. Blood! [looks intently at the blot]	All of the red especially here [lower D] looks like mixed with other liquids (w). [Again the response "blood" is an uncontrolled color response. It is interpreted as a breakdown in intellectual and impulse control over omission here and we begin to speculate that Mr. Sirhan is having trouble managing his aggressiveness, terrific impulses, he is disturbed by his own hostile destructive impulses.]
7. A face of a person. Glass.	Profile [red at top] It projects no feeling to me. (?) Madness(?), anger – the teeth are showing, they look more like women than men. [So here is a person seeing a couple of angry women. That is not too bad, I could see, I think it would move and you could see a couple of profiles which might be angry at each other.]

8. An elephant or bear.	The GOP elephant [popular area] Maybe it could be just a bear. [You look down here again and you look very intently at the blot. You see blood and then you say...]
CARD III	
1. A couple of dancers.	A jovial bunch of Negro drum players, Watusi, although up here (pointing) – this much looks like foxes – more animal than human – looks like a werewolf (sexy). Oh, men [Let's take Card 3. We expect a person in response to this to color by saying he is going to use color and by perhaps a red bow tie, and so he sees these people here. Now the perception of "people" in the Rorschach is interpreted by Rorschachers as indicating the extent to which a person can include other people into his life, to identify with other people, to have common feelings, to feel comfortable with others. To the Rorschacher what has happened here is that something that started out to be jovial and human has become cunning, shrewd, hostile and aggressive, and we say this is a breakdown in Mr. Sirhan's own basic feeling of human in relation to others and in relation to others and in relation to himself; that is, there is a severe loss of the ability to identify to sympathize, to have compassion for himself or for others.]
2. Lungs	[Center D lower] Looks like a cauliflower really. I see all fine edges – the edge of it looks like cauliflower. Also looks like the trachea, leading to the bronchial tubes.[Next we see the lungs – this side down here (indicating) – the lung response, and anatomy response, is interpreted in the Rorschach as indicating a preoccupation of the body which arises out of anxiety about the integrity and safety of the body. This kind of response is given by people who are afraid of their welfare and expect harm from others].
3. Cauliflower	No inquiry
4. Sternum. This is the sternum, isn't it? [long pause]	[Side d] Maybe a turkey – Red made me think of it.
5. A rooster	Maybe a turkey – Red made me think of it.

CARD IV	
1. Underwater plantations – plant life-kelp [grimace]	Looks like seeing through kelp, this depth thing here. I see it. Looking through it all. (additional comment). Now I feel like saying it looks like a casket to me. It represents death. [Mr. Sihan gives a very deep hint to his response by going to an area right there (pointing) in the inside shading of the blot (indicating) it's very seldom used – about half of one percent will anybody come up with this (response) and he says, "It looks like seeing through kelp, this is depth here. I see it." In the inquiry he says, "Now I feel like saying 'it looks like a casket to me.'" Now in the final and a separate place he has gone down to this area (indicating) and seen a fairly well shaped casket in this area on the card which has been called the "father" card.]
2. A medieval castle, abandoned	[Small detail, top dd] [Then he looked in the performance proper in this area (indicating) at a very tiny detail, and looking far off from the distance he says, "It is a medieval castle abandoned." These areas are highly unusual and this response sequence is highly unusual, and it is quoted by Phillips and Smith in the literature, indicating a distorted thought process, to have this kind of response process in these unusual areas suggesting personal alienation.]
3. An X-ray of the chest [grimace]	Well, going down the center here (top 1/3) in the shading it looks like the muscles around the neck. [He sees an X-ray. The X-ray is associated with intense feelings about the integrity of the body, again a feeling of worry about whether one is in danger or not, up in this area] [indicating]
4. [Points at own stomach] I see these muscles, the abdominal muscles.	[Center line just above--CENTER D]The shading in here looks like the abdominal muscles. [Additional comment] This much here is way out beyond. It goes beyond. I can't describe it. [Again, with the intense feelings of worry about whether one is in danger or not.... Similarly to the abdominal muscles going down.]
CARD V	
1. A bird. A big eagle like. Flying head-on.	[W, FM, A, P responses]
2. A chicken leg. Fried chicken	You know these advertisements for fried chicken. Some old man has all these franchises for fried chicken.
3. Horns, looks like the ears of a kangaroo.	Looks like horns and ears of a kangaroo, looking straight at me. Right in here.

4. A ballet dancer	The legs are here, the skirt and all that floating around. [Gestures] Just the legs and standing on the toes. Just the center bottom legs.
5. A seal	? [written in]
CARD VI	
1. A cat	[Just the tip of the top d.) Eyes, whiskers. Ad [written in]
2. Chicken. This chicken comes in here again	No inquiry
3. A lamp	It's the brightest spot in the blot. [dd on center line]
4. A rocket	[The center line, lower 2/3, F+]
5. An owl	No inquiry
6. Cliffs. I have a feeling of high altitude.	From the cliffs. Very high. Looks like looking very high and from a high altitude.
7. The bust of a female from the chest up.	[Tip of outer extension dd] [Handwritten in]
8. The claws of an eagle or predatory bird.	Just these claws here [Ad written in]
9. Walking in a very dense forest, a lot of foliage	Looks like an aerial view what you might see around the equator. [Center, both sides in shading]
10. Vertebrae	No inquiry [limits] Can you find anything of a sexual nature in this particular blot? "Yeah, you mean this being the vagina?" What about an animal skin or a hide that's often seen on this card? "Oh, yeah, the whole thing. That's beautiful. Looks like the fur side – " Again this foliage.
CARD VII	
1. Monkey with [handwritten in] tail	Heads, playful. The heads [Letter A handwritten in] and the tails [tail is the usual ear]
2. Bears. Stuffed bears	A bear's head. The expression is wicked, mean, mad. [Ad written in]
3. A jigsaw puzzle.	A jigsaw puzzle [W no inquiry].
4. A dam	A dam. Inquiry-a canal, more like Egypt.
5. A canal	No inquiry
6. A map of Egypt, you know, the boundaries	[One side of lower D]
7. The Delta River, no, a delta, a river.	No inquiry
8. Towers [very ruminative here]	The towers very distant. [At top of the center] Very mountainous--might be a church on a cliff.
CARD VIII	
1. The California bear	D, F, A, P. No inquiry

2. Flags	(Blue area.) Is that blue or green – like the United Nations flags at the top of the buildings.
3. The spine. The vertical column. Is it vertical?	The spine, the center line – the spinal column.
4. I don't know, it's a desert plant. Grows very tall–not a cactus. I don't know the name.	Patient suddenly verbalizes, "The color shocks me – no–I don't know – I feel very jittery – I can't hold still, – it stirs me. I read this magazine article on the twentieth anniversary of the State of Israel. It was in color – that color–I hate the Jews. There was jubilation – I felt they were saying in the article, we beat the Arabs – it burns the shit out of me, there was happiness and jubilation. ["The deep resentment and envy stimulated by card VIII of the Rorschach were expressed with an increasing sense of disturbance and loss of control. Mr. Sirhan responded to this card with the statement, "The colors shock me." I'm not used to it. There are too many of them at the same time (colors). It confuses me. It has depth. It's too deep. The card stimulates a memory of colored, pictorial magazine articles depicting the twentieth anniversary of the State of Israel. The bright colors remind him of the victory celebration of the Israelis and the defeat of the Arabs. He said, 'It meant to me the Israelis were saying we beat the Arabs.'] His increasing emotional disturbance continued on the next card."]
5. Guns – Mortars	No inquiry
6. Boats	No inquiry
CARD IX [Head in hands]	
1. In school class – in biology – plant life under a microscope. I don't remember the name of this plant.	The smear of a botanical slide (W). The color clashes – I am not used to it – too many of them at the same time – it confuses me. It just increases in degrees! [A distinct sense of disturbance and a loss control on Card 9 and also brightly colored card. In school class Card 9 where he says, "In biology--plant life under a microscope – Now that's for the whole card."]
2. Apples	No inquiry. Comment, Dr. Richardson on card IX: ["For example, the apples which Mr. Sirhan sees on card 9 of my Rorschach are seen as 'rotting' on Dr. Schorr's Rorschach some months later; that is, the evidence of illness we saw in August is still more apparent in November"]
3. Fire. It's weird [shakes head]. Whew! It has depth-it's too deep. Whew!	No inquiry.
CARD X	

SIRHAN'S RORSCHACH CODING

This whole color – it throws me off: Monster! [60-second interval) It's really about all on this one? (You seem upset.) It's frightening – it frightens me-they all seem the same wickedness! Too many entanglements!	It's a cacophony of colors, a hodgepodge. All those legs! This here looks like some kind of rat [brown area]. No, not a rat – it flies – a bat. The whole thing looks like monstrosities. It's more vulgar–I'd avoid it. Everybody wants to catch on to you-with all those legs! The minute you're within reach you're in their clutches. (What about the blood?) I seem to associate the whole thing negatively with blood. (What about the red area?) It looks like liver to me–some kind of meat [grimace]. I'd rather not even discuss it-I'd rather not even discuss it. All those legs. It confuses me. It has depth. It's too deep. His continued emotional disturbance continued.... It looks like monsters – frightening – it is wickedness – entanglements – I see blood. In this response, what is apparent is a sudden, gross breakdown in emotional control, reality testing and discrimination created by a stimulating, complex, emotion – provoking readiness to react with overwhelming anger in a context of bitter rivalry, envy and fear. Also he has the very rare uncontrolled color response, a so-called pure C color. This is the total blood response to card 10 on the Rorschach, which is called by David Rapport, a deterioration scene. That is also a patho-monic sign for schizophrenia. This is an intense disorganized response .... where this whole scene becomes a mass of things which are attacking, devouring; which are wicked, which constitutes a paranoid environment ; and so the deep illness really spurts through on this card.]

385

Index

ABOUT THE AUTHOR

Dr. John C. Brady II, a California-licensed forensic psychologist, is the author of seven true crime books in his Bad Actor Series. He is a psychologist and criminologist with a masters and doctorate in criminology from UC Berkeley. He has used both disciplines and his forty-plus years in private practice to discover why ordinary, law-abiding people suddenly begin to engage in criminal acts.

In his forensic psychology practice, he has worked with various criminal populations having analyzed hundreds of "bad actor" cases, including celebrity offenders in addition to this retrospective analysis of Sirhan Sirhan. He is the executive producer of the true crime TV show, *Silicon Valley Confidential*.

Please visit
www.johncbradyphd